Teaching ELLs
Across Content Areas

Teaching ELLs Across Content Areas

Issues and Strategies

edited by

Nan Li
Claflin University

INFORMATION AGE PUBLISHING, INC.
Charlotte, NC • www.infoagepub.com

Library of Congress Cataloging-in-Publication Data

A CIP record for this book is available from the Library of Congress
http://www.loc.gov

ISBN: 978-1-68123-487-8 (Paperback)
978-1-68123-488-5 (Hardcover)
978-1-68123-489-2 (ebook)

CONTENTS

PART III

OTHER ISSUES ON TEACHING ELLs

PREFACE

The book, *Teaching ELLs Across Content Areas: Issues and Strategies,* is a unique, useful text written for K–12 teachers. This book is the culmination of the professional knowledge, expertise, and experience from the distinguished authors who represent the entire range of the content areas, including: language arts, science, mathematics, technology, arts, psychology, and Hispanic studies. Each author also has extensive experience working in the K–12 classrooms in the content areas. The impetus for writing this book emanates also from our experiences working with K–12 teachers and it provides them with professional training through our federally-funded projects. Several authors have served as project directors of the grant programs funded by the U.S. Department of Education to provide professional training that is intended to prepare the K–12 teachers to work effectively with English Language Learners (ELLs). This interaction with practicing teachers and ELL students has guided the development of this edited book. In recent years, the ELL school population has increased exponentially and it shows every sign of continuing to increase. It is projected that, by Year 2025, one out of every four public school students will be ELLs (NEA, 2013). Thus, providing the ELLs with high-quality services and programs is an important investment in America's future.

We decided to work together on this book project because each author has unique professional experience, expertise, and absolute authority in each content area. We wanted to invest our time and contribute a text that is helpful for K–12 teachers to meet the challenges and to better serve the ELLs in classrooms. The book focuses on two areas: issues and strategies.

Teaching ELLs Across Content Areas, pages ix–xvii
Copyright © 2016 by Information Age Publishing
All rights of reproduction in any form reserved.

Issues refer to challenges that teachers frequently face in content area class-rooms while strategies refer to pedagogical approaches that are both practical and helpful. In addition, the book provides useful information from a second language (L2) theoretical perspective to help teachers understand ELLs and better serve them (i.e., Chapter 2: ELLs & L2 Acquisition Theories). The book also provides tips on teaching academic vocabulary to ELLs in Chapter 9: Increasing Academic Vocabulary for ELLs. Tips and strategies to increase the cultural awareness for the teachers are discussed in Chapter 10: Increasing Cultural Awareness for Teachers. The book includes even discussion from a psychological perspective for teaching ELLs (i.e., Chapter 11: Motivating ELLs Using a Psychological Approach) by the author with authority.

UNIQUENESS OF THE BOOK

This book makes a contribution to the field in four ways. First, it discusses issues on teaching ELLs in content classrooms, which are important for teachers to know in order to work effectively with their students. Second, the book updates professional educators' knowledge about ways to meet the immediate needs of ELLs in various content areas. Third, the material in this book is presented in a practical and reader-friendly way that speaks directly to pre-service and in-service teachers. For example, this book combines L2 theories, teaching strategies, and professional knowledge into one book. The book can be used as daily text and reference by teachers or for professional training materials. Finally, the book is carefully crafted with twelve chapters, each with focus that is useful for teachers in content area classrooms. For example, each chapter begins with a real case scenario of ELLs. The relevant information and strategies are provided in each chapter.

Through our various programs working with the teachers to provide them with professional training, finding appropriate training materials is the first difficulty that we have encountered. To address this need, we typically buy hundreds of copies of books to support teachers' professional development each year. Despite this investment, the books fall short of expectations for several reasons. Some textbooks on teaching ELLs are too voluminous and do not meet our program needs. Others, while very practical and full of teaching ideas, fall short when it comes to furthering teachers' understanding of key issues. Still others have in-depth discussion of L2 theories but no discussion of vocabulary or culturally responsive teaching. Our response has been to produce a new book that fills that gap by combining useful information, L2 theories, and teaching strategies to meet the immediate needs of the teachers of ELLs in classrooms. Our goal in writing this book is thus to fill that gap.

AUDIENCE FOR THE BOOK

The book is designed for the K–12 teachers who are responsible for teaching ELLs. It is best used by the teachers who have ELLs in content classrooms and who seek knowledge and teaching strategies to work effectively with their ELLs for their academic success. With this design, teachers can use the books as a daily text or reference book.

According to the national data, ELL school enrollment has increased dramatically across the nation in the recent years (NCES, 2013). Nationally, the increase of the ELL population was 105% (U.S. Department of Education, 2008). In the state of South Carolina, for example, the ELL school enrollment increased 714% between 1995 and 2005. In light of these trends, the teaching force is generally underprepared to meet the needs of this rapidly growing group of students. Through our training programs, we have worked with the K–12 teachers on a frequent basis to provide them with training workshops in various school districts. The teachers who participate in our training also come to university campus. Through these ongoing interactions, we have established a professional collaboration with the teachers that has made us acutely aware of their needs when teaching ELLs in classrooms. This regular, sustained interaction with practicing teachers is the foundation for the book.

This book can also be adopted as the text for professional training of pre-service educators. Teachers are the most important factor for ELLs' academic success. The ELL school population will continue to increase in the coming decades. With this, there is a current trend of preparing teachers through professional development training. Thus, comprehensive books for the training programs are in great demand. Through our professional training programs and working with in-service teachers on a daily basis, we can "work backwards" to identify what would have prepared them to be more effective teachers of ELLs. By sharing this in advance of a pre-service teacher's assignment to a classroom of students, the book can serve as a tool in better preparing the next generation of teachers. Thus, this book can be adopted as the text in the TESOL programs or teacher education programs at the university level for pre-service teachers. In addition, it can be used by any prospective educator who is interested in teaching ELLs.

ORGANIZATION OF THE BOOK

The book has three parts with twelve chapters. Part I includes two chapters that focus on the basic information on ELL school population and strategies to engage the ELLs' participation in the classrooms. This part also includes L2 theories and approaches for teachers to understand the learning process from a theoretic perspective to work with the ELLs effectively. Part II includes six chapters that focus on teaching ELLs in content area classrooms. These content areas include: the Language Arts, Science, Mathematics, Technology, Social Studies, and Arts. Challenges are discussed and strategies on how to meet the challenges are provided with useful teaching tips by authors with expertise in these content areas. Part III includes four chapters that focus on increasing academic words, becoming more culturally responsive, and understanding psychological issues related to teaching ELLs. These chapters provide much needed information for teachers to work with ELLs. This part also provides information related to the professional requirements, standards, and statistics for the teachers.

Twelve chapters are embedded in the three parts. Each chapter provides the basic information and useful strategies relevant in the content classrooms. For example, Chapter 2 provides the basic theories in second language acquisition to help teachers know the basic L2 theories and concepts to better serve the ELLs. These basic L2 acquisition concepts include BICS & CALPL, Comprehensive Input, Affective Filter, and Theories of Interaction. Chapter 2 also introduces several other popular L2 approaches on teaching ELLs, such as TPR (Total Physical Response), and WIDA (World Class Instructional Design and Assessment). These basic L2 theoretical approaches are useful because they explain the L2 learning stages and can serve as a foundation to guide teachers to work with the ELLs. Chapter 2 also includes a popular lesson model, the Sheltered Instruction Observation Protocol (SIOP), which is an empirically-validated approach useful for not only working with ELLs but teaching all students in classrooms.

If teachers choose to teach a specific lesson in a content area (e.g., science or language arts), they can refer to the chapter title and subtitle as an index to select the topic for the lesson. For example, Chapter 3: Teaching Language Arts to ELLs, provides useful information and hands-on strategies on teaching language arts in the four language domains (i.e., listening, speaking, reading and writing). Chapter 5 provides hands-on tips on teaching math lessons to ELLs, such as Creating Vocabulary Banks, Using Differentiated Instruction, Modifying Speech, and Eliciting Nonverbal Responses. Chapter 7 provides useful information and strategies on teaching social studies lessons, such as Creating T-Notes, Applying Analogy and Comparison, and Using Chains and Concept Circles. Chapter 9 provides information and strategies on teaching academic words. The ELLs need to have basic academic vocabulary and word knowledge to support their academic success. ELLs also need to learn about American traditions and holidays. Chapter 10 focuses on cultural awareness and also provides basic information on Latino/Hispanic family traditions, food, and holidays. The teacher can use Chapter 10 as a starting point to continue their cultural and linguistic quest or to use the strategies to teach ELLs. Chapter 11 provides useful information that teachers need from a psychological perspective to work with ELLs. This chapter discusses useful theories and strategies related to teaching ELLs in classrooms and help teachers in a psychological way.

CHAPTER SUMMARIES

Chapter 1 focuses on basic information on the ELLs. The chapter begins with a case scenario about Tom as a snapshot to help teachers understand who the ELLs are and what possible problems they may face. Then the chapter provides the background knowledge on the fast growth of the ELL school enrollment, tracing the immigration law in 1924 (i.e., Johnson-Reed Act). The chapter discusses common characteristics of the ELLs so that teachers can meet the unique needs of this school population. The chapter also discusses the types of ELL students (e.g., Generation 1.5 vs. U.S. born ELL students). Academic attainment related issues are addressed with an examination of common terminology and myths about the ELLs. The chapter also provides the sample profiles of the ELLs with their work samples. Teachers must understand that the ELLs have diverse backgrounds, different needs, and learning styles. Having a better understanding of the ELLs is an initial step for teachers to work effectively with their ELLs to enhance the learning success of the ELLs and all students.

Chapter 2 focuses on the second language (L2) theories and perspectives, such as Basic Interpersonal Communication Skills (BICS), Cognitive Academic Language Proficiency (CALP), Affective Filter, and Comprehensive Input. Like the process of learning the first language (L2) or the native language, ELL students develop their English language proficiency through interaction and meaningful input in a contextualized linguistic environment. ELLs develop BICS and CALP at different paces. It takes about six months to two years to develop BICS but three to five years to develop CALP. Providing context embedded support helps ELLs gain access to the cognitively demanding content areas. Meaningful, comprehensive input at the learners' instructional level and slightly beyond is essential to help ELLs continuously develop their English proficiency. Lowering the affective filter (e.g., anxiety) in classrooms motivates ELLs to learn and seek input and to be more willing to meet the challenge. The chapter also explores other L2 theories and approaches that are important for teachers and that are useful to teaching ELLs in classrooms, such as TPR and Theories of Interaction, SIOP Lesson Model, and the WIDA framework, in order for teachers to work successfully on lesson planning and assessment to assist ELLs in classrooms.

Chapter 3 focuses on teaching the language arts to ELLs. This chapter discusses the characteristics of the four language domains: listening, speaking, reading, and writing. The chapter also discusses how these four language skills are interdependent rather than discrete. The chapter addresses how oral language proficiency has a strong impact on ELLs' text-level literacy skills and why it is important for teachers to provide opportunities for the ELLs to develop all four skills simultaneously in order to attain high levels of proficiency in English. The chapter also describes the unique challenges that ELLs face in acquiring each of the four language skills and shares some best practices to overcome the difficulties and to meet the needs of these students in each of the four areas. The chapter also provides examples of specific strategies for teachers to help ELLs strengthen their proficiency in each of the four language domains (i.e., strategies for teaching listening, speaking, reading, and writing). Additionally, the chapter emphasizes the importance of the English language arts to all areas of the curriculum and how they should be integrated throughout the curriculum as much as possible.

Chapter 4 focuses on teaching science to ELLs. The chapter begins with a case scenario related to an eleven-year old ELL student, Adera, who is challenged in learning, especially in her science classroom. The chapter urges teachers that, when teaching science to ELLs, they are expected to focus on both science content and language development. Many issues can make learning science challenging for ELLs, including the nature of inquiry, varying language demands, and negative attitudes toward science. Teachers can use a variety of tools and strategies to enhance instruction of the science lessons and to engage ELLs' participation. For example, the 5E instructional model provides a useful structure for inquiry lessons. Science videos, demonstrations, and field trips can be used effectively to provide meaningful science experiences to ELL students. Teachers can organize small group work to maximize the involvement of ELLs. Most importantly, teachers can help students develop positive views on science by infusing culture and focusing on diverse contributions to science.

Chapter 5 focuses on teaching mathematics to ELLs. In this chapter we discuss some of the key challenges in teaching mathematics to ELLs. Teachers, such as Ms. Anita, want to know "how" to support ELLs. We advocate for a core value of creating linguistically and culturally responsive learning environments. This ideal requires grappling with conceptions of mathematics teaching and learning. Furthermore, developing these environments requires a commitment to learners even given the demands on teachers to align curriculum and instruction to state content and language standards. Some teaching strategies include: (a) the use of vocabulary banks as an embedded and contextualized form for learners to access discipline specific terminology; (b) foregrounding differentiated instruction to tap into various modes of learning, sensory experiences, and levels of language and content proficiency; (c) modifying spoken and written speech; and (d) eliciting nonverbal responses from learners.

Chapter 6 focuses on using technology to teach ELLs. The chapter provides an overview of the importance of technology integration in teaching ELLs in the content areas. The role of the teacher is crucial for successful integration of technology into the curriculum. Teachers should design learning activities that align with academic standards, find appropriate technology tools that are available in the classroom and tailor activities to their learners depending on the topic. The review of the literature has shown that technology supports teaching and could be used to make second language learning experiences more student-centered and more effective for ELLs; technology is not meant to replace the teacher. Even though researchers tend to focus now more on the positive outcomes of teachers' technology integration in the classroom, teachers still deal with challenges to the implementation of technology in real practice.

Chapter 7 focuses on teaching social studies to ELL students. The chapter provides relevant information and strategies for teachers. Teachers who service ELLs in the social studies classrooms have a wealth of cultural knowledge at their fingertips that can enhance any social studies curriculum. By utilizing culturally responsive pedagogy and backwards planning, teachers can help students connect their experiences to abstract social studies concepts. If teachers use the repertoire of teaching strategies available they can help ELLs overcome many of the challenges they face in the classroom. Graphic organizers and other visual resources help make content accessible for ELLs. The use of realia and hands-on learning experiences help develop a context for learning. It is important that social studies teachers also incorporate both language and content objectives when planning lessons. Literacy instruction and social studies content needs to be intertwined in order for ELLs to successfully navigate the information.

Chapter 8 focuses on using arts to teach ELLs. The visual arts are an excellent vehicle through which ELLs can gain access to concepts, ideas, vocabulary applications, and new linguistic contexts for terms heard in daily conversations. Developing visual literacy (i.e., awareness, critical and evaluative skills), and learning to articulate inner narratives and observations, are a significant contribution provided by the incorporation of visual materials with language learning opportunities. Approaches to studio-based activities, centered in demonstration, are a natural asset for teachers of ELLs. Clear, succinct instructions and simple guidelines for art projects allow the students to develop creative skills and apply challenging new conceptual information. Teachers must also pay attention to clarity and simplicity for project guidelines. Quiet interview is a good strategy to help teachers make an adequate assessment of an ELL's language skill mastery. Instructors must also provide a safe environment for questions, consider the possibility of differing cultural contexts and acculturation process for ELL students, and offer modifications as needed to help integrate ELL students into the culture of the individual classrooms as well as the school as a holistic institution. Teachers in the art classes must support ELLs in the translation of the art tools into other areas of learning with linguistic expressiveness and enhanced self-expression via the fabrication of arts objects.

Chapter 9 focuses on teaching academic vocabulary words to ELLs. The chapter begins with a case scenario about Juan, a gregarious ELL from Ecuador to indicate the importance of vocabulary. It then continues with the importance of academic vocabulary building. We went over how learning vocabulary is much more than recognizing, memorizing, and being able to pronounce a list of words. In order to help ELLs, teachers have to help students go beyond this and learn how to decode words. Students should have multiple exposures to the new vocabulary words, with adequate time to discus and practice them. Teachers need to keep in mind *form* (word's spelling and pronunciation), *meaning* (the literal meaning of a word and the meaning of a word within the reading's context), and *use* (when and why a word is being used). The chapter continues with several strategies, such as scaling words, making cognate connections, using semantic features and graphic organizers, creating comprehensive word lists, and including music in the classroom. It ends with Reading, Grammar, and Writing (RGW)—An Integrated Approach to learning vocabulary.

Chapter 10 focuses on cultural awareness. The chapter opens with a personal vignette that illustrates the need for ideologically clear teachers of ELLs to work toward continually developing an elevated critical consciousness of their students' linguistic, social, and familial capital. This chapter discusses the role of culturally, linguistically competent educators, Community School Scan Process (CSSP). This chapter introduces classroom practice for creating curriculum access and equity for ELLs. This chapter also introduces basic Latino and Hispanic vocabulary, traditions, food, and holidays, serving as a starting point for teachers to continue their cultural and linguistic quest for knowledge. Teachers must be aware when teaching linguistic minority students using "cultural wealth" pedagogical approaches so they can ultimately appropriate new language varieties in an additive and self-empowering fashion. Teaching standard academic discourse in English cannot be adequately accomplished without taking a detour through the richness of students' cultural wealth and funds of knowledge.

Chapter 11 focuses on how to motivate ELLs from psychological perspectives. We discuss the theories on motivation. We review some of the best strategies and approaches to motivate ELLs in our classrooms. One of the first strategies we may want to employ is to make the students feel comfortable in the classroom setting. This can be thought of as inclusion. An inclusive teaching strategy can refer to any teaching approach that addresses the needs of the individual students. This would include their different backgrounds, varied learning styles, and differing abilities. This can also allow the students to feel valued. Feeling valued will increase one's feelings of self-efficacy. Teachers need to insure that their lesson material has content relevance for the students. This can facilitate a healthy learning environment. There should be continuity between lessons, with relatedness from one topic to the next. ELLs need to see the value of the new information being presented. The material should be challenging and thought provoking. The teacher needs to be able to aid the students in finding out about any possible personal meaning they can derive from the material being studied. Finally, structure will help provide a strong base from which students can feel comfortable in their lessons.

Chapter 12 focuses on professional standards, requirements, and information. It first introduces the framework for the P-12 CAEP/ESOL standards, common core standards. It then discusses trends and programs in teaching ELLs, assessment and related issues, ELL population data and statistics, and suggestions for teacher education programs. In order to prepare a TESOL professional, competence in five domains that lead to the profession is discussed. The five domains that are interrelated and support each other are: language, culture, instruction, assessment, and professionalism. With the implementation of the Common Core State Standards (CCSS), the role of ESOL teachers are not limited to teaching English, but advocating for ELLs and collaborating with mainstream teachers to provide the academic language needed for ELLs to succeed. The shift from teaching the four language skills only to incorporating content knowledge, academic language, and assessment in ESOL into teaching ELLs has taken place. Different types of programs for ELLs are discussed. Finally, suggestions for teacher education programs to effectively prepare for teachers to work with ELLs are discussed.

REFERENCES

National Educational Association. (2013). *A NEA policy brief: Professional development for general education teachers of English Language Learners.* Retrieved from http://www.nea.org/assets/docs/PB32_ELL11.pdf

U.S. Department of Education. (2008). For example, the increase of the ELL school enrollment was 714 percent in South Carolina from 1995 to 2005 and the increase of the ELL population was 105 percent nationally in the same period (U.S. Department of Education, 2008).

ACKNOWLEDGMENTS

We are pleased to present this unique volume on teaching ELLs in content areas. We would like to take this opportunity to thank a group of professionals, who are chapter authors, editorial board members, publisher, and classroom teachers, for their knowledge, support, expertise, contribution, and much more help provided in creating this book.

We first would like to give our thanks to our chapter authors for their dedicated time, hard work, and contribution with professional knowledge and expertise to make this book possible for our readers, the K–12 teachers. The authors who contributed chapters include:

Dr. Cristina Alfaro (San Diego State University)
Dr. Ron Collins (Mars Hills University)
Dr. Angela Cozart (College of Charleston)
Dr. Thomas Destino (Mars Hills University)
Dr. Tolulope Filani (South Carolina State University)
Dr. Courtney Howard (College of Charleston)
Dr. Jennifer Kohnke (Aurora University)
Mr. Frank Martin (South Carolina State University)
Dr. Larisa Olesova (George Mason University)
Dr. Luciana de Oliveira (University of Miami)
Dr. Aria Razfar (University of Illinois at Chicago)
Ms. Barbara Ragin (Summerton Early Childhood Center)
Dr. Lynn Smolen (University of Akron)
Dr. Zayoni Torres (University of Illinois at Chicago)
Dr. Wei Zhang (University of Akron)

We must also thank our editorial board members as our consultant editors contributing equally their valuable time and hard work with editorial suggestions. Their contributions played an integral role. Without it, this book would be otherwise impossible. Our editorial board consists of these prominent national scholars:

Dr. Christine Sleeter (California State University Monterey Bay, Emerita)
Dr. Mary Jalongo (Springer International, Editor)
Dr. Rossan Boyd (University of North Texas, Denton)
Dr. Judy Beck (University of South Carolina, Aiken)
Dr. James Cohen (Northern Illinois University)
Dr. Sara Kingge (Aurora University)
Dr. Belinda Louie (University of Washington)
Dr. Louise Lockard (Northern Arizona University)
Dr. Aria Razfar (University of Illinois at Chicago)
Dr. Sheryl Santos (University of North Texas at Dallas)

Our thanks also need to go to our publisher at Information Age Publishing, Mr. George Johnson, who has been most encouraging and supportive; to our ESOL coordinators who are always the best friends in need; to our mainstream teachers who are our inspiration to embark on this book journey. Without the support and contributions from this diverse group of professionals, this book might never have found its way to the final publication and meet the readers.

Best Regards,
Dr. Nan Li, Editor

PART I

KNOWING ELLs

CHAPTER 1

WHO ARE THE ELLs?

Nan Li
Claflin University

CASE SCENARIO

Tom is a seventh grader. He came to the United States from China six months ago with his mother and sister to join his father. The parents now both work in a restaurant, leaving for work in the morning and returning home late. Tom stays at home after school with his sister and occasionally also visits the restaurant to provide any help as needed. Tom has been attending the ESOL class daily to learn English. ESOL stands for English Speakers of Other Languages. An ESOL class is a resource classroom where the ELLs are provided additional English language support so that they can improve their English skills. The ESOL programs are required in school by the *Lau v. Nichols* decision made by the Supreme Court in 1974. Tom stays in the ESOL class for one hour daily and then returns to mainstream classrooms. He often sits silently in the mainstream classrooms. It is difficult for him to understand the basic concepts presented by teachers in the content-area classrooms and he does not know how to ask questions or to interact with peers due to his limited English. He tries to improve English by watching TV and listening to tapes in English daily at home. He does not have many friends in school or after school to socialize with. Yet, Tom is polite and has never been a behavior problem and most teachers comment that Tom is a "good kid" but he does not speak English. Academically, he lags behind his grade level.

Teaching ELLs Across Content Areas, pages 3–20
Copyright © 2016 by Information Age Publishing
All rights of reproduction in any form reserved.

LIFE EXPERIENCES AND CULTURES

In the above scenario, Tom is one of the 5.3 million ELLs who are attend-ing our schools with various academic challenges. The term ELLs stands for the English Language Learners, formerly known as the LEP (i.e., Limited English Proficiency). The fast increase in the ELL school population is one of the major trends in our schools across the nation. The ELL school enroll-ment has increased rapidly in comparison to the general school population. Based on the National Center for Educational Statistics (NCES, 2012), the ELL school population has reached 5.3 million in 2010 with the increase rate of 29.7% since 2000. The NCES data further reveals that the general school enrollment in the United States reached to 49.5 million in 2010 from 46.6 million in 2000 with the increase rate of 5.7%. According to the NCES data, the ELL population took 18% of the total school enrollment in the United States in 2010, 21% in large cities, and about 30% in some states (e.g., Texas, New Mexico, Nevada, and California) (NCES, 2012). The data from the National Clearinghouse for English Language Acquisition also reveals that, from the 1997–1998 school year to the 2008–2009 school year, the number of ELLs enrolled in public schools increased by 51% from 3.5 million to 5.3 million and this was the highest increase in the last three decades (NCELA, 2011). The fast growth rate of the ELL school population poses a unique challenge for K–12 teachers who strive to ensure that these linguistic-minority students get access to the core curriculum in schools and learn academic content knowledge as well as the English-language skills.

Teachers may ask what has caused the ELL school enrollment to grow so fast. The burgeoning increase in ELL school population has its back-ground. In 1968, Congress voted to eliminate the Johnson–Reed Act, an immigration law created in 1924 that had a quota system to discriminate against the non-European immigrants. Since the elimination of this dis-crimination law, immigration population has evidenced the increase with a noticeable change in country sources (i.e., the immigration population represents more diversity in its country source) (Li, 2015; Ovando, Collier, & Combs, 2005). The immigration demographics affect school population. The students whose primary language is not English have thus increased fast, mainly from non-European countries. Data reveals that the ELL school enrollment increased by 105% from 1995 to 2005 when the general school population growth was less than 10% (NCELA, 2011) and over five million school-aged students are ELLs (NCES, 2012; Zelasko & Antunez, 2000). With the new demographics in schools, how to educate this ELL population effectively becomes a challenging issue for K–12 teachers in classrooms.

So who are the ELLs? Typically, an ELL refers to a student whose first language (L1) is not English, who is in the process of learning English but not yet able to profit fully from English-only instruction, and who needs instructional support in order to access academic content in school (Bardack, 2010; Li, 2015; Li, Howard, & Mitchell, 2011; Singhal, 2006). The ELLs are the fastest growing segment of the school population and also a most heterogeneous group of students. The ELLs come with different life experiences and cultural backgrounds. The ELLs also have diverse educational needs and goals as well as different gifts and family backgrounds. Some ELLs may live in their own cultural community while other ELLs may live in a non-ELL environment; some ELL families may live in the United States for over a generation while others may be new comers; some ELLs can be high achievers while others can be struggling readers. Thus, it is hard to adequately describe all ELLs with one simple definition or sentence because no single profile can represent the needs of all ELLs. Yet, the ELL students do share some characteristics that teachers can use to get to know their ELLs in order to accommodate their learning needs based on these following factors:

- Length of residence in the United States
- Literacy skills in the primary language(s)
- Previous schooling
- Education background of parents
- Socioeconomic status & resources available at home
- Personal life experiences
- Cultural norms

Each of these factors has an effect on ELLs to acquire the English language skills and content knowledge as they enter their new schools in the United States.

The length of the residence in the United States is an important factor that affects the ELLs' English proficiency and acculturation. The term of Generation 1.5 is often used to describe some ELLs. This term refers to the ELLs who immigrated to the United States in elementary school or high school years, who are U.S. educated but do not have English as a home language, and who may be orally proficient in English but do not have the adequate academic English proficiency (Li, 2015; Mikesell, 2008; Roberge, 2002; Short & Fitzsimmons, 2007). These ELLs can have diverse educational experiences and a wide range of language proficiency and literacy skills. In a sense, these ELLs are caught by generations (i.e., they belong to neither the first nor the second generation of immigrants). That is why they are classified by the term Generation 1.5. In comparison to the U.S. born ELLs, they bring with them the characteristics from their home country but continue the assimilation and socialization in the new country. Thus, Generation 1.5 ELL students are often identified as having a combination of new and old cultural tradition. Depending on the age of immigration, the community into which they settle, and the extent of education in their native country along with some other factors, Generation 1.5 ELLs identify with their countries of origin to varying degrees (Li, 2015; Mikesell, 2008; Oudenhoven, 2006). Yet, this identification is also affected by their experiences growing up in the new country. These ELLs are usually bilingual and are more easily assimilated into the local culture and society than people who are adult immigrants such as their parents.

Although some ELLs are immigrants coming with their families to the United States, many ELL students are born in the United States. According to data, a growing number of ELLs in fact, are U.S. born (Flannery, 2009; Li, Howard, & Mitchell, 2011; NCES 2012). These U.S. born ELLs may have lived in the United States for many years in households where family members or caretakers speak a language other than English. Thus, although English may be the dominant language for these ELLs, they may not have developed the academic English skills and vocabulary needed to function successfully at their grade level in the English-speaking environments in schools. They are likely to suffer the same achievement gaps as other ELLs because of the fact that they are from a home where no English language support is available. Yet, as the second generation of the immigrants, these U.S. born ELLs do have some advantages in overcoming the academic challenges because they emerge into the English-speaking context from the early stage as they start schooling. With the proper support from teachers, educators, and policy-makers to implement the high-quality early educational support programs, such as appropriate dual-language or ESOL programs, and with good assessments, these ELLs have the potential to do better in school than the other ELL students.

The *literacy skills in the primary language* and *previous schooling* can affect the ELLs' learning English and academic content knowledge, especially for those ELLs immigrating to the United States with their families. Even if the ELLs are U.S. born, they still face such a challenge. For example, some young ELLs in the primary grades of U.S. schools must acquire the initial literacy concepts and skills through the medium of English, a language that they have not mastered orally before their schooling because they often lack the emergent literacy support at home due to the non-English speaking home environments. Some ELLs may have developed literacy and academic skills in their home language(s). For these ELLs, the major challenge is that they must learn to read in English. Once they know how to read in English, they can transfer their L1 skills to the second language (L2). Yet, some ELLs may have not experienced consistent previous schooling or appropriate instruction in the primary language(s). This compounds the difficulties because they must learn to read and write in English when they have the challenge to learn academic content at the same time. Some ELLs may already know some English when they arrive in the United States and have also strong literacy skills in the home language and adequate previous schooling. For these students, they usually grasp the concepts more easily in the L2 than the other ELLs and are likely to become high achievers in schools.

In addition to the literacy skills in the primary language, some ELLs may have a L1 that is totally different from English in terms of language structure, word order, sound system, or word formation patterns (Freeman & Freeman, 2003; Jalongo & Li, 2010; Li, 2015). For example, some ELLs' L1 may greatly differ from English in a non-alphabetic writing system (e.g., Chinese), in alphabets (e.g., Russian), or in directionalities (e.g., Hebrew). Other ELLs' home languages may be similar to English in these respects. For example, Spanish, French, and Portuguese have more in common with English than do Swahili or Vietnamese. Some ELLs may have a L1 that shares some commonalties with English in terms of the usage of Roman alphabet or grammar (e.g., Italian and Polish). Other ELLs may have the L1 that shares even cognate words with English. For example, many words in English and Spanish are cognates, such as: observe vs. observar, anniversary vs. aniversario, stomach vs. estómago. Similarities between ELLs' home languages and the English language tend to make learning of English easier while differences tend to make the process more difficult or complicated (Callahan, Wilkinson, & Muller, 2010; Li, 2015; Meltzer & Hamann, 2005).

The other factors, such as, *the education of parents, socioeconomic status (SES),* and *resources available at home,* also can affect the ELLs' acquiring the L2 skills and academic content knowledge. The education of the ELL parents has an impact on the ELLs' learning the L2 and literacy skills. Research has documented that parents' education has a long-term effect on children's learning and academic success and that the parent's education, especially on the mother's level of education, is one of the important factors influencing children's reading levels and school achievements (NCFL, 2003; Roeser & Peck, 2009; Sticht & McDonald, 2009). Other studies find that the parent education is one of the indicators to predict the quality of family interactions and child behavior and thus further shape, by late adolescence, educational achievement and aspirations for future educational and occupational success of their children (Davis-Kean, 2005; Eccles, Templeton, & Barber, 2005; Guerra & Huesmann, 2004; Li, 2015). These studies believe that it is possible that, in addition to lower parental educational levels, lower socioeconomic status also affect positive family interaction patterns. It may result in child behavior problems, such as aggression as measured by these studies. In turn, it causes lowered achievement-oriented attitudes and thus affects academic outcomes.

Although many variables may affect student academic success, the SES often predicts resources available at home and is among the factors associated with student school attainment. For example, the SES of a family may determine learning resources available at home. Many ELLs are likely to live in the low SES conditions to afford learning tools and provide the needed family literacy support and this can affect the ELLs' performance in schools (Abedi, Leon, & Mirocha, 2005; Batalova & McHugh, 2010). Research also shows that some ELL parents with the lower-educational level may face barriers to support children's schooling. These barriers include inability to understand English, unfamiliarity with the school system, and differences in cultural norms and cultural capital (Abedi et al., 2005; Arias & Morillo-Campbell, 2008; Callahan, 2005). Some ELL parents may have significant communication challenges that impact their lives and that of their children. When teachers try to involve the parents in their children's learning, these factors can limit the parents' school participation.

However, research indicates that the ELL parents do have the desire to participate in and support their children's education (Mikesell, 2008; Roberge, 2002). Research also suggests the importance of parental involvement for the improved student attainment, better school attendance, and reduced dropout rate (Arias & Morillo-Campbell, 2008; Batalova & McHugh, 2010; Callahan, 2005). Thus, the parental involvement in education plays a crucial role for children to learn. It is therefore important to ensure appropriate communication between the school and parents to involve the ELL parents who can be an aspiration for their children to meet the ELLs' educational goals. It is also important that teachers establish a climate that encourages growth in cultural responsiveness, sensitivity, and appreciation to involve ELL parents in important school functions such as parent conferences and meetings.

Educators therefore must find ways to communicate with ELL parents and involve their school participation. To effectively involve the ELL parents, good communication skills are required. The following are some communication techniques when involving ELL parents:

- Have an interpreter involved for the school meetings with parents so that immediate communication is available to prevent misunderstanding.
- Translate the frequently-used school documents for the ELL parents such as an invitation letter or other school documents for parents.
- Provide the ELL parents with choices, such as using non-verbal feedback, to make the communication easier in order to improve their participation.
- Use the telephone conference with an interpreter available in the conference meetings with ELL parents if they are unable to come due to transportation.

- Use technology-based media (e.g., website and internet techniques) to involve the ELL parents' participation with a reliable design and an easy access so that ELL parents can participate in and support for their children's schooling.
- Encourage the ELL parents' participation by giving them more opportunities, such as involving them in working with their children on some class projects.

Finally, the *life experiences* and *cultural norms* of the ELLs also affect how they learn English and literacy skills. For example, Generation 1.5 ELL students, especially those who are Latino, may come from family backgrounds that place a premium importance on the family value. These ELLs may be expected to take priority over the family instead of school. As a result, some ELLs may have to drop out of school to help their parents and support their family in time of financial needs. In the Case Scenario, Tom had to sacrifice some of his time and provide help with some restaurant work to support his parents and fulfill family responsibilities when he needed that time for his academic work. In his own words, he had the responsibility to help his parents and support his family because they would have no way to survive if the parents did not work. ELLs bring with them not only different life experiences but also cultural norms that may have shaped their notions of appropriate teacher–student relationship. For example, the ELLs from some cultures may have learned to show respect for adults by listening quietly instead of asking questions or displaying knowledge by volunteering answers. Some ELL students may have the desire for closeness with their teachers through physical proximity and hugs, while others may expect a more formal or distant relationship with their teachers.

Some ELLs may even come from a refugee background. According to the Geneva Convention definition, a refugee is a person who, due to fear of persecution or due to war, violence, or natural disaster, is forced outside the country of his or her nationality, and seeks refuge or asylum (Kanno & Varghese, 2010; Li, 2015). Since 1980, when the formal U.S. refugee resettlement began, 1.8 million refugees have been invited to live in the United States, with annual refugee arrival typically between 40,000 to 75,000 (NHCR, 2009; USCIS, 2013). The refugee ELLs not only have limited English proficiency but also constraints unique to this population. For example, they may have limited financial resources, tendency of self-eliminate or suffering from grief, anxiety, depression, guilt, or symptoms of post-traumatic stress disorder (Kanno & Varghese, 2010; Li, 2015). Compared to other ELLs, the refugee ELLs are more likely to have difficulties with school work or adjustment issues related to these facts:

- Their education may be interrupted or postponed due to war in their home country or a waiting period of settlement in a refugee camp.
- They are faced with a sudden, unexpected transition to a new culture and new country that may create confusion, difficulty, or uncertainty for them; it is thus difficult for them to adjust to school codes of conduct.
- These ELLs may have a sense of loss and trauma that could be profound for them; for instance, the loss may include family members or personal property, which can have psychological and emotional impacts.
- The family business in the home country may be left unsettled after leaving in a hurry; thus, basic needs and requirements, such as food, housing, and immediate medical and dental care, may be an urgent issue.
- They may be even without parents or family guardians, experience some dramatic emotional and physical difficulties, and returning home is not an option for them.

Educators need to be sensitive to the needs of the ELLs and all students and strive to help them succeed academically and socially. Due to the difference in the life experiences and cultural norms of the ELLs who come to school with different backgrounds, it is up to teachers to get to know their students and make necessary adjustment in instructional aspects and learning environments to accommodate the needs of all students so that they can succeed.

ACADEMIC RELATED ISSUES

As the fast growing segment of the school population, the ELL students' academic attainments and related issues concern many educators. Achievement data suggest that ELL students generally lag behind their English-speaking peers and the performance gap between ELLs and their English-speaking peers (non-ELLs) is persistent. For example, the NCES on student achievement reveals that the students of the nation's second largest ethnic group (i.e., the Hispanic students) are underperforming their Caucasian peers (NCES, 2012). This NCES data released in June 2012 by the U.S. Department of Education shows that scores have gone up for both groups. For instance, at the 4th grade level, the average mathematics scores in 2011 for Caucasian students increased by 249 points and Hispanic students by 229 points, which were higher for both groups than their respective scores in 1990. However, Hispanic students still lagged behind their Caucasian peers by the same points as they did in 1990. This means that the achievement gap between Hispanic and Caucasian students has been unchanged for the past two decades while 80% of the ELL population are Hispanic speaking (Batalova &

McHugh, 2010; Flannery, 2009). Generally, 4th grade ELL students are about three years behind 4th grade Caucasian students in reading; 8th grade ELLs are about four years behind (Fry, 2007; Ortiz & Pagan, 2009).

Furthermore, between 1990 and 2010, the percentage of public school students who were White decreased from 67% to 54%, and the percentage of those who were Hispanic increased from 12% or 5.1 million students to 23% or 12.1 million students (NCES, 2012). The NCES data shows that the Hispanic students are also less likely to complete high school than their Caucasian peers with the high school graduation rate for White students to be 75% and 53.2% for the Hispanic students. Nationally, only 12% of students with LEP scored "at or above proficient" in mathematics in the 4th grade on the 2009 National Assessment of Educational Progress, compared with 42% of students who were not classified as ELLs (Ortiz & Pagan, 2009; Slavin, Madden, Calderon, Chamberlain, & Hennessy, 2010). Therefore, it is crucial that teachers build capacity for learning success and seek strategies to support the ELLs so that the academic attainment of this school population can be achieved. In this respect, it is imperative that the content area teachers know the basics in the L2 acquisition and teaching strategies in order to work this unique student body.

To begin with, teachers need to understand basic terminologies related to ELLs and the programs within the school system. These terms are provided in Table 1.1 with the purpose of helping the K–12 teachers know the basics information and resources in the schools to better work with the ELLs and help them with learning success.

In the process of working with the ELLs and understanding their needs, teachers need to distinguish truth from some misconceptions about the ELL students that can affect the teachers' attitude to serve ELLs. In Table 1.2, seven common myths are provided. The purpose is to help teachers have a better understanding of ELLs to help them achieve success.

ELL PROFILES AND WORK SAMPLES

Julio Gonzales Profile

Julio, a kindergartener and U.S.-born ELL, is energetic and enjoys active learning. He looks forward to the sessions with his English tutor who works with him twice a week for supplementary L2 support. Julio has made an improvement on recognizing a majority of the letters in the alphabet. Flash cards are used as a great tool to work with him. On a Monday morning, Julio and his tutor were working on alphabets. They used flash cards to identify the different alphabets and sounds. Each alphabet circle had diverse letters and pictures of items for each letter. Julio and the tutor also played the "Name that Letter" game. This game allowed Julio to shuffle the

TABLE 1.1 Common Terms Related to ELLs and Programs

	Acronym	Definition	Context
Terminologies Related to ELLs	EL	*English Learners:* This term is exchangeable with the term ELLs	U.S. Department of Education has started to use this term to substitute the previous term *LEP*.
	ELL	*English Language Learner:* who is in the process of acquiring English; whose primary language is not English	This term is used more frequently in recent years to substitute other terms, e.g., LEP or ESL students.
	LEP	*Limited English Proficiency:* A student who has limited English proficiency	Educators believe that this term has a connotation focusing on limitation. It is substituted with other terms (e.g., ELs or ELLs) in recent years.
	Generation 1.5	*Generation 1.5 students:* U.S. educated ELLs but belong to neither Generation 1 nor Generation 2 of immigrants	They may have limited skills in L1 but strong oral skills in L2; yet, they are less proficient in academic language related to school achievement.
ELL Related Programs	EFL	*English as a Foreign Language:* English is taught by teachers whose native language is not English.	A program for students who learn English as a foreign language in a country where English is not the L1.
	ESL	*English as a Second Language:* English is taught by teachers whose native language is English.	The ESL student is now a less common term than the ELL and is more often used to refer to an educational approach to support ELLs to learn English.
	ESOL	*English for Speakers of Other Languages:* English is taught by teachers whose native language is English.	It is also referred to as ENL, *English as a New Language;* the program offered in public schools often pulls ELLs out of regular classes to learn English.
	TESOL	Teaching English to Speakers of Other Languages: *Teaching English to non-English speakers*	It is an international association with the mission to advance professional expertise in English language teaching and learning for students of other languages than English.

Note: This table is modified based on information from Bardack (2010).

flash cards, close his eyes, and then select one card. After selecting the card, he excitingly announced that it was the letter "A." Julio informed the tutor that "A" was the first letter in the alphabet and made the "ah" sound. Next, they used the *Oxford Picture Dictionary* to identify some items that begin with the letter "A." Julio pointed to a red apple, an ant, and a green alligator and he drew a picture (see Figure 1.1). He truly enjoyed this session. They also read *Silly Monsters ABC* by Gearld Hawksley. Julio was ecstatic and excited when he saw the different monsters. His favorite monster, the "J" monster, played jump rope, ate a jellybean, and juggled balls. Julio recognized that

TABLE 1.2 Seven Common Myths With Truth Related to the ELLs

Myth	Truth	Rationale
Myth #1: *ELLs can learn English easily by being simply exposed to the L2 contexts*	Exposure to the L2 context alone is insufficient. An ELL may appear proficient in basic communication skills but he or she may not have developed the academic language proficiency to function in schools (Ovando et al., 2005).	Good lesson planning and teaching strategies apply to all students including ELLs.
Myth #2: *The ability to speak fluently in English indicates that an ELL should do well in classroom.*	Proficiency in social language cannot be used to judge an ELL's academic proficiency; Spoken English may be acquired in 2 or 3 years; yet, cognitive academic language proficiency takes about 5 to 7 years to be developed (Cummins, 2000).	Oral English has different rhetoric, structure, vocabulary, and requirements from that of academic L2.
Myth #3: *All ELLs learn English in the same way and thus can be taught in the same manner.*	ELLs are a heterogeneous group and different in many ways, such as previous schooling, family background, L1 knowledge, and immigration status; all these factors can affect how ELLs learn a L2 and they learn in varied paces and ways (McCarthey, Garcia, Lopez-Velasquez, & Guo, 2004).	No one strategy can fit all ELLs; teachers must use multiple ways to assess and meet the ELL students' needs.
Myth #4: *ELLs have disabilities; that is why they are often overrepresented in special education.*	Inappropriate placement of ELLs in special education classes can limit the growth of ELLs when they have no disabilities; they can perform better if placed accordingly; quality instruction and inclusive environments are more effective for ELLs (Callahan, 2005; Ariles & Ortiz, 2002).	Overrepresentation reflects the assessment system problem that does not differentiate disabilities from the ELLs' L2 needs.
Myth #5: *Teaching ELLs focus on teaching them vocabulary.*	Learning a L2 is a recursive process and integrating listening, speaking, reading, and writing skills into instruction from the start helps ELLs, who need to learn not only forms and structures of academic language but also understand the relationship between forms and meanings; need the opportunities to express complex meanings in written English (Callahan, 2005; Schleppegrell & Go, 2007).	Curricula organized around authentic reading and writing experiences provide textual choices and meaningful content for ELL students.
Myth #6: *Providing accommodations for ELLs benefits these students only.*	Making mainstream classrooms more responsive to ELLs will also help other under-served students in general because many cognitive aspects of teaching to ELLs are common to the native English speakers although teachers should pay additional attention to background knowledge, interaction, and word use with ELLs (Meltzer &. Hamann, 2005).	ELLs tend to perform much better when teaching respond to their needs and the environment is supportive to learn.
Myth #7: *ELL students should concentrate on English and stop speaking their L1.*	Proficiency in the L1 facilitates L2 development; academic achievement is significantly enhanced when ELL students are able to use their L1 knowledge to learn academic content in the L2 context (Cummins, 2000; Li, 2015).	Denying the native language of an individual is to deny his or her existence.

Note: Common myths are modified from Espinosa's (2008).

Figure 1.1 Julio focused on recognizing the letters in the above session. He was given many opportunities to practice in a meaningful way by reading, writing, listening, and playing the game. The drawing is his sample work after learning Letter "A."

the monster participated in activities that began with the letter "J." He identified most of the letters in the book! Reading with Julio was an adventure. The joy in his eyes showed that he was happy and enjoyed learning.

Edwin Perez Profile

Edwin, a first grader and also U.S. born, enjoys learning but can become distracted. Edwin works better with one-on-one guidance. He is focused when there is less distraction such as in the ESOL resource room. It was at the beginning of the school year and Edwin was working with his tutor who assisted Edwin with learning sessions twice a week as supplementary support. This was an afternoon session inside the mainstream classroom reviewing the new vocabulary words before his one-on-one session. Students were doing independent work while the teacher prepared for the next lesson. Edwin seemed to be unable to concentrate on his work. The assignment was for all the students to review the ten vocabulary words. After the students completed this review assignment, Edwin and the tutor worked in a quiet location so that Edwin would feel comfortable and not be distracted. They reviewed the vocabulary words again. Edwin knew some of the words; yet, did not comprehend others.

Figure 1.2   This is Edwin's sample work. After reading the story, *The Fence* by Debra Blenus, Edwin drew a picture of the different animals in the story. He also described what happened in the story with a brief summary. As a first grader, he was beginning to enjoy learning although there appeared to be the need for him to improve his writing skills.

He was guided to create sentences for each word and drew pictures for some words (see Figure 1.2). He was able to enunciate some words with ease while needing more assistance with the others. Edwin also needed to improve his writing skills. Practice was key in helping Edwin with word development. Edwin enjoyed the session with the tutor and appeared eager to learn.

Ann Sanchez Profile

Ann is a fifth-grade ELL who has recently immigrated to the United States with her parents and younger brother. Although she was a good student in her home country, it is not easy for Ann to keep the pace with the academic work in her new school. In all, Ann is experiencing some difficulty getting good grades due to not being able to understand the content covered by her teachers in English. This is also the unfortunate situation for many other ELLs because they cannot comprehend the content due to the English language barrier. Although many teachers want to help, they seem to feel the limitation for what they can do in terms of helping Ann because Ann cannot speak or understand English. However, Mrs. Daniels (pseudonym), Ann's 5th grade teacher, went out of her way and provided Ann with additional assistance whenever she could, such as translating versions of assignments and assessments and giving Ann more time, so that Ann could have an opportunity to complete her assignments (see Figure 1.3). This did require the teacher to go beyond her normal work. Yet, Ann accelerated with her academic work once the language barrier was overcome.

These ELL profiles provide further information on ELLs who have different learning needs and their needs were accommodated accordingly. As a diverse, fast growing student body, the ELL school population offers both challenges and opportunities to American education (Nieto, 2000). They bring diversity and rich cultures with them to our school and classrooms. It is important for teachers to recognize that the ELLs' L1 and home cultures should be positioned as resources so that teachers can help ELLs see that their L1s and cultures are valued and contributing to education rather than something to be overcome. Involving ELL students in activities, such as writing about home and school, helps them develop abilities in text comprehension, collaboration with peers, and construction of a writer identity (Nieto, 2000; Yi, 2007). Teachers

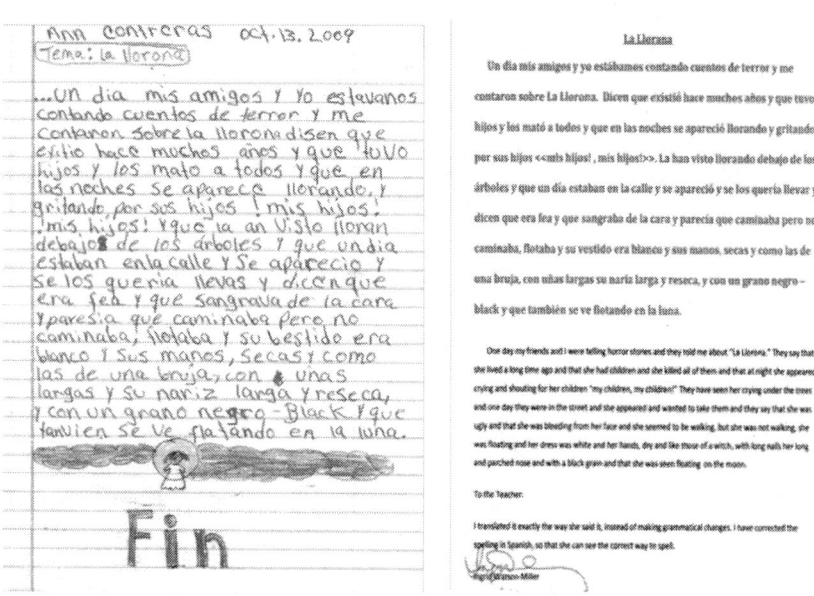

Figure 1.3 This is Ann's sample work. On the left is a story that Ann wrote in Spanish as an assignment on her first day in school. The teacher allows her to express in the language she understands. Under the story is the picture Ann drew, which depicted a ghost floating in the night sky because it was around Halloween. The word "Fin" at the bottom represents "The End" in Spanish. The translated version of the story is provided on the right with the help of another Spanish teacher. This is an example of the teacher going beyond her way to help her student.

can use different strategies to reduce the distance between home and school, while helping ELLs to become more invested in school learning.

Continuing to engage teachers in professional development to ensure that all teachers are adequately prepared to work with ELLs is important in the next few years. Teachers need to know basic knowledge and strategies to work with ELLs. Research indicates that a low percentage of teachers received professional development on teaching ELLs despite the growing numbers of ELLs and fewer states have policies that have requirements for K–12 teachers to obtain certain expertise in teaching ELLs (Freeman & Freeman, 2003; Karabenick & Noda, 2004). As a result, many ELLs find themselves in mainstream classrooms taught by teachers with no formal preparation to work with these linguistically-diverse students. Thus, it is imperative that teachers of the ELLs gain knowledge and skills through various efforts so that they can produce positive effects. In this process, getting to the ELLs and their educational needs is the initial step for teachers to devise strategies and work with them.

SUMMARY

Chapter 1 focused on basic information about the ELLs. The chapter began with a case scenario about an ELL, Tom, as a snapshot to help teachers understand who the ELLs are and what possible problems they may face. Then the chapter provided the background information on the fast growth of the ELL school enrollment, tracing the immigration law (i.e., Johnson-Reed Act in 1924). The chapter also discussed common characteristics of the ELLs so that teachers can meet the needs of this unique school population. The chapter discussed the types of ELL students (e.g., Generation 1.5 vs. U.S. born ELL students). Academic attainment related issues are addressed with an examination of common terms and myths related to the ELLs. The chapter also provided the sample profiles of the ELLs with their work samples. The intention is to help teachers understand that the ELLs have different educational needs and learning styles. It is up to teachers to be engaged in professional development and preparation to meet the special needs of ELLs as this school population is and will be continuing to increase. Having a better understanding of the ELLs is an initial step for teachers to work effectively with their ELLs to enhance the learning outcomes of ELLs and all students.

REFERENCES

Abedi, J., Leon, S., & Mirocha, J. (2005). Examining ELL and non-ELL student performance differences and their relationship to background factors:

Continued analyses of extant data. In *The validity of administering large-scale content assessments to english language learners: An investigation from three perspectives* (pp. 1–43). Los Angeles, CA: NCRESST.

Arias, B., & Morillo-Campbell, M. (2008). Promoting ELL parental involvement: Challenges in contested times. *Educational Research Policy.* Retrieved on December 12, 2012 from: http://epsl.asu.edu/epru/documents/EPSL-0801-250-EPRU.pdf.

Artiles, A. J., & Ortiz, A. A. (2002). English language learners with special education needs. McHenry, IL: Center for Applied Linguistics and Delta Systems.

Bardack, S. (2010). Common ELL terms and definitions. *English Language Learner Center: American Institute for Research.* Washington, DC: AIR. Retrieved on December 29, 2012 from http://www.air.org/files/NEW_-_Common_ELL_TERMS.

Batalova, J., & McHugh, M. (2010). Top languages spoken by English Language Learners nationally and by state. National Center on Immigrant Integration Policy. *Immigration Policy Institute: ELL Information Center Fact Series, 3*(1), 1–5.

Callahan, R. M., Wilkinson, L., & Muller, C. (2010). Academic achievement and course taking among language minority youth in U.S. schools: Effects of ESL placement. *Educational Evaluation and Policy Analysis, 32*(1), 84–117.

Callahan, R. M. (2005). Tracking and high school English learners: Limiting opportunities to learn. *American Educational Research Journal, 42*(2), 305–328.

Cummins, J. (2000). *Language, power, and pedagogy: Bilingual children in the crossfire.* Clevedon, England: Multilingual Matters.

Davis-Kean, P. E. (2005). The influence of parent education and family income on child achievement: The indirect role of parental expectations and the home environment. *Journal of Family Psychology, 19*(2), 294–304.

Eccles J., Templeton J., & Barber B. (2005). Adolescence and emerging adulthood: The critical passage ways to adulthood. In M. Bornstein, L. Davidson, & N. J. Mahwah (Eds.), *Well-being: Positive development across the life course* (pp. 383–406). Hillsdale, NJ: Lawrence Erlbaum Associates.

Espinosa, L. M. (2008). *Challenging common myths about young English language learners.* [PCD Policy Brief-Advancing PK–3, Number 8]. New York, NY: Foundation for Child Development.

Flannery, M. E. (2009). *A new look at America's English language learners.* Washington, DC: National Education Association. Retrieved from http://www.nea.org/home/29160.htm

Fry, R. (2007). *How far behind in math and reading are English language learners?* Washington, DC: Pew Hispanic Center. Retrieved from http://www.pewhispanic.org/2007/06/06/how-far-behind-in-math-and-reading-are-english-language-learners/

Freeman, D. E., & Freeman, Y. S. (2003). *Essential linguistics: What you need to know to teach reading, ESL, spelling, phonics, grammar.* Portsmouth, NH: Heinemann.

Guerra, N. G., & Huesmann, L. R. (2004). A cognitive-ecological model of aggression. *International Review of Social Psychology, 17*(3), 177–203.

Jalongo, M., & Li, N. (2010). Young English language learners as listeners: Theoretical perspectives, research stands, and implications for instruction. In B. Spodek & O. Saracho (Eds.), *Contemporary Perspectives on Language and*

Cultural Diversity in Childhood Education (pp. 95–115). Charlotte, NC: Information Age.

Kanno, Y., & Varghese, M. M. (2010). Immigrant and refugee ESL students' challenge to assess four year college education: Language policy and educational policy. *Journal of Language, 9*(5), 310–328.

Karabenick, A. S., & Noda, P. A. (2004). Professional development implications of teachers beliefs and attitudes toward English language learners. *Bilingual Research Journal, 28*(1), 55–75.

Li, N. (2015). *A book for every teacher: Teaching to English Language Learners.* Charlotte, NC: Information Age.

Li, N., Howard, C., & Mitchell, Y. (2011). What a case study reveals: Facing the new challenge and learning the basics in L2 acquisition. *The National Teacher Education Journal, 3*(2), 57–69.

McCarthey, S. J., Garcia, G. E., Lopez-Velasquez, A. M., & Guo, S. H. (2004). Understanding contexts for English language learners. *Research in Teaching of English, 38*(4), 351–394.

Meltzer, J., &. Hamann, E. T. (2005). *Meeting the literacy development needs of adolescent English language learners through content-area learning.* Providence, RI: The Education Alliance at Brown University.

Mikesell, L. (2008, December). Generation 1.5 and ESL learners' use of past participles: A corpus-based comparison. *CATESOL State Conference Proceedings.* Retrieved from http://www.catesol.org/06Mikesell.pdf

National Center for Educational Statistics. (2012). *The Condition of Education 2012* (NCES 2012–045), National Center for Education Statistics, Institute of Education Sciences. Washington, DC: U.S. Department of Education.

National Center for Family Literacy. (2003). *Dissemination process submission to the Program Effectiveness Panel of the U.S. Department of Education.* Louisville, KY: NCFL.

National Clearinghouse for English Language Acquisition (2011). *The Growing Numbers of English Learner Students, 1998/99–2008/09.* Washington, DC: NCELA.

Nieto, S. (2012). Linguistic diversity in multicultural classrooms. In S. Nieto & P. Bode (Eds.), *Affirming diversity: Creating multicultural communities* (pp. 189–217). New York, NY: Addison Wesley, and Longman.

Office of the United Nations High Commissioner for Refugees (2009). Students from refugee backgrounds: A guide for teachers and schools. *Convention and Protocol Relating to the Status of Refugees (UNHCR).* British Columbia, Canada: Ministry of Education.

Ortiz, T., & Pagan, M. (2009). *Closing the ELL achievement gap: A leader's guide to making schools effective for culturally and linguistically diverse students.* Rexford, NY: International Center for Leadership in Education.

Oudenhoven, E. D. (2006). *Caught in the middle: Generation 1.5 Latino students and English language learning at a community college* (Doctoral dissertation). Loyola University, Chicago, IL: *Digital Dissertations,* AAT 3212980.

Ovando, C. J., Collier, V. P., & Combs, M. C. (2005). *Bilingual & ESL classrooms: Teaching in multicultural contexts.* New York, NY: McGraw Hill.

Roberge, M. M. (2002). California's generation 1.5 immigrants: What experiences, characteristics, and needs do they bring to our English classes? *The CATESOL Journal, 14*(1), 107–129.

Roeser, R.W., & Peck, S. C. (2009). Education in awareness: Self-motivation and self-regulated learning in contemplative perspective. *Educational Psychologist, 44(2),* 119–136.

Schleppegrell, M. J., & Go, A. L. (2007). Analyzing the writing of English learners: A functional approach. *Language Arts, 84* (6), 529–538.

Short, P. J., & Fitzsimmons, S. (2007). *Double the work: Challenges and solutions to ac-quiring language and academic literacy for adolescent English Language Learners-Report to Carnegie Corporation.* New York, NY: Alliance for Excellence Education.

Singhal, M. (2006). Academic writing and Generation 1.5: Pedagogical goals and instructional issues in the college composition classrooms. *The Reading Matrix, 4*(3), 3–15.

Slavin, R. E., Madden, N., Calderon, M., Chamberlain, A., & Hennessy, M. (2010). *Reading and language outcomes of a five-year randomized evaluation of transitional bilingual education* (Report submitted to Institute for Education Sciences). Washington DC: U.S. Department of Education.

Sticht, T. G., & McDonald, B. A. (2009). *Teach the mother and reach the child: Literacy across generations. Literacy Lessons.* Geneva, NY: International Bureau of Education.

Yi, Y. (2007). Engaging literacy: A biliterate student's composing practices beyond school. *Journal of Second Language Writing, 16(1),* 23–39.

Zelasko, N., & Antunez, B., (2000). *If your child learns in two languages.* Washington, DC: National Clearinghouse for Bilingual Education, George Washington University.

CHAPTER 2

ELLs AND L2
ACQUISITION THEORIES

Nan Li
Claflin University

Thomas Destino
Mars Hill University

CASE SCENARIO

Samantha Ortíz came to the United States from Honduras when she was six years old. Samantha started school from the first grade. She was required to receive the daily ESOL service because she didn't speak English. Her father spoke some English and worked on a sod farm; her mother did not speak any English and stayed home to take care of the children. Every day Samantha's mother checked her schoolwork and that of her siblings to make sure that the children completed their homework. Samantha was shy but polite. By the end of the second grade, Samantha was able to speak English. In fact, her oral English became very good and she could tell stories in English. In the third grade, Samantha was mainstreamed. However, at the beginning of the fourth grade, her teacher noticed that Samantha struggled with her social studies, math, and science lesson content. She could not understand the concepts in these subject areas. Her teacher was confused about why she could speak English so well but could not understand the content lessons

Teaching ELLs Across Content Areas, pages 21–46
Copyright © 2016 by Information Age Publishing
All rights of reproduction in any form reserved.

in English. What Samantha struggled with most was understanding math or science concepts. This made the teacher think that Samantha could have a learning disability. According to the teacher, if Samantha had fluent oral English, she should be able to understand the lesson content in English. The teacher knew that Samantha had been in America for four years and thus began to think that Samantha might need to be diagnosed to see what her learning disability issue was.

Many content area teachers may find their ELLs struggle in a similar way in the content area classrooms as shown in the above scenario. These ELLs may have quite fluent oral English skills after two years of schooling in the content area classrooms; yet, they continue struggling to understand the content area lessons in the classrooms. This chapter will discuss why this can happen from a second language (L2) theoretical perspective. Based on Jim Cummins (1984) and his L2 acquisition theories, oral English is easier to acquire than academic English. He refers to oral English as social language that can be acquired in a relatively shorter period, from six months to two years. Yet, academic language takes a longer period to acquire because academic language requires specific vocabulary related to each content area. For example, to understand algebraic concepts, academic mathematics language is required.

The above scenario thus tells educators that they should not expect that an ELL can meet all academic challenges in the mainstream classroom solely based on their oral English fluency. As the scenario shows, teachers could easily think that the ELLs have a learning disability or that they might not work hard enough. Without receiving appropriate instructional and language support, these ELLs are likely to continue to struggle in mainstream classrooms. Teachers have the obligation to help their ELLs and all students succeed so that they can make yearly academic progress in the content areas. Learning about the basics of the L2 acquisition from a theoretical perspective can help teachers understand how to better assist their ELLs.

BICS AND CALP

Cummins (1984) proposes his L2 acquisition theories defining two types of L2 proficiencies. The two types are: Basic Interpersonal Communication Skills (BICS) and Cognitive Academic Language Proficiency (CALP). BICS refers to the oral, social language skills, or the "surface" L2 skills of listening and speaking. These are typically acquired in informal settings by many ELL students; particularly, by those from language backgrounds similar to the English language who spend a lot of their school time interacting with native speakers. CALP is the basis of an ELL's ability to address the academic demands of the various subject areas. According to Cummins, the language used in school has a broad range of competencies and he makes a distinction between conversational English language skills, which takes the ELL from six months to two years to develop, and cognitive academic English language competency, which takes five to seven years (Collier, 1987; Cummins, 1984).

Cummins further explains that children can reach the autonomous stage called plateau, where they feel that no more progress can be made in learning the second language. The causes for plateaus can be for different reasons; yet, it is believed that a major cause is sticking to the same habits, whether it's writing, typing, or programming. This often results in failing to progress, despite investing a lot of time learning language (Ericsson, 2006). In a nutshell, people feel that they are fine with their proficiency level and stop improving. Also, they allow evident flaws and lose control of what they are doing. However, experts tend to engage in a directed, highly focused routine, something called, deliberate practice. These experts and top achievers in various fields tend to follow the same general pattern of development. There are three attitudes that are common for them: focusing on their technique, staying goal-oriented, and receiving constant and immediate feedback on their performance. Applying this to L2 learning, it means that ELLs can reach near-nativelike oral skills. However, the proficiency in the academic language requires deliberate practice and it takes a longer period for ELLs to reach and to meet the demands of schoolwork at the same level as a native English speaker.

Understanding the basic concepts of BICS and CALP explains why it is challenging for Samantha to understand the vocabulary of the subject areas even though she is able to speak English very well. It takes longer for an ELL to develop CALP although the ELL may have gained BICS. For example, without any context clues, an ELL could associate the word table with a chair while a native speaker may already know the multiple meanings of the word table and can relate it to a mathematics concept more easily (see Figure 2.1).

Figure 2.1 Multiple meanings of an English word, such as "Table."

Basic Interpersonal Communicative Skills (BICS)

According to Cummins (1984), BICS refers to social language skills of everyday English that people use in conversational contexts. Thus, BICS is gained through communication and interaction. Lev Vygotsky (1978), a twentieth century Soviet psychologist, also believes language acquisition involves a child's exposure to words and the interdependent process of growth between thought and language. According to Vygotsky, children develop the first language (L1) skills through social interaction. By interacting with others in the environment, a child develops the ability for inner speech. Through inner speech, children straddle the divide between thought and language, eventually being able to express their thoughts coherently to others. Consistent with Vygotsky's theory, Donato (1994) and Lantolf (2000) believe that ELLs acquire the English language through interaction with others just like when they learn their L1. ELLs interact with their teachers and peers in the English-speaking environments, such as classrooms, playground, school cafeteria, libraries, watching videos, television shows, movies, sports, games, computer games, reading magazines, or through the use of electronic devices, such iPods, iPads, and iPhones.

Therefore, ELLs need to be exposed to a rich English language environment to retell stories, describe activities, share personal experiences, tell their preferences and opinions, and talk about events to develop their oral English. Yet, BICS does not assure that they have acquired the academic English proficiency that is crucial for them to function successfully in content area classrooms (e.g., to understand math or science concepts and terminology).

Cognitive Academic Language Proficiency (CALP)

According to L2 acquisition theories, CALP is the academic English language needed to understand subject matter related concepts. It is about cognitively demanding language skills and it takes five to seven years to develop. Schools usually measure the ELLs' L2 proficiency based on four language skills: listening, speaking, reading, and writing. The ELLs can be competent in having a face-to-face conversation by listening and speaking, but they may still lack the academic proficiency to read and write well. Also, they may have difficulty comprehending concepts that are cognitively demanding and require a significant amount of background knowledge and specific vocabulary related to the content areas. Thus, it is important that the classroom teachers do not assume that ELLs who have attained a certain degree of fluency in spoken English have the corresponding academic language proficiency (Collier, 1987; Cummins, 1984). Although ELLs have exited from the ESOL program, they may still be in the process of acquiring their academic language proficiency.

These L2 acquisition theories concur with educational theories. Bloom's Taxonomy, first developed in 1956 under the leadership of educational psychologist Benjamin Bloom, was further constructed to promote higher levels of thinking skills, such as analyzing and evaluating concepts instead of simply remembering facts (Bloom, 1956). Based on Bloom's Taxonomy, academic activities that require students to accomplish are different from those in the social context. See examples in Table 2.1. For handling academically demanding tasks, cognitive competence is needed at the six levels: (a) knowledge to remember previously learned information (e.g., define, describe, identify, state, select, label, list, outline, reproduce); (b)

Table 2.1 Examples of Social and Academic Language Based on Bloom's Taxonomy in 1956

Social Language	Academic Language
Everyday conversation: – "Hello!" – "It is cold today." – "Tom likes to play football."	Knowledge: define, describe, identify, state, select, label, list, outline, etc. – "Please name three natural disasters based on our reading yesterday."
Culturally related: – "They are invited to a cocktail party to celebrate their class reunion." – "We had a birthday party for my younger brother last week and she turned 7." – "Please bring your brownbag for the planning meeting tomorrow."	Comprehension: classify, describe, discuss, explain, identify, paraphrase, predict, recognize, summarize, review, etc. – "Please summarize the author's main ideas in one or two paragraphs." Application: apply, choose, demonstrate, illustrate, interpret, predict, produce, show, solve, use, write, etc. – "Please predict what happens next in the story by writing it down a sentence."
Instructionally related: – "Please raise your hand if you have any question before we move on." – "Let's turn to Page 12 and read the first paragraph of this book." – "Please remember to use double-space and the font size 12 for this research paper."	Analysis: analyze, categorize, compare, distinguish, examine, identify, infer, model – "Please compare the differences between the amphibians and reptiles based on your reading." Synthesis: arrange, assemble, categorize, collect, combine, construct, develop, generate, rearrange, reconstruct, rewrite, summarize, synthesize, etc. – "Please provide three categories of food discussed in the text." Evaluation: appraise, assess, judge, evaluate, justify, rate, summarize, support, etc. – "Please summarize the main ideas of the author with one sentence."

Note: Please also see those action words in the revised Bloom's Taxonomy in Chapter 3.

comprehension to demonstrate understanding (e.g., classify, describe, discuss, explain, identify, paraphrase, predict, recognize, summarize, select, rewrite, review); (c) application to apply knowledge in the actual situation (e.g., apply, choose, demonstrate, illustrate, interpret, predict, produce, show, solve, use, write); (d) analysis to break down ideas to find evidence (e.g., analyze, categorize, compare, distinguish, examine, identify, infer, model); (e) synthesis to compile ideas into a new whole (e.g., arrange, assemble, categorize, collect, combine, construct, develop, generate, rearrange, reconstruct, rewrite, summarize, synthesize); (f) evaluation to make a judgment (e.g., appraise, assess, choose, evaluate, judge, justify, rate, support). In order to accomplish the academic assignments, students need to have these higher-order thinking skills in order for the ELL students to apply different forms of language.

Cummins, in addition to contributing to the concepts of BICS and CALP also developed a graphic (see Figure 2.2) to understand what makes language easier or not easier for ELLs to learn. Difficulty is based on the relationship between two factors: the cognitive demand of the task and the amount of available contextual support. In Figure 2.2, the BICS and CALP are further illustrated. The first factor, the degree of cognitive challenge, is represented in Cummins's framework as basically easy or hard. The two quadrants (Quadrant I & II) on the top of Cummins's chart represent oral

	Context-Embedded	Context-Reduced
Undemanding	**I** Cognitively Undemanding + Context-Embedded	**II** Cognitively Undemanding + Context-Reduced
Demanding	**III** Cognitively Demanding + Context-Embedded	**IV** Cognitively Demanding + Context-Reduced

Figure 2.2 This is the modified format of Cummin's quadrants. Teachers can help their ELLs understand the information by providing contextual support.
Source: The chart is created based on Cummins's framework to evaluate language demand in content activities (Cummins, 1984).

or written tasks that are cognitively undemanding as in blue color (i.e., they can be either socially or academically easy tasks, such as read with picture cues, get lunch from the lunch line, play on the playground, talk on the phone, or shop for the school supplies). The two lower quadrants (Quadrant III and IV) of the chart represent tasks that are cognitively demanding as in red color. These tasks are academically difficult, requiring higher levels of thinking processing and language skills.

The second factor in Cummins's framework evaluates the amount of contextual support inherent in the task. Contextual supports offer clues to the meaning of words. The more spoken and written words are embedded in context, the easier they are to understand. Spoken language can be given contextual support through facial expressions, gestures, body language, demonstrations, visual cues, and physical environment. Written language can offer contextual support through pictures, graphs, charts, tables, and textbook aids. Oral and written tasks with these kinds of supports are called context-embedded. The two quadrants (Quadrant I & III) on the left side of the chart represent tasks that are contextually embedded as in green color. Tasks in which students have only the spoken or written words alone to work with are termed context-reduced as in Quadrant II and IV as in yellow color. Combining the two elements of cognitive challenge and contextual support, the quadrants move in difficulty from I to IV. ELLs will find Quadrant I tasks easy because they are low in cognitive demand and high in contextual support. Quadrant IV tasks will be most difficult because they are academically demanding and lack contextual support. The standardized assessment falls into this category. Therefore, to provide the contextual support and scaffolding strategies, such as visual aids, hands-on activities, and working with peers, can help ELLs understand better.

The following are some example activities that illustrate Cummins' quadrants. Teachers can help their ELLs understand the information by providing contextual support:

Quadrant I: Cognitively Undemanding and Context Embedded
   a. Engaging in face-to-face social conversation with peers.
   b. Ordering lunch from a picture menu in a fast food restaurant.
   c. Listening to a presentation about pet animals with pictures and videos.
   d. Participating in physical education classes.
   e. Participating in shows and games.
   f. Learning to play baseball with coaching demonstration.

Quadrant II: Cognitively Undemanding and Context Reduced
   a. Engaging in social conversation on the telephone.
   b. Getting travel direction via the telephone.

    c. Ordering dinner from a menu in a formal restaurant with no picture clues.

    d. Listening to a presentation about caring for pets without visual aids.

    e. Reading a list of required school supplies.

    f. Talking with friends about shows and games.

Quadrant III: Cognitively Demanding and Context Embedded

    a. Solving mathematics word problems with manipulatives and/or pictures.

    b. Solving simple math computation problems.

    c. Doing a science experiment by following a demonstration.

    d. Understanding written text through pictures, graphics, and small group discussion.

    e. Reading the illustrated (comic book) version of Shakespeare's *Romeo and Juliet*.

    f. Listening to a lecture with visual aids (e.g., gesture and PowerPoint).

    g. Writing a report paper with detailed explanation and ample examples.

Quadrants IV: Cognitively Demanding and Context Reduced

    a. Solving mathematics word problems without manipulatives and/or pictures.

    b. Conducting a science experiment by reading directions from a textbook.

    c. Writing research reports on assigned topics in social studies.

    d. Listening to a lecture about an unfamiliar topic.

    e. Reading Shakespeare's *Romeo and Juliet* in its original format.

    f. Taking a standard test, such SAT, ACT, and TOFEL.

Source: Adapted from Gardner (2012)

To summarize the chart in Figure 2.2, it is clear that a context-embedded task is one in which an ELL has access to additional visual and oral cues. For example, an ELL can look at illustrations of what is being talked about to confirm understanding. A context-reduced task is one such as listening to a lecture or reading difficult text, where there are no other sources of support or help other than the language itself. Therefore, providing contextual clues is very important to help ELLs develop CALP. Cummins' contribution to the distinction between BICS and CALP is influential. However, his framework of BICS and CALP also received some criticism. Some critics believe that language is always "contextualized" as opposed to Cummins' definition that CALP is "decontextualized" language (Bartolomé, 1998; Gee, 1990). Others argue that Cummins' framework does not provide enough specific information to help teachers meet the diverse needs of ELLs and the framework of BICS and CALP emphasizes the weaknesses of the low cognitive skills of the ELLs rather than the fund of knowledge that students can bring to the classroom (MacSwan & Rolstad, 2003; Edelsky, 2006; Scarcella, 2003). Yet, BICS and CALP contribute greatly to help teachers understand the differences between social and academic languages and the process of the ELLs' academic growth in content areas.

COMPREHENSIBLE INPUT AND AFFECTIVE FILTER

Comprehensible input refers to the language message that can be understood by the ELLs despite their not understanding all the words and structures in it. It is described as one level above that of the learners if it can only just be understood. Krashen (1982), an American linguist and an educational researcher, proposes this theory of the L2 Acquisition. In this chapter, his hypotheses of the Comprehensible Input and Affective Filter are introduced as the basic concepts of L2 acquisition needed for helping the ELLs in classrooms.

Comprehensible Input Hypothesis

According to Krashen (1982), providing ELLs with the comprehensive input helps the ELLs acquire language naturally, rather than learn it consciously. For example, the teacher can select a reading text for upper-intermediate level ELLs that is from a lower advanced level course book. Based on what the teacher knows about the learners, the teacher believes that this will give them comprehensible input to help them acquire more language. In the classroom, it is important that teachers understand that language slightly above their level encourages ELLs to use natural learning strategies, such as guessing words from context and inferring meaning. As the example suggests, a teacher needs to know the level of the learners very well in order to select comprehensible input, and in a large class of mixed ability, different learners will need different texts. Krashen (1982) proposes this Comprehensible Input Hypothesis and states that language acquisition requires meaningful interaction in the target language through natural communication. By natural communication, he means that speakers should not be concerned with the form of their utterances but with the messages they are conveying and understanding. He believes that the best ways to learn a second language is to supply comprehensible input in low anxiety situations. In other words, the input conveyed to the ELLs must be comprehensible. This further indicates that the ELLs should not be forced for early production in learning the second language, but produce when they are ready. This requires teachers to understand that ELLs' learning progress largely comes from supplying communicative and comprehensible input, and not from forcing and correcting production.

Krashen further explains that languages are learned in context through the learner's knowledge of the world. Knowing the structure of a language will not help an ELL to develop the communication competence. His comprehensive input hypothesis proposes that ELLs acquire the L2 through understanding the meaning before they learn the structure. He also presents an idea using the formula $i + 1$, in which i stands for input, the meaningful and comprehensible communication in a context that is understood by the ELLs immediately; and +1 refers to the level that is slightly beyond the current level of the learners, but challenging enough for the learners to advance their language proficiency. In other words, if the lesson content is at the level of $i + 0$ or $i + 2$, it will be either lack of challenge or too difficult. In classrooms, teachers can enhance ELLs and all students' comprehension by using the $i + 1$ formula through incorporating strategies, such as using scaffolding strategies, embedding rich context, linking to the learner's prior knowledge, using graphic organizers, providing modeling, visual aids, and ample examples, pre-teaching the content, and collaborating with the ESOL teachers.

Affective Filter Hypothesis

An effective language teacher is someone who can provide input and help make language comprehensible in a low anxiety environment. Krashen (1982) also proposes the Affective Filter hypothesis. According to this theory, emotional factors can affect ELLs ability to learn the second language. Comprehensible input is not enough to ensure language acquisition and an ELL must also be receptive to that input. In the human brain, there is a *language acquisition device* (LAD) that functions to process the L2. However, if the ELLs are nervous, unmotivated, bored, frustrated, or stressed, the ELLs may not be receptive to language input; in other words, they may filter the input to reach LAD. This filter is called the *Affective Filter*. It includes several variables, such as motivation, self-esteem, confidence, and anxiety. Krashen believes that when learners have high motivation, self-esteem, confidence, a good self-image, and low anxiety, they are more receptive to learning content and thus better equipped for success in L2 acquisition. On the other hand, low motivation, low self-esteem, and debilitating anxiety can cause the learners to increase the affective filter and form a *mental block* that prevents comprehensible input from being used for acquisition. In other words, when the affective filter is high, it impedes language acquisition.

When applying this hypothesis in classrooms, teachers can see that ELLs can learn better in the learning environment that makes them feel motivated and that builds their self-esteem and confidence because such a positive environment lowers their anxiety. This L2 acquisition theory has a practical implication for all K–12 mainstream teachers in terms of creating a supportive classroom atmosphere for ELLs and designing lessons that motivate ELLs to learn while lowering their affective filter (i.e., reducing anxiety for students). If a learner's Affective Filter is high, he or she is less likely to take risks; therefore, he or she will perceive less input. The Affective Filter Hypothesis Chart is illustrated in Figure 2.3.

What can content area teachers do to lower ELLs' anxiety and motivate them to learn? The initial interaction between the ELLs and the teacher and peers play an important role in helping them get adjusted to the new learning environment. Whether they feel being accepted as valued members of the learning community or not is significantly important to decrease their anxiety or motivate them to participate in class activities. Some of the things that the teachers can do to welcome the new ELLs may include giving ELLs a tour of campus, introducing them to the school personnel, assigning them a buddy, embracing their cultures by inviting them to share aspects of their culture and languages through lesson activities.

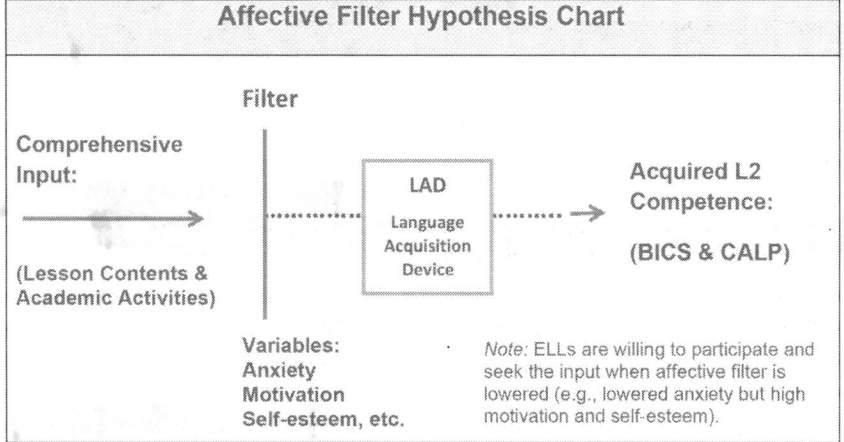

Figure 2.3 The Affective Filter Hypothesis Chart. *Source:* Based on Krashen (1982).

OTHER L2 THEORIES AND APPROACHES
FOR TEACHING ELLs

Several other successful theoretically-based approaches to teaching ELLs were developed in the late 20th century. This chapter will introduce these four: (a) Total Physical Response (TPR), developed by psychologist James Asher in the 1960s; (b) Theories of Interaction, based on applied linguistics research expanded in the 1970; (c) Sheltered Instruction Observation Protocol, a large-scale research-based pedagogical theory of the teaching of English learners in academic settings; and (d) World Class Instructional Design and Assessment (WIDA), a comprehensive analytic framework that summarizes the challenges to improving educational outcomes for ELLs.

Total Physical Response

The TPR approach emphasizes the importance of a low anxiety environment and the coherence of teacher and student relation (Asher, 1965). The TPR theory is based on the way in which children learn the native language. The central theme of this theory is that children learn the coordination of speech and action in a low-anxiety setting (Asher, 1972; Li, 2015). Asher believes that when learning a second language, there are three critical principles that we should draw from native language acquisition. The first of these principles is that listening precedes speaking. This is a clearly observable phenomenon in the sense that children demonstrate a listening comprehension of many complex spoken utterances before they actually produce any real intelligible speech. Secondly, Asher contends that listening comprehension develops through an intimate relationship between language and bodily movement. The utterances of adults, usually in the form of commands, are used to direct the child's body in an effort to get things done, accomplish tasks, etc. In other words, language learning in early childhood often is in response to adult commands such as, "Please come here! "Walk over to Jim!" "Get out of the street!" Thirdly, Asher believes the development of listening comprehension produces in the child a "readiness" for speaking. Speaking should not be rushed and attempts to advance its development may be futile. Finally, children will decide when to speak at some point as their listening comprehension grows.

As a strategy for teaching ELLs, Asher believes language in action (i.e., the verb) is the central linguistic structure around which language learning and language use is organized. Thus, TPR is especially helpful for teaching vocabulary and grammar to the beginner ELLs. Teachers introduce a few new concepts at one time in carefully sequenced commands based on ELLs' readiness. Students demonstrate comprehension of the commands by physical performance. In addition, commands follow a developmental trajectory from simple one word commands, ("Stand" or "Sit"), to increasingly complex imperative sentences. Naturally, the teacher must determine the nature of the content used in a TPR approach, though any content is possible assuming it is developmentally appropriate both from a linguistic and academic perspective. Teachers should only address errors when they make speech incomprehensible. Reading and writing materials are initially based on the commands, but it is expected that over time ELLs are able to read short passages from a variety of genres.

Based on over 30 years of research, Asher explains that about 80 percent of students are able to internalize the structure of a language and vocabulary when language is synchronized with body movement. Without question, TPR has had a strong influence on second language acquisition and on the teaching and learning of languages in general. Considering the pressure on ELLs and their teachers today to build proficiency as quickly as possible, teachers across the content areas should experiment with TPR in their classrooms.

Theories of Interaction

The role of interaction in L2 learning is important. Applied linguistics research expanded in the 1970s, and one result was the work of Evelyn Hatch. Hatch (1978) began to work from the perspective that interaction is the central means by which learners gain grammatical knowledge. Hatch's new perspective departed from the early perspective that grammatical knowledge should be obtained first so that ELLs may then engage in interaction. The new perspective is referred to as the input–output model with three central issues: (a) in what ways does interaction/input contribute to L2 acquisition, (b) which types of interaction/input promote L2 acquisition, and (c) what kinds of language pedagogy are needed to ensure that classroom learners experience acquisition-rich interactions.

Theoretically, interaction has two meanings in the context of L2 acquisition: *interpersonal* and *intrapersonal.* The most common meaning of interaction is the one where people communicate with each other orally or in writing. In this sense, interaction is interpersonal. However, interaction can also occur in the individual's mind. This happens, for example, when we engage with text and make connections with prior knowledge or with the world. We also engage in "private speech" (Vygotsky, 1978) and regularly build understandings of different phenomena over time. In these cases, interaction is intrapersonal.

The Interaction Hypothesis

The Interaction Hypothesis (IH) is concerned with negotiating meaning in spoken language. This refers to the strategies speakers use in order to prevent communication breakdowns and to fix actual breakdowns when they happen. When speakers are trying to negotiate meaning, they make *interactional modifications* and *input modifications* (Long, 1980). The former type involves changes to the structure of the conversation to prevent actual or potential problems of understanding, whereas the latter type is specifically made to language learners. For example, content area teachers make input modifications all day long in school when they see that students do not understand:

> **Student:** Photosynthesis, wait what... why is the sun part of this?
> **Teacher:** Oh, OK, look at these pictures of plants of trees and we can talk about it again...

What is significant in the above example is that teachers and students use language orally and make modifications in conversations and dialogues, which in turn helps learners to advance their proficiency (Varonis and Gass, 1985).

In addition, in interactive classrooms, learners are able to test out their own hypotheses about the second language. For example, when learners use inaccurate grammar such as the wrong verb tense or the wrong word form, they are "testing out" the new language. Teachers in interactive classrooms are able to use this student talk as data to determine the kind of responses they should give. By *seeing* student talk as data, teachers can decide if they need to focus on aspects of language itself, such as grammar and vocabulary, aspects of academic content, or the combination of language and content issues. Thus, across content areas and grade levels, current best practices include student–student and student–teacher interaction. A brief look at the IH reminds us of the major role that interaction plays in creating the conditions under which second language acquisition takes place. Moreover, interaction must be seen at both the interpersonal and intrapersonal dimensions. Therefore teachers of ELLs in the content areas must facilitate acquisition for their students when they create interactive classrooms that encourage exchanges around academic material (Li, 2015; Peregoy & Boyle, 2008).

Deep Processing Theory

Deep Processing (DP) is a cognitive theory, influenced by the tradition of information processing. This theory has attracted less attention in the field of L2 acquisition but has a great potential both as a theoretical inspiration for researchers and a pedagogical inspiration for teachers. The potential influence and usefulness of DP for second language learning in academic contexts, centers on its possibility to serve as a bridge between academic tasks and securing knowledge in long term memory. Moreover, whereas the IH was mainly concerned with oral language development and language acquisition, DP reminds teachers to use reading and writing as essential to build academic literacy.

Traditional information processing models have focused on different types of stored memory (e.g., sensory registers, short and long term). Craik and Lockhart (1972) expanded the thinking of information processing by drawing attention away from storing memory to a focus on the nature of processing in which people engage when faced with new material and input. In their view of building knowledge, Craik and Lockhart claim that input can be processed at different levels, from the superficial recognition of shapes to deeper levels that construct meaning by building on existing knowledge (see Figure 2.4). For example, we can process visual images at the structural level, based on how something looks or appears. We also process input phonemically, based on how it sounds. Additionally, we process information graphemically, as in the letters that make up words, as well as orthographically, based on the shape of words. These are examples of perceptual processing, which is considered *shallow* processing. Shallow processing results in short-term memory. Deep processing, however, is about semantics, is meaning based and occurs when we relate new information to something else. Figure 2.1 illustrates these levels of processing. In the case of phonetics, it is possible for information to be retained in long-term memory based on phonetics, but only if conditions are right. In other words, when we engage in activities that focus our attention on the meaning of new content we are more likely to learn the content (i.e., hold the information for long-term recall). This latter type is what we hope happens for the students in our classrooms.

Research has shown that learning best occurs when the learner is required to generate or elaborate on input (Wittrock, 1974). When learners engage in this kind of generative processing, learning is seen as a function

Depth of Processing Chart

Structural (looks like)	Shallow	
Graphemic (letters)	Shallow	
Orthographic (word shape)	Shallow	
Phonetic (sounds like)	Short-Term Memory	→ Long-Term Memory Possible
Semantic (meaning)	Deep	

Figure 2.4 Depth of Processing Chart. *Source:* Based on Craik & Tulving (1975).

of the concrete and abstract associations made between the new input and existing knowledge. Scholars suggest that when these connections are made, long-term memory occurs and learners are able to apply and use the new information in new contexts. The research on depth of processing connects very directly to the work of teachers with regard to the kind of data gathered and analyzed. For example, research has shown that two key types of tasks encourage deep processing. One task type is recall and summary of new materials. Deeper processing results from recall and summary tasks where learners are explicitly required to integrate knowledge from the text with existing schemata. The other type of task requires learners to write questions based on texts they have read. After writing questions, learners then answer their own questions. Scholars investigating these tasks in research with native speakers have demonstrated positive results for learning as well as a variety of cognitive activities necessary to complete tasks, such as focusing attention, organizing new material, and of course integrating new knowledge with existing (Pressley, Johnson, Symons, McGoldrick, & Kurita, 1989).

Scholars researching DP among second language learners have discovered that information processed at the semantic level also leads to better memory than information merely processed at the acoustic/visual level and learning is deepened when learners are required to generate sentences with new words they have read in the context of text (Brown & Perry, 1991). When we think about connecting theory to practice, this kind of active learning, with strategies like those used in the research, may not be new information for teachers who already require their students to engage with text materials in very deliberate ways. DP theory, however, certainly suggests that content area teachers of ELLs should engage students with texts and should very intentionally require students to generate sentences, summaries, outlines, etc. as a means of deepening learning. In other words, it is not enough to assign reading and expect learners to grasp content and be able to recall it in the long term.

Although DP still needs more research like the other theories of interaction, the content area teachers can use it as a tool to support their ELLs for the academic literacy development in their L2 learning process. Teachers who encourage students to negotiate meaning with one another and provide students with opportunities for deep processing provide solid opportunities for authentic learning to occur. Negotiating meaning encourages learners to share ideas about familiar and unfamiliar topics in the input and actively connect them to existing knowledge. The theory of DP sensitizes us to the intrapersonal learning needs of students, which can help English learners make sense of academic materials.

In all, interaction benefits second language acquisition. The IH theory shows the dynamic nature of this influence. The DP theory demonstrates the value of focusing instruction on interpersonal and intrapersonal interaction. Moreover, the content areas offer motivational, rich materials to do this. Therefore, teachers should experiment with both types of interaction and provide the supportive environment that allows interaction for ELLs to achieve success.

Sheltered Instruction Observation Protocol (SIOP)

SIOP is a large-scale research-based pedagogical theory of the teaching of ELLs in academic settings. The work of SIOP began as a research project (Short, 1999) and has ballooned into a wide-ranging movement. State and local educational agencies have embraced SIOP, engaging professional development nationwide. For example, Pearson Education lists many books aimed at teachers, instructional coaches, and administrators on SIOP. This same website indicates that SIOP is "trusted by more than 600,000 educators" and that all students are in need of an "empirically-based instructional model to improve student achievement and get our students college and career ready."

Over the years, teachers and scholars have devised various approaches to best help ELLs make sense of academic content through the second language. Since the early 1980s, the predominant approach to meeting this double challenge has been sheltered instruction (Freeman & Freeman, 1988). When this term was first used, students were considered "sheltered" because they were in separate classes from native English speakers and, technically, did not compete academically with native speakers. That is, students were not expected to meet the grade-level norms until some time had passed.

In sheltered academic classrooms, teachers use clear, direct, simplified English and various scaffolding techniques to make content comprehensible. Skilled sheltered teachers are able to modify their speech rate and tone, teach by demonstration, with plenty of visuals, graphic organizers, all strategies aimed at providing context for meaning. Sheltered instructional techniques gained credibility as more and more educators believed it to be a way to advance both English learner proficiency in the language as well as academic achievement. Research began to show that English learners made better academic achievement gains in sheltered classes than in traditional, stand-alone classes that merely focused on the English language per se (Thomas & Collier, 2001). Academic content came to be seen as the most effective approach to teaching English learners due to its motivation value and for the meaningful learning context it provides.

During this same period, the authors who would eventually develop SIOP began to conduct research on effective ways to meet the academic needs of English learners (Short, 1999). The research program has resulted in a model of teaching that consists of eight components, which subsume 30 features and can be seen in Figure 2.5. The model, essentially, provides a structure to what had previously been known as sheltered methods. Following are the eight components of SIOP (Echevarria & Short, 2011).

These eight components represent an approach that most teachers would agree is a thorough framework. The theory is based on a foundation of objectives for academic content as well as for the kinds of language students will need in order to comprehend lesson content. Teachers are also encouraged to connect to students' background knowledge and to take

Eight SIOP Components	Explanation
Lesson Preparation	Examines the lesson planning process, including the language and content objectives, the use of supplemental materials, and the meaningfulness of the activities.
Building Background	Focuses on making connections with students' background experiences and prior learning and developing academic vocabulary.
Comprehensible Input	Considers adjusting teacher speech, modeling academic tasks, and using multimodal techniques to enhance comprehension.
Strategies	Emphasizes teaching learning strategies to students, scaffolding instruction, and promoting higher-order thinking skills.
Interaction	Reminds teachers to encourage elaborated speech and to group students appropriately for language and content development.
Practice/Application	Provides activities to practice and extend language and content learning.
Lesson Delivery	Ensures that teachers present a lesson that meets the planned objectives, promotes students' engagement and paces the lesson appropriately.
Review and Assessment	Considers whether the teacher reviewed the key vocabulary and content concepts, assessed student learning, and provided feedback to students on their output.

Figure 2.5 The SIOP Components Chart. *Source:* Based on Echevarria, Vogt, and Short (2012).

measures to make content comprehensible through the teaching of learning strategies. Furthermore, interaction is seen as playing a critical role in learning. Finally, any segment of teaching should close with some sort of review and assessment.

Clearly, SIOP attends to significant theoretical and research work such as that discussed above (e.g., Cummins, Krashen, Hatch, Long, and Wittrock). It is important to note, however, that some SIOP components are more focused on skills building while others are more comprehension focused. "Skills building depends on conscious learning, output, and correction" (Krashen, 2013). In contrast to skills building, the comprehension hypothesis claims that we acquire language when we understand messages both orally and through reading. This hypothesis indicates that we do not acquire language simply by using it or studying the rules of grammar and vocabulary. ELLs acquire comprehension through context and comprehensible input, coupled with our current linguistic competence and background knowledge. While research continues to work out the details of these two approaches most facilitates second language learning, content area teachers must realize they need to help students build certain academic skills while helping students to comprehend oral and written academic language. The most important challenge is to figure out when to focus student attention on skills-building issues and when to focus them on comprehension issues.

In a broad summary of research on ELLs in public schools, Saunders, Goldenberg, and Marcelletti (2013) offer a range of research-based recommendations for teachers. Some of these recommendations overlap with those of SIOP as listed below:

1. Teachers should attend to communication and language-learning strategies and incorporate them into English language development (ELD) instruction.
   a. Provide opportunities for students to use a variety of strategies that are metacognitive, cognitive, and social/affective.
      i. Previewing and predicting, summarizing, problem solving, self-monitoring, categorizing, think aloud.
      ii. Scaffolding—providing the right amount of support to move comprehension from lower levels to higher.
      iii. Questioning—use a variety of question types (literal, analytical, and interpretive).

2. Teachers should provide students with constructive feedback through clarification, and make instructional decisions based on student response.
   a. Provide feedback to students regularly on their output (e.g., language, work).

      i. Providing feedback clarifies and corrects misconceptions, helps students develop English proficiency, and allows teachers to paraphrase and model correct grammar and usage.

  b. Conduct assessments of student comprehension throughout lessons on all objectives (e.g., spot checking, group response).

      ii. Engage comprehensive review of lesson vocabulary and key content concepts.

3. Instruction should include interactive activities among students, but they must be carefully planned and carried out.

  a. Provide frequent opportunities for interactions and discussion between teacher/student and among students, and encourage elaborated responses.

  b. Use group configurations that support language and content objectives of the lesson. Provide sufficient wait time for student response consistently.

  c. Give ample opportunities for students to clarify key concepts in L1 as needed with aide, peer, or L1 text.

4. Instruction should be planned and delivered with specific L2 objectives in mind.

  a. L2 objectives describe how the ELLs will learn the lesson content. They are based on ELLs' needs to determine which of 4 language domains (listening, speaking, reading, and writing) ELLs will use to accomplish the objectives.

  b. L2 objectives should be stated orally and be written where all will see, preferably in the same space each time. L2 objectives can be specific academic concepts and vocabulary recognizable during lessons.

5. Instruction should integrate meaning and communication to support explicit teaching.

  a. Use speech appropriate to students' proficiency levels.

  b. Use body language, gestures, realia, pictures, and visuals to accompany spoken words.

  c. Give clear explanations of tasks, including repetition, and step-by-step directions when necessary.

6. Instruction should emphasize academic language as well as conversational language.

  a. New content and abstract concepts need to be presented in personally relevant ways that spark a student's prior knowledge and experiences. Examples:

      i. Keeping personal learning journals.

      ii. Making/playing a game for reviewing content (Bingo, Jeopardy etc).
     iii. Writing test questions or creating math problems for another ELL.
     iv. Teaching a concept to another student.
  b. Encouraging students to discuss, interact, and work together makes abstract concepts more concrete. These are some ways to do this:
      i. Making and using graphic organizers.
     ii. Solving problems in cooperative groups.
     iii. Engaging in discussion circles.
     iv. Partnering students for a project.

Saunders et al. (2013) provide a salient summary of teaching English learners in content areas. However, no one guideline will be sufficient to help ELLs gain access to high-level, mainstream academic curriculum. Thus, teachers must test individual components and guidelines to construct comprehensive ELD programs and test the proposition that they help students acquire high levels of English language proficiency, regardless of whether they are in bilingual or English-only programs. From our experience, strong opinion too often trumps careful weighing of evidence in what remains a volatile and politically charged field.

World-Class Instructional Design and Assessment (WIDA)

Short and Fitzsimmons (2007) provide a comprehensive analytic framework that summarizes the challenges to improving educational outcomes for ELLs. One of the major challenged areas is a lack of coherent means for assessing L2 proficiency and the validity and reliability of the assessment measures. Another critical concerned area is the lack of common criteria for identifying ELLs and tracking their academic progress. WIDA, as the large-scale effort, addresses both of these two issues and it provides a standards framework for English language development in the content areas and an accompanying proficiency test.

WIDA began as a multi-state, grant-funded partnership between Wisconsin, Delaware, and Arkansas as an effort to improve assessment of ELLs. Inspired by Title III in what was at that time the new No Child Left Behind Act (2006), and the pressure it placed on states to develop language proficiency standards for English learners; WIDA quickly produced a set of ELD standards and an accompanying proficiency test. The next several years would see many revisions to both the standards and the test. According to the WIDA website, the ELD standards now serve as the curriculum for 31 states and the ACCESS exam serves as the accompanying proficiency test. That same website indicates that in 2013–14, WIDA conducted 218 professional development workshops across the country. If there is to be anything close to a national curriculum framework for English learners, it surely appears to be WIDA.

The WIDA standards are considered as framework with a firm theoretical and research foundation. The standards address social, instructional, and academic language that students need to fully engage ELLs in the K–12 endeavor. Several guiding principles of language development highlight the theoretical assumptions. The first principle centers on the communicative purpose of language. Language is used to accomplish tasks, including academic ones. Academic content area tasks have unique communicative functions (Schleppegrell, 2004). These functions are related to the ways in which grammar is used and how text is organized and structured to communicate meaning. Another WIDA principle focuses on student learning L2 through meaningful use and interaction. The third WIDA principle concerns the interdependency of language and literacy development. This principle reminds us of the variety of individual and environmental factors that impact second language acquisition, such as age, time in the country, educational background, etc. (Spolsky, 1989; Lightbown & Spada, 2006). These WIDA principles of academic language development are presented in Figure 2.6.

	Performance Criteria	**Features**
Discourse Level	Linguistic Complexity (Quantity and variety of oral and written text)	Amount of speech/written text Structure of speech/written text Density of speech/written text Organization and cohesion of ideas Variety of sentence types
Sentence Level	Language Forms and Conventions (Types, array, and use of language structures)	Types and variety of grammatical structures Conventions, mechanics, and fluency Match of language forms to purpose/perspective
Word/Phrase Level	Vocabulary Usage (Specificity of word or phrase choice)	General, specific, and technical language Multiple meanings of words and phrases Formulaic and idiomatic expressions Nuances and shades of meaning Collocations

Figure 2.6 The features of academic language chart. *Source:* Based on WIDA ELD Standards (www.wida.us).

With these principles as a foundation, the WIDA standards framework includes five stages of academic language proficiency. The stages are measured by the WIDA, ACCESS test which gives an ELL scores in each of the domains or reading, writing, speaking, and listening. Like SIOP, WIDA takes a range of theories and brings them to bear on the circumstances of English learners in content area settings. But unlike SIOP, WIDA is a curriculum framework that engages teachers in a study of the nature of how language is used to accomplish academic and social tasks in school. WIDA provides teachers with exemplars of language processing and use as students gain proficiency. Moreover, the standards are aligned to the Common Core State Standards (CCSS) and Next Generation Science Standards. In addition, the standards illustrate for teachers the value of addressing the contexts for language use in the content areas as well as the types of language and cognitive functions they will require of their students on content area tasks (description, analysis, synthesis, explanation, etc.).

In summary, the goal of the WIDA standards is to improve comprehension and meaning-making in the specific contexts of language development and use across content areas. WIDA offers the most advanced approach to a genuine ELD curriculum to date. In the case of English learners, language expectations based in the content areas serve to help teachers and students alike to set targets for academic growth and grade-level achievement. When we reflect on the major challenges and issues of improving the educational outcomes for English learners mentioned at the beginning of this section, we see that WIDA offers a valid and reliable proficiency test based in the standards as well as giving educational agencies a common criteria for identifying English learners and tracking their academic progress.

SUMMARY

This chapter focused on the theoretical perspectives in the L2 acquisition theories, such as BICS, CALP, Affective Filter, and Comprehensive Input. Like the process of learning the first language or the native language, ELL students develop their English language proficiency through interaction and meaningful input in a contextualized linguistic environment. ELLs develop BICS and CALP at different paces. It takes about six months to two years to develop BICS (Basic Interpersonal Communication Skills) but three to five years to develop CALP (Cognitive Academic Language Proficiency). Providing context embedded support helps ELLs have access to the cognitively demanding content areas. Meaningful, comprehensive input at the learners' instructional level and slightly beyond is essential to help ELLs continuously develop their English proficiency level. Lowering the affective filter in the classroom motivates ELL students to seek more input and to be more willing to meet the challenge. The chapter also explored other L2 theories and approaches that are important for teachers to know and that are useful related to teaching ELLs in classrooms. TPR and Theories of Interaction, SIOP Model, and WIDA framework are explained in this chapter to help teachers with successful lesson planning and assessment to work with ELLs.

REFERENCES

Asher, J. J. (1965). The strategy of the total physical response: An application to learning *Russian International Review of Applied Linguistics, 3*(4), 291–300.

Asher, J. J. (1972). Children's first language as a model for second language learning. *Modern Language Journal, 56,* 133–139.

Bartolomé, L. I. (1998). *The misteaching of academic discourses.* Boulder, CO: Westview Press.

Bloom, B. (1956). Bloom's Taxonomy. Retrieved from http://www.bloomstaxonomy.org/Blooms%20Taxonomy%20questions.pdf

Bloom, B. S. (1956). *Taxonomy of educational objectives, handbook I: The cognitive domain.* New York, NY: David McKay.

Brown, T. S., & Perry, F. L. (1991). A comparison of three learning strategies for ESL vocabulary acquisition. *TESOL Quarterly, 25*(3), 655–670.

Collier, V. P. (1987). Age and rate of acquisition of second language for academic purposes. *TESOL Quarterly, 21,* 617–641.

Craik, F. I. M., & Lockhart, R. S. (1972). Levels of processing: A framework for memory research. *Journal of Verbal Learning and Verbal Behavior, 11,* 671–684.

Craik, F. I. M., & Tulving, E. (1975). Depth of processing and the retention of words in episodic memory. *Journal of Experimental Psychology: General, 104,* 268–294.

Cummins, J. (1984). *Bilingualism and special education: Issues in assessment pedagogy.* San Francisco, CA: College-Hill Press.

Donato, R. (1994). Collective scaffolding in second language learning. In J. Lantolf & G. Apple. (Eds.), *Vygotskyan approaches to second language research* (pp. 33–56). Norwood, NJ: Ablex.

Echevarria, J., & Short, D. (2011). *The SIOP® model: A professional development framework for comprehensive schoolwide intervention.* Washington, DC: Center for Research on the Educational Achievement and Teaching of English Language Learners.

Echevarria, J., Vogt, M., & Short, D. J. (2012). *Making content comprehensible for secondary English learners: The SIOP model.* Boston, MA: Allyn & Bacon.

Edelsky, C. (2006). *With literacy and justice for all: Rethinking the social in language and education* (3rd ed.). London, England: The Falmer Press.

Ericsson, K. A. (2006). The influence of experience and deliberate practice on the development of superior expert performance. In K. A. Ericsson, N. Charness, P. Feltovich, & R. R. Hoffman (Eds.), *Cambridge handbook of expertise and expert performance* (pp. 685–706). Cambridge, England: Cambridge University Press.

Freeman, D., & Freeman, Y. (1988). *Sheltered English instruction.* Washington, DC: ERIC Clearinghouse on Languages and Linguistics.

Gardner, P. (2012). *Teaching and Learning in Multicultural Classrooms.* New York, NY: Routledge.

Gee, J. P. (1990). *Sociolinguistics and illiteracies: Idealogy in discourses.* London, England: Falmer Press.

Hatch, E. (Ed.). (1978). *Second language acquisition: A book of readings.* Rowley, MA: Newbury House.

Krashen, S. (1982). *Principles and practice in second language acquisition.* London, England: Prentice-hall International.

Krashen, S. (2013). Does SIOP research support SIOP claims? *International Journal of Foreign Language Teaching, 8*(1), 11924.

Lantolf, J. P. (2000). *Socialcultural theory and second language learning.* Oxford, England: Oxford University Press.

Li, N. (2015). *A book for every teacher: Teaching to English Language Learners.* Charlotte, NC: Information Age.

Lightbown, P. M., & Spada, N. (2006). *How languages are learned* (3rd ed.). New York, NY: Oxford University Press.

Long, M. H. (1980). *Input, interaction, and second language acquisition* (PhD dissertation). University of California, Los Angeles, CA.

MacSwan, J., & Rolstad, K. (2003). Linguistic diversity, schooling, and social class: Rethinking our conception of language proficiency in language minority education. In C. B. Paulston & R. Tucker (Eds.), *Sociolinguistics: The essential readings* (pp. 329–340). Oxford, England: Blackwell.

No Child Left Behind Act (2006). *No child left behind act: Assistance from education could help states better measure progress of students with limited English Proficiency.* GAO-16-85. Washington DC: Committee on Education and Labor, House of Representatives.

Peregoy, S. F., & Boyle, O. F. (2008). *Reading, writing, and learning in ESL: A resource book for K–12 teachers* (5th ed.). New York, NY: Addison-Wesley.

Pressley, M., Johnson, C. J., Symons, S., McGoldrick, J. A., & Kurita, J. A. (1989). Strategies that improve children's memory and comprehension. *Elementary School Journal, 90,* 3–32.

Saunders, W., Goldenberg, C., & Marcelletti, D. (2013, Summer). English language development: Guidelines for instruction. *American Educator, 37*(2), 13–39.

Scarcella, R. (2003). *Accelerating academic English: A focus on English language learners.* Oakland, CA: Regents of the University of California.

Schleppegrell, M. J. (2004). *The language of schooling: A functional linguistics perspective.* Mahwah, NJ: Erlbaum.

Short, D. (1999). *The sheltered instruction observation protocol: A tool for teacher–researcher collaboration and professional development.* Washington, DC: Center for Applied Linguistics.

Short, D., & Fitzsimmons, S. (2007). *Double the work: Challenges and solutions to acquiring language and academic literacy for adolescent English language learners—A report to Carnegie Corporation of New York.* Washington, DC: Alliance for Excellent Education.

Spolsky, B. (1989). *Conditions for the second language learning: Introduction to a general theory.* Oxford, United Kingdom: Oxford University Press.

Thomas, W., & Collier, V. (2001). *A national study of school effectiveness for language minority students long-term academic achievement.* Center for Research Excellence in Diversity Education. Berkeley, CA: UC.

Varonis, E. M., & Gass, S. (1985). Non-native/non-native conversations: A model for negotiation of meaning. *Applied Linguistics, 6*(1), 71–90.

Vygotsky, L. S. (1978). *Mind in society: Development of higher psychological processes.* Cambridge, MA: Harvard University Press.

Wittrock, M. C. (1974). Learning as a generative process. *Educational Psychologist, 1*, 87–95.

PART II

TEACHING ELLs ACROSS CONTENT AREAS

CHAPTER 3

TEACHING
LANGUAGE ARTS TO ELLs

Lynn A. Smolen and Wei Zhang
The University of Akron

CASE SCENARIO

Racine was a young adolescent from Congo whose first experience in a classroom was when she stepped into Sam Román's 6th grade science class at Thomas Jefferson International Newcomer's Academy. At age 16, she towered over the other students in the class, but her smile and warmth won everyone's hearts. She spoke no English and had not had any formal schooling in any language. As a result, she was illiterate. She understood some basic French, but her native language was Swahili. The first month of school was rather traumatic for her as she struggled to understand English with very little success. Mr. Román was able to help her navigate daily activities using conversational French, but she was unable to understand academic content in French. The Swahili instructional aide was only available to come to the class for one period a day to assist Racine and when he did, Racine bombarded him with questions on every subject area. As she began to utter basic words in English, she asked Mr. Román for a math book to practice. When he gave her a workbook with basic arithmetic, she returned it fully completed in less than two weeks. Her determination and dedication propelled

Teaching ELLs Across Content Areas, pages 49–82
Copyright © 2016 by Information Age Publishing
All rights of reproduction in any form reserved.

her to improve by leaps and bounds. From a pre-primer reading level in August, she progressed to a mid-first grade level by December. She was so determined to learn that by the end of the school year she was reading at a mid-third grade level. Due to her age and her progress, she was placed in the ninth grade for the next school year. Today she is on track to graduate from high school in two years.

Racine's case illustrates that English Language Learners (ELLs) can be academically successful despite tremendous obstacles that they face. She had no prior education when she stepped into Sam Román's sixth grade class, yet with the support of dedicated caring teachers and staff and her own determination, Racine was able to accelerate her progress in acquiring English and learning academic content to catch up with her peers. Teachers' knowledge and understanding of how to support ELLs are the keys to the success of these students. This is particularly true in the English language arts, as literacy is the basis for all subject areas. Regardless of the grade level or subject matter, teachers must understand the challenges that ELLs face and the ways to help them acquire English language and literacy in the subject areas they teach.

ISSUES FOR TEACHING ELLs LANGUAGE ARTS

In this chapter, we focus on teaching language arts to ELLs. This is an important topic to begin with discussing teaching ELLs across the content areas because the development of the language arts, specifically teaching listening, speaking, reading, and writing, is critical for the academic success of the English learners. The acquisition of knowledge and skills in math, science, social studies, and the visual and performing arts is dependent on proficiency in oral language, reading, and writing, and particularly on the ability to use academic language in these areas. In order for ELLs to succeed academically, they need to learn content (math, science, and social studies) and the English language skills needed to learn that content at the same time. In essence they have to do double the work that native speaking students have to do at the same grade level. This is very challenging given the fact that they also have to learn academic content through a different cultural lens from the mainstream culture and with a language that they are still in the process of acquiring. ELLs at various grade levels perform at a range of the English proficiency levels. It is important that teachers can provide differentiated instruction for the ELLs at their appropriate proficiency levels. For example, the teacher must have a differentiated method for a middle-school ELL with the minimal proficiency vs. another middle-school ELL at a more proficient level in English (Goldenberg, 2008).

In the age of high stakes testing and new state standards, ELLs are especially challenged with language arts. The Common Core State Standards (CCSS) call for rigorous teaching and learning, yet ELLs often come to U.S. schools with limited proficiency in English. Furthermore, many of these students come to school with limited schooling experiences and from homes in which parents know little about the structure of American schools and the requirements of the curricula. Parents often lack an understanding of how they can help their children and are frequently told that they should not speak their home language to their children. To further exacerbate this situation, ELLs often are in classrooms in which teachers have had limited training in how to adapt instruction to meet their needs. This chapter provides teachers with guidelines on how to effectively teach English language arts to ELLs.

To begin with this discussion, it is important for teachers to know that many of the strategies they use to teach language arts to native speakers of English are appropriate for ELLs. For example, it is quite appropriate for them to use literature circles and reader's theatre to promote collaborative literacy development while providing opportunities for peer interaction. It is also valuable for the teachers to teach strategies such as visualizing, predicting, inferring, synthesizing, and summarizing to teach reading comprehension. However, they need to understand that these strategies may have to be modified for ELLs since the ELL students are likely to require more scaffolding and explicit, direct instruction with background knowledge, cultural nuances, vocabulary, and complex grammatical structures.

Teachers also need to understand that ELLs are in the process of learning English, therefore, they are operating with an interlanguage (a language that is somewhere between their first language and their second language) and as a result, their oral and written production will not sound like the English language produced by a native speaker. Furthermore, it is important to realize that it takes time to acquire English oral and written skills, especially academic English language skills (Short & Echevarría, 2016).

CHALLENGES FOR ELLs IN CLASSROOMS

Although ELLs often bring strengths to learning English, such as the knowledge of how language works and the ability to listen and read for meaning in their first language, they also face many challenges which can be greater if they are expected to learn in classrooms where instruction is directed towards native speakers of English and insufficient attention is devoted to differentiation of instruction. These challenges and ways to meet them for the four language domains (i.e., listening, speaking, reading, and writing) are discussed in the sections below.

Listening Challenges for ELLs

Listening is receiving language through the ears. In the listening process, we identify the sounds of speech and process them into words and sentences (Li, 2015). When we listen, we use our ears to receive individual sounds (letters, stress, rhythm, and pauses) and use our brain to convert these into messages that mean something to us. Listening requires focus and attention. It is a skill that some people need to work at harder than others related to focus and attention.

Listening in a second language requires even greater focus. Although listening is an active and integrative process, listening in a second language environment can be difficult for ELLs because they hear English through the filter of their native language that has different sound patterns and may use stress in a different way from their native language. The ELLs are also challenged by sounds in English that may not exist in their native language or are articulated differently from English. For example, the sounds of th, dh, r, h, and l are difficult for many non-native speakers of English from different language backgrounds.

Also, ELLs may not be used to the stress, rhythm, and intonation patterns in English because stress may be conveyed in a very different manner from their native language. English is a stress-timed language and a listener needs to pay careful attention to the stressed words in a sentence in order to understand what the speaker considers to be important. For example, in the sentence: "There are *five main* causes of the Civil War," the words that have a tonic syllable (the stressed syllable in a word in a sentence that carries the most important meaning) are *five* and *main*. A native English speaker is likely to know that he/she should pay attention to the words in the sentence that are stressed by the speaker and will expect the statement to be followed by a discussion of the five main causes of the Civil War. On the other hand, an ELL is less likely to pay attention to the words in the sentence that are stressed by the speaker and may miss the intended meaning.

ELL's listening is also challenged by reduced forms, disfluent speech, fast-paced speech with few pauses, and speech interlaced with colloquial language (Brown, 2015). English speakers use reduced forms in a variety of ways, such as phonologically (e.g., "Gimme it" for "Give me it."); morphologically (e.g., "he'd" and "she'll"); and pragmatically (e.g., "Books away" for "Put your books away."). Disfluent speech contains a lot of false starts, fillers (e.g., "um," "well," "OK"), and awkward pauses. Some speakers speak very fast and have few pauses, which make it challenging for ELLs to listen with comprehension.

Colloquial language also makes speech difficult to comprehend. It includes idioms (e.g., "Hit the lights."), slang (e.g., "She's hot!"), and cultural references such sports terms (e.g., "down to the wire" and "Monday morning quarterback"). Additionally, by its very nature listening is evanescent; once something is said, the speaker moves on. There is no opportunity for the listener to go back to listen again to what was just said, so if there is no written or audio recorded version of what was said by the teacher the ELL has no way to recapture it.

Speaking Challenges for ELLs

Speaking can be defined as to deliver language through our mouth. To speak, we create sounds using many parts of our body, including the lungs, vocal tract, vocal chords, tongue, teeth, and lips to utter and express (Li, 2015). Speaking usually requires at least a listener. When two or more people speak or talk to each other, the conversation is formed and called a dialogue. Speaking is one of the four language skills and it requires practice.

Like listening, speaking is challenging for ELLs as it is far more complex than learning vocabulary and grammar rules. In order for ELLs to be understood, they need to have acceptable pronunciation, fluency, vocabulary, and grammar. They also need to have some understanding of how to say things in a socially and culturally appropriate way. Speech acts involve knowing how to speak for different purposes such as in conversations (two-way communication); formal presentations (one-way communication); and participation in whole class discussions by asking and answering questions, sharing ideas, and offering opinions. Additionally, they need to understand how to use nonverbal communication so that there is no cross-cultural misunderstanding (Wright, 2015).

In its review of research on oral language development, the Center for Research on Education, Diversity, and Excellence (CREDE), found that ELLs take a number of years to develop oral English proficiency and tend to make more rapid advances in proficiency in Levels 1 through 3 and slower progress beyond Level 3. They suspect that the slowdown at higher levels may be due to a lack of instructional attention to oral language development once ELLs reach an intermediate level of oral proficiency (Genesee, Lindholm-Leary, Saunders, & Christian, 2006). This finding emphasizes the importance of building ELLs' oral language at all five levels of second language development.

Reading Challenges for ELLs

Reading can be explained as the process of looking at a series of written symbols and getting meaning from them (Li, 2015). When we read, we use our eyes to receive written symbols (letters, punctuation marks, and spaces) and we use our brain to convert them into words, sentences, and paragraphs that communicate something to us. Reading is a receptive skill and it is through that we receive information.

Reading presents a challenge to ELLs, just as do listening, speaking, and writing. It shares some important characteristics with listening. Like listening, reading is a receptive skill that is active and integrative. Its successful performance draws on a language learner's world knowledge, knowledge of the English language, and alphabetic system. It is also affected by the learner's short-term and long-term memory (Arrington, Kulesz, Francis, Fletcher, & Barnes, 2014; Hall, Jarrold, Towse, & Zarandi, 2015). As with listening, both bottom-up processing and top-down processing are involved. In bottom-up processing, the reader decodes and encodes words and reads and interprets phrases and sentences, that is, she reads from parts to the whole; in top down processing the reader activates her schema to determine what prior knowledge she has on the topic and genre she will read, that is, she previews the text and develops an overview of what she is about to read. Both top down and bottom up processing are necessary and an effective reader uses an interactive process, going back and forth between top down and bottom up processing. Second language readers tend to use either bottom up or top down processing when reading which makes their reading less effective (Brown, 2015).

According to Kenneth Goodman (1967), reading is a psycholinguistic guessing game in which the reader uses his prior knowledge and knowledge of the phonological, syntactic, and semantic structure of the language to predict what the author will say, then samples enough text to confirm or disconfirm his predictions. The reading process is much the same in the first and second language (Carrell, Devine, & Eskey, 1988; Goodman & Goodman, 1978; Grabe, 1991). However, there are some significant differences.

First and second language readers bring different resources to the reading task. First language readers are familiar with the English language and usually have background knowledge that they can connect to the text. On the other hand, second language readers have limited English proficiency and often lack relevant background knowledge and cultural knowledge to connect to a text that has been written in English on a topic that is culturally bound by the English-speaking environment. Lacking relevant background knowledge that is pertinent to the text often results in limited comprehension of what they read. Another limitation is their vocabulary knowledge in English. Inadequate knowledge of the meanings of words in a text can negatively impact comprehension (Anderson, 2014; Graves, August, & Mancilla-Martinez, 2013; Peregoy & Boyle, 2013).

Writing Challenges for ELLs

Writing is the process of using symbols (letters of the alphabet, punctuation, and spaces) to communicate thoughts and ideas in a readable form (Li, 2015). We usually write with a pen or pencil (handwriting) or a keyboard (typing). With a pen or pencil we usually write on a surface such as paper or whiteboard. A keyboard is normally attached to a typewriter, computer, or mobile device. To write correctly, we must understand the basic system of a language. For example, we must have the knowledge of grammar, punctuation, and sentence structure. Vocabulary is also necessary for correct spelling and formatting.

Second language writers spend less time planning writing than native speakers do, and are less fluent and accurate in vocabulary and grammar. Also, they are slower and more laborious in all stages of composing in the target language than first language writers. Most use their native language at some point in the composing process, which makes the process less automatic. They pay more attention to language issues as they write, focusing mostly on the sentence level. As a result, they have difficulty paying enough attention to the composing process and consideration of the overall organization of what they are writing (Williams, 2005).

MEETING THE CHALLENGES AND PLANNING TO TEACH

Meeting the Challenges of Listening in a Second Language

It is helpful when teachers become aware of the challenges of listening in a second language and make modifications in their speech by slowing down; using pauses after making key points; reducing the number of colloquialisms, slang words, and idioms; and providing contextual support for listening with PowerPoint slides, pictures of key ideas, realia (real objects), word walls, concrete demonstrations, and outlines of lectures. They can also demonstrate how stress is used to emphasize important ideas in lectures and discussions, and point out how the mouth forms to pronounce different sounds.

An important way to promote listening comprehension is to provide opportunities for students to listen to authentic language from network television websites and video-sharing systems such as YouTube. For example, the "Friends" (2016) series on YouTube provides students with short, entertaining skits that relate to their everyday lives. For older students who are more proficient in English, short TED Talks (www.ted.com/talks) are excellent for developing listening comprehension. There is also a variety of listening comprehension tasks offered by Randall's ESL Cyber Listening Lab (www.esl-lab.com). When creating listening activities it is advisable to have students listen to a video or podcast at least twice. The first time they should listen to get the gist of what is said and the second time they should listen for specific details. Additionally, it is beneficial for teachers to guide ELLs' listening before, during, and after listening. For pre-listening the teacher could provide students with the topic of the listening text and ask them to activate their knowledge about it through brainstorming. They can then write down predictions about what they think they will learn. During listening, students can monitor their listening to see if their predictions are correct and after listening they can discuss the main ideas and supporting details of the text. More information about how to help ELLs with pronunciation of English is discussed in the section in this chapter under teaching strategies.

Meeting the Challenges of Speaking in a Second Language

An important way to promote speaking skills of ELLs is to pay attention to the amount of teacher talk versus student talk. If teachers do most of the talking in class, students will not have an opportunity to practice speaking. Teachers should cut back on the time they spend lecturing and provide opportunities for students to engage in guided class discussions. They can ask open-ended and higher-order questions such as:

"Why do you think _____ happened?"
"How does the author create a sense of suspense in the novel?"
"Do you agree with what _____ said about _____?" "Why or why not?"

Teachers should also encourage ELLs to develop their speaking skills with cooperative learning, think-pair-share, role play, readers' theater, and information gap activities. Heterogeneous groups should be the norm so that ELLs have the opportunity to talk with students who are more proficient in English than they are. It is best if teachers plan lessons so that students have many opportunities to engage in meaningful conversations with peers about important concepts they are learning in each content area across the curriculum so that they can develop academic language in English (Zwiers, O'Hara, & Pritchard, 2014).

Meeting the Challenges of Reading in a Second Language

Having well-developed oral language in English is vital for ELLs' development of reading and writing. Therefore, it is important that teachers support ELL's in developing oral language as they are taught literacy skills. Additionally, it is beneficial for teachers to emphasize making meaning in all reading instruction, use scaffolding techniques, and promote extensive reading (Peregoy & Boyle, 2013; Ediger, 2014). To promote understanding, language should be presented in context rather than in isolation. Context can be developed by teaching vocabulary using examples of words in sentences or with pictures. Providing background knowledge on a topic, helping students relate new concepts to their own life experiences, and providing concrete examples to illustrate key ideas are other ways in which context can be provided.

Due to ELL's limited English proficiency, some teachers tend to emphasize bottom-up strategies, such as learning sight words, phonics, and syllabication, and de-emphasize or ignore the development of top down strategies such as activating background knowledge and making predictions. It is essential for teachers to teach reading comprehension regularly and consistently to all ELLs throughout the curriculum, even to beginning level ELLs and emergent readers. With pictures, stress and intonation, and gestures, meaning can be emphasized using shared reading, guided reading, and interactive read aloud activities.

In shared reading, an approach that is commonly used with emergent and early readers, the teacher focuses on a picture book, usually in a large format such as a big book, reads the book to a group of children several times, engaging them in a book walk and a variety of activities such as predicting events in a story, learning letter-sound associations, finding rhyming words, and reading repetitive phrases. One example of shared reading is when a teacher reads the big book, *Have You Seen My Cat?* by Eric Carle (2012). In this book, a little boy loses his cat and travels around the world asking, "Have you seen my cat?" For the first reading, the teacher could engage the children in a book walk, pointing to the pictures and asking them questions about what is happening in the story. During the second reading, the teacher could ask the students to listen to her read the story aloud. For the third reading the teacher could ask the students to notice the repetitive question, "Have you seen my cat?" As she reads, the teacher could emphasize this repetitive question, model how to read it, and ask students to join her in reading this part chorally. After reading, the teacher could ask the students to discuss their favorite part of the story.

Interactive read alouds are an excellent way for teachers to model good reading strategies and emphasize comprehension. In an interactive read aloud, teachers read a book aloud to a small group or whole class and engage students in discussion of the story. For example, with the book *Pink and Say* by Patricia Polacco (1994), the teacher could read the book aloud and stop at key points to ask questions about the concepts and events in the story. In this story, a young White boy and a young African American boy fight in the Civil War side by side. At one point in the story, the young African American boy's mother is killed. In this section, the teacher could ask students questions about how African American people were treated during this time period and whether or not they think this was fair and just.

Guided reading is a reading approach in which a teacher guides a small group of readers to read the same book using before reading, during reading, and after reading activities. Before reading activities include previewing the book, having students discuss their background knowledge and personal connections with the topic of the book, reviewing key vocabulary, and practicing pre-reading strategies such as predicting and questioning. During reading activities include discussion of key events and ideas, summarizing important ideas in the book, and practicing fluent reading. After reading activities include discussion of key points in the book, answering questions about characters or events in the story, summarizing the key ideas of the story, and making personal responses by writing about their favorite part of the story or dramatizing an event in the story. Guidance and prompting provided by the teacher support the readers and help them build their comprehension of the text.

Extensive reading is to provide opportunities for students to read as much as possible over an extended period of time for enjoyment and to use texts at an easy, comfortable level. Students should have choice in what they read and should be encouraged to select books that they can read smoothly and at a reasonable rate without having to look up words or needing to translate them from English to their own language. Extensive reading of books written at a comfortable level provides ELLs with lots of practice and fosters more proficient reading. To promote extensive reading, teachers should introduce students to a variety of books on different topics and in different genres by doing book talks, read alouds, and encouraging visits to the library. It is also effective to immerse the classroom in a variety of different kinds of print: nonfiction, poetry, children's and adolescent magazines, big books, word walls, and bulletin boards with displays of interesting words.

Meeting the Challenges of Writing in a Second Language

Since ELLs have more difficulty in composing than native speakers, it is very important that teachers provide direct instruction in all aspects of the writing process and support ELLs with scaffolding techniques. Modeled writing, shared writing, and guided writing are examples of instructional strategies that are very helpful for beginning and younger ELL writers. Modeled writing is a way for teachers to provide direct demonstration of how writers think as they write a message. With this technique, teachers write a message on the Smartboard or chalkboard and think aloud as they compose, making sure to be clear and accurate. For example, the teacher could write a summary of a field trip that the students took. Below is a short example.

> I am going to write a summary of our field trip to Hale Farm and Village last week. In the first paragraph I should make it clear where and when the field trip took place and who participated in the trip. Let's see … On October 10th the class took a field trip to Hale Farm and Village. The class had a wonderful time. Hmmm. I think I need to include in the first sentence which class it was and where the village was located …

Modeled writing is particularly beneficial for ELLs because they may not have models of English writing at home (Wright, 2015). The writing sample can be posted on the classroom wall as an example for students to follow. Supporting information could be added to the text by highlighting punctuation in yellow and labeling sections in a contrasting color with reminders such as, "The first paragraph introduces the topic;" "This paragraph tells who, when, and where."

Shared writing is similar to modeled writing except that it invites students to participate in the composing process. The teacher writes on the board and asks the students to suggest words and content to include. Throughout the process, the teacher scaffolds the students' attempts by making suggestions for vocabulary and grammar. For example, when writing a group response to Strega Nona by Tomie dePaola (1979), a student might suggest that the teacher writes, "Strega Nona was an awesome story!" The teacher could then have the students brainstorm what they thought was awesome about the story and guide them to generate more specific descriptive adjectives such as hilarious, amusing, engaging, and so forth.

Guided writing is similar to shared writing except that it usually focuses on an area of need. For example, teachers can begin by examining students' writing to determine an area of weakness that needs to be addressed, such as sentence clarity, organization of ideas, or descriptive details. They can then provide direct instruction in that area to an individual or group of students with a 10- to 15-minute mini lesson and encourage them to practice the skill or strategy in their own writing. Providing students with feedback and opportunities to share their writing is also important in guided writing.

For ELLs who are at the intermediate or advanced stages of writing, teaching the writing process through an approach such as writer's workshop can be helpful. In writer's workshop teachers provide direct instruction and scaffolding as they guide students through prewriting, drafting, revising, editing, and publishing. This approach is particularly appropriate for ELLs because it allows them to focus on the expression of ideas first and work on corrections later (Peregoy & Boyle, 2013). Additionally, it provides a collaborative support system for students as they engage frequently with their writing group to discuss and share their writing.

Teachers who use the writing process approach may want to use corrective feedback judiciously so that students do not feel overwhelmed by the challenges of writing in a language they do not yet command. They may want to focus on errors students are ready to self-correct and those that interfere with meaning. In students' compositions, they could underline errors students are ready to self-correct and directly correct those errors that students are not yet competent to correct themselves. Recurring grammatical and mechanical issues that are found in students' writing can be taught with direct instruction in mini-lessons (Wright, 2015).

TEACHING STRATEGIES

The four skills of listening, speaking, reading, and writing are the domains of language teaching and learning. Listening and reading are receptive skills; speaking and writing are productive skills. Similar to the developmental trajectory in first language acquisition, the productive skills seem to develop at a slower pace than the receptive skills for second language learners. In spite of this distinction, the four skills are interdependent rather than discrete. For instance, research has shown that oral English fluency has a strong impact on language learners' text-level literacy skills (Wright, 2015). In an education system driven by standardized testing, the importance of reading and writing overshadows that of listening and speaking, but language instruction should provide opportunities for language learners to develop all four skills simultaneously as they attain proficiency in English.

Driven by current research in second language teaching and learning, the teaching strategies presented in this section take into consideration both the language arts teacher and the language learner. First, effective instruction of the four skills is grounded in the language instructor's understanding of how language works (Echevarría & Graves, 2011). This is the explicit knowledge of which sounds are used in English, how these sounds are combined into words, how words are formed, how they are combined into sentences, and how meanings are conveyed in speaking and writing as well as what words should be taught and learned. Key concepts about language related to the development of each of the four skills thus are integrated into the discussion of teaching strategies. Second, effective instruction of the four skills should target how ELLs learn a second language. Unlike learning a first language in which learning takes place intuitively and implicitly, second language learners tend to approach the task of learning a second language analytically (Lightbown & Spada, 2013; Pinter, 2013). They are consciously or unconsciously

seeking patterns as they constantly compare and contrast the language they know and the language they are learning. Explicit instruction of the four skills thus is considered important to ELLs.

LISTENING STRATEGIES

Even though listening is a receptive skill, it is nevertheless an active and integrative activity. Its successful performance draws on a language learner's world knowledge and knowledge of the English language and its appropriate use (pragmatics); it is also affected by the learner's short-term and long-term memory (Richards, 1985). When listening to a second language, the language learner is engaged constantly in constructing and reconstructing the message through developing, testing, accepting, rejecting, or revising what is being said and what it means. Both bottom-up processing and top-down processing are involved. In bottom-up processing, the learner assembles the message piece by piece from the speech stream, going from the parts to the whole, beginning with sounds to words to sentences in an effort to comprehend the message; in top-down processing, the learner starts from prior knowledge of the topic to gain comprehension of the parts that construct the message by means of predicting and inferring (Scrivener, 2011). Strategies for teaching listening therefore should include the following three components:

- a component allowing the learner to develop the necessary background knowledge for a topic, including the more general world knowledge and the more specific knowledge of a particular academic topic;
- a component allowing the learner to develop the schema of a genre; and
- a component allowing the learner to focus attention on the key words that carry the most essential meaning for the comprehension of a text.

The listening strategies explained below are examples of ways to teach listening based on these three components. They provide practical examples that teachers can apply directly in their classrooms.

Contextualizing for Key Words

Context is important for us to convey and understand a message, but academic texts typically are context reduced (Cummings, 2008; Schleppegrell, 2004). For instance, when the sentence *"The President wants more icebreakers"*

is said out of context, it could mean a number of things: that the president wants more Ice Breaker mints, he wants more warm-up games for social gatherings, or he wants more ships designed for clearing a passage through ice. Only when the context is made clear that the president made comments about "keeping up" in the Arctic against Russia's fleet of icebreakers during his recent trip to Alaska is given, does the meaning of the key word *icebreaker* become clear. Language learners, with the pressure of trying to make meaning in a second language or limited by their lack of experience with a topic, could easily misinterpret the context and fail to focus on the key words that are important for understanding a message. So the often-used key words approach to listening comprehension needs to be modified so it is contextualized for ELLs.

Key words in academic texts tend to be content words, such as nouns, verbs, adjectives, and adverbs. They are the meaning-making units of a sentence (Fromkin, Rodman, & Hyams, 2011). To prepare ELLs for a listening task, such as understanding an academic text read to them, teachers should first carry out a two-step text analysis of the academic text to identify the world knowledge and topic-specific knowledge needed for comprehending the text as well as the words in the text that expand on the topic and relate to the knowledge demand. Second, teachers should prepare students for the new vocabulary with focused instruction. Third, teachers should match students' age and proficiency level with the listening task for the key words in the text.

Below is an illustration of the strategy of contextualizing for key words with, "A Day at the Beach," a poem for first graders (Froese, 2013). The italicized words in the poem are the key words that need explicit instruction.

A Day at the Beach
by Charon Froese

A day at the beach
What could be
More <u>fun</u>
Than <u>playing</u> in
The <u>sand</u>
The <u>surf</u>
The <u>sun</u>
<u>Building</u> <u>castles</u>
And <u>rivers</u>
And <u>splashing</u>
In the <u>waves</u>
There's <u>no</u> better
<u>Way</u> to spend
Hot <u>summer</u> <u>days</u>.

First, the two-step text analysis shows that the title of the poem speaks clearly about the topic: A day at the beach. In particular, the poem is structured in a question–answer format: It starts with the question, "What could be more fun than . . . " and ends with the answer, "There's no better way to spend hot summer days." Based on this analysis, the italicized key words expand on the topic and relate to the question–answer structure of this poem.

Second, to prepare ELLs to listen to the poem, the teacher can show students pictures or video clips of beach scenes to activate their experiences or imagination about playing on a beach on a hot summer day. Next, the teacher can introduce beach-related vocabulary in focused instruction, including objects on a beach and activities that people engage in at the beach such as playing in the sand and splashing in the waves. While the focused instruction on vocabulary does not have to be limited to the key words in the poem, the teacher should at least make sure that students know the key words. After that, the teacher conducts a series of listening activities:

1. The teacher reads the poem to students for the first time and students listen.
2. The teacher shows the poem with the key words missing to students.
3. The teacher reads the poem for the second time and students complete a cloze activity to fill in the missing words with pictures.
4. The teacher initiates a discussion on the parts of speech of the key words to draw students' attention to the meaning-making function of these words.
5. The teacher reads the poem with the students followed by students reading the poem on their own.

Third, to match the listening task to students' age and proficiency level, the above-mentioned cloze activity can take a number of different forms. For instance, intermediate students can choose words from a word bank to complete the cloze activity, and more proficient learners can fill in the missing key words directly. In addition, a discussion on what the author thinks is the best way to spend a hot summer day can be used to assess students' comprehension. For less proficient students, the discussion can be initiated and guided by the teacher. For more proficient students, the discussion can be extended to what students themselves think are the most enjoyable things to do on a beach and how they can justify their opinions. Such a discussion can also lead to a writing assignment for students to write or draw about their own "perfect summer day" to elicit more language production from them.

Constructing for Text Frame

When listening to a text in English, ELLs may wrestle with each word and lose track of what is being said. It is thus important that they are explicitly taught how to tolerate ambiguity and focus on the overall meaning of a text rather than individual words and sentences (Richards, 1985). Furthermore, teachers should bring their attention to the overall organization and linguistic features of a text to facilitate and deepen understanding. Genre-based studies on text structure have yielded a rich literature on the organization and linguistic features of different types of texts. If students know the typical pattern of a text, they are able to activate their prior knowledge and knowledge of lexical sets associated with a topic in an effort to understand the text. Therefore, teaching the text structure of the most commonly taught genres can be an effective strategy to prepare ELLs to grasp the main idea and important details.

For example, narratives and arguments are two commonly taught genres in English language classrooms. As summarized in Figure 3.1, the two genres have their unique text organizational patterns. It is effective to pre-teach the text organization patterns using annotated sample texts before asking ELLs to listen to a target text. Then in the actual listening session, the teacher can divide the listening text into sections based on its text organization. This offers the teacher opportunities to scaffold the content of the text and allows ELLs time to process what has been taught and heard. To accompany the listening activity, worksheets derived from the text structures can be used for note taking, which could be reviewed one section at a time.

Focusing on Cohesion Devices

Texts are often connected by linking words or special classes of words. They are the cohesion devices of a text that connect ideas together (Eggins, 2004; Lukin, 2008). The cohesion devices employed by academic texts often are the following types: (a) nouns and pronouns; (b) transitional words (e.g., *for example* and *in other words* for elaboration; *on the other hand* and *however* for extension; and *then, still, because,* and *similarly* for enhancement); and (c) purposeful choice of words that are typically related nouns and verbs (e.g., *professor/teach*) or words of certain semantic relations such as synonyms and antonyms (Eggins, 2004). Directing ELLs' attention to words and phrases that carry the ideas of a text forward helps to emphasize the key points of a text. For instance, the conjunction *however* is used in between two parts of a sentence with the actual or more important meaning resting on the second part, the part that immediately follows this word. In argumentative writing, apart from the thesis statement, the message

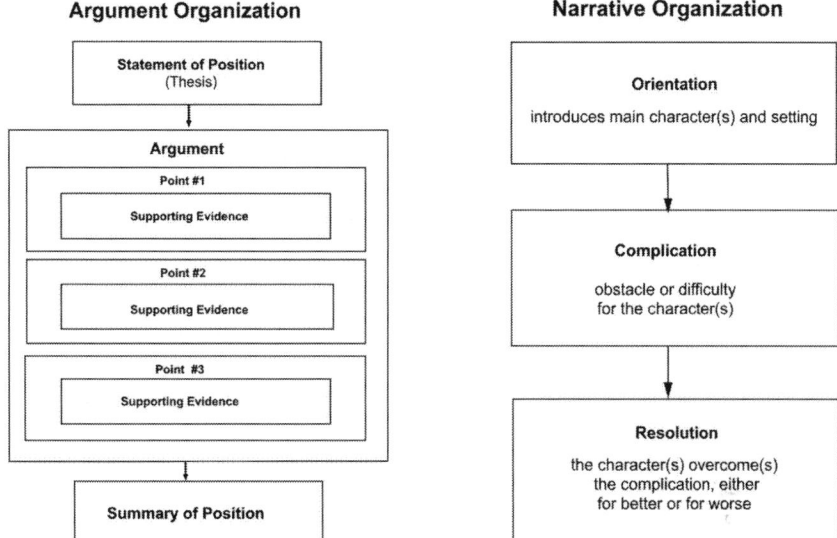

Figure 3.1   This figure is the Text Organization of Narratives and Arguments.
Source: Based on Derewianka (1990, pp. 40–42; p. 75–76).

immediately following transitional words and phrases that advances the argument calls for special attention because it expresses the main points supporting the thesis statement.

To implement the Focusing on Cohesion Devices strategy for listening, teachers need to first identify words and phrases that are used as the cohesion device in a text. Then a tiered listening task can be used in which students listen to a text multiple times to complete a series of tasks that are increasingly more demanding. For instance, in the first listening session of an argument, students are asked to write down only the transitional words or phrases that they have heard. In the second listening session, students are asked to write down three to five key words in the sentence immediately following each transitional word or phrase. In the third listening session, students fill in other information in the sentence immediately following each transitional word or phrase. Finally, students construct a thesis statement based on what has been written down and compare the thesis statement with the actual thesis statement found in the text.

SPEAKING STRATEGIES

Speech is fundamental to human communication. Learning to talk seems effortless with guaranteed success in first language acquisition, but learning to speak fluently in a second language is considerably more difficult. Unlike other language skills, speaking is not just a brain function; it is also a neuromuscular skill. Its processing involves both the motor control of the speech organs and a speaker's phonological knowledge (Moyer, 2013). Successful performance in speaking involves the speaker's phonological, grammatical, sociolinguistic, and world knowledge as well as the processing capacities of the individual at the time of speaking. To be a competent speaker in a second language, a learner needs to demonstrate four interactive competences proposed by Hymes (1972) as communicative competence: (a) grammatical competence (the correctness and accuracy of utterances); (b) sociolinguistic competence (the appropriateness of utterances); (c) discourse competence (the coherence and cohesiveness of utterances); and (d) strategic competence (the use of communicative strategies, such as paraphrasing). Hymes's theory of communicative competence defines what a speaker needs to know in order to be communicatively competent in a speech community. According to Hymes, a person who acquires communicative competence acquires both knowledge and ability for language use.

Speaking becomes even more challenging in the case of learning to discuss academic content in a second language. It not only requires general speaking skills, it also demands knowledge of academic vocabulary and content as well as discourse organization and planning, specific to a content area. At the minimum, in order to teach pronunciation and speaking effectively, teachers should know the vowels and consonants in English, how the pronunciation of vowels can vary according to context, and how these sounds co-articulate in a sentence (Derwing & Munro, 2015). In the English language arts classroom, explicit instruction in speaking can be integrated into read-aloud activities and reading fluency practices. The following strategies are designed with integrated teaching of speaking in the content areas.

Articulating for Vocabulary Building

Academic vocabulary in English language arts, similar to academic vocabulary in other content areas, typically comprises the key words used in academic texts and in discussions of academic content. These words are often content words with more than one syllable. Being able to say these words facilitates the mental retention of these words and enables academic conversation as learners build up a repertoire of words at their disposal.

In English, if a word has more than one syllable, one of the syllables receives more prominence. This is the primary stress of the word. The stressed syllable is pronounced relatively longer and louder than other syllables. In particular, stress can also carry lexical meaning in English, or differentiate one word from another. For instance, stress on bi-syllabic words can differentiate the part of speech as in ***pro*duce** (noun) and *pro'duce* (verb), ***im*port** (noun) and *im'port* (verb). What's more, ELLs often find words with three or more syllables difficult to pronounce, especially when they occur in a sentence with other words, such as *characteri'zation* and ***an**notated bibli'ography*.

Given ELLs' potential difficulty with multi-syllabic words, these words should be highlighted and practiced so that ELLs can use them to access content knowledge and engage in academic conversations. When first introduced, the teacher should enunciate these words more than once with appropriate hand gestures and emphatic pronunciation, such as in a louder and clearer voice, to draw students' attention to them. Students should also repeat these words orally after the teacher while clapping for the stressed syllable. In focused instruction on multi-syllabic content words such as in a review class, lists of multi-syllabic words can be grouped together based on parts of speech (e.g., adjectives) or stress patterns (e.g., four syllable words with the primary stress on the second syllable, x X x x). Then a chant can be created for students to clap for the primary stress as listed in Table 3.1. More advanced students can mark the primary stress on the words before reading them in a chant with accompanying musical beats.

Annotating for Comprehensibility

As a stress-timed language, the rhythm of English speech is created by the alternation between stressed and unstressed words. Stressed words in a sentence are mostly content words, such as nouns, verbs, adjectives, and adverbs. Other words in a sentence, such as articles, pronouns, prepositions, conjunctions, and auxiliary verbs are typically not stressed and are grouped together with a stressed word to form phonological phrases, each of which receives about an equal amount of time in an utterance. The intonation of speech, or the pitch movement gliding through the stressed and unstressed words in a sentence, together with rhythm, function as the "road signs" of English. They direct listeners' attention to the emphasis in a sentence and make the

TABLE 3.1 Adverbs With Stress Pattern X x x x and x X x x

X x x x	x X x x
'consequently	e'normously
'personally	a'pparently
'permanently	a'ccordingly
'practically	in'creasingly

relationship between ideas clear "so that listeners can readily identify these relationships and understand the speaker's meaning" (Gilbert, 2008, p. 2).

In focused pronunciation instruction, teachers often emphasize accurate pronunciation of individual sounds, but rhythm and intonation are actually more important for the comprehensibility of a message, that is, how easy a message is to understand from the listener's perspective (Derwing & Munro, 2015; Gilbert, 2008). ELLs whose native languages are not stress timed, or ELLs with relatively lower oral proficiency, might lack the intuition to tune into the stress pattern marked by stressed words that would facilitate a listener's comprehension of an utterance.

An emphasis on teaching the rhythm and intonation of English thus enables students to actively engage in predicting and catching up with the meaning of what they are reading. It has also been shown to have a positive effect on their listening comprehension, even when explicit instruction is not given (Bradlow, Pisoni, Akahane-Yamada, & Tohkura, 1997). So to raise students' awareness of the essentials of English speech, the following should be demonstrated explicitly with concrete examples:

- English sentences should be parsed phrase by phrase with the marker on the stressed words;
- unstressed words should be pronounced with relatively lower volume of the voice and relatively fast; and
- the pitch movement of intonation should fall on the stressed words to give emphasis.

In focused instruction on the rhythm and intonation of English sentences, the teacher can first choose materials with relatively low vocabulary and knowledge demand so that attention can be concentrated on the pronunciation itself. Second, the teacher can underline the stressed words and stressed syllables in each sentence. Third, the teacher can parse each sentence into phrases around the stressed syllables. Fourth, the teacher can read the annotated text with students. Fifth, students can read the annotated text on their own. Finally, when students have had enough experience in annotating texts, they can annotate the reading text on their own.

Poems are often taught in English language arts classes. With their built-in rhythmic patterns, poems offer many opportunities for pronunciation instruction. Actions can also be added to the reading of poems to differentiate the stressed and unstressed words. Younger students would enjoy tapping the desk for stressed words and tapping their shoulders for unstressed words; older students can take one shoe off and then stomp the foot with a shoe for stressed words and the foot without a shoe for unstressed words. Once students have a better grasp of how stressed and unstressed words alternate in a sentence, the teacher can challenge them with texts with less regular rhythmical patterns. Below, the poem, "Little Things" (Carney, 2010) and the excerpt from "A Courtroom in the Classroom" (Stahl, 2014) illustrate one way to mark the stress patterns of texts (bolded, underlined words are the stressed words and equal length should be assigned to words between slashes. Also note that the marking is for pronunciation practice and therefore follows the rules of syllabification of English speech, which is not the same for syllabication for reading instruction. For example, the word *wanted* can be divided as ***want**-ed* in reading instruction).

Little Things
by Julia A. Carney

Little /**drops** of /**wa**ter,
Little /**grains** of /**sand**,
Make the /**migh**ty /**o**cean
And the /**beau**teous /**land**.

And the /**lit**tle /**mo**ments,
Humble /**though** they /**be**,
Make the /**migh**ty /**a**ges
Of e/**ter**nity.

So our /**lit**tle /**e**rrors
Lead the **soul** a/**way**,
From the /**paths** of /**vir**tue
Into/**sin** to /**stray**

Little /**deeds** of /**kind**ness,
Little /**words** of /**love**,
Make our /**ear**th an /**E**den
Like the /**hea**ven a/**bove**.

*A **Court**room /in the **Class**room*
by Michael Stahl

Miss **Blake** /**want**ed /to **show** /her **third** grade /**class** /**what** it's **like** /inside a **court**room/ of the U**ni**ted /**States**/, so she de**ci**ded /to **stage** /a **role** play/. There are **ma**ny /**di**fferent/ **peo**ple /in the **court**room/ during a **tri**al/. **All** of them /have **di**fferent /but im**por**tant /**jobs**/ or **roles**

Fast Reading for Fluency

Languages differ from one another in their sound inventories and the specific ways to put those sounds together. Speakers of different languages accordingly form a habitual way to bring together the speech organs to suit the sound inventory and its combinations. When speaking a second language, learners need to re-configure their speech organs for the second language. Fast reading forces very active movement of the speech organs. It can be an effective way to help students gain better motor control of the flow of speech. To begin this practice, the teacher should choose a short text that has been previously annotated and read. The teacher can then ask students to read the text multiple times, each time at a faster speed. To make this practice more interesting, a fast reading competition can be held at regular times to encourage practice outside of class. Students can also form fast reading pairs and enter the competition in pairs.

READING COMPREHENSION STRATEGIES

ELLs learning to read in English, just like their native English-speaking peers, benefit from a balanced approach to reading instruction, and specifically, with explicit teaching of the components of literacy such as phonemic awareness, phonics, vocabulary, fluency, reading comprehension, and writing (Goldenberg, 2008; Peregoy & Boyle, 2013; Wright 2015). It is important that teachers teach ELLs how to become good readers by focusing on meaningful contexts using interesting literature and nonfiction texts at students' instructional level. When possible, it is helpful for students to be taught how to read in their native language and supported in transferring literacy skills from their first language to their second language. Additionally, it has been found that materials that are culturally relevant to ELLs facilitate reading comprehension (Wright, 2015).

ELLs benefit from being taught reading strategies that will facilitate their comprehension of texts. Good readers typically use many strategies to comprehend texts (Pressley, 2002), as listed in Table 3.2.

When good readers read challenging texts they use a variety of strategies with an increased metacognitive awareness (Grabe & Stoller, 2014). Metacognitive strategies help them to become aware of their own thinking as they read, monitor their reading as they encounter words and ideas that are challenging, and employ fix-up strategies such as rereading and reading ahead to help themselves understand when meaning breaks down.

An instructional model that has been found to improve student engagement and achievement for ELLs is the Gradual Release of Responsibility (GRR) model (Fisher & Frey, 2008; Frey & Fisher, 2009). This model has four components: focus lessons, teacher guided instruction, collaborative learning, and independent application (Frey & Fisher, 2008). During focus lessons teachers model thinking, ask students questions to scaffold their learning, and build metacognitive awareness of how they are to use a particular skill or strategy. In the guided instruction phase, teachers and students engage in dialogue so students become aware of how they should apply the skill or strategy. During the collaborative learning phase, students work in small groups and interact

TABLE 3.2   Strategies Used by Good Readers to Comprehend Text

- Planning and forming goals before reading
- Forming predictions before reading
- Reading selectively according to goals
- Rereading as appropriate
- Monitoring reading continuously
- Identifying important information
- Filling in gaps in the text through inferences and prior knowledge
- Making guesses about unknown words to be able to continue reading without major disruptions
- Using discourse-structure information to guide understanding
- Integrating ideas from different parts of the text
- Building interpretations of the text while reading
- Building main idea summaries
- Evaluating the text and the author, and forming feelings about the text
- Attempting to resolve difficulties
- Reflecting on information in the text

Source: Pressley, 2002, pp. 294–296

with group members to complete a task. They are held individually account-able for their contributions to the goals of the group. Finally, during independent learning, students engage in independent tasks that extend their learning (Frey & Fisher, 2008). Teachers often call this model I do it, we do it, you do it together, you do it alone. When introducing a new reading strategy to ELLs it is valuable for teachers to use the GRR model so they have the necessary support to comprehend text. Some examples of activities that help students learn good reader strategies are described below. Each of these activities should be used with modeling and explanations from the teacher and meaningful collaboration and discussion amongst students before and after reading.

KWHL: What Do I Know? What Do I Want to Know? How Will I Meet My Goals? What Have I Learned?

KWHL is a widely applicable activity that is designed to promote strategic reading and motivate students to engage with text. K stands for "What do I know?" W stands for "What do I want to know?" H stands for "How will I meet my goals while reading?" and L stands for "What have I learned?" This strategy encourages students to activate their background knowledge, set goals for reading, monitor their reading to focus on important ideas, evaluate the information they have learned, connect back to their goals, and list what they have learned. It is particularly useful with nonfiction. Table 3.3 provides an illustration of a KWHL chart on the topic of immigrants.

TABLE 3.3 Example of KWHL Chart Used With Passage on Immigrants in the United States. Sample Shows Possible Student Responses Before and After Reading

K	W	H	L
• People who have come from a different place to our country • People who have to learn our laws • People who have to adjust to our way of life	• Why do come here? • What problems do they cause? • Do they bring some good things to our country? • How do they become U.S. citizens?	• Preview text to find main ideas. • Write questions to answer when reading the text. • Read to find answers to my questions. • Evaluate whether or not I have answered the questions by rereading sections.	• Immigrants come to the United States to find a better way of life or to flee war, oppression, or poverty. • Sometimes they cause problems because the people who already live in the United States are afraid they will take their jobs. • They bring good things such as skills, knowledge, and willingness to work hard. • They have to pass a citizenship test.

Source: Based on Grabe and Stoller (2014, p. 199)

Anticipation–Reaction Guide

Anticipation–Reaction Guide is a comprehension activity that encourages students to use cognitive and metacognitive strategies as they actively engage with reading a text before, during, and after reading. Figure 3.2 provides an example of this activity on the topic of Leonardo da Vinci. With this activity students make predictions about what they will read, read to verify their predictions, and then find evidence in the text to support their answers. To prepare for this activity, the teacher reads the text to determine the main ideas and supporting details and then develops an anticipation guide with statements to be used to predict information in the text. Before reading, the teacher asks students to read the statements on the guide and mark whether or not they agree (A) or disagree (D) with them. Then the students share their responses with a partner and read the text to determine if their predictions are correct. After reading, they return to the statements to mark whether or not the author agreed or disagreed with the statements. The final step is for the students to provide evidence from the

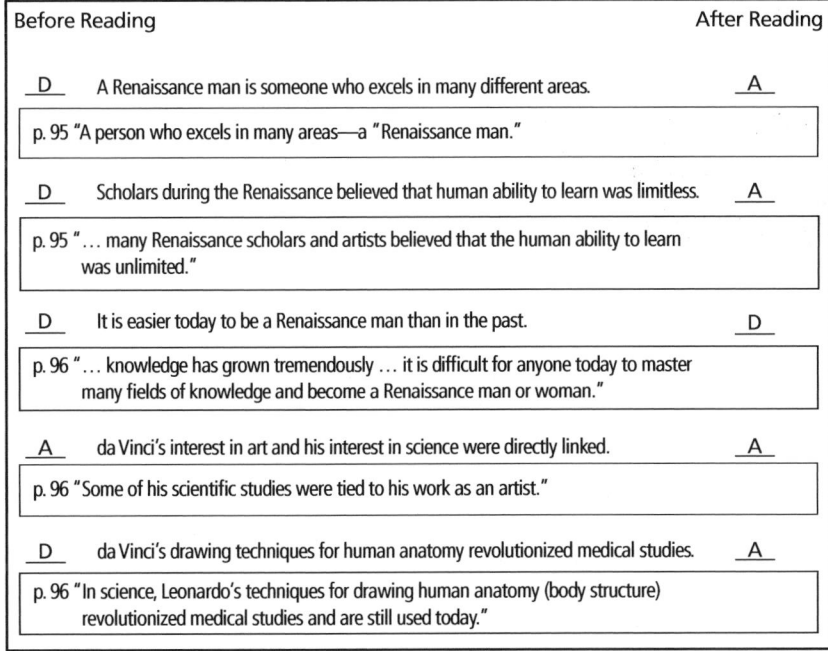

Before Reading	After Reading
D A Renaissance man is someone who excels in many different areas.	**A**
p. 95 "A person who excels in many areas—a "Renaissance man.""	
D Scholars during the Renaissance believed that human ability to learn was limitless.	**A**
p. 95 "… many Renaissance scholars and artists believed that the human ability to learn was unlimited."	
D It is easier today to be a Renaissance man than in the past.	**D**
p. 96 "… knowledge has grown tremendously … it is difficult for anyone today to master many fields of knowledge and become a Renaissance man or woman."	
A da Vinci's interest in art and his interest in science were directly linked.	**A**
p. 96 "Some of his scientific studies were tied to his work as an artist."	
D da Vinci's drawing techniques for human anatomy revolutionized medical studies.	**A**
p. 96 "In science, Leonardo's techniques for drawing human anatomy (body structure) revolutionized medical studies and are still used today."	

Figure 3.2 Sample Anticipation Guide used with *Leonardo da Vinci, Renaissance Man.* The sample shows possible student responses before and after reading. *Source:* Based on Baltas and Nessel (1999, p. 93–96).

text to support their after-reading answers and to discuss what they learned with the whole class.

Survey, Question, Predict, Read, Respond, and Summarize (SQP2RS)

SQP2RS is an activity described by Echevarría, Vogt, & Short (2013) which engages students in before, during, and after reading to build their comprehension. It is usually used with expository text and can often be used as a study guide. This before reading, during reading, and after reading strategy helps students use metacognitive thinking skills as they set goals for their reading, approach the text with an inquiring mind, and summarize what they have learned.

The steps of the SQP2RS strategy are as follows:

1. *Survey:* Students survey the text by looking at the title, headings, subheadings, and other graphic features to get an overview of what it is about.
2. *Question:* In groups, students come up with questions they think will be answered in the text and write them on a template or post them on a large classroom chart.
3. *Predict:* Based on their questions, the students as a small group or whole class generate key ideas they think will be discussed in the text.
4. *Read:* Students read the text with a partner or in a small group, searching for answers to their questions and attempting to verify or disconfirm their predictions.
5. *Respond:* Students answer their questions in small groups and discuss the key concepts in the text.
6. *Summarize:* Students work with a partner or a small group to summarize the main ideas in the text. This summary can be written on their template or on a large classroom chart.

Tiered Texts

Another way for teachers to provide students with scaffolding for their reading comprehension is to have them read texts of gradually increasing difficulty or tiered texts. Tiered texts are texts related to the same topic or story that gradually build readers' background knowledge and understanding of the events in a story to provide access to a more challenging text. This activity is an excellent way to scaffold reading comprehension because it builds students' background knowledge and exposes them to similar vocabulary and academic language across texts to prepare them to comprehend a target text. An example is a tiered text set for Shakespeare's *Romeo and Juliet* as described by Moss, Lapp, and O'Shea (2011). Their model uses a three-tiered system. In tier one, the teacher builds background knowledge about Shakespeare and the Elizabethan period with a read aloud of the picture book, *William Shakespeare and the Globe* by Aliki (2000). After discussing this book, the teacher follows up by having students view Franco Zeffirelli's (1995) film version of *Romeo and Juliet* to learn about the plot and the characters in the play by viewing. In tier two, students practice and prepare to read a challenging text by reading the graphic novel, *Picture this! Shakespeare: Romeo and Juliet* (Page & Petit, 2005). This is followed up by having students create a sociogram of the characters in the play so that they have the opportunity to explore the characters at a deeper level. After this scaffolding, the students are ready to read and discuss the target text, *Romeo and Juliet* by William Shakespeare (2004). After reading the original play, they respond to it by either creating a PowerPoint that retells the story or by developing an iMovie that illustrates the point of view of a particular character in the play (Moss, Lapp, & O'Shea, 2011). This three-tiered approach is an excellent example of literacy instruction based on the GRR model (Fisher & Frey, 2008; Pearson & Gallagher, 1983).

WRITING INSTRUCTION STRATEGIES

Writing is a complex literacy skill. Just as in speaking, writing is a productive process, so fluency (flow of ideas) and accuracy (correct sentences) share the same importance. It requires competence in four different areas:

- linguistic knowledge (grammar and vocabulary);
- functional discourse knowledge (differences between written and spoken English);
- rhetorical knowledge (conventions of writing); and
- composing and thinking skills.

The linguistic forms of written English discourse are different in many ways from that of spoken English discourse. Written English is based on the sentence, paragraph, and text. Furthermore, complex written sentences replace the chains of coordinately linked phrases and clauses of oral language to suit a neutral and formal style. Just as in speaking, composition differs substantially from one culture to another and the conventions of writing also differ (Connor, 2002). Due to this difference, writing instruction should be based on an examination of the forms of authentic English and should be linked to reading (Carrell, 1996; Nation, 2009). Furthermore, it is important that teachers establish an appropriate balance of instruction to foster the development of language skills (vocabulary and grammar) and other skills, especially higher-level thinking skills, so that ELLs' writing contains a logical flow of ideas. Finally, writing tasks should be at the same level of learners' cognitive development even though there is often a discrepancy between learners' cognitive level and second language skills.

Spontaneous Writing for Fluency

Writing about daily life is a low-stakes, low anxiety form of writing practice. Encouraging students to write on a regular basis for real communication motivates them to express themselves in words. For instance, a student can write in English to an English-speaking pen pal who is learning the student's native language, such as Spanish. This also provides an opportunity for the native-speaking Spanish student to write back in Spanish, making this a reciprocally rewarding experience for both students. Students can also write to other students in other classes about what happened in each other's classroom. As long as the writing is understandable, no correction of writing errors is necessary. However, depending on students' ages and English proficiency levels, the teacher should set a reasonable goal of word count to provide guidance for these activities.

One-Page Grammar for Accuracy

Error correction is a reality in teaching writing to learners. ELLs' writing errors might seem to be chaotic at first glance; and yet, research shows that these errors are often systematic and reflect their developing grammar in a second language (Corder, 1967; Ferris, 2011). The most common errors in ELLs' writing range from misuse of punctuation and words to grammatical morphemes (such as the articles *a, an, the;* the third person singular *-s;* and the copula *be*) and tenses. An efficient way to deal with these learners' writing errors is to provide them with a checklist of the most commonly made mistakes in their own writing called a "one-page grammar." The checklist might need to be personalized or could be applicable to students with similar proficiency levels or the same native language backgrounds. To use the checklist, the teacher can number each item and reference the numbers when giving feedback to a learner's writing. The numbers can direct students' attention to the type of errors in their own writing without directly providing the correction. This procedure transforms students from passively receiving feedback to actively participating in the process of improving their own grammar in English.

Blending Reading and Writing for Genre Writing

As mentioned earlier, ELLs tend to approach the task of learning a second language analytically. Writing instruction that is categorized, for example by focusing on specific genres, can be useful for learners to develop the required writing skills. Focus on form, or the linguistic features of each genre, is also important as ELLs are also learning how to use the surface features of the target language.

The English language arts writing standards of the CCSS clearly state that narratives, expository writing, and arguments are the key genres required for reading and writing instruction for students at all levels, from kindergarten to high school, with differentiated requirements (National Governors Association Center for Best Practices & Council of Chief State School Officers, 2010a). Appendix C of the same document provides annotated samples of students' writing that match up to the standards specified for each grade level. Figure 3.3 shows an example of an annotated sample of a narrative written by a second grader that illustrates the standards (National Governors Association Center for Best Practices & Council of Chief State School Officers (2010b, p. 12).

This sample narrative also includes the general linguistic feature of narratives (Derewianka, 1990, p. 42):

1. Specific, individual participants (*I, my sister, my mom and dad*)
2. Use of action verbs (*running, cry, bleeding, lying, put, found...*) mainly and feeling words (*felt, was surprised*)
3. Past tenses (*happened, were (running), did... cry, was (bleeding), put...*)
4. Linking words of time (*So that night... and in the morning*).
5. Descriptive language (*Boy! Did we cry...*)
6. First person or third person point of view (*I, my*)

To teach students to write a narrative similar to the example, the teacher can plan a unit using three to four short stories at a similar reading level about things that happened in the past. These stories should also share most of the same linguistic features described above. The teacher can annotate each story to highlight the linguistic features. Then the teacher can provide specific guidelines or rubrics for students to write in the same style and manner as the example shown in Figure 3.4. The rubric should be

Student Sample: Grade 2, Narrative

This narrative was produced in class, and the writer likely received support from the teacher.

My first tooth is gone

I recall one winter night. I was four. My sister and I were running down the hall and something happend. It was my sister and I had run right into each other. Boy! did we cry. But not only did I cry, my tooth was bleeding. Then it felt funny. Then plop! There it was lying in my hand. So that night I put it under my pillow and in the morning I found something. It was not my tooth it was two dollars. So I ran down the hall, like I wasn't supposed to, and showed my mom and dad. They were suprised because when they lost teeth the only thing they got is 50¢.

Annotation

The writer of this piece

- establishes a situation in time and place appropriate for what is to come.
  - *I recall one winter night. I was four. My sister and I were running down the hall and something happend.*
- recounts a well-elaborated sequence of events using temporal words to signal event order.
  - *My sister and I were running down the hall and something happend.... **But not only did I** cry ... **Then** it felt funny. **Then** plop! There it was lying in my hand.*
- includes details to describe actions, thoughts, and feelings.
  - *Boy! did we cry.*
  - *Then it felt funny.*
  - *So I ran down the hall, like I wasn't supposed to, and showed my mom and dad*
- provides a sense of closure.
  - *They were suprised because when they lost teeth the only thing they got is 50¢.*
- demonstrates growing command of the conventions of standard written English.
  - This piece illustrates the writer's largely consistent use of beginning-of-sentence capitalization and end-of-sentence punctuation (both periods and exclamation points). The pronoun *I* is also capitalized consistently, and almost all the words are spelled correctly. The writer sets off a parenthetical element with commas and uses an apostrophe correctly.

Figure 3.3 This figure is an example of student work sample: Grade 2 narrative.

explained with one of the short stories that students read in this unit to provide specific examples of what each item means.

SUMMARY

This chapter focused on teaching the language arts to ELL students. The chapter began with a real case scenario. This chapter then described the characteristics of each of the four language arts domains: listening, speaking, reading, and writing. We have discussed how these four language skills are interdependent rather than discrete. We have also discussed how oral language proficiency has a strong impact on ELLs' text-level literacy skills (Wright, 2015) and why it is important for teachers to provide opportunities

RECOUNT RUBRIC—SECOND GRADE

1. Title: Describe what happened in a phrase ____
2. Story:

One or two sentences:	When did it happen?	____
One or two sentences:	What were you doing when it happened?	____
One or two sentences:	What were others doing when it happened?	____
Two to three sentences:	What happened exactly?	____
	What were the details?	____
One or two sentences:	What happened next?	____
One or two sentences:	How did you or others feel?	____

3. Mechanics

Does each sentence start with a capital letter? ____
Does each sentence end with punctuation? ____
Does each sentence have a subject? ____
Do most sentences have a verb in past tense? ____
Are there words and phrases about time? ____

Figure 3.4 Example rubric.

for language learners to develop all four skills simultaneously in order to attain high levels of proficiency in English. We have also described the unique challenges that ELLs face in acquiring each of the four language skills and some best practices to overcome the difficulties and to meet the needs of these students in each of the four areas. We have also provided examples of specific strategies that can be used for teachers to help ELLs strengthen their proficiency in each of the four language domains (i.e., strategies for teaching listening, speaking, reading, and writing). Additionally, we have emphasized the importance of the English language arts to all areas of the curriculum and how they should be integrated throughout the curriculum as much as possible.

REFERENCES

Aliki. (2000). *William Shakespeare and the Globe.* New York, NY: HarperCollins.

Anderson, N. J. (2014). Developing engaged second language readers. In M. Celce-Murcia, D. M. Brinton, & M. A. Snow (Eds.), *Teaching English as a second or foreign language, 4th ed.* (pp. 170–188). Boston, MA: National Geographic Learning.

Arrington, C. N., Kulesz, P. A., Francis, D. J., Fletcher, J. M., & Barnes, M. A. (2014). The contribution of attentional control and working memory to reading comprehension and decoding. *Scientific Studies of Reading, 118*(5), 325–346.

Baltas, J. G., & Nessel, D. (1999). *Easy strategies & lessons that build content area reading skills.* New York, NY: Scholastic.

Brown, H. D. (2015). *Teaching by principles: An interactive approach to language pedagogy*. White Plains, NY: Pearson Education.

Bradlow, A. R., Pisoni, D. B., Akahane-Yamada, R., & Tohkura, Y. (1997). Training Japanese listeners to identify English /r/ and /l/: IV. Some effects of perceptual learning on speech production. *The Journal of the Acoustical Society of America, 101*(4), 2299–2310.

Carle, E. (2012). *Have you seen my cat?* New York, NY: Simon and Schuster.

Carney, J. A. F. (2010). *Little things*. Retrieved from http://www.poemhunter.com/poem/little-things-23/

Carrell, P. L. (1996). Text as interaction: Some implications of text analysis and reading research for ESL composition. In B. Leeds (Ed.), *Writing in a second language: Insights from first and second language teaching and research* (pp. 40–47). Boston, MA: Addison-Wesley.

Carrell, P. L., Devine, J., & Eskey, D. (1988). *Interactive approaches to second language reading*. Cambridge, England: Cambridge University Press.

Corder, S. P. (1967). The significance of learner's errors. *International Review of Applied Linguistics in Language Teaching, 5*(4), 161–170.

Cummings, J. (2008). BICS and CALP: Empirical and theoretical status of the distinction. In B. Street & N. H. Hornberger (Eds.), *Encyclopedia of language and education (2nd ed.) Volume 2: Literacy* (pp. 71–83). New York, NY: Springer Science Business Media LLC.

Connor, U. (2002). New directions in contrastive rhetoric. *TESOL Quarterly, 36*(4), 493–510.

dePaola, T. (1979). *Strega Nona*. New York, NY: Aladdin.

Derewianka, B. (1990). *Exploring how texts work*. Newtown, AU: Primary English Teaching Association.

Derwing, T. M., & Munro, M. J. (2015). *Pronunciation fundamentals: Evidence-based perspectives for L2 teaching and research*. Philadelphia, PA: John Benjamins.

Echevarría, J., & Graves, A. (2011). *Sheltered content instruction: Teaching English learners with diverse abilities* (4th ed.). Boston, MA: Pearson Education.

Echevarría, J., Vogt, M. E., & Short, D. J. (2013). *Making content comprehensible for English learners: The SIOP Model*. Boston, MA: Pearson.

Ediger, A. M. (2014). Teaching second/foreign language literacy to school-age learners. In M. Celce-Murcia, D. M. Brinton, & M. A. Snow (Eds.), *Teaching English as a second or foreign language*, 4th ed. (pp. 154–169). Boston, MA: National Geographic Learning.

Eggins, S. (2004). *An introduction to systemic functional linguistics* (2nd ed.). New York, NY: Bloomsbury.

Ferris, D. R. (2011). *Treatment of error in second language student writing* (2nd ed.). Ann Arbor, MI: The University of Michigan Press.

Fisher, D., & Frey, N. (2008). Homework and the gradual release of responsibility: Making "responsibility" possible. *English Journal, 98*(2), 40–45.

Frey, N., & Fisher, D. (2009). The release of learning. *Principal Leadership, 9*(6), 18–22.

Friends. (2016, March 11). Seasons (Episodes by seasons). Retrieved from https://www.youtube.com/show/friends

Froese, S. (2013, March 17). A day at the beach. Retrieved from http://bluebell-books.blogspot.com/2013/03/a-day-at-beach-by-sharon-froese.html

Fromkin, V. A., Rodman, R., & Hyams, N. (2011). *An introduction to language,* (9th ed.). Boston, MA: Wadsworth.

Genesse, F., Linholm-Leary, K., Saunders, W. M., & Christian, D. (2006). *Educating English language learners: A synthesis of research evidence.* New York, NY: Cambridge University Press.

Gilbert, J. B. (2008). *Teaching pronunciation: Using the prosody pyramid.* New York, NY: Cambridge University Press.

Goldenberg, C. (2008, Summer). Teaching English language learners: What the research does—and does not—say. *American Educator,* 8–44.

Goodman, K. S. (1967). Reading: A psycholinguistic guessing game. *Literacy Research and Instruction, 6*(4), 126–135.

Goodman, K. S., & Goodman, Y. (1978). *Reading of American children whose language is a rural dialect of English or a language other than English* (Final Report No. C–0003–0087). Washington, DC: National Institute of Education.

Grabe, W. (1991). Current developments in second language reading research. *TESOL Quarterly, 25*(3), 375–406.

Grabe, W., & Stoller, F. L. (2014). Teaching reading for academic purposes. In M. Celce-Murcia, D. M. Brinton, & M. A. Snow (Eds.), *Teaching English as a second or foreign language* (4th ed.; pp. 189–205). Boston, MA: National Geographic Learning.

Graves, M. F., August, D., & Mancilla-Martinez, J. (2013). *Teaching vocabulary to English language learners.* New York, NY: Teachers College Press.

Hall, D., Jarrold, C., Towse, J. N., & Zarandi, A. L. (2015). The developmental influence of primary memory capacity on working memory and academic achievement. *Developmental Psychology, 51*(8), 1131–1147.

Hymes, D. (1972). On communicative competence. In J. B. Pride & J. Holmes (Eds.), *Sociolinguistics: Selected Readings* (pp. 269–293). Harmondsworth, England: Penguin Books.

Li, N. (2015). A book for every teacher: Teaching to English Language Learners. Charlotte, NC: Information Age.

Lightbown, P. M., & Spada, N. (2013). *How languages are learned* (4th ed.). Oxford, England: Oxford University Press.

Lukin, A. (2008). Reading literary texts: Beyond personal responses. In Z. Fang & M. J. Schleppegrell (Eds.), *Reading in secondary content areas: A language-based pedagogy* (pp. 84–103). Ann Arbor, MI: University of Michigan Press.

Moss, B., Lapp, D., & O'Shea, M. (2011). Tiered texts: Supporting knowledge and language learning for English learners and struggling readers. *English Journal, 100*(5), 54–60.

Moyer, A. (2013). *Foreign accent: The phenomenon of non-native speech.* New York, NY: Cambridge University Press.

Nation, I. S. P. (2009). *Teaching ESL/EFL reading and writing.* New York, NY: Routledge.

National Governors Association Center for Best Practices & Council of Chief State School Officers. (2010a). Common Core State Standards for English language arts and literacy. Washington, DC: Authors.

National Governors Association Center for Best Practices & Council of Chief State School Officers. (2010b). Common Core State Standards for English language arts and literacy in history/social studies, science, and technical subjects: *Appendix C: Samples of student writing.* Washington, DC: Authors.

Page, P., & Petit, M. (Eds.). (2005). *Romeo and Juliet (Picture this! Shakespeare).* Hauppauge, NY: Barron's Educational Series.

Pearson, P. D., & Gallagher, M. C. (1983). The instruction of reading comprehension. *Contemporary Educational Psychology, 8*(3), 317–344.

Pinter, A. (2013). Teaching young learners. In A. Burns & J. C. Richards (Eds.), *The Cambridge guide to pedagogy and practice in second language teaching* (pp. 103–111). New York, NY: Cambridge University Press.

Peregoy, S. F., & Boyle, O. F. (2013). *Reading, writing, and learning in ESL: A resource book for teaching K–12 English learners,* (6th ed.). Boston, MA: Pearson.

Polacco, P. (1994). *Pink and Say.* New York, NY: Philomel Books.

Pressley, M. (2002). Metacognitive and self-regulated comprehension. In A. Farstrup & S. Samuels (Eds.), *What research has to say about reading instruction* (pp. 291–309). Newark, NJ: International Reading Association.

Richards, J. C. (1985). *The context of language teaching.* New York, NY: Cambridge University Press.

Schleppegrell, M. J. (2004). *The language of schooling: A functional linguistic perspective.* Mahwah, NJ: Lawrence Erlbaum Associates.

Scrivener, J. (2011). *Learning teaching: The essential guide to English language teaching* (3rd ed.). London, England: Macmillan Education.

Shakespeare, W. (2004). *Romeo and Juliet.* New York, NY: NY: Simon & Schuster.

Short, D., & Echevarría, J. (2016). *Developing academic language with the SIOP model.* Boston, MA: Pearson.

Stahl, M. (2014). A courtroom in the classroom. Retrieved from http://www.readworks.org/passages/courtroom-classroom

Williams, J. (2005). *Teaching writing in second and foreign language classrooms.* Boston, MA: McGraw-Hill.

Wright, W. E. (2015). *Foundations for teaching English language learners: Research, theory, policy, and practice.* Philadelphia, PA: Caslon.

Zeffirelli, F., Hussey, O., Whiting, L., & Shakespeare, W. (1995). *Romeo and Juliet.* Videocassette. Paramount Pictures Corporation, Hollywood, CA.

Zwiers, J., O'Hara, S., & Pritchard, R. (2014). *Common core standards in diverse classrooms: Essential practices for developing academic language and disciplinary literacy.* Portland, MA: Stenhouse.

CHAPTER 4

TEACHING SCIENCE TO ELLs

Courtney A. Howard
College of Charleston

CASE SCENARIO

Adera is eleven years old and a fifth grader from rural Ethiopia. She and her family moved to the United States last year. They live in a tight-knit immigrant community where her parents run a small grocery store. The family primarily speaks Amharic, their native language. Adera's father is proficient in English, but he frequently travels for business. Her mother speaks very limited English. She and three women from the neighborhood recently enrolled in adult ESL classes offered at the local library. Each week, the women take turns hosting dinner so they can practice speaking English. Adera always attends the dinners with her mother, as do the other children in the group. Her ESOL teacher says she is making good progress with speaking and listening, but Adera is very uncomfortable speaking aloud in front of her native English-speaking classmates. She rarely raises her hand in class and she has few friends at school. Adera's favorite subject is science and she understands most of the concepts she is taught. Her writing proficiency is at the beginner level but improving, and she struggles most with reading. During science investigations, Adera has trouble reading the instructions. She does not say much during group work. This frustrates her peers, so they often exclude her from the activity or only let her help with menial tasks. When she is called on by her teacher, her nervousness makes it hard to think of the right words to say. Adera wishes she could better communicate with others in class.

Teaching ELLs Across Content Areas, pages 83–108
Copyright © 2016 by Information Age Publishing
All rights of reproduction in any form reserved.

ISSUES FOR TEACHING ELLs IN SCIENCE

The United States is undergoing a resurgence of interest in science, technology, engineering, and mathematics (STEM) education. While the origin of this rebirth is debatable, President Obama's 2009 Educate to Innovate initiative played a role in bringing the current status of the STEM education to the nation's attention (McCormack, 2010). STEM fields are credited as pathways to the innovation that will help maintain the U.S position as a world superpower. Advancements in technology lead to solutions to some of the most pressing energy, healthcare, environmental, and national security challenges. National reports project that STEM jobs are growing at a much faster rate than non-STEM jobs. Many of these jobs require technical skills that are rewarded with high wages (U.S. Chamber of Commerce Foundation, 2015).

A recent large-scale collaboration, aimed at ensuring high quality science education for today's students, resulted in the revision of existing national guidelines for teaching science. The lead partners were the National Research Council, National Science Teachers Association, American Association for the Advancement of Science, and Achieve. The result of their work is the Next Generation Science Standards (NGSS), a set of evidence-based curriculum standards that detail the science knowledge and skills all K–12 students should know. The NGSS document was approved in April 2013. Since then, it has been adopted by 14 states and portions have been adapted by several others. Rather than focusing on many discrete facts, NGSS emphasizes (a) deep understanding of core concepts, (b) the process of developing and testing ideas, and (c) evaluating scientific evidence (NGSS Lead States, 2013). NGSS also addresses the habits of mind and practices of scientists and engineers. These practices represent the range of cognitive, social, and physical norms that comprise the culture of science inquiry. These eight practices are not intended to be isolated skills that are taught separately. Rather, they are to be developed within the context of learning science content. The eight science and engineering practices are:

1. Asking questions (for science) and defining problems (for engineering)
2. Developing and using models
3. Planning and carrying out investigations
4. Analyzing and interpreting data
5. Using mathematics and computational thinking
6. Constructing explanations (for science) and designing solutions (for engineering)
7. Engaging in argument from evidence
8. Obtaining, evaluating, and communicating information

The NGSS and scientific practices are language intensive (Hakuta, Santos, & Fang, 2013; Tretter, Ardasheva, & Bookstrom, 2014). This presents a potential challenge for English Language Learners (ELLs); however, teachers can adopt strategies that support language development. It is important that these strategies maintain high standards of academic rigor and that teachers not view language differences as academic deficiencies. In addition, teachers can establish a classroom culture that values students' backgrounds and perspectives and helps them feel comfortable in an inquiry-based learning environment. Teachers can also be intentional about presenting science in an inclusive manner to combat negative attitudes toward science. Some students might have negative predispositions towards science that are based on stereotypes or their cultural experiences. For example, female students might believe that science is a male endeavor. The ethnic minorities may feel under-represented because they do not learn about scientists to whom they can relate. Still, other students might not enjoy science because they consider it too challenging to learn. Teachers can work to identify and address students' attitudes toward science.

CHALLENGES FOR ELLS IN CLASSROOMS

ELLs' prior learning impacts how they acquire both English and science content. It is important that teachers of ELLs also consider a student's literacy skills in their native language and any relevant cultural experiences or knowledge (Yu Ren, 2013). Content and literacy skills are generally transferable. This means that a student who is literate in his native language can expect the same potential in English. Likewise, most of a student's conceptual understanding of science is not dependent on the language in which it was learned. Teachers can make a distinction between content knowledge and vocabulary knowledge when evaluating students' prior learning. A student's lack of familiarity with specific terminology is not necessarily an indication that they also lack understanding of a science concept. It is important that teachers acknowledge students' informal learning, or the many ways in which they interact with particular science concepts in their everyday life. For example, on a pre-assessment given by her teacher, Adera might not be able to articulate formal knowledge of the impact of water on the earth's processes. She may not know the definition of hydrosphere or be able to graph the distribution of water on earth. What Adera does know is how to find and collect water in drought-stricken Ethiopia. This knowledge and experience are meaningful to her and they provide the foundation on which she can learn the formal concepts of the unit.

Inquiry Science

The culture of science instruction in U.S. classrooms involves questioning, investigating, and explaining. In short, this is known as inquiry. Scientific inquiry refers to the many ways scientists study and explain the natural world. Inquiry involves active learning, a process that may be uncomfortable for students with experience in passive learning environments. Students in an inquiry-based science classroom learn to ask questions, conduct investigations, and use evidence from multiple sources to answer those questions. They also learn to substantiate their explanations and defend their conclusions. Inquiry lessons are characterized by discovery, collaboration, and dialogue. Discovery refers to the process of finding new information and perceiving conceptual relationships to build understanding. Students work together (collaboration) to try to make sense of science phenomena. Because they each bring different perspectives and past experiences, they are expected to talk about their observations and understandings within the context of the available evidence. This process can be challenging for ELLs who struggle to communicate with their peers or whose cultural differences are not valued in the science classroom.

For ELLs receiving support through sheltered instruction and other highly sequenced models, the structure of inquiry can be difficult for them to manage (Bergman, 2013). Inquiry learning often occurs in a non-sequenced manner. Learning objectives may not be articulated at the beginning of a lesson, and students might feel disoriented because of the unpredictable nature of the learning experience. Additionally, inquiry learning can be in conflict with the cultural norms of some ELLs (McDonnough & Cho, 2009). For example, a student might view the expectation to question information from adults as disrespectful (Okhee, 2005) or students might think they are insulting others when they defend their conclusions. Teachers can consider these and other perspectives, and use instructional models that support both ELLs and science inquiry.

One such instructional model is the 5E model (Bass, Contant, & Carin, 2009), named after its five phases—engage, explore, explain, elaborate, and evaluate. In this model, teachers sequence the lesson so that students can build conceptual understanding on their prior knowledge and experiences. In the Engage phase, teachers find out what students already know and think about the topic. They also pique students' interests and invite them to ask questions on the subject. During Explore, students interact with materials and ideas. Teachers create a common experience on which students build their understanding. This common experience can be lab investigation or some other hands-on activity. In Explain, students articulate their own ideas, receive new information, and revise their ideas. Teachers introduce formal language, provide content, and clarify meanings. During

Elaborate, students apply what they have learned to new situations. They use academic language while solving problems and communicating their ideas and findings. In Evaluate, students demonstrate what they know and understand. Students also identify deeper questions to explore. They even assess their own progress.

All components of the 5E model are collaborative, so students interact with each other and/or the teacher. The 5E model of instruction is useful when teaching ELLs because it starts with an acknowledgement of students' own culture and experiences (Engage). Students are invited to share what they know without fear of being incorrect. In this phase, teachers can allow different forms of communication, including drawing, writing, and speaking. Some teachers may even host show-and-tell sessions so that students can bring relevant items from home. In this way, teachers can use the Engage phase to infuse students' culture and help them make personal connections to the lesson. For example, at the start of a unit on the role of water on earth's processes, Adera might bring a clay pot that she or other Ethiopian village dwellers use to collect water. Teachers can also engage students by bringing attention to diverse scientists who have studied the topic to be learned. This phase is followed by the Explore phase, in which teachers facilitate a common interactive experience for students. They can use various models of cooperative learning and strategies to support ELLs.

During the Explain phase, science concepts are formally presented. This can occur via direct instruction. The teacher can determine the best way to deliver the information, whether through lecture, reading, video, guest speaker, or other means. To make this decision, the teacher can consider the learning needs of the students and the structure of the content. For example, when the material is dense with new terminology, a teacher may find that lecture is the most effective way to reach the class. Another teacher may prefer guided reading using science trade books and small reading groups.

In the Elaborate phase, students apply the new knowledge to new but similar situations. This allows them to extend their knowledge as they build conceptual understanding prior to being assessed. Teachers can check for understanding and help students to use evidence to support their thinking. Also, students use academic language in their explanations. The Evaluate phase requires students to demonstrate their understanding of the new information they have received. For ELLs, teachers can consider English proficiency when deciding which form of productive communication skill to target—speaking, writing, or drawing. Teachers can set up multiple stations in the classroom for small group work, with each one emphasizing a different mode of communication. For example, during the unit on the impact of water on the earth's processes, the writing station can prompt students to write a fact-based story about the life of a raindrop under different conditions. The drawing station can ask for an illustration of the distribution of water on earth. If her teacher assigns her to the speaking station, then Adera can engage in a science chat.

A science chat is a small group activity during which students sit in a circle and talk about a particular science concept. Ideally, the teacher forms the chat groups, being sure they include a range of science and language abilities. Each chat lasts no more than five to seven minutes and is guided by a series of questions about the material. The questions can be a mix of low-level through higher-order thinking questions written by the teacher. Science chat rules include the following:

1. Each group member must respond to each question;
2. allow the speaker to talk without interruption or help; and
3. the speaker can refer to, but not rely on, materials such as the textbook, handouts, class notes, etc.

Science chats are most useful if teachers are able to listen and make note of any science misconceptions to address later during instruction. To aid with this, teachers can show students how to record their chat using equipment in the classroom. This can ensure that teachers have a record of students' responses that can be used to learn more about how students understand the topic. Also, teachers can share the recordings with the school's ESOL specialist to document language development. Table 4.1 summarizes the 5E Instructional Model and includes tips for using it with ELLs.

Although their overall structures differ, both inquiry and sheltered instruction use similar strategies to engage students (Bergman, 2013). For example, both value students' prior experiences and cultural background. They involve interactions with visual aids and manipulatives, as well as with the teacher and peers. Teachers can use these and other strategies that complement sheltered instruction or use other inquiry models to help ELLs learn science content.

Language Demands

Language is a significant feature in science classrooms. Teachers convey information and instructions. Students write their predictions and hypotheses. They talk to each other about their science readings, activities, and ideas. Students present their projects and ask questions to one another. Though these types of interactions stimulate concept development, they can also be barriers to learning if appropriate language supports are not available to ELLs.

The science classroom can be particularly ominous for ELLs because of the language demands. Science academic language includes words with broad use (e.g., pressure, cycle, force), content-specific terms (e.g., stamen, igneous, cardiovascular), and the language structures used to develop

TABLE 4.1   Summary of 5E Instructional Model

5E Phase	What the Teacher Does	What the Student Does	Working With ELLs
Engage	Generates interest and curiosity; Asks questions; Finds out what students already know or think; Welcomes diverse cultural perspectives and experiences	Asks questions; Shares prior experiences and knowledge in ways that are personally meaningful	Value their cultural knowledge; Allow them to communicate comfortably
Explore	Facilitates hands-on activities; Establishes student groups that maximize individual participation; Monitors students as they interact; Asks probing questions to redirect students' thinking, when needed	Works with classmates to interact with materials and conduct investigations; Records observations and ideas; Clarifies their own understanding of concepts	Give students specific roles within the group. Be sure the role supports language development
Explain	Encourages students' explanations and definitions; Formally explains concepts and definitions; Introduces academic language	Clarifies their ideas based on their understanding and evidence; Listens critically and questions others' ideas; Tries to understand teacher's formal explanations	Use structured notes, word walls, graphic organizers, and other strategies to organize new information; Infuse culturally relevant examples and evidence to support new information
Elaborate	Expects students to use academic language; Provides opportunities for students to apply knowledge to new situations; Guides students to build conceptual knowledge	Applies new knowledge to new situations; Conducts investigations and develops conclusions based on evidence; Records observations and ideas; Helps peers build conceptual knowledge	In addition to the content objectives, focus on language objectives based on students' language proficiency
Evaluate	Observes students as they apply new knowledge and skills; Assesses students; Provides constructive and timely feedback to students	Demonstrates understanding of new information; Reflects on his own progress and knowledge; Receives and responds to teacher feedback	Provide multiple options of how students can demonstrate knowledge, if possible; Select or allow student to select the option that supports a target level or skillset of language proficiency

Source: Adapted from CSCOPE (n.d.)

hypotheses, make inferences, and ask questions. Many common words have different meanings when used in a science context. Some examples are tissue, organic, and model.

"To create an equitable learning environment during inquiry, teachers must be aware of their students' proficiency levels in English and determine the language demands of science lessons to plan for appropriate support during instruction." (Bresser & Fargason, 2014). Teachers can incorporate a number of instructional strategies to promote comprehension. Examples of these strategies are (Bergman, 2013):

- Describe, not define, new vocabulary words. The language and structure of definitions can be challenging for some ELLs. For example, rather than defining gravity as "the force of attraction between two objects," a teacher can describe it using informal and formal language and examples that resonate with the students.
- Use visual aids such as diagrams, photos, videos, and graphic organizers.
- Provide instructions and explanations in written and spoken forms.
- Clarify information by first simplifying and then building on each component.

Teachers can also pay attention to the importance of legible handwriting. Writing on the board is a daily activity for most teachers. Early childhood and elementary educators tend to be conscious of their handwriting. They acknowledge their role in modeling proper handwriting technique for their young learners. These teachers take great pride in making sure their board notes are large, legible, straight, and maybe even color coded. Middle and high school teachers may not exhibit the same level of care with their handwriting, which can be problematic for ELLs. Some teachers write using a combination of cursive, print, capital, and lowercase letters or form letters in non-standard ways. In classrooms with limited board space, teachers might shrink the size of their writing, abbreviate words, write on a slant, or make arrows to show the continuation of a phrase or sentence. This can be confusing for ELLs who are still learning to decipher written English or who take longer than their classmates to copy board notes. As these students copy, they might miss the explanation of the words or shapes, leading to notes they do not understand. In middle and secondary science classrooms especially, teachers often use abbreviations and symbols to convey scientific information.

Figure 4.1 shows two different ways information can be written on a classroom board. The example on the left shows board notes written in a consistent writing style. All words are spelled out completely and information is presented in complete phrases or sentences. The example on the right might be difficult for some ELLs to understand because of the abbreviations and

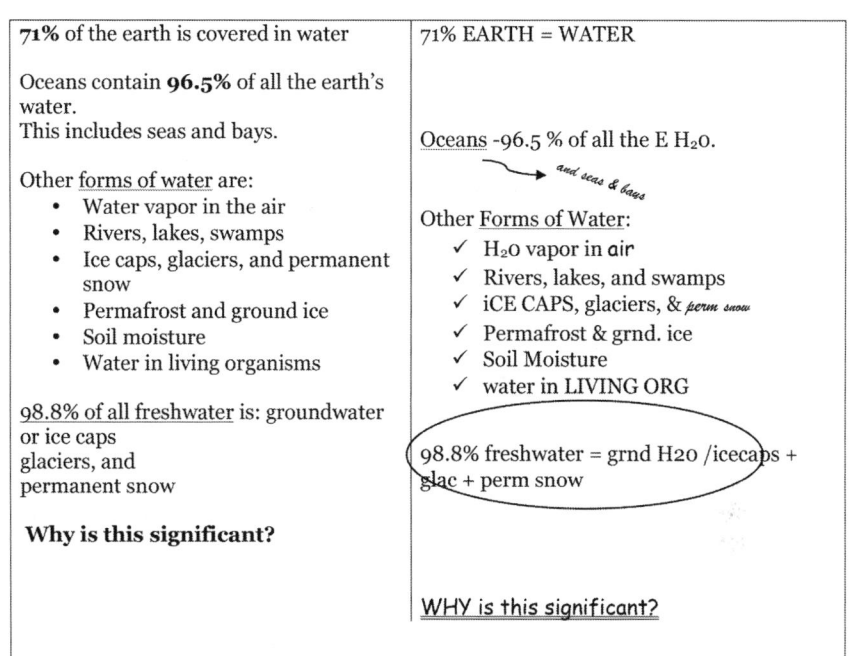

Figure 4.1 Example of legible versus less legible board notes that can impact learning. Legible notes are on the left and less legible notes are on the right.

different writing styles. Maintaining a chart of frequently used abbreviations and symbols might be helpful. It can be used to explain the word origin as it might help an ELL who speaks a language with the same derivation. Teachers can explain the abbreviations and symbols as they write and periodically check if students can make out what has been written (Case, 2009).

Attitudes Toward Science

Historically in the United States, science and scientists have been stereotypically viewed as boring, too hard, and only for the very smart. Scientists are seen as unflattering, quirky, and reclusive nerds or mad scientists. They work in laboratories and are mostly old, Caucasian males (Movahedzadeh, 2011). Developed at home, school, and through the media, these attitudes have been blamed partially for the under-participation of women and ethnic minorities in U.S. science careers. A recent international study shows that the male-dominated image of science is prevalent beyond the United States (Miller, Eagley, & Linn, 2015). This suggests that even ELLs can have stereotypes that inhibit their participation in science. Some ELLs may also be influenced by other views of science that are reinforced in their home culture. Factors such as ethnicity, social economic status, religion, disability, and age may determine who they see represented in science. The earlier teachers can begin to understand their students' attitudes toward science, the sooner they can intervene, if necessary.

Two activities for learning about students' perceptions of science and scientists are (a) to define the word(s) "science" and/or "scientist" and (b) to draw a scientist. Both of these can be implemented early in the school year to find out how students feel about science.

In define the word, the teacher asks students to think of all the words that come to mind when they hear the word "science" or "scientist." Students work individually or in pairs to generate a list. Groups with ELLs can use a bilingual dictionary so that all members' contributions can be included. The teacher tells students to work with a partner or small group to write a definition of science that uses as many words from their lists as possible. After allowing each group to share its definition, the teacher identifies similarities and differences. The class then works together to create a definition that incorporates the students' ideas. An alternative is for teachers to tell students to list all the nouns, verbs, and adjectives that come to mind when they hear "science" or "scientist." With this method, teachers can require that the definitions include words representing the three parts of speech.

Based on years of research, the Draw a Scientist test gives students a chance to illustrate their perception of a scientist (Chambers, 1983; Zhai, Jocz, Aik-Ling, & Tan, 2014). Teachers can provide drawing paper and crayons. This activity works best if teachers give very few instructions. For example, a teacher might say "Draw a scientist. It does not have to be a picture of a specific person, but it should represent what you think a scientist looks like." Afterwards, the teacher can ask students to place their drawing on their desks and allow everyone to walk around to view the illustrations. Students can talk about similarities amongst the drawings. Teachers might notice that common features are: Caucasian, male, bald or messy hair, eyeglasses, and lab coat. Some students might also include a laboratory bench, beaker, test tube, or flame.

Teachers who conduct these activities learn more about their students' perspectives of science. It is equally important for teachers to evaluate their own ideas of what science is, who does it, and how it should be taught. Early childhood and elementary teachers, especially, are more likely to hold negative views of science (Bass et al., 2013; Bresser & Fargason, 2014). In most cases, they are not science specialists so their attitudes are shaped by their own schooling and science experiences. Many of these teachers have limited content knowledge, confidence, or interest in science. Teachers with poor understanding of science concepts are able to focus less on structuring the lesson to meet the needs of ELLs. Also, teachers can hold biased views of different cultures that can impact their teaching. For example, Adera's science teacher might have different expectations from Adera and her Chinese ELL classmate, based solely on stereotypes. It is important for teachers to examine their own views of science and to develop ways to present science positively in their classrooms.

TEACHING STRATEGIES

Teaching science to ELLs involves rich sensory experiences that allow students to interact with science concepts through multiple modalities. Learning modalities refer to the many ways students use their senses to process, remember, and communicate new information. The term learning modality is often used interchangeably with learning style, and a student can be described as a visual, auditory, tactile, or kinesthetic learner. These descriptions fuel the misconceptions that learning occurs through one sense (or mode) at a time and that, for example, visual learners can only learn through sight. The term learning style is more accurately replaced with primary learning preference to suggest that the student favors a particular sense that works in conjunction with the other senses to learn new information. ELLs grapple with both second language acquisition and science content, therefore instruction should involve multiple senses to accommodate this simultaneous learning. More senses gives the student more ways to process the new language and the new content. Students who see, hear, touch, and smell science in action have more opportunities to make personal connections that help them to remember and understand what they are learning. For safety and health reasons, teachers should never allow tasting during science instruction. Also, surfaces and items used for science activities should not come into contact with food and drink that are meant to be consumed.

SHOWING SCIENCE VIDEOS

Science teachers searching for ways to "bring science to the students" may turn to educational videos. Videos can be found on the internet and at the school or local library. The benefits of using videos are many—engaging visual effects, clear explanations, and the chance to view scientific phenomena that cannot be replicated in the classroom. In some cases, short video segments may be more useful than an entire recording because teachers can focus on a particular topic. Regardless of length, there are several factors to consider when selecting an appropriate video. First, teachers need to be aware of their students' levels of English proficiency. Second, videos should present content accurately. Third, the format and language of the video must support language learners. Videos that hold the attention and interest of students probably entertain as much as they educate. Music, animation, and narration can help students relate to the material, but can also be distracting. Fast-paced videos with many transitions may not adequately build science content or reiterate key terminology. ELL students benefit when important terms are repeated and displayed, and when concepts are developed progressively. Teachers should never show a video to students without prior screening, and a video should only be used to supplement (not replace) the teacher. To screen a video, teachers can watch and answer these questions:

- Does the video cover the content at the same level as the teacher's instruction? Look for videos that do not oversimplify concepts or explain them in more detail than necessary. For instance, an elementary lesson on differences between plants and animals might teach that plants use sunlight to make their own food. A video that describes each step of photosynthesis is not helpful at this level.
- Does the vocabulary match? It is helpful if science terms introduced during instruction are reinforced in the video, or vice versa. The use of different words can lead to confusion. For example, during a unit on the butterfly lifecycle, a sudden shift from the word pupa to chrysalis can interfere with concept development if the teacher does not explicitly link the words and their meaning using strategies that address synonyms.
- What non-academic comparisons does the video use to explain science concepts? A comparison works only if students have experience with at least one of the items being compared. Be prepared to introduce the necessary background knowledge to ELLs. Teachers can stop the video at strategic points to provide hands-on experiences that support the comparison or may find it more useful to prepare students before showing the video. For example, a geology video might compare the layers of the Earth to a hard-boiled egg. Dissect and slice boiled eggs to demonstrate what the video is describing. If possible, give students time to manipulate their own hard boiled eggs.
- Is the language inclusive? Videos with narration may use humor, sarcasm, and colloquialisms while presenting information. Witty communication can confuse ELLs with limited English proficiency because of the double meanings that are involved. Teachers should monitor videos for this type of language and be prepared to clarify for students. In addition to academic benefits, interpreting entertaining language may reduce ELLs' awkward feelings of not "getting the joke" when everyone else is laughing.

Once a video has been selected, teachers can create an anticipation guide with key terms and concepts. Fill-in-the-blank items and other interactive components reinforce the material and encourage ELLs to carefully listen to the video. It is helpful to stop the recording periodically to check for understanding and give students time to complete portions of the sheet. Teachers can make the videos available for ELLs to re-watch independently or in pairs during a unit. This is especially useful for students who need more time with a particular concept, or for students who were absent when the video was first shown to the class. Teachers can limit re-screenings to a specific film or portion of a video. Teachers can set up a viewing station on a classroom computer, with headphones and a time-stamped outline of the concepts covered. Whenever possible, teachers can provide a transcript of the video or subtitles. They should consider ELL students' level of English proficiency when considering what language is appropriate for the subtitles. As they watch the video again, students can make changes to their anticipation guides.

PLANNING SCIENCE DEMONSTRATIONS

During science demonstrations, teachers model a particular science concept or process to students. Demonstrations can be suitable when dangerous, expensive, or scarce materials are involved, but also when the goal is to focus students' observations on a particular scientific phenomenon. The theatrics and special effects often associated with demonstrations on television or at tourist attractions are not necessary in the science classroom. Effective demonstrations take on the personality of the teacher and students, and should emphasize concept development rather than surprises. In addition to safety and visibility, consider how to scaffold learning for ELLs and other students. Good science demonstrations engage students in observing and explaining science phenomena. Although they are interactive, they are not improvisational. Teachers should write a script and practice it several times before the lesson. The script includes each step of the demonstration:

Step 1: Activate prior knowledge. Teachers can make explicit connections to previous lessons or experiences that focus students' thinking on the relevant concept. Reminders such as, "Yesterday we learned that..." and questions like, "Based on what we saw in our lab earlier this week, what is the relationship between X and Y?" can be helpful. A quick review of pertinent vocabulary may also remind ELLs of key terms to use.

Step 2: Focus the observation. Introduce the materials and equipment that will be used during the demonstration to be sure students can follow the narration. If knowing the formal names of the materials is important at this stage, then a pictorial guide can be useful for ELLs. Otherwise, use familiar terms such as jar and flame, rather than specialized terms like beaker and Bunsen burner. This allows students to focus on observing the scientific phenomenon itself, not on figuring out which item on the table to watch. Similarly to a television cooking show, provide step-by-step narration of the demonstration with a steady pace. When writing the demonstration script, teachers can determine the balance of conversational and academic language that best meets the language goals of each ELL student. Be careful not to spoil the educational value of the demonstration by giving hints or information too soon. It is acceptable to direct students' observations (e.g., "Watch the food coloring as I drop it into the water."), but it is unacceptable to reveal what they will see (e.g., "The food coloring will move faster in hot water than in cold water.").

Step 3: Engage to explain. When learning science, classroom discussions help students to process ideas and practice using new terminology. These opportunities are often lost to ELLs reluctant to participate in class discussions or who teachers rarely call on. When planning the demonstration, teachers can include time for students to discuss their observations via think-pair-share or other collaborative learning strategies. Student pairs or groups should be heterogeneous so that ELLs have opportunities to interact with non-ELLs or with more proficient ELLs. In pairs or small groups, students can talk generally about their observations at first, but also teachers can guide their conversations with focus questions, such as, "What did you notice about the food coloring? Was it the same in each bowl of water?" These focus questions can be used in conjunction with a "sharing script" that can facilitate whole class discussions (see Figure 4.2). The sharing script is a mostly fill-in-the-blank template, though some of the fields may have multiple choices. The purpose of the sharing script is to help students organize their thoughts and words before whole-class sharing. This can be especially useful to ELLs who are reluctant speakers.

After each group presents its observations, the teacher can offer a summary statement, such as, "Most of you saw the food coloring spread through the hot water faster than it did in the cold water." Ask specific follow up questions that stimulate deeper thinking and give time for small group discussion. Questions like, "What makes hot and cold water different and how might that affect the food coloring?" are more effective than simply, "Why did that happen?" This phase of the lesson is important for the development of conceptual understanding, so teachers should scaffold learning. For ELLs, this phase also encourages verbal participation and supports language development. When appropriate, encourage students to use academic language to enhance their descriptions of what they see (e.g., "I hear you saying that the food coloring moved faster in the hot water. How can you explain that using the terms heat energy and molecules?").

MANAGING SMALL GROUP WORK

Students often conduct science activities in pairs or small groups, and teachers can strategically organize students to maximize the participation

---

Sample of Sharing Script

The people in my group are _____.

We noticed that the food coloring behaved _____ in hot and cold water.
pick one: the same or differently

In the hot water, the food coloring_____.
describe what it did

We think this is because _____.
explain why it did that

In the cold water, the food coloring _____.
describe what it did

We think this is because_____.
explain why it did that

We noticed some other things that we think are important. They are:
  1.
  2.
  3.

We also thought of some questions. They were:
  1.
  2.
  3.

Figure 4.2 Sample sharing script to assist ELLs in organizing thoughts and words prior to whole-class sharing.

of ELLs. To start, create heterogeneous groups that combine different ability levels and language proficiencies. Assigning a role to each student sends the message that everyone is important and accountable to the group. Clarify expectations by creating role cards with the name of the role, its duties, and why it is important. Recall Adera, the student from Ethiopia, who was introduced at the beginning of the chapter. See Figure 4.3 for Adera's role card. Notice that her role has a creative name, as do all the other roles. Using inventive names can prevent students from perceiving the jobs as hierarchical. Be sure the role card is written with ELLs in mind and use language appropriate to their level of proficiency. Although each role has a specific job, every student in the group is expected to help analyze the findings. This is explicitly stated so that students do not excuse themselves from their cognitive responsibility.

Teachers can hold brief meetings for all students with the same role prior to the activity to clarify responsibilities, go over the materials, and to

---

Role Name: Hero

Duties:
1. Clean the work table
2. Wash the equipment
3. Get safety items for my group
4. Remind others of safety rules
5. Help my group understand the findings of our investigation

Importance:
The Hero keeps the group safe. This is important so that nobody gets hurt. The Hero also keeps the work area clean. This is important so our lab table and equipment are not dirty. If they are dirty, then our investigation can be ruined. We cannot be sure our findings are correct.

Figure 4.3   Adera's role card for a small group science investigation.

address questions and concerns. For example, Adera's teacher calls a meeting for all Heroes in the back of the classroom. While they meet, the rest of the class is working on their pre-lab assignment. The teacher reviews the duties of the role and their importance. He guides the Heroes in discussing details of their job. They talk about which safety equipment is needed and where it is stored. They review how to properly clean the work space and items that will be used. They also review the safety rules and expectations. The teacher instructs the students to make sure they are familiar with their fellow Heroes so they can help each other as needed. In this example, Adera's teacher uses the role meetings to prepare students for the upcoming lab investigation and to establish a community among all of the Heroes. He repeats this for each of the roles, even those with no ELLs. In some cases, teachers can also have problem-solving role meetings to discuss challenges that may be impacting a particular role. A reflective role meeting after the activity can give students a chance to talk about ways to improve the efficiency of that role for future investigations.

The process for assigning roles can be strategic, rather than random or by student selection. For ELLs, teachers might prefer to assign a role that can support a target area of language proficiency. For example, an ELL who reads fairly fluently but struggles with comprehension may make a good "navigator," the person responsible for finding the section of the reading that relates to the question. The ELL then works with their group to make sense of the passage to determine the correct answer. On the other hand, a student with beginning language proficiency might be a well-suited "materials tech" who gathers the items needed by the group. Teachers can form groups that remain for an entire unit, grading period, or change them more frequently. In either case, teachers can monitor ELLs' progress and rotate them through group roles that challenge them at appropriate levels.

Teachers can encourage students to work outside of their comfort zone, but avoid assigning roles that are so challenging that they become counterproductive to student progress.

EXPLORING SCIENCE FIELD TRIPS

Field trips enhance science learning for all students if they are well-planned, interactive, and meaningfully integrated into the curriculum. Teachers can arrange field trips to local places of interest, the schoolyard, or other campus spots as a way to supplement classroom instruction. Field trips can be led by the classroom teacher or by a guide who is knowledgeable of the site. In either case, teachers should prepare by visiting in advance, previewing all activities that will occur during the class trip, and beginning to plan pre- and post-trip activities to underscore the learning goals. When selecting a field trip site, teachers may consider many factors, including relevance, cost, distance from school, and class size. Teachers may also think about how well the location can meet the needs of ELLs.

During the advance visit, obtain a copy of all the materials students will use during their trip. Take photographs or make note of words, objects, skills, and concepts to include in the pre-visit lessons. Consider the language demands of the tour and the interactive experiences students will have during the trip. Also, picture how students will be grouped. It may be helpful to complete a Site Features Checklist (Figure 4.4) to identify potential barriers and supports for ELLs. This tool can be useful when trying to select the most accommodating field trip location for ELLs. The checklist divides site features into four categories: video/audio guides, signage, museum staff, and interactive activities. Teachers can check each category for each of the listed features. The features on the right are potential barriers for ELLs and the features on the left are potential supports for ELLs.

Teacher-guided field trips may offer the most flexibility to meet the individual needs of ELLs; however, they are not always practical. Field trips to established educational institutions such as aquariums, science museums, planetariums, and botanical gardens can be led by staff members who are knowledgeable of the exhibits and relevant science content. These individuals may work in the site's education department, where they develop and implement site-specific lessons, and they might be trained to address the needs of ELLs. To be sure, teachers can discuss this when making the reservation. Any accommodations made by site staff might be general in nature, so teachers can prepare their own supplements and personalized supports. On the other hand, staff at non-traditional field trips are likely not educators and they may never have been trained to work with ELLs. Non-traditional field trip sites include local service institutions and businesses

Video/Audio Guide	
Available in multiple languages	Available in English only
No cost to use listening device	Rental fee to use listening device
Captions or written transcripts are available	Captions or written transcripts are not available
Level of guide matches level of instruction	Level of guide is more complex or simple than level of instruction
Signage	
Available in multiple languages	Available in English only
Level of text matches level of instruction	Level of text does not match level of instruction
Museum Staff	
Easily accessible and available to help	Hard to locate and/or unhelpful
Knowledgeable and able to clarify content	Not knowledgeable of relevant content
Prepared to address the needs of ELLs	Unprepared to address the needs of ELLs
Interactive Experiences	
Focus on a few big ideas	Focus on many ideas
Develops conceptual understanding	Develops knowledge of facts
Incorporates diverse cultures	Does not incorporate diverse cultures
Notes:	

Figure 4.4 Site Features Checklist for identifying potential barriers and supports for ELLs. Supports are listed on the left and barriers are listed on the right. Teachers can use this checklist when previewing a prospective field trip site.

such as a recycling center, animal shelter, or grocery store. For these visits, teachers should work with staff in advance to ensure the experience will meet the needs of all students.

INFUSING CULTURE

Science is a human endeavor and good science teaching calls attention to the people and circumstances that impact science discovery. This type of focus can be motivating for students from under-represented groups, including ELLs, because it reflects the diversity of ideas, personal stories, and cultures that have contributed to science. Teachers can infuse culture into the science classroom in a number of ways. One way is to highlight particular scientists, particularly those whose lives might resonate with students in the class. Other ways to infuse cultural diversity are acknowledging the contributions of various cultural/ethnic groups and the geographic locations in which significant discoveries have occurred.

Teachers can engage their class in creating a "science wall of fame" with posters representing a range of diverse scientists. To start, the teacher generates a list of male and female life, earth, and physical scientists. The list should include historical and contemporary researchers. As much as possible, be sure to include representations that mirror the students in the class. For example, Adera's teacher might include Dr. Segenet Kelemu, a plant pathologist and Dr. Sossina M. Haile, a chemist. Both are contemporary Ethiopian female scientists. The teacher identifies several reputable websites and other approved resources that students can access. Assign one scientist to each student or pair of students, and allow time for them to conduct research. Though it may be preferred in some cases, it is not necessary for students to study a scientist who shares their national background. Because the students can present and display their posters to each other, all students will be exposed to all of the scientists on the list. Teachers instruct students to find a photograph and gather information such as birthday, place of birth, education, area of expertise, professional accomplishments, and unique challenges or experiences. Using a world map, teachers can help the class identify the many places from which the scientists hail. After in-class presentations, the teacher displays the posters in the classroom or hallway. Some teachers prefer to conduct this lesson early in the school year to inspire student learning. Also, these teachers can later refer to particular scientists whose work relates to the unit of study.

Another approach to infusing diversity into the science classroom is to discuss the role of various non-dominant groups in scientific discovery. Teachers can show how a science idea progresses over many years based on the work of multiple scientists. For example, planetary motion was studied by ancient Babylonians, Greeks, Indians, Arabs, and Chinese. Here are some names: Ma Yize (China), Kublai Khan (Iran), Al- Khawarizmi, and the concept of planetary motion was also studied by Tycho Brahe (Dutch), Nicolas Copernicus (Polish), Johannes Kepler (German), and Galileo Galilei (Italian) over a period of nearly 100 years. Teachers can explain how each of these astronomers advanced the ideas of the previous one. They can also highlight how international conflict has impacted science, such as the space race and nuclear arms race between the United States and Russia. This can be contrasted with the many examples of international cooperation in science, including the International Space Station (United States,

Russia, Japan, Canada, and Europe) and the Large Millimeter Telescope (Mexico and United States). Other examples of collaboration address endangered species, the environment, and disease.

In addition to emphasizing diverse scientists, teachers can also bring attention to the location of many science discoveries. For example, Adera's teacher might share news stories about Ethiopia as a site of several significant human fossil discoveries. The most recent discovery in March 2015 is considered to be of the oldest known human fossil. Teachers are cautioned to be mindful of the sensitive and sometimes controversial nature of certain topics, such as global warming and human evolution. They are advised to consult their state education guidelines to find out how these topics should be approached, if at all. Also, teachers need to be aware of different and often conflicting historical perspectives, and take care to present past events in an unbiased manner.

Table 4.2 provides a list of diverse scientists and scientific discoveries based on country of origin. The countries listed are among the most common origins of U.S. immigrants, according to various reports of the Migration Policy Institute (Auclair & Batalova, 2013; Batalova, 2011; Russell & Batalova, 2012; Stoney, Batalova, & Russell, 2013; Terrazas, 2009). This list is not intended to be exhaustive.

OTHER TIPS & STRATEGIES

Teachers can enhance science teaching by involving parents through family assignments. These assignments can reinforce classroom instruction, give ELLs practice explaining science concepts to parents, and provide a means of supporting other parent engagement initiatives at the school. Whenever possible, teachers can provide the materials needed and give adequate time for families to complete the assignments. These types of experiences help parents know what the students are learning, and they also give the student a structured platform on which to talk to family about science concepts. It may be necessary to tailor the assignment to individual students' English proficiency. Family science assignments are great ways to acknowledge the role, culture, and knowledge-base of students' families. Some suggestions for how to engage ELLs' families are: home-based science investigations, art interviews, and science-themed children's movies.

Home-Based Science Investigations

Teachers can assign home-based science investigations for parents and ELLs to work on together. In some cases, the science activity can occur

TABLE 4.2 List of Diverse Science Contributions

Country	Selected Contribution to Science
Brazil	Carlos Chagas (physician who discovered Chagas Disease)
China	Chien-Shiung Wu (nuclear physicist known as the "First Lady of Physics")
Colombia	Salomón Hakim Dow (neurosurgeon, researcher, and inventor)
Equador	Clodoveo Carrión Mora (paleontologist and naturalist)
Egypt	Ahmed Hassan Zewail (1999 Nobel Prize in Chemistry)
El Salvador	David Joaquín Guzmán (archaeologist)
Ethiopia	Segenet Kelemu (plant pathologist)
Germany	Maria Sibylla Merian (naturalist and scientific illustrator)
Ghana	Ave K. P. Kludze, Jr (rocket scientist)
Guatemala	Monica Pellecer Alecio (archaeologist)
Honduras	Home of one of the first programs to protect amphibians in the wild from extinction due to disease
India	Kamal Ranadive (cancer researcher)
Iraq	Ancient Babylonian astronomical observations are the origins of modern Western astronomy
Italy	Marcello Malpigi (Father of Microscopic Anatomy)
Kenya	Kamoya Kimeu (fossil collector who worked with the Leakey's, a famous paleontogist husband–wife team)
Mexico	Home of one of the world's largest telescopes used to study how stars are formed
Nigeria	Debrework Zewdie (public health immunologist responsible for the world's first global HIV/AIDS strategy)
Peru	Ancient Incas are known for inventing elaborate highway systems, terrace farming, rope bridges, and freeze dried foods
Philippines	Leonardo Legaspi Co (botanist and plant taxonomist who discovered eight new species of plants)
Russia	Boris Schwanwitsch (entomologist who studies the color pattern of the wings of butterflies and moths)
Saudi Arabia, Syria, and Yemen	The Islamic Golden Age was an era with high scientific activity, including the development of forms of experimentation

Note: Information compiled from various pages within http://en.wikipedia

prior to the start of a new unit, as a way to pique families' interest. In other cases, the activity might culminate the unit, to allow students the chance to explain science concepts to their families. It is best when the investigation involves common household materials and items that, whenever possible, the teacher provides. Clear, simply stated instructions with diagrams are important, and some teachers may find value in creating a companion video that demonstrates each step of the activity. Teachers should ensure that students are familiar enough with the activity to explain it to their parents. It is important to note that some ELLs will prefer or need to communicate with their parents using their native language, therefore teachers should not confuse difficulty explaining in English with lack of understanding.

An example of a science investigation that can be adapted for use at home is popularly referred to as dancing raisins. This activity is commonly used while teaching about density and buoyancy, or more simply, that air bubbles cause objects to float. The materials are inexpensive and easy to find—raisins, clear carbonated beverage, and a tall clear glass or plastic cup. To do the activity, families simply pour the beverage in the glass, observe the bubbles, add several raisins, and continue to observe. Teachers can create an activity sheet on which families document their observations and explanations.

Art Interviews

An art interview can be an engaging way for students to learn more about their parents' experience with a particular science concept. This assignment can be an excellent way to learn how different cultures interact with or perceive a science topic. The only materials needed are crayons or markers and one sheet of drawing paper. This activity works well for students and parents with no or very low English proficiency. To develop an art interview assignment, teachers first identify the science concept to be studied and one key word. At home, the student draws a picture that represents their experience with or perception of that word. They then show the picture to their parent, who responds by drawing on the same page. The parent's response can be a separate image or an extension of the student's illustration. This exchange can continue until the page is filled or other criteria set by the teacher are reached. Families can be encouraged to discuss each drawing so that, when the students return to school, they can explain what they learned from the art interview. For example, if the key word is water, Adera might draw a picture of a river and her mother might respond with a drawing of a container used to collect water. Adera might then draw a picture of a girl tending to feet calluses caused by walking long distances in search of water. As the art interview continues, a unique portrait emerges that details the relationship between Adera's family and water. Adera's teacher can use the students' art interviews to understand and acknowledge the diversity of experiences in the class.

SCIENCE-THEMED CHILDREN'S MOVIES

Teachers can incorporate popular children's movies into instruction as a home-based family assignment. This activity is useful as an exercise for students to showcase their near the end of one or several related instructional units. The goal of this assignment is for the student to lead his family in determining how accurately a children's movie portrays science concepts. Teachers can first generate a list of movies that address or depict the science topics addressed in the instructional unit. Several animated movies (with release year) to consider are:

- Ferngully: The Last Rainforest (1992)
- The Lion King (1994)
- A Bug's Life (1998)
- Antz (1998)
- Osmosis Jones (2001)
- Ice Age (2002)
- Finding Nemo (2003)
- Madagascar (2005)
- Happy Feet (2006)
- Bee Movie (2007)
- Ice Age: Contintental Drift (2012)
- Zambezia (2012)

Teachers are encouraged to preview the movies to ensure appropriateness and to gain familiarity with what and how the science concepts are represented. It may be preferable to assign the same movie to all families or students can be permitted to select a movie from the list. Whenever possible, teachers can provide legitimate DVDs or links to websites with the full movie. This activity can be time-consuming, so teachers are encouraged to give families ample time to complete this assignment. Also, teachers can consider alternate viewing arrangements for families without movie-watching equipment. Teachers can create a handout (Figure 4.5) for families to rate how the science concepts are depicted in the movie. Individual science concepts can be listed, with each followed by a rating scale. Families can then provide evidence from the movie to support their rating.

Concept #1 Predator–Prey Relationships

Rating Scale (circle one):
    4 – Real science   3 – Mostly real science   2 – A little real   1 – Not real science at all

Evidence from the movie:

Concept #2 Nocturnal Animals
Rating Scale (circle one):
    4 – Real science   3 – Mostly real science   2 – A little real   1 – Not real science at all

Evidence from the movie:

Figure 4.5   Excerpt from sample handout for families to use while rating how accurately science concepts are portrayed in a children's movie.

SUMMARY

This chapter focused on teaching science to ELLs. The chapter began with a case scenario related to an eleven-year old ELL, Adera, who is challenged in learning, especially in her science classroom. The chapter urged teachers to focus on both science content and language development when teaching science to ELLs. Many issues can make learning science challenging for ELLs, including the nature of inquiry, varying language demands, and negative attitudes toward science. Teachers can use a variety of tools and strategies to enhance instruction of the science lessons and to engage ELLs' participation. For example, the 5E instructional model provides a useful structure for inquiry lessons. Science videos, demonstrations, and field trips can be used effectively to provide meaningful science experiences to ELL students. Teachers can organize small group work to maximize the involvement of ELLs. Most importantly, teachers can help students develop positive views on science by infusing culture and focusing on diverse contributions to science.

REFERENCES

Auclair, G., & Batalova, J. (2013, Sept 26). Middle Eastern and North African immigrants in the United States. Retrieved from Migration Policy Institute website: http://www.migrationpolicy.org/article/middle-eastern-and-north-africanimmigrants-united-states-0

Bass, J. E., Contant, T. L., & Carin, A. A. (2009). *Teaching science as inquiry* (11th ed.). New York, NY: Pearson.

Batalova, J. (2011, May 24). *Asian immigrants in the United States.* Retrieved from Migration Policy Institute website: http://www.migrationpolicy.org/article/asian-immigrants-united states

Bergman, D. (2013). Blending language learning with science. *Science Teacher, 80*(4), 46–50.

Bresser, R., & Fargason, S. (2014). Opportunities and challenges for ELLs in the science Inquiry classroom (Part 1). Washington, DC: Colorin Colorado. Retrieved from http://www.colorincolorado.org/article/61273/

Case, A. (2009). Classroom language when using the board. Retrieved from http://www.usingenglish.com/articles/classroom-language-when-using-board.html

Chambers, D. W. (1983). Stereotypic images of the scientist: The draw-a-scientist test. *Science Education 67*(3), 255–265. doi: 10.1002/sce.3730670213

CSCOPE (n.d.). *The 5E model of instruction.* Retrieved from http://www.wisd.org/users/0001/docs/GVC/5E%20Model.pdf

Hakuta, K., Santos, M., & Fang, Z. (2013). Challenges and opportunities for language learning in the context of the CCSS and the NGSS. *Journal of Adolescent & Adult Literacy, 56*(6), 451–454. doi:10.1002/JAAL.164

McCormack, A. (2010). Imagine and invent: Create a great future. *Science Teacher, 77*(6), 8–9.

McDonnough, J. T., & Cho, S. (2009). Making the connection. *Science Teacher, 76*(3), 34–37.

Miller, D. I., Eagley, A. H., & Linn, M. C. (2015). Women's representation in science predicts national gender-science stereotypes: Evidence from 66 nations. *Journal of Educational Psychology, 107*(3), 632–644.

Movahedzadeh, F. (2011). Improving students' attitude toward science through blended learning. *Science Education & Civic Engagement—An International Journal, 3*(2), 13–19. Retrieved from http://seceij.net/seceij/summer11/movahedzadeh_im.html

NGSS Lead States (2013). *Next generation science standards: For states, by states.* Washington, DC: The National Academies Press. Retrieved from http://www.nextgenscience.org/

Okhee, L. (2005). Science education with English language learners: Synthesis and research agenda. *Review of Educational Research, 75*(4), 491–530.

Russell, J., & Batalova, J. (2012, July 26). *European immigrants in the United States.* Retrieved online from Migration Policy website: http://www.migrationpolicy.org/article/europeanimmigrants-united-states

Stoney, S., Batalova, J., & Russell, J. (2013, May 2). *South American immigrants in the United States.* Retrieved from Migration Policy Institute website: http://www.migrationpolicy.org/article/south-american-immigrants-united-states

Terrazas, A. (2009, Feb. 10). *African immigrants in the United States.* Retrieved from Migration Policy Institute website: http://www.migrationpolicy.org/article/africanimmigrants-united-states-0

Tretter, T., Ardasheva, Y., & Bookstrom, E. (2014). A brick and mortar approach. *Science Teacher, 81*(4), 39–44.

U.S. Chamber of Commerce Foundation. (2015, October 19). STEM education talking points. Retrieved from http://www.uschamberfoundation.org/content/stem-education-talking-points

Wikipedia (2015, October 5). Information. Retrieved from http://en.wikipedia.org

Yu Ren, D. (2013). Powerful learning tools for ELLs. *Science Teacher, 80*(4), 51–57.

Zhai, J., Jocz, J. A, & Tana, A. (2014). Am I like a scientist?' Primary children's images of doing science. *International Journal of Science Education, 36*(4), 553–576.

CHAPTER 5

TEACHING MATH TO ELLs

Aria Razfar and Zayoni Torres
University of Illinois at Chicago

CASE SCENARIO

Ms. Anita is a 6th grade bilingual teacher. All instructional time in her classroom is in English. She has a newly arrived learner from Mexico. His name is Juan. Juan's home language is Spanish. Each day at school, Juan has the same routine. He enters the classroom, sits at his desk, and stares down at his book(s) as the instruction continues. At times, he will open his notebook and start scribbling. Sometimes he will look up at the Promethean Board when something is displayed on the board that catches his eye. Other than that, he mostly sits at his seat quietly. Once everyone gets started on individual, partner, or group work after given instruction to do so, Juan asks the bilingual (Spanish-English) learner that sits next to him for instructions. Since Ms. Anita speaks Spanish, Juan will approach her during this time to have her clarify the task at hand. He usually only participates during individual, partner, or group work. During this time, he talks to the bilingual learner that sits next to him. He then copies down responses based on what that learner says. Ms. Anita has tried desperately to figure out ways to better support Juan. Her bilingual lead teacher simply tells her that as a bilingual teacher her job is to provide a certain amount of time a day when Juan can have a teacher who speaks his home language.

Teaching ELLs Across Content Areas, pages 109–129

ISSUES FOR TEACHING ELLs IN MATHEMATICS

In the above scenario, Ms. Anita has been teaching for 4 years. Her teaching strategies to support her English Language Learners (ELLs), such as Juan, have come as a result of trial and error. She has recently completed her master's degree and is familiar with the research literature's recommendations for supporting ELLs. After attempting various strategies, she is still confused about what practical steps to take as a bilingual teacher. For her, understanding that home language can be a valuable resource for instruction and comprehension is not enough. For example, Juan mainly sits quietly during most of the instructional time. He is able to use his home language to express himself and to ask questions. He has other bilingual learners in the classroom that can provide assistance. Ms. Anita speaks and understands Juan's home language. However, simply allowing this home language and other bilingual learners to serve as resources in the classroom does not seem to be enough to further Juan's progress. Juan relies heavily on the bilingual learner sitting next to him to translate information. Ms. Anita intentionally placed Juan next to this bilingual learner to provide assistance. This move seemed to help. However, she is unsure if he is grasping any of the content since Juan's reliance on that bilingual learner is evident as he copies down what the learner says. Ms. Anita faces one of the common challenges of teachers—How do I support learners just like Juan? Furthermore, how do I ensure that these learners are learning something and not just keeping preoccupied?

Challenges for ELLs in Classrooms

These challenges in findings ways to support ELLs are particularly common when teaching literacy skills, such as reading and writing. It is not uncommon to hear teachers mention, "My ELLs struggle with reading and writing, but they excel at math." Implicit in this statement is that literacy is separate from content areas. Rather, literacy is a fundamental component of all content areas, such as mathematics. Learners need to be able to listen, read, write, understand, and think mathematically. Furthermore, statements such as the one above indicate a misconception that mathematics is a universal content area. This misconception includes fixed rules and answers, where there are few differences across language(s) and cultural groups (Razfar, 2012). Even the slightest nuances can change the entire meaning for ELLs and other learners. For example, a widely cited mathematics problem that questions this universality is the bus pass problem:

It costs $1.50 each way to ride the bus between home and work. A weekly pass is $16. Which is the better deal, paying the daily fare or buying the weekly pass? (Tate, 1994, p. 480)

Since ELLs will rely on their personal experience in responding to word problems such as the one above, answers may vary. For the above example, this problem and the anticipated response only apply to a subset of people—those who work a 5-day workweek and make one trip to work and back (Tate, 1994). Therefore, the problem does not take into account the cultural differences of learners' interpretations.

Vocabulary and Context

These nuances further extend to the discursive practices required for particular problems. In teaching discipline specific content to ELLs, in this case mathematics, it is easy to view building vocabulary as the sole strategy to help learners understand the content. Rather, vocabulary is a part of this larger foundation learners need. One mathematics teacher explained what she views as mathematical language, "For me mathematical language is more than just the terminology or words, but how to put it together. How we think. How we think about thinking in math or how we explain our reasoning. The whole process." Mathematical thinking and reasoning is a process.

Vomvoridi-Ivanovic and Razfar (2013) reported on their experience with pre-service teachers (PSTs) attempting to solve "the baseball problem." Ultimately, the interaction of PSTs around the baseball problem demonstrates how knowledge of vocabulary is not enough. Rather, learners need to understand the practices surrounding the target topics to even begin to problem solve.

PSTs were grouped based on their knowledge of baseball. The three resulting groups are the following, with group 3 identifying as "Baseball Language Learners" (BLLs):

- *Group 1: Baseball Experts.* PSTs who are very knowledgeable about baseball and can fluently talk about the sport.
- *Group 2: Baseball Novices.* PSTs who have only basic knowledge about baseball.
- *Group 3: Foreign to Baseball.* PSTs with no or almost no knowledge of baseball, other than that it is a sport. They could not explain how the game is played. (Vomvoridi-Ivanovic & Razfar, 2013, p. 9)

Next, group members were asked to define the baseball terms—slug, bat, batting three hundred, ball, strike, diamond, base, steal, stealing home, hit and run, Triple Crown, run, out, balk, and save. Groups shared out their responses. All groups were then given the same working definitions to assist with the next part of the activity. Third, PSTs were asked to solve the following baseball problem:

> Barry Bonds, one of the most prolific home run hitters of the modern era, slugged over "eight hundred" in one season. If he had six hundred at bats, how many total bases did he get? (p. 9)

In the end, PSTs were asked to share their solution and the process in which they went through in attempting to solve the baseball problem. As expected, those PSTs who were knowledgeable about baseball had no difficulties solving the problem. On the other hand, those who had no knowledge or limited knowledge of baseball struggled (i.e., BLLs) with the response. This was the case even though all groups were provided with common working definitions for key vocabulary words. For example, all groups at this point in the activity knew what run, slug, batting three hundred, and base are. However, not all groups had the "baseball" knowledge required to solve the problem.

Linguistically and Culturally Responsive

Given the diversity in our schools, there continues to be a need to create linguistically and culturally responsive learning environments. These environments can help support ELLs to more fully participate in mathematical discourse communities. Within these discourse communities, learners develop ways of communicating that mediate the process of mathematical learning. This form of communication extends beyond simply the use of home language. Ms. Anita found that allowing a space for home language use is not enough. In order for Juan to more fully participate, where he is gaining knowledge and utilizing it in the classroom, other meditational tools need to be established.

Therefore, our approach is mathematics as a way for learners to view and understand the world (Gutstein, 2006; Tate, 1994). The more recent Common Core State Standards (CCSS), which is a state-led initiative that has been adopted by nearly all U.S. states, pushes for conceptual understanding and the mastering of specific topics in each mathematics content category (i.e., geometry, number and measurement, etc.). Within this framework, teachers are encouraged to focus on these skills to prepare learners for college, career, and life. Furthermore, some states have adopted language standards. These standards have been aligned with assessments that determine the English language proficiency of ELLs. Teachers can continue to provide meaningful learning opportunities for ELLs for the sake of learning mathematics and for real-world application. This responsibility comes even with continued requirements and demands on teachers.

Meeting Challenges and Planning to Teach

Two of the biggest challenges teachers face are: (a) conceptions of mathematics and how that translates into classroom instruction for ELLs (i.e., vocabulary in context, developing communities of learners, awareness of verbal and non-verbal cues); and (b) how to ensure that the content, curriculum, and instruction provided are in alignment with national and state requirements, while also maintaining this core value of creating linguistically and culturally responsive learning environments. The former challenge requires teachers to change conceptions of mathematics that include universality and route memorization. The latter challenge requires a balance between what is meaningful to the ELLs and what is important for success on mandated assessments.

TEACHING STRATEGIES

There are a number of teaching strategies that teachers can use as common practices to develop linguistically and culturally responsive learning environments when working with ELLs. The first one is the use of vocabulary banks as an embedded and contextualized form for learners to access discipline specific terminology. The second one is foregrounding differentiated instruction to tap into various modes of learning, sensory experiences, and levels of language and content proficiency. The third is modifying spoken and written speech. The fourth is eliciting nonverbal responses from learners as a way for them to demonstrate their thinking without an overreliance on spoken language. There are also a number of other teaching strategies to support ELLs. Here we focus on the aforementioned teaching strategies.

Creating Vocabulary Banks

In terms of vocabulary banks, teachers need to both strategize for the creation of these resources and be aware of the purpose they serve. Using vocabulary banks can help learners to move toward more specialized approaches that advance content specific meaning making (Moschkovich, 2002). They provide ELLs with vocabulary words and phrases that can be useful to reference (Bresser, Melanese, & Sphar, 2009). Furthermore, they serve as mediational tools to enhance verbal discussions and when writing about the process of problem solving. Razfar and Rumenapp (2013) provide suggestions when it comes to a similar approach, word walls. Word walls can be organized thematically or discretely. When word walls are organized thematically, ELLs have better opportunities to contextualize the meanings. Similarly, vocabulary banks can take many forms; for example, digitally accessible boards, bulletin boards, charts, posters, and/or personal word banks. A personal word bank can take the form of a mathematics notebook. Learners can write words and key phrases, draw pictures, and paste images.

To begin, it is important to build awareness of those nuances in terminology and mathematical expression. This includes knowledge of some of the differences in symbols and algorithms, for particularly immigrant learners (Moschkovich, 2013). For example, the comma and period serve diverse purposes in some countries. A period can be used to mark the thousands place, while a comma can be used to mark a decimals place (e.g., 1.500 rather than 1,500 to represent one thousand, five hundred; and 12,23 rather than 12.23 to represent twelve and twenty-three hundredths respectively). Teachers can find these variations in learners' written work. One example is a few methods for solving long division problems (Moschkovich, 2013). These strategies are shown in Figure 5.1.

For Strategy 1, the divisor (i.e., 7) is placed at the upper right corner in a box, while the dividend (i.e., 123) is written to the left of the divisor. The learner places a number (which makes up the quotient) (i.e., 17) underneath the box. The process of division alternates from the right hand side to the left hand side. In Strategy 2, the learner excludes the in between steps of subtracting a quantity. These strategies still result in the expected answer.

```
123        | 7
  7          17
 53
 49
  4
```

Strategy 1

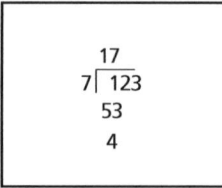

Strategy 2

Figure 5.1 Division strategies.

When introducing new words, ensure that the words are thematically relevant and regularly used. It is recommended to introduce no more than 5–7 words related to the mathematical concept. Some schools introduce vocabulary words that are consistent across subject areas. These vocabulary words are separated into different tiers based on difficulty. This strategy provides consistency across subject areas, where learners are able to see the application of vocabulary words across these various domains. Learners are then able to expand on their own definition of these key terms. Begin with concepts. For example, learners will come across terms such as "product," "multiply," "times," and symbols such as "x," "*," and "·," that are used interchangeably. As learners begin to understand the process of multiplication (i.e., not simply lining up numbers and going through the step by step of producing an answer, but understanding what it means to have a quantity that is increased a certain number of times through repeated addition), terms can be introduced.

Learners should be able to clearly see and make out the word. Therefore, words should be printed or written in a font and size that learners are comfortable with. If possible, add the learners' home language(s) translation of the vocabulary words. ELLs may or may not be literate in their native tongue. It is important to know the language and educational history of the learner (Moschkovich, 2013). Some questions to ask are: What grade levels did the learner attend? Where? In what language(s)?, and Are they literate in their home language? Knowing this history can assist the teacher in planning supports. For each vocabulary word include accompanying images, gestures, and/or phrases. Colors can be used to distinguish words by topic or category. Learners can work in groups to write sentences and definitions, draw pictures, or create gestures for new vocabulary words. What these groups produce can become a part of the vocabulary bank.

Using Vocabulary Banks

ELLs can be given vocabulary words and asked to create categories for the words. Learners can then place the vocabulary words under the category of choice and explain or justify why the word(s) belongs under that category. Learners can also group the vocabulary words as they see fit. They will discuss how they grouped the words and why they grouped them in such a way. These approaches can help with word association. Another strategy is to begin with some type of image (i.e., photo, drawing, etc.) that learners are familiar with. Have them describe this image drawing from their toolkit of vocabulary words and phrases. This can be done orally or in written form. These strategies can help teachers to better understand the meaning learners are associating with the vocabulary words and to modify their own display/organization of the vocabulary bank if necessary. In Figure 5.2, we provide examples of how to display three vocabulary words—tally marks, frequency, and percent. The ELLs' home language in this classroom is

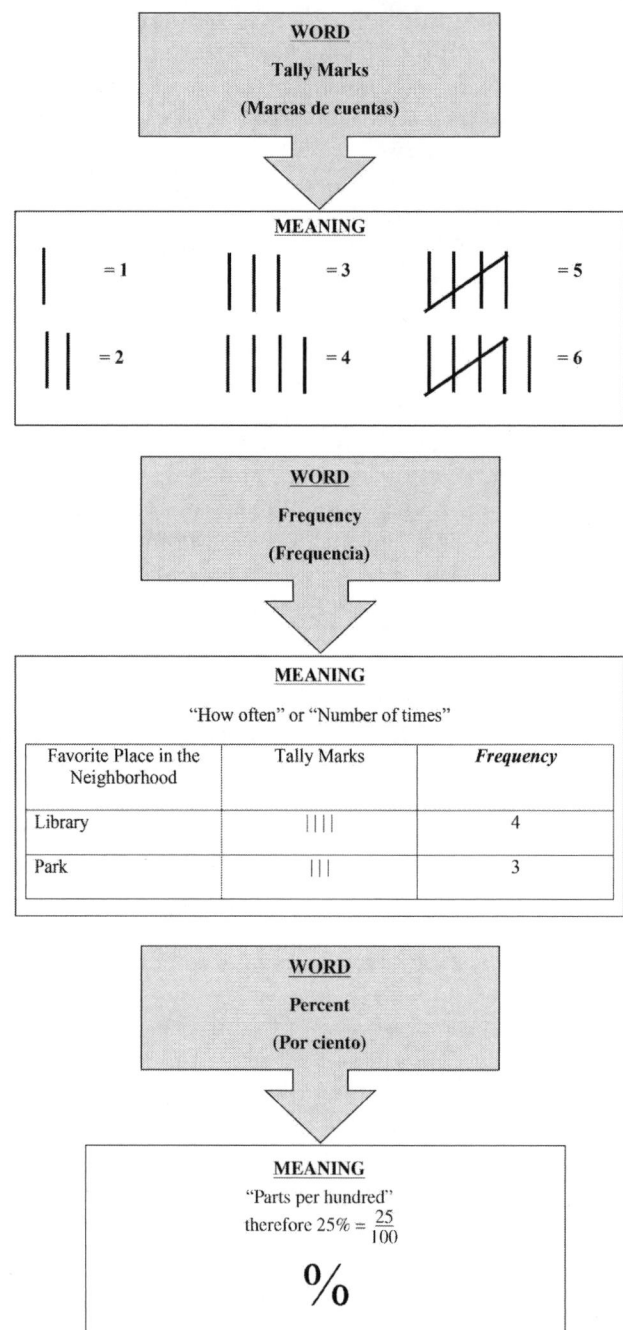

Figure 5.2 Sample vocabulary bank.

Spanish. The Spanish translation of each word is included. Images, short phrases, and numbers also accompany each vocabulary word.

Vocabulary Bank in Context

Vocabulary banks should always be used in context. An example of the use of the above vocabulary words (i.e., tally marks, frequency, and percent) in context is shown below (Figure 5.3). The teacher who created this instructional handout took an integrated approach of reading and

---

Instructions: Read through the following questions carefully. Answer question 1 and 3 by yourself. We will answer question 2 and 4 together.

1. What can you share about the fire hydrants in [neighborhood name] during the summer months?

2.

Word	Tally Marks	Frequency	Percent

3. Approximately how many fire hydrants are on your block?

4.

Number of Hydrants	Tally Marks	Frequency	Percent

Figure 5.3 Vocabulary in context.

mathematics. As a pre-reading assignment learners responded to the following questions (questions 1 and 3 individually and questions 2 and 4 as a class). This activity was derived from learners' own experiences with fire hydrants in their community. Their community is located in the center of an urban context. Learners first described what they knew about fire hydrants during the summer months (responses could be in any language) (Question 1). Setati (2005) found that in classes where the discourse was limited in nature to solely English, learners did not develop conceptual understandings of mathematical strategies. Rather, where multiple discourses were encouraged, learners demonstrated greater conceptual discourse. After completing Question 1, learners shared out key words that they used to describe fire hydrants in their neighborhood. The number of times key words were used was then documented by tally marks, frequency, and percent (Question 2). The teacher filled in the table for Question 2 based on learners' responses. For Question 3, learners jotted down the number of fire hydrants on their residential block. Learners shared out their responses by a show of raised hands. Volunteer learners then went up to the front of the class to fill in the corresponding tally marks, frequency, and percent (table for Question 4).

Vocabulary words need to become a part of the daily communicative practices of learners. In specific, these words should be used by learners in talking and writing about mathematics. Learners can also use these new terms outside of the classroom to affirm their real-world application. Razfar, Khisty, and Chval (2011) recalled a statement by a teacher when asking about her use of sophisticated language with ELLs. She replied, "When are they going to learn it? How are they going to learn it? They encounter those words in books. I'm angry with the notion that students are not competent to learn" (p. 202). ELLs need access to this sophisticated language.

Using Differentiated Instruction

Differentiated instruction refers to the accommodations or adaptations made to curriculum and instruction that provide opportunities for learners of differing learning styles, proficiency levels, and background experiences (Reyhner & Davison, 1993). If we take learning to be a mediated activity, then the differentiation becomes the meditational tools that support learners reaching their learning goal. Learners can benefit from having differentiated instruction such as (a) questions, prompts, and activities that gauge different proficiency levels, (b) activities that tap into various sensory inputs, (c) organization of learning that enhances active participation in the learning environment, and (d) a wealth of resources or meditational tools that learners can draw from in participating in these learning environments.

Questioning, Prompts, and Activities

ELLs can be at different proficiency levels in language—home language and English—and in content knowledge. When designing questions, prompts, and activities, these levels of proficiency need to be taken into consideration. Questioning ELLs provides them an opportunity to demonstrate their knowledge. Yet, questions need to be structured in a way where learners can produce a response. Open-ended questions and prompts challenge learners who have more of a grasp of the language and content. Questions and prompts should not be convoluted. This means that they should be clear, concise, and avoid connecting two extensive thoughts with "and," "but," or "or" (Miller, Linn, & Gronlund, 2012). Most words should be familiar to them. There should be enough context clues so that ELLs can have some indication of what the task is asking of them. Numbers, symbols, capital letters, bold font, underlined font, and italicized font should be used to point out important information (Miller et al., 2012). For example, if there is a key word or phrase that is necessary for the learner to point out before even beginning the task, then that can be indicated by the previously mentioned means. Questions and prompts should be in the active voice and should avoid the negative form, such as "not" (Miller et al., 2012). If a negative form is used ensure to underline these key terms. In the following example, learners were provided with 4 maps of different sections of their community. ELLs were asked these questions (Figure 5.4).

Here the teacher tapped into learners' knowledge by asking if they recognized a location on the map and to record the location. Learners needed to have a grasp of maps and the purpose of a key. Learners were asked to compare the maps. Questions 2, 3, and 4 have consistency in how the questions are presented (i.e., What can you say . . . ? How do . . . ?).

Mathematics sentence frames. Sentence frames, sentence stems, or sentence starters can support learners that are moving towards full explanations and sentences. Mathematics sentence frames serve a variety of purposes. First, they help the learner to more fully participate in discussions by providing some guidance. Second, they afford a context for applying key words and phrases. Third, the structure helps extend English language skills that can lead to the development of complete thoughts and sentences. The goal is for learners to transfer this practice into expressing mathematical thinking in written and verbal form. Here we further develop the activity with open-ended questions in Figure 5.4 into an activity of sentence frames (Figure 5.5). Learners refer to the maps to respond to the questions. They begin by listing locations (Question 1). They then draw a symbol for each

Instructions: Refer to the maps on the following pages. Answer the questions below.

1. Is there a place on the map that you recognize? If so, please make a key and record the location.

2. What can you say about the scale of Map #1 in comparison with Map #2? How do you know?

3. What can you say about the scale of Map #1 in comparison with Map #3? How do you know?

4. What can you say about the scale of Map #1 in comparison with Map #4? How do you know?

Figure 5.4 Mapping questions.

location (Question 2). Lastly, they compare and contrast Map #1 and Map #2 by completing the sentence starter (Question 3 and 4).

We can opt to make the sentence frames more structured and provide some possible options for learners. Figure 5.6 shows an alternate format for a related question to the previous activity (see p. 122). Learners can fill in the blank(s) inserting words that they view fit best. Learners are given the information that the scales are different and asked to tell what they see. They are given three options in parentheses.

Multi-Sensory and Multi-Modal

Drawing on various sensory inputs in lesson planning provides a fuller and more meaningful experience for learners (Reyhner & Davison, 1993). Learners can touch, see, feel, and hear all simultaneously. By doing this, it increases neural connections and enhances learning and memory (Willis, 2006). Furthermore, learners should be provided with opportunities to engage with different modes of learning (i.e., listening, writing, speaking, and reading). For instance, Moschkovich (2013) suggests that, "teachers should not assume that proficiency in one mode implies proficiency in another

---

Instructions: Refer to the maps on the following page. Fill in the blanks below.

1. I recognize the following places on the map.

    A _____

    B _____

    C _____

2. I will use this symbol _____ (*draw a symbol*) to show where place A is located on the map.

    I will use this symbol _____ (*draw another symbol*) to show where place B is located on the map.

    I will use this symbol _____ (*draw another symbol*) to show where place C is located on the map.

3. What is the **same** about the *scale* of Map #1 and the *scale* of Map #2?

    The scale of Map #1 _____

    The scale of Map #2 _____

4. What is **different** about the *scale* of Map #1 and the *scale* of Map #2?

    The scale of Map #1 _____

    The scale of Map #2 _____

Figure 5.5 Mathematics sentence frames.

mode and should provide mathematics assessment and instruction across all modes" (p. 31).

Returning to the fire hydrant activity in Figure 5.5 of this chapter, the teacher designed a multitude of activities where learners would listen, read, write, and speak. Learners were also able to hear, see, and touch materials to further their understanding. First, the teacher began with an activity where learners would describe (in writing) the fire hydrants in their neighborhood. Second, volunteer learners would share out their responses verbally. Third, as a whole class, learners figured the tally, frequency, and percent of each word. They jotted down these responses. Next, learners wrote a number indicating the fire hydrants on their residential block.

Instructions: Fill in the blanks below.

Look at the two maps below. They are of **different scales**. Tell me what you see. *Choose one of the options in parentheses to complete the statement.*

insert map of one scale

insert map of another scale

Scale #1   Scale #2

Scale #1 is _____ in comparison to Scale #2. (*larger, smaller, the same*)

Scale #1 is covering _____ **area** in comparison to Scale #2. (*more, less, the same*)

Figure 5.6 Mathematics sentence frames (more structured).

When responding to this question, learners tended to talk to other learners who lived on their residential block to ensure they were making an accurate prediction. Fifth, learners determined the tally, frequency and percent of the number of fire hydrants as proportional to the whole class.

The next part of the lesson consisted of learners listening to a read aloud of an excerpt of a book. Within the excerpt, the author pointed out street names and landmarks in the community in which the learners live. Learners listened as the teacher read and were asked to:

> Please take notes during the read aloud, highlight any information you may want to discuss further with a peer or in a small group.

At the conclusion of the read aloud, learners discussed the text in small groups. As a post-reading assignment, learners were asked to discuss if they recognized any of the landmarks and streets mentioned in the text. Furthermore, they were asked if they knew anyone from the neighborhood that resembled one of the main characters of the text. Again learners needed to rely on community knowledge to make connections to the text.

The last part of the lesson consisted of a map activity. Learners were provided with four maps (of different scales) of the neighborhood. Outlined in these maps were some of the street names mentioned in the text. Learners completed the activity in Figure 5.4 of this chapter. Here they were afforded a means to visualize these locations and to manipulative the given maps by recording landmarks in which they are familiar.

Modifying Speech

Another strategy to support ELLs is to modify teacher speech. This strategy includes being conscious of responses to ELLs. First, when ELLs speak, focus more so on the message that they are trying to convey, rather than sentence structure and grammar. Respond using a correct form. Paraphrase learner responses and questions, rather than overtly re-voicing and correcting these same responses and questions. Second, use familiar language rather than specialized mathematical terms and syntax structures. In this case it is okay to repeat, rephrase, and paraphrase what you say as the teacher. Third, as was mentioned earlier with vocabulary, use key words frequently so that they become a part of the daily communicative practices of the classroom. Fourth, not all learners have mastered the cultural practices of a language group. This means that not all learners understand idioms and slang words (Razfar & Rumenapp, 2013). Try to avoid their usage. For example, one teacher used the expression "pick up the pace" with her grade 2 ELLs. One learner looked down to the floor to try to make sense of what the teacher was asking her to pick up. It is easy for learners to attempt to interpret idioms such as "pick up the pace" literally.

Fifth, pause between sentences and thoughts. Learners, particularly ELLs, need enough time to process questions and problems and to formulate some type of response. It is tempting to call on the same learner all the time and/or the first learner to raise her/his hand. Learners need time to think; therefore, enough wait time is necessary (it is suggested to count to 20 in your head before calling on someone). Sixth, speak clearly and slowly without raising your voice. Here, you can focus on the enunciation of words. Seventh, use gestures and visuals to assist learners. Visuals can even be used on handouts. Furthermore, help learners to see the instructions. This can be done by having instructions displayed in written form in short concise points somewhere that is visible to all learners. Eighth, reduce the amount of teacher talk. Talking too much and giving too much direction can cause confusion. Again, clear concise instructions are important.

Eliciting Nonverbal Responses

Nonverbal responses serve a multitude of purposes. They are intended to check for a learners understanding without them needing to produce oral language. In specific:

ELLs can participate and show that they understand a concept, or agree or disagree with an idea, without having to talk. This is especially important for students whose comprehension of English is more advanced than their ability to speak the language. (Bresser et al., 2009, p. 12)

Eliciting nonverbal responses can tap into various cognitive resources by allowing learners to participate in mathematical "talk" in different ways (Moschkovich, 2013). Leaners can draw, write about mathematics, demonstrate mathematical representation, use gestures, use manipulative objects, among other means. Learners can also participate in physical activities. These activities can be movement along an imaginary line or a number line. Alternatively, learners themselves can be used as representations to explain a mathematical concept. Learners can have individual boards where they write down their response and show it to the teacher. Learners can be asked to raise their hand depending on their response. For example, for the fire hydrant activity, the teacher had volunteer learners first raise their hand to provide a verbal response. Then she asked if anyone had the same response to raise her or his hand. She then took note of the number of learners who shared a similar response. This approach ensured that all learners were participating and engaged in the activity, while not requiring a verbal response from learners in order to be a participant.

Hand gestures and ASL. Learners can also use hand gestures to provide a response. For example, learners can give a thumbs-up, thumbs to the side for agreement/disagreement or to show certainty/uncertainty. American Sign Language (ASL) is another resource for learner non-verbal responses. In specific, learners can make use of the ASL alphabet. For example, for multiple choice questions, learners can respond with an "a," "b," "c," or "d." Furthermore, learners can demonstrate agreement/disagreement by the show of an "a" for agree and "d" for disagree (Figure 5.7). Alternatively learners can show an "a" to indicate an answer; while they can use another letter, say "r" for simplicity, to indicate a question (Figure 5.7).

Other Tips and Strategies

Organization of Learning/Grouping

The organization of learning has implications for how the dynamic of the classroom unfolds. A teacher needs to consider how the space of the classroom is physically organized and how learning is socially organized. For example, desks arranged where learners are in rows facing towards the teacher allows for more initiation-response-evaluation discourse (IRE). Alternatively, learners seated in pairs or in clusters of a few to several students allows for more partner and group work. Heterogeneous (mixed-linguistic ability) groups

	= Letter "a" to indicate a response to a multiple choice question, to show agreement, or to indicate an answer
	= Letter "d" to show disagreement
	= Letter "r" to indicate a question

Figure 5.7 ASL alphabet—"a," "d," and "r."

are beneficial for all learners. It is advised to partner/group learners with limited proficiency with those who have moderate proficiency. Within these groups, learners should be given roles and responsibilities that allow them to participate. Roles can take the form of facilitator, recorder, reporter, and participant. Learners should be given opportunities to fill all roles. Therefore, it is crucial to suppress any underlying preferences in choosing which learners will fulfill which roles. Knowledge of cultural/community practices is needed to understand a learners' form of participation. Teachers should be mindful of the learners' language practices at home and in community settings (Moschkovich, 2013). For example, some forms of common participation are more observing than talking. Moschkovich (2013) provides some of the typical mathematics communication practices of bilingual students:

Using arithmetic facts in first language, doing arithmetic computation in their first language and then translating the answer, and code-switching, using two languages during one conversation. (p. 30)

Thus, in organizing learning (physically and socially) it is crucial to understand the goal of the interactions and to be aware of any tensions in participation practices from home and school for learners. Color-coded index cards or individual slits of paper can be posted on the wall (example in Figure 5.8). They should contain the table number, group name if applicable, role/

Table 1 [Group Name]
1. Facilitator—[Name of learner]
2. Recorder—[Name of learner]
3. Reporter—[Name of learner]
4. Participant—[Name of learner]
5. Participant—[Name of learner]

Table 2 [Group Name]
1. Facilitator—[Name of learner]
2. Recorder—[Name of learner]
3. Reporter—[Name of learner]
4. Participant—[Name of learner]
5. Participant—[Name of learner]

Table 3 [Group Name]
1. Facilitator—[Name of learner]
2. Recorder—[Name of learner]
3. Reporter—[Name of learner]
4. Participant—[Name of learner]
5. Participant—[Name of learner]

Figure 5.8 Example group roles.

responsibility of each learner, and the learner's name. One of the "partici-pants" can fill the vacant role of facilitator, recorder, or reporter in the event that a learner is absent on that day.

Using Technology. An alternate form of soliciting nonverbal responses from learners is through the use of technology. Some forms include Smart Boards, Promethean Boards, laptops, Chrome Pads, I-Pads, Internet, cellphones, video games, and calculators. Razfar et al. (2011) explored the strategy of calculator keystrokes. The purpose of calculator keystrokes is for learners to produce written explanations. For example, a teacher gave learners the following representation (Figure 5.9) and asked them to find the area of the "ice cream cone" (Razfar et al., 2011, p. 24). The use of calculators was common practice in this classroom.

Learners used the calculator to help in problem solving. They then pro-ceeded to write out their problem solving process. The following is an ex-ample of the use of these calculator keystrokes (Figure 5.10, Razfar, et al., 2011, p. 211). Even if learners cannot find the word(s) to describe their thinking, they know the keystroke to demonstrate the process. This strategy can help learners form more complete thoughts without being limited by words. In the example in Figure 5.10, the learner drew a sketch of 3/4 of a circle. To accompany the drawing, she also included boxes with numbers, symbols, and words. These boxes represent the keystrokes. The learner then wrote out her mathematical problem solving process. This learner is familiar with terms such as "multiply" and "divide." She used keystrokes for numbers, for words such as sum, and for symbols such as p. An extension activity is for learners to switch their problem solving strategies and to ex-plain another learner's approach in writing (see Razfar et al., 2011).

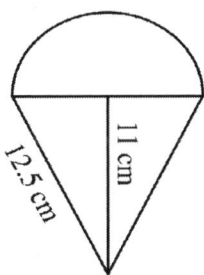

Figure 5.9 Ice cream cone problem.

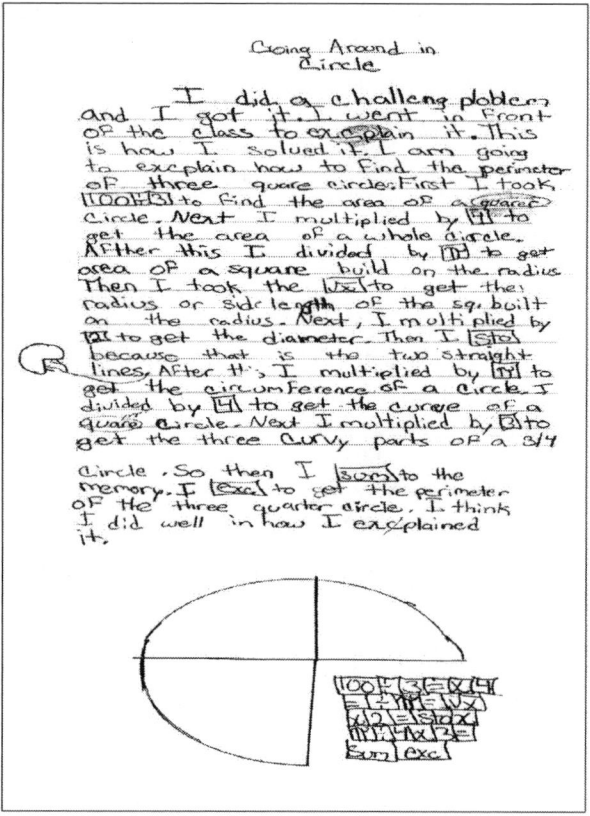

Figure 5.10 Example key strokes for mathematical explanation.

SUMMARY

This chapter focuses on teaching mathematics to ELLs. In this chapter we discussed some of the key challenges in teaching mathematics to ELLs. Teachers, such as Ms. Anita, want to know "how" to support ELLs. We advocate for a core value of creating linguistically and culturally responsive learning environments. This ideal requires grappling with conceptions of mathematics teaching and learning. Furthermore, developing these environments requires a commitment to learners even given the demands on teachers to align curriculum and instruction to state content and language standards. Some teaching strategies include (a) the use of vocabulary banks as an embedded and contextualized form for learners to access discipline specific terminology; (b) foregrounding differentiated instruction to tap into various modes of learning, sensory experiences, and levels of language and content proficiency; (c) modifying spoken and written speech; and (d) eliciting nonverbal responses from learners.

REFERENCES

Bresser, R., Melanese, K., & Sphar, C. (2009). *Supporting English language learners in math class, grades K–2.* Sausalito, CA: Math Solutions Publications.

Gutstein, E. (2006). *Reading and writing the world with mathematics: Toward a pedagogy for social justice.* New York, NY: Taylor & Francis Group.

Miller, M. D., Linn, R. L., & Gronlund, N. E. (2012). *Measurement and assessment in teaching* (11th ed.). Upper Saddle River, NJ: Pearson Education.

Moschkovich, J. N. (2002). A situated and sociocultural perspective on bilingual mathematics learners. *Mathematics Thinking and Learning, 4*(2/3), 189–212.

Moschkovich, J. (2013). Equitable practices in mathematics classrooms: Research-based recommendations. *Teaching for Excellence and Equity in Mathematics, 5*(1), 26–33.

Razfar, A. (2012). Discoursing mathematically: Using discourse analysis to develop a sociocritical perspective of mathematics education. *The Mathematics Educator, 22*(1), 39–62.

Razfar, A., Khisty, L. L., & Chval, K. (2011). Re-mediating second language acquisition: A sociocultural perspective for language development. *Mind, Culture, and Activity, 18*(3), 195–215.

Razfar, A., & Rumenapp, J. (2013). *Applying linguistics in the classroom: A sociocultural approach.* New York, NY: Routledge.

Reyhner, J., & Davison, D. M. (1993). *Improving mathematics and science instruction for LEP middle and high school students through language activities.* Proceedings of the third national research symposium on LEP student issues: Focus on middle and high school issues (Vol. II). Washington, DC: U.S. Department of Education, Office of Bilingual Education and Minority Language Affairs.

Setati, M. (2005). Learning and teaching mathematics in a primary multilingual classroom. *Journal for Research in Mathematics Education, 36*(5), 447–466.

Tate, W. F. (1994). Race, retrenchment, and the reform of school mathematics. *Phi Delta Kappan, 75*(6), 477–484.

Vomvoridi-Ivanovic, E., & Razfar, A. (2013). In the shoes of English language learners: Using baseball to help pre-service teachers understand some complexities of language in mathematics instruction. *Teaching for Excellence and Equity in Mathematics, 5*(1), 8–15.

Willis, J. (2006). *Research-based strategies to ignite student learning: Insights from a neurologist and classroom teacher.* Alexandria, VA: Association for Supervision and Curriculum Development (ASCD).

CHAPTER 6

TEACHING SOCIAL STUDIES TO ELLs

Jennifer Kohnke
Aurora University

CASE SCENARIO

My first encounter with teaching social studies to English language learners (ELLs) began when I taught a combination reading and social studies methods course for education majors at the university. The course was held at an elementary school, which made it convenient to do our practicums in the fourth and fifth grade classrooms. The demographic of the school was 97% Latino. At the beginning of the semester the teacher candidates went into sheltered and mainstream classrooms with high populations of ELLs to do observations. During one of our first visits we observed a 5th grade social studies lesson. The lesson consisted of the classroom teacher who played a CD of the chapter while the students followed along in their own copy of the textbook. When the text had questions the teacher would pause the CD and ask for volunteers to answer. If no one volunteered she would give the class the answer. During the lesson I witnessed some students following along, others looking around the room, some staring at the ceiling, and others pondering what type of mischief they could get into at their seats. When the teacher finally stopped the CD, she asked some follow-up questions. The answers she received were very vague and she ended up having to summarize

Teaching ELLs Across Content Areas, pages 131–155
Copyright © 2016 by Information Age Publishing
131

132 • J. KOHNKE

the information for the students. Afterwards the classroom teacher expressed her grief about the participation of students and their lack of recall of the content knowledge. Unfortunately, this classroom experience is seen in many social studies classrooms and can pose a struggle for many ELLs.

ISSUES FOR TEACHING ELLs IN SOCIAL STUDIES

Teaching social studies to ELLs is inspiring but it can also bring about issues that teachers of native students might not have to face. The inspiration comes from teaching someone from another country about the culture, traditions, geography, and history of America while also exploring global perspectives. One of the issues teachers will encounter is finding resources and strategies to deliver the curriculum in a way to best support ELLs. Unfortunately, social studies has traditionally been taught using a textbook which poses a few problems. First of all, textbooks are often written at a reading level that would far exceed the English language proficiency of many ELLs. Secondly, the lack of an inquiry-based approach to teaching would hinder the learning process for these students.

The issue then becomes where to find resources outside of the textbook that would help teach the major concepts in social studies units. Then it also becomes imperative to provide information in a variety of reading levels to reach all learners. With the increased responsibilities teachers have, finding the time to prepare such material can be a challenge.

Another major issue for teaching social studies to ELLs is the lack of background knowledge for some students concerning the content being taught. In America, beginning in the early grades and up through high school many social studies concepts build upon each other. When students lack that scaffolding they are devoid of the connections that make learning meaningful. Dewey (1916) felt strongly that when ideas and topics were separated from experience it was difficult for real thinking to occur. A teacher needs to be sensitive to the fact that some ELLs might not have the basic knowledge necessary for a new unit of study. Therefore, some pre-teaching is helpful before launching into the topic or theme being taught.

Along with the lack of background knowledge would be the issue that students will not always have the necessary base vocabulary needed in order to comprehend new concepts that are centralized around the main topics being studied. This would then require the classroom teacher to combine language lessons along with the content. For example, in an upper elementary unit on the Civil Rights, students would be expected to already understand vocabulary such as unfair, unequal, segregation, discrimination, and the meaning of rights of citizens. Without that basic knowledge, even providing students with the definition of the Jim Crow Laws would not do them any good because it would have no meaning to them.

The implementation of the Common Core State Standards (CCSS) is another issue that impacts the teaching of social studies to ELLs. Since a large portion of the school day is devoted to language arts, often times these standards need to be covered during content classes such as social studies. One reason why social studies is a good fit for covering the standards is the recommended focus on informational text. This can be accomplished during social studies through the use of historical fiction texts and the use of primary source documents. Therefore, teachers need to be explicit when planning how to meet both the content and language objectives for students.

Challenges for ELLs in Classrooms

Parallel to the issues that a teacher faces when teaching ELLs are the challenges ELLs encounter when they are in a social studies classroom. The subject of social studies can put ELLs at a disadvantage because the content assumes that students have proficiency in English language skills. Such skills are necessary for comprehending the material and for acculturation and socialization in the dominant culture (Haynes, 2005). A lack of literacy skills will make learning abstract concepts difficult. Social studies derives its content from a variety of academic disciplines, such as the natural sciences and the humanities. Each area has specialized terminology and concepts that students must learn, and early socialization into American civic life will give American-born children an advantage over ELLs (Szpara & Ahmad, 2007). Many parents of ELLs are not accustomed to the inner-workings of American society and will not be able to aide their children in the understanding of certain social studies topics at home. The lack of the home–school support can hinder homework assignments and put an extra burden on the student to independently complete all of the schoolwork.

Many ELLs will come to school knowing conversational English, but will struggle with academic language. This can pose a challenge if the classroom teacher assumes that by hearing the student converse with others that they are capable of comprehending grade-level material. It is imperative that the classroom teacher understands the difference between basic interpersonal communication skills (BICS) and cognitive academic language proficiency (CALP). If the language being spoken is not in a context-embedded situation, ELLs will have difficulty using higher-order thinking skills to deconstruct the information and process any learning. This can prove to be even more debilitating when students have to present their understanding through discussions, debates, and oral reports (Weisman & Hansen, 2007).

These linguistic demands can be a roadblock to participation and understanding. If the classroom teacher has not differentiated the curriculum to include various forms and levels of assessment it can put ELLs in a situation to be unsuccessful.

Oftentimes social studies textbooks have a decontextualized discourse style that contains complex syntax, abstract concepts, and technical vocabulary specific to the subject matter. For example, Brown (2007) points out that, "In history texts, sentences are often written in the passive voice when describing events or explaining cause and effect. This can be troubling for ELLs because the passive voice is not used in daily conversation" (pp. 186–187). The vocabulary in the textbooks often highlights complex ideas. Without concrete examples and the necessary background knowledge it becomes difficult for ELLs to navigate the text. When social studies is taught through the textbook without extra support it automatically puts ELLs in a negative learning environment.

There are a plethora of challenges ELLs face when reading textbooks besides the written discourse. First of all, students will not have the benefits of facial features, intonation, gestures, or feedback when reading. These types of cues would help clarify content and questions about the material that students might have. Secondly, many texts contain few graphic cues, less predictable sequences, and an assumption of necessary background knowledge (Brown, 2007). Such elements make it difficult for ELLs to follow along in the text and connect any new learning to prior experiences. Another problem that occurs is that the worldview presented in the text can differ significantly from the ELLs native countries' perspectives (Szpara & Ahmad, 2007). This can cause confusion and resistance in learning. Coinciding with that is the possibility that some ELLs may not have received formal schooling in their native country so will be lacking any type of connection to concepts and the process of critical thinking. Even ELLs who have extensive knowledge of their culture might have it ignored as a resource because teachers are unfamiliar with it and unsure of how to bring it into the curriculum (Weisman & Hansen, 2007). These problems make it increasingly challenging for ELLs to be successful in the social studies classroom.

A lack of connection between the home culture of ELLs and the social studies curriculum can contribute to academic failure and psychological problems including low self-esteem and/or identity confusion (Salazar & Fránquiz, 2008). Students need to have their own identity valued in the classroom without feeling like the curriculum is focused on changing or demeaning their culture. The environment of the social studies classroom can be a challenge if it is not culturally relevant and anti-oppressive by bridging the gap between ELLs' home culture and the curriculum in order to facilitate understandings of how students see themselves in the world

(Almarza, 2001; Salinas, 2006). According to Choi (2013), social studies has been criticized for its marginalization of stories of immigrants and Cho and Reich (2008) also explain that inadequate images and prejudices against immigrant groups and a tokenistic approach to diversity and social justice (Banks, 2007; Landson-Billings, 2003). The combination of those issues can make ELLs feel like outsiders in the social studies classroom.

Another challenge ELLs can face in the social studies classroom is the cultural differences that can affect participation and the fostering of critical and independent thinking. Depending upon the cultures of their native countries, some ELLs may not question authority, "speak in the classroom without fear of reprisal, or assert their point of view on controversial issues" (Szpara & Ahmad, 2007, p. 190). This can make it difficult when studying areas of social justice or when students are asked to look at historical events from different points of view.

Meeting Challenges and Planning to Teach

Luckily for ELLs, there are a myriad of ways teachers can meet the challenges non-native speaking students might have in the social studies classroom. It's important for teachers to differentiate their teaching to meet the needs of all students regardless of their level of English language proficiency. However, the specific issues and challenges that were presented earlier are areas of concern for ELLs that need to be taken into consideration when planning curriculum and assessment for social studies lessons.

First of all, teachers need to address the roadblocks that using traditional social studies textbooks can have on the ability of ELLs to understand the content. As stated before, they can have many struggles with learning abstract concepts, lacking sufficient background knowledge and understanding some specialized terminology. Utilizing the textbook as a guide to create a scope and sequence for the school year can be helpful. However, teachers need to look outside of the textbook for material to teach each unit. Although gathering resources can be tedious, the benefits will outweigh the negatives and will provide a solid foundation for future lessons.

To begin meeting this challenge and planning to adequately teach ELLs, teachers need to utilize the backwards planning and adopt culturally relevant pedagogy (CRP). Research suggests that a social-studies curriculum should begin with students' relevant life experiences and current progress to antecedent knowledge and experiences that explain why things are the way they are (Misco & Castaneda, 2009). This is especially important for ELLs who oftentimes have no prior knowledge relating to the learning content about American history and culture. It's also imperative to find connections that students can make to their current knowledge in order for the concepts they're learning to make sense and have importance. Reverse chronology helps focus curricula into areas that have current relevance to students.

In *Pedagogy of the Oppressed* (1970) Paulo Freire promotes critical pedagogy. His writings enforce the need for a socially just curriculum for students. Looking at injustices and instances of inequality today and comparing them to inequities and social injustices of the past can help students bridge the gap between the ways historical events have influenced the present in either positive or negative ways. For example, when studying the Civil Rights Movement, students will learn about the landmark case of *Brown v. The Board of Education* (1954) and the desegregation of schools. However, they can study today how many of the major cities in the country have a high segregation rate and oftentimes schools named after Martin Luther King and Rosa Parks are some of the most segregated schools. In *Savage Inequalities* (1991), Jonathan Kozol brings to light instances of injustices among schools and districts. Critical pedagogy can pave the way for ELLs to start social studies units with important questions to guide their learning. Such questions can help make the information relevant and interesting to students.

In order to teach with critical pedagogy by utilizing backwards planning, the teacher must first get to know the students and understand their culture. Choi (2013) highlighted a successful teacher who focused on global multicultural citizenship and strove to understand the social cultural contexts of his students by capitalizing on their diversity and incorporating it into the curriculum. The promotion of critical perspectives to tolerate diversity helped students broaden their worldviews (Choi, 2013). Embracing the experiences of students in the classroom can lead to rich discussions and strengthen the classroom environment. When students know that they are valued it will help build mutual respect among everyone.

Having students do a beginning of the year culture bag activity can be an easy way for teachers to get to know everyone and for students to recognize similarities and differences among each other. To do this activity students decorate the outside of a bag with things people would readily notice, or assume, about them. Then, the inside of the bag should be filled with things that represent their "inner" culture. The items they place inside the bag are unique to themselves and can represent family, hobbies, collections, religion, and anything personally meaningful to them. This activity is a great way to start off a school year and to build relationships in the classroom. Creating an environment where ELLs feel safe participating and sharing their identity can make them feel more comfortable asking questions, along with answering questions about controversial social studies topics.

Milner (2014) points out how Moll and Gonzalez's (2004) research enforces the need to learn with and from the families of students, even so far as having the family share home practices with the teacher. In order to do this, the classroom teacher needs to be open to family involvement in the classroom and flexible enough to tweak the curriculum in order to capitalize on such lived experiences. "Through culturally relevant teaching, teachers help students develop the skills needed to question inequity and to fight against the many isms and phobias that they encounter" (Milner, 2014, p. 10). This helps bring a social justice connection to the classroom. By using the five Ws (who, what, where, when, and why), teachers can help ELLs form a deeper understanding of the complexities surrounding the various facets of social studies.

When students exhibit sociopolitical consciousness they can use skills they are learning in the classroom to try and understand their social position (Ladson-Billings, 2006). Being able to understand and critique the context in which they live can aide ELLs in their comprehension of broader social studies topics. Sociopolitical consciousness is about, "the micro-, meso-, and macro-level matters that have a bearing on teachers' and students' lived experiences and educational interactions" (Milner, 2014, p. 10). For instance, when studying the government, the curriculum can look at how particular issues can have implications at both the national and local level and therefore teachers can help make those connections with the students' consciousness.

When students can connect what they are learning to their own lives and the broader world it makes social studies more relevant to them. In Milner's (2014) study he followed a teacher who believed that when we teach students that they are a part of a broader school social context, "...students will be more willing to build pride in their school while simultaneously assembling and enhancing pride in themselves" (p. 15). That type of pride can lead to greater confidence in and outside of the classroom. In return, that confidence can help promote more academic risk-taking in the classroom. In social studies, teachers can focus on both home and school pride. By including the student's culture and family heritage in the curriculum and embracing the diversity of the classroom environment, many topics can be supported and looked at with a deeper lens. School pride can be developed by looking at how public education affords students the benefits of citizenship and how the state and federal government play a role in education.

All these prior ideas link back to the importance of joining background knowledge with the content being taught in the social studies classroom. Allowing students to develop connections to the material will help them process the information better. Beginning with concepts that are familiar to students will ease their comfort level. Then the teacher can gradually branch out into broader topics. For example, having students interview one of their family members can be an excellent way to bridge the connection between home and school and is a great way to begin studying immigration and migration. After interviewing the family member, students can draw their journey on a map and bring in any items that relate to that experience (Weisman & Hansen, 2007). Anstrom, DiCerbo, & National Clearinghouse for Bilingual Education (1999) cite that using an oral history approach that includes the background and experience of students can, "...form the raw historical data from which a social studies curriculum can be built" (Olemedo, 1993; p. 12). When a teacher develops curriculum in this manner it will help lay the foundation for authentic learning in the classroom.

Part of backwards planning also involves looking at the academic strategies students might need to learn in order to be successful. This explicit instruction is imperative for ELLs who are learning both the English language and social studies content at the same time. That is why it is important for teachers to create both content and language objectives for each lesson. The content objectives should focus on the social studies standards and the main ideas that encompass the core subject matter. The language objectives should focus on the reading, writing, listening, and speaking skills needed to complete the lesson. The sheltered instruction observation protocol (SIOP) method stresses the important of reviewing both the language and content objectives in the beginning and end of the class (Echevarria, Vogt, & Short, 2013). This helps students know what they are accountable for in the lesson.

Providing instructional supports to meet both types of objectives is a way to make the lesson accessible to all students (Reutebuch, 2010). When referring back to culturally relevant pedagogy it is important for teachers to begin their planning with a guiding question that will keep the experiences of students in mind while providing a focus for the lesson. It is also helpful to include vocabulary that will be introduced in order to highlight the academic language needed to understand the lesson (Figure 6.1). Creating

Guiding Question(s): Why were people passionate in standing up for civil rights? What are dreams that you have?		Lesson Topic: The Civil Rights Movement
Objectives		**Key Vocabulary**
Content – Students will: • Learn why Martin Luther King Jr. is an important historical figure relating to The Civil Right Movement. **Language** – Students will: • Use key vocabulary to read, write, listen and speak during the lesson. • Discuss how Martin Luther King Jr.'s dream is similar or different to their own dream.		• Dream • Rights • Segregation • Protest

Figure 6.1 Planning chart.

a chart like this for each lesson is a way for teachers to stay on track and to meet the needs of all students. It is also a good way to utilize backwards planning so that the lesson is structured around helping students make connections while supporting their academic language needs.

Once teachers have planned out the guiding question, objectives, and key vocabulary for the lesson, it's imperative that they search for ways to reduce the cognitive load for students. In order to do this there also needs to be a shift in presentation style and strategies used to deliver the information. In doing so, the teacher needs to be careful not to simplify and water down the content material and make it less rigorous therefore leaving out, "...the richness and nuances of a particular period or event; rather, the goal is to identify the key aspects of that period or event and describe the information in the simplest terms possible" (Szpara & Ahmad, 2007, p. 192). Therefore, the teacher needs to do a lot of pre-examination of the content and the variety of methods used to deliver it.

As stated earlier, textbooks in general are not user-friendly for ELLs. This is the first area of concern when looking at how to deliver the content to students. It is important that teachers take the information in the textbook and put it in a form that breaks down main points into manageable chunks for ELLs. Once the information is broken down there are a variety of ways to present it to the students. Depending on the amount and type of information, it can be displayed on a bulletin board, in a graphic organizer, as an outline, in a technology presentation, or any other way that would help ELLs comprehend what is in the textbook. Specific strategies that can be used with ELLs will be identified in the next section of this chapter.

Words and concepts that are able to be displayed through pictures should be highlighted in the lesson. "...Visual teaching aids ensure that learners attach meaning and mental images to words and concepts through the use of concrete instructional materials" (Curtain, as cited in Allison & Rehm, 2007; p. 18). Therefore, teachers need to deliberately plan how to incorporate visual learning into the social studies lesson in a way that enhances the learning for ELLs. All of this becomes important when deciding what academic language students need for a particular lesson. The standards set forth for students have created high expectations regarding student's ability to read and comprehend complex texts, which makes understanding unfamiliar words and expressions crucial for ELLs (Maxwell, 2012). Since ELLs might not have been exposed to academic language, or the vocabulary necessary to understand new concepts, teachers must pre-assess students and decide what needs to be taught prior to the lesson.

Social studies teachers should imbed literacy strategies in such a way that both content and literacy instruction are taught simultaneously (Perin et al., 2009). When planning to meet the challenge ELLs face with linguistic demands, literacy instruction needs to be implemented as part of the entire lesson. Reutebuch (2010) describes a seven step process for teaching new vocabulary words, which consists of displaying the word; pronouncing the word; providing a definition of the word; discussing how the visual is representative of the word; providing two sentences using the word, " ... one showing a historical context and the other in a context that is more relevant to students' experiences;" having students make connections; and lastly having students use the word (p. 3). That seven step process (Figure 6.2) uses visuals and repetition along with peer and teacher support, which are all strategies that help meet the challenges ELLs face in the social studies classroom.

In their study, Vaughn et al. (2010) found that instructional practices for ELLs consisting of vocabulary and concept instruction, media use for comprehension and concept knowledge, graphic organizers and peer support create solid lessons for ELLs and are generally just good teaching strategies for any student. Teachers are expected to differentiate every lesson regardless of whether students are native or non-native speakers. However, it is important to keep in mind that ELLs have specific challenges that must be taken into consideration when planning social studies lessons. The lesson plan featured here (Figure 6.3) addresses the needs of English language learners by being explicit in teaching core concepts and using teaching strategies that help break down information into manageable chunks for students to process better.

ELL students come with challenges that must be met by the classroom teacher. The culturally relevant pedagogy and backwards planning are two major avenues that lay the foundation for a successful lesson. Once

Unit: Civil Rights **Word: Protest**
1. Display the word (Protest) on the board. Also put the word on a social studies word wall or word bank. If students have their own social studies dictionary have them add the word (Protest) to it.
2. Say the word (Protest) and have students pronounce it in a choral-like fashion. Then have them say the word to a partner.
3. Tell students that to "protest" something means to make an expression of disagreement or a complaint about something.
4. Under the word (Protest) display a picture of a group of people holding up signs during a protest to end segregation.
5. Display and discuss the following two sentences with students: In the mid-1950's African Americans protested against the legal segregation of the buses in Birmingham, Alabama. Our football coach protested against the call the referees made on the last play of the game.
6. Ask students the following: What do you think causes people to protest something? How is a protest similar or different to a riot?
7. Ask students to turn and talk to a partner about how they think a protest can make a change in society.

Figure 6.2 Example of explicitly teaching vocabulary.

Guiding Question (s):	Lesson Topic:
What were some instances of dehumanization that occurred during the Holocaust? What are the perils of indifference?	The Holocaust

Objectives	Key Vocabulary
Content—Students will: • Learn ways Jewish people were dehumanized during the Holocaust. • Understand the consequences of being indifferent towards others. **Language**—Students will: • Discuss instances of dehumanization that occurred during the Holocaust. • Debate whether or not being indifferent in certain situations is acceptable.	• Dehumanize • Indifference

Lesson Introduction (Building Background):

Give students an outline of a suitcase. Tell them to write and/or draw the items they would take if they were forced to leave their homes with only a suitcase, just as the Jewish people were. When students are finished have them share their suitcases with a partner. Have them discuss how it would feel to have their suitcases taken away from them.

Main Lesson Activity:

1. Review the content and language objectives with the students.
2. Use a 7-step vocabulary process to teach the vocabulary words (dehumanize & indifference). After going through the 7-steps, ask students how these two words relate to the Holocaust.
3. Hand-out a venn diagram to students. Have them compare the life people lived before being forced out of their homes, and then their lives during their time in a concentration camp. Point out instances of dehumanization.
4. Have students list the incidents of dehumanization on a chain organizer.
5. Have students complete a role-play where one person is a bully, one person is getting bullied, and one person is an indifferent bystander. Afterwards, discuss the significance of the bystander. Then compare that to instances in the Holocaust where people were indifferent.
6. Have students complete a concept circle on "indifference" choosing words that describe the effects indifference can have on people.

Lesson Conclusion:

Have students write a diary entry as if they were a person living in a concentration camp. Tell them to write about instances of dehumanization they are experiencing and how it makes them feel.

Materials Needed:

• Worksheet of an outline of a suitcase
• Venn Diagram
• Concept Circle
• Chain Organizer
• Diary Entry Paper

Figure 6.3 Sample lesson plan on the Holocaust.

teachers adopt these modes of thinking then they can move on to outlining objectives, highlighting vocabulary, condensing textbook information, and using strategies to deliver content in the best possible way for ELLs. In reverse-chronological teaching, "teachers act as more-empowered curricular gatekeepers, exercising increased discretion to modify, discard, and include content" (Misco & Castaneda, 2009; p. 187). From there, teachers utilize best practices to create the lessons.

TEACHING STRATEGIES

In order to meet the challenges that have been mentioned in social studies class-rooms, teachers must use a variety of strategies specifically aimed at delivering content to ELLs in the best way possible. One thing to always keep in mind is the use of different learning styles. When giving directions it is helpful to explain the directions for auditory learners, to write the directions down for visual learn-ers, and then to model what students should do for the kinesthetic learners. It's also invaluable for ELLs because even if they are unsure of the language a teacher is using, by visually seeing the task it becomes easier to understand.

The strategies outlined in this section can be used with any social studies topic. Each one helps deliver content in a way that aides in the organization of information without being inundated with dense academic language that is found by simply reading textbooks. Depending on the objectives of each lesson, some strategies might lend themselves more useful than others. When specifi-cally teaching academic vocabulary, it is important that instruction is explicit, ongoing, contextually-bound, and student centered (Perez & Holmes, 2010). The strategies explained in this section can support this type of instruction and therefore they can be used merging content and language instruction.

Teachers can provide opportunities in the social studies classroom for stu-dents to learn about and use cognitive, metacognitive, and social/affective strategies. "Cognitive strategies help learners manipulate information, meta-cognitive strategies help students monitor their own learning, and social/affec-tive strategies help students affectively influence their learning processes..." (Chamot & O'Malley, as stated in Perez & Holmes, 2010). A curriculum that is designed with these strategies in mind will help ELLs become independent in acquiring and understanding the oftentimes complex social studies content.

Cognitive strategies consist of helping students make connections to what they are learning in order to make information accessible and to give it mean-ing. It also consists of strategies that help students summarize and highlight key information. Various types of outlines, graphic organizers, and charts, which break down information into meaningful chunks are useful metacognitive strategies. Graphic organizers can help students, especially ELLs, sort, show re-lationships, make meaning, and manage data quickly and easily before, during, and after reading and discussion (Gallavan & Kottler, 2007). Peer grouping and critical thinking activities are helpful social/affective strategies.

Before using any of the strategies in this section it is imperative that teach-ers do a pre-assessment of the students to see what they already know about the topic and also have a clear understanding of the levels of English language proficiency of the students. Then, carefully look at the content and decide the critical vocabulary that needs to be explicitly taught. Finally, a clear understand-ing of the content and language objectives is necessary as a building block for any lesson.

Creating T-Notes

T-notes can be used in a variety of ways in the social studies classroom. They are helpful for organizing material. One way they can be used is to segment main ideas from a chapter or worksheet, along with new vocabulary (Figure 6.4). Fagan (2003) had students write down main ideas from what they read and then discuss. She then modeled her own t-chart for students and had them reread to reinforce comprehension. She also had her students list unfamiliar words. After modeling this for students, eventually she moved to using sticky notes to place in the chart. The use of sticky notes allows for more flexibility. Students can write the main ideas and vocabulary words as they read and then stick them on the pages. Then when they are done they can take them all out and organize them onto the t-note chart. They could also be used on one large chart in the front of the classroom therefore making the activity more interactive.

T-notes can also be used to compare and contrast ideas, events, or people in social studies. It is a good way for students to make connections and pull out main ideas. For example, students can compare two historical figures such as George Washington and Thomas Jefferson (Figure 6.5). Depending on the level of English language proficiency, students can also include drawings in the charts. This is also an activity that can be supported by cooperative grouping.

Applying Compare and Contrast

Social studies texts are informational texts and that type of rhetorical structure has challenges for ELLs. Implementing a compare and contrast strategy to help students navigate the text can be beneficial in that it helps link new

Main Idea	New Vocabulary
• People vote to choose leaders • People vote on issues • People have to register to vote	• Candidate • Election • Ballot

Figure 6.4 T-note: Example #1.

George Washington	Thomas Jefferson
• 1st President • In office for 2 terms • Supported the plan for a National Bank	• 3rd President • In office for 2 terms • Advocated states' rights over national institutions

Figure 6.5 T-note: Example #2.

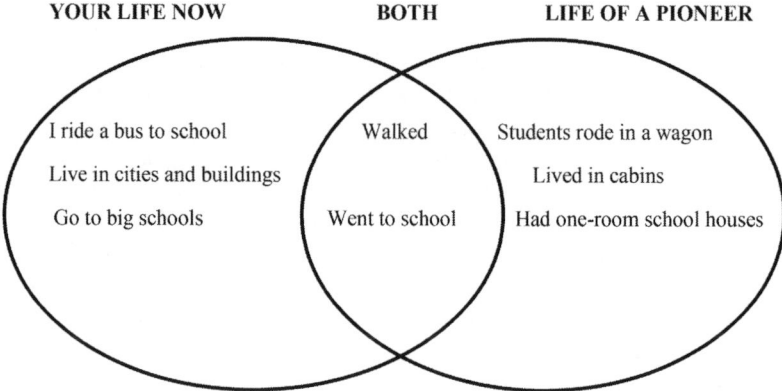

Figure 6.6 Compare–Contrast Venn Diagram.

content with student's background knowledge (Figure 6.6). Dreher and Gray (2009) outline the following steps for a compare–contrast structure:

1. The teacher conducts a brief think-aloud activity, modeling the thinking that he or she does when reading a compare–contrast text. The teacher also records the similarities and differences between things being compared and contrasted using a graphic organizer such as a Venn diagram. The students' role in this first think-aloud activity is to watch and listen to the model that the teacher provides. The teacher also points out features of the compare–contrast text structure itself, and creates a list of words or phrases in the text that students can look for to help them understand that they are being asked to compare and contrast two or more different things or ideas.
2. The teacher engages the student in a second think-aloud activity. At this stage, the teacher involves students by asking direct questions about the things or ideas that are being compared and contrasted in the text, and then supports students as they complete a graphic organizer either in small groups or as a class.
3. The teacher provides students with the opportunity to practice reading compare–contrast texts, either in small groups or individually. Students are instructed to use the same strategies modeled by the teacher during the think-aloud activities, and are given a graphic organizer to help them record and think about the similarities and differences between the things or ideas that are being compared and contrasted in the text (p. 135).

Using Chains and Organizers

Chains and concept circles are great ways for ELL students to see how specific ideas or events connect and relate to one another. "...Thoughtful reorganization and presentation of facts can lead to significant understanding" (Peregoy & Boyle, as stated in Jenks 2002, p. 6). Chains are useful for showing the order of events that are linked together (Figure 6.7). Once students see how the progression of events link together they can make connections and have a visual to help them better understand the way one thing leads to another. A chain organizer helps students break down information as they arrange important developments and events in history into chronological order.

Chaining is also a way for students to understand cause and effect concerning social studies issues. This type of chain would be a vertical parallel chain (Figure 6.8). Part to whole and whole to part relationships can be shown with a linked chain organizer showing how events, ideas, or topics connect to one another (Figure 6.9). Another way to show students how ideas relate to one

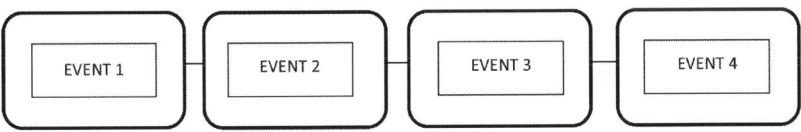

Figure 6.7 Chain example #1.

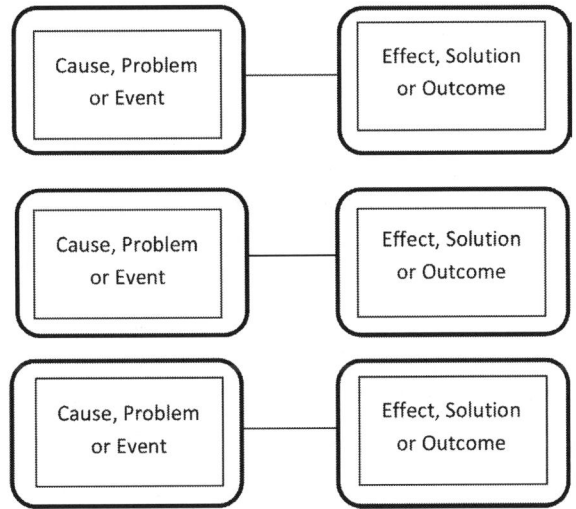

Figure 6.8 Chain example #2.

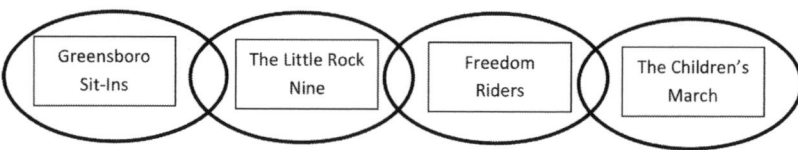

Figure 6.9 Chain example #3 on important events of the Civil Rights Movement.

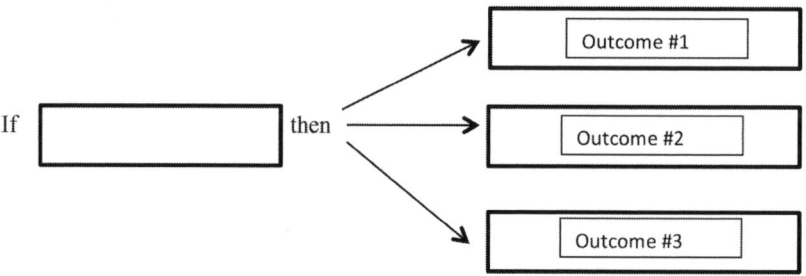

Figure 6.10 If/then organizer.

another is to create an if/then organizer (Figure 6.10). Teachers could fill these out with students while reading or delivering the lesson.

Other Tips and Strategies

Using Concept Circles and Content Maps

Concept circles are useful to highlight important facts, events, or people surrounding a social studies topic and specific vocabulary. They can be used as word clusters to help students understand social studies vocabulary that is pertinent to a lesson or unit. In each section of the circle students can write a word that goes along with the chosen social studies topic (Figure 6.11). This activity can connect, "...reading to writing through description, explanation, comparison, or summarization of important information covered in the lesson" (Reutebuch, 2010, p. 4). Teachers could also use this activity by writing words in the circle that go together, but then including one word that does not and see if the students can figure out which word doesn't belong and then justify their reasoning.

Content maps show how parts of the text are related and break down information into main ideas (Figure 6.12). Brown (2007) stresses the effectiveness of using content maps to show the hierarchical relationship of facts that teachers can use to introduce key points in a lesson or present to students as an outline of the text. These graphic organizers help students understand how an idea is associated with an overarching concept or

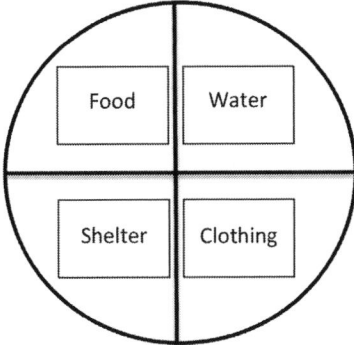

Figure 6.11 Concept circle on needs and wants.

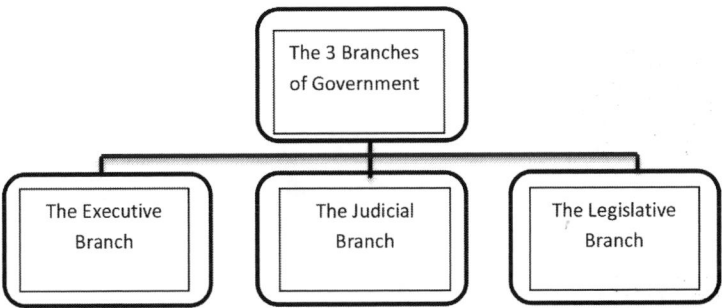

Figure 6.12 Content map of the branches of government.

purpose" (Gallavan & Kottler, 2007; p. 118). Content maps can also be used as a note-taking resource (Figure 6.13).

Using Analogies and Other Vocabulary Techniques

Analogies are a good way to have students use critical thinking to compare the relationships of words. Such relationships can help students make connections between words and concepts in order to better understand them. Analogies can also compare concepts to students' personal lives. For ELLs this is beneficial because they might not have the background knowledge to understand the words separate from experience. Depending on a student's level of English language proficiency, analogies can also be used with pictures. Some common types of analogy relationships include looking at the part to whole, cause and effect, and person to situation. An example would be showing a student that race is to runner, as election is to candidate.

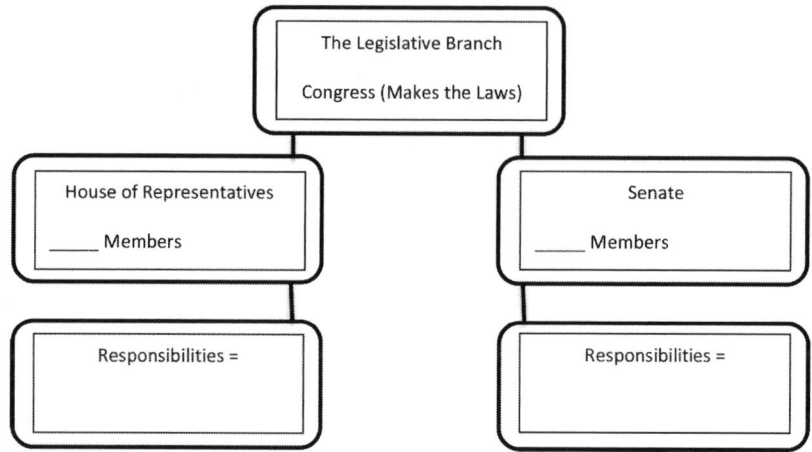

Figure 6.13 Content map for note taking.

Mnemonic instruction is another vocabulary strategy in which students create words, sentences, or pictures to remember the meaning of words. Ekiaka Nzai and Reyna (2014) suggest finding a key word that can be represented in a drawing that sounds similar to the word being taught. They used the example of the word carline ("witch") in which students visualized a car with a witch driving it. Hall, Kent, McCulley, Davis, and Wanzek (2013) describe three types of mnemonics: acoustic elaborations, symbolic elaborations, and mimetic elaborations. Acoustic elaborations use keywords and illustrations that focus on the sound of the information students need to remember. For example, President Lincoln could be represented as a Lincoln town car. Symbolic elaborations use symbols to represent information. For example, President Lincoln could be represented as a tall black top hat like the ones he wore. Mimetic elaborations are exact drawings of the information students need to remember. Therefore, with mimetic elaborations if students wanted to remember that President Lincoln was against slavery they could draw a picture of him next to a sign that said, "Abolish Slavery."

Weisman and Hansen (2007) offer the idea of using word walls in the classroom where the teacher can explain the meaning of the word, and then provide examples and pictures. Students then collect the words and write down the definition and draw a picture in their own student dictionary. Students can also complete a word map (Figure 6.14) with the necessary information. For review, groups of students write down definitions to be used in a Jeopardy game. The repetitive use of the social studies words give students the opportunity to engage in a lot of practice with the language.

Using the word cluster charts is a way to have students use adjectives or other words to describe a social studies vocabulary word. The main word is

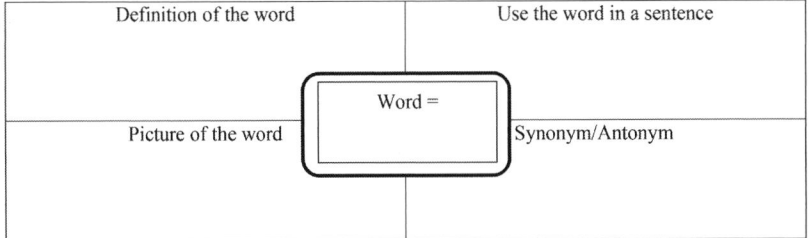

Figure 6.14 Word map.

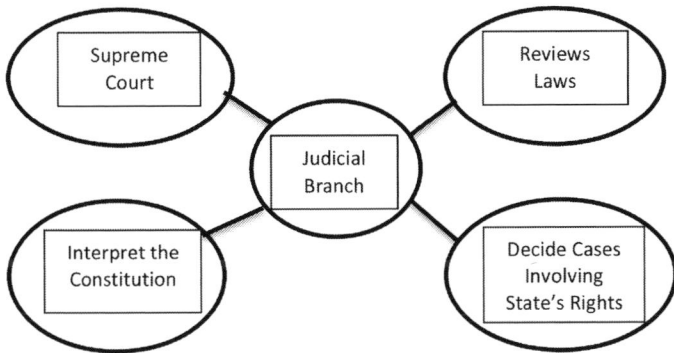

Figure 6.15 Word cluster chart on government.

put into the middle circle and then words that describe it are connected to it (Figure 6.15). Jenks (2002) suggests leaving the middle word blank and allowing the students to guess the word after being given the examples.

Using Timelines

Time and place are important concepts in social studies. "Time presents an overwhelming concept to young learners as historical events are perceived as long ago, occurring in isolation, and disconnected from today's world" (Gallavan & Kottler, 2010, p. 95). As stated earlier, making connections is an important strategy for English language learners. Timelines offer students a visual measurement of events and relationships to help students make those important connections (Figure 6.16). Timelines can also include pictures to go along with events in order to make the information even more accessible for students.

Using Anticipation Guides

Anticipation guides are used with a unit of study or when introducing a new event, person, or concept in a lesson. They are especially effective

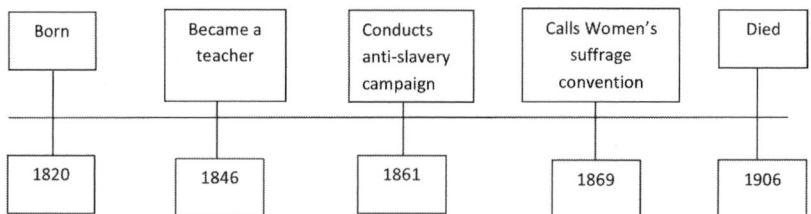

Figure 6.16 Susan B. Anthony simplified timeline.

Anticipation Guide for the Civil Rights Movement			

Directions: Read the statements below and respond once before reading, once during reading, and once after reading. For each response write whether you **agree** or **disagree**.

Response Before Reading	Statement	Response During Reading	Response After Reading
	Martin Luther King Jr. was an important person during this time in history.		
	Black people always had the same rights as white people.		
	Separate but equal in schools was fair.		
	By 1950 most schools were integrated.		
	Nonviolent protests were common during the Civil Rights Movement.		
	The "Freedom Riders" were a group of people who rode the buses for free in the South.		

Figure 6.17 Anticipation guide for the Civil Rights Movement.

when using with textbooks. "This strategy highlights the importance of anticipating meanings of a text before reading, thinking, and rethinking these meanings during reading, and reflecting and taking a position on confirmed meanings after reading" (Bintz, 2011, p. 50). To begin with, students are provided with statements that are either correct or incorrect. Then students read them and can either agree or disagree, mark yes or no, or true or false, depending on how the guide is set up (Figure 6.17). This part is done before reading a section of the text. Then while reading they can keep their original answer or change their minds. After reading they mark the guide again and use evidence from the text to support their position.

Utilizing Visual Resources

As stated earlier, visuals are an important resource for ELLs. When words elude them, visuals can help make concrete connections. Szpara and

Ahmad (2007) give the example of a teacher discussing the Renaissance by downloading and printing copies of Renaissance paintings. Students then analyzed the paintings and used this as the basis for discussion. Another example was using pictures and also an ink pad and stamps to explain how a printing press worked. Combining pictures with realia makes the concepts more realistic to students. According to Szpara and Ahmad (2007) "Social studies teachers can also use role playing and dramatizations to make abstract concepts and important historical figures come alive" (Szpara and Ahmad, 2007, p. 194).

Maps, video clips, cultural artifacts and graphs make social studies more comprehensible (Choi, 2013). Videos are a great resource because they can help provide background knowledge for certain topics that ELLs might be unfamiliar with because of their experiences. Reutebuch (2010) suggests that teachers first "introduce the video clip either before students have read a textbook passage or before they have begun the supplemental reading that supports (i.e., explains, describes, reiterates) the big idea of the lesson" (p. 3). Then they should preview the clip, play the clip while students take notes, and finally conduct a brief discussion about the video. The following is an example of how the steps would look when introducing the video, The Children's March to go along with a unit on The Civil Rights Movement:

1. The teacher may say, "Now you are going to watch a video about The Children's March that happened in Birmingham, Alabama in 1963. Later you will read about it. Instead of staying home and doing nothing, it was kids who decided to do something to try to end the struggle of segregation."

2. Then the teacher would review the video and set the purpose for viewing. For example, the teacher may say, "In this video you will see hundreds of children faced with police dogs, water hoses, angry mobs, and arrests. Watch and listen in order to answer the question, "What inspired these children to risk harm in order to stand up for this cause?"

3. Next, the teacher will show the video while students take notes and think about the question posed to them. Afterwards, students can discuss their thoughts with their peers.

4. Finally, the teacher would hold a discussion about the video. After circling the room the teacher can highlight some of the student's responses and have them justify their thought process. She could also use a graphic organizer to write down main ideas that were brought up in the video.

PowerPoints, videos, websites, blogs, and web animation can be used as teaching strategies as well as assessment pieces. "These formats not only allow teachers to see what their ELLs know in ways that go beyond traditional assessments, they also allow ELLs to develop the necessary and current technological skills needed for success in their new society" (DelliCarpini, 2009, p. 119). Providing ELLs with a variety of avenues to receive information and to showcase their learning can help bridge the gap between language and academic goals.

Applying Directed Reading-Thinking Activities (DR-TA)

Successful support for ELLs is necessary to help them navigate social studies textbooks and content that can be challenging even for a native English speaker. The DR-TA strategy is a comprehension strategy that works well with social studies content. According to El-Koumy (2006) the DR-TA is defined operationally as a reading strategy, which consists of the following six steps:

1. The teacher writes the title of the reading passage on the board and asks students to read it.

2. The teacher asks students to make predictions about the title using these questions:
   a. What do you think a passage with a title like this might be about?
   b. Why do you think so?

3. The teacher lists predictions on the board and initiates a discussion with the students by asking them to respond to the following questions:
   a. Which of these predictions do you think would be the likely one?
   b. Why do you think this prediction is a good one?

4. The teacher invites students to work in small groups to complete the discussion following the same format.

5. The teacher asks students to read the passage silently and to confirm or reject their own predictions. Then he asks them the following questions:
   a. Were you correct?
   b. What do you think now?
   c. Why do you think so?

6. The teacher asks students to reflect on their predictions through responding to the following questions:
   a. What prediction did you make?
   b. What made you think of this prediction?
   c. What in the passage supports this prediction?
   d. Do you still agree with this prediction? Why? (pp. 3–4)

This type of strategy promotes critical thinking and allows ELLs to have the support of their peers when discussing their ideas. It "...requires students to engage in prediction, verification, interpretation, and judgment" (Vaca and Vaca, as stated in DelliCarpini, 2011, p. 110). It is important for ELLs to continually be challenged in class while being provided the scaffolding needed to support their learning.

SUMMARY

This chapter focuses on teaching social studies to ELLs. The chapter provides information and strategies for teachers. Teachers who service ELLs in the social studies classrooms have a wealth of cultural knowledge at their fingertips that can enhance any social studies curriculum. By utilizing culturally responsive pedagogy and backwards planning, teachers can help students connect their experiences to abstract social studies concepts. If teachers use the repertoire of teaching strategies available they can help ELLs overcome many of the challenges they face in the classroom. Graphic organizers and other visual resources help make content accessible for ELLs. The use of realia and hands-on learning experiences help develop a context for learning. It is important that social studies teachers also incorporate both language and content objectives when planning lessons. Literacy instruction and social studies content needs to be intertwined in order for ELLs to successfully navigate the information.

REFERENCES

Allison, B. N., & Rehm, M. L. (2007). Effective teaching strategies for middle school learners in multicultural, multilingual classrooms. *Middle School Journal, 39*(2), 12–18.

Almarza, D. J. (2001). Contexts shaping minority language students' perceptions of American history. *Journal of Social Studies Research, 25,* 4–22.

Anstrom, K., DiCerbo, P., & National Clearinghouse for Bilingual Education, W. D. (1999). Preparing secondary education teachers to work with English Language Learners: Social studies. *NCBE Resource Collection Series,* No. 13.

Banks, J. A. (2007). *Educating citizens in a multicultural society* (2nd ed.). New York, NY: Teachers College Press.

Bintz, W. (2011). Teaching vocabulary across the curriculum. *Middle School Journal, 42*(4), 44–53.

Brown, C. L. (2007). Strategies for making social studies texts more comprehensible for English-Language Learners. *Social Studies, 98*(5), 185–188.

Cho, S., & Reich, B. A. (2008). New immigrants, new challenges: High school social studies teachers and English language learner instruction. *The Social Studies, 99,* 235–242.

Choi, Y. (2013). Teaching social studies for newcomer English Language Learners: Toward culturally relevant pedagogy. *Multicultural Perspectives, 15*(1), 12–18.

DelliCarpini, M. (2009). Success with ELLs: Authentic assessment for ELLs in the ELA Classroom. *English Journal, 98*(5), 116–119.

DelliCarpini, M. (2011). Success with ELLs. *English Journal, 100*(5), 108.

Dewey, J. (1916). *Democracy and education: An introduction to the philosophy of education* New York, NY: Macmillan.

Dreher, M. J., & Gray, J. L. (2009). Compare, contrast, comprehend: Using compare-contrast text structures with ELLs in K–3 Classrooms. *Reading Teacher, 63*(2), 132–141.

Echevarria, J., Short, D., & Vogt, M. (2013). *Making content comprehensible for English learners: The SIOP model* (4th Ed.). Boston, MA: Pearson.

Ekiaka Nzai, V., & Reyna, C. (2014). Teaching English vocabulary to elementary Mexican American students in south Texas: Some responsive modern instructional strategies. *Journal of Latinos & Education, 13*(1), 44–45.

El-Koumy, A. S. A. K. (2006). *The effects of the directed reading-thinking activity on EFL students' referential and inferential comprehension.* Retrieved from http://www.eric. ed.gov/ERICWebPortal/contentdelivery/servlet/ERICServlet?accno=ED 502645

Fagan, B. (2003). Scaffolds to help ELL readers. *Voices From The Middle, 11*(1), 38–42.

Freire, P. (1970). *Pedagogy of the oppressed.* New York, NY: Continuum.

Gallavan, N., & Kottler, E. (2007). Eight types of graphic organizers for empowering social studies students and teachers. *The Social Studies, 98*(3), 117–123.

Gallavan, N., & Kottler, E. (2010). Visualizing the life and legacy of Henry VIII: Guiding students with eight types of graphic organizers. *The Social Studies, 101*, 93–102.

Hall, C., Kent, S. C., McCulley, L., Davis, A., & Wanzek, J. (2013). A new look at mnemonics and graphic organizers in the secondary social studies classroom. *Teaching Exceptional Children, 46*(1), 47–55.

Haynes, J. (2003, March). *Challenges for ELLs in content area learning.* Paper presented at the 2003 TESOL Annual Convention, Baltimore, MD.

Jenks, C. J. (2002). Teaching reading strategies to English Language Learners. *ERIC, EBSCO host* (accessed August 21, 2015).

Kozol, J. (1991). *Savage inequalities: Children in America's schools.* New York, NY: Crown.

Ladson-Billings, G. (2003). *Critical race theory perspectives on social studies: The profession, policies and curriculum.* Greenwich, CT: Information Age.

Ladson-Billings, G. (2006). From the achievement gap to the education debt: Understanding achievement in U.S. Schools. *Educational Researcher, 35*(7), 3–12.

Maxwell, L. A. (2012). Building bridges for ELLs. *Education Week, 32*(12), 23.

Milner, H. I. (2014). Culturally relevant, purpose-driven learning & teaching in a middle school social studies classroom. *Multicultural Education, 21*(2), 9–17.

Misco, T., & Castaneda, M. E. (2009). "Now, what should I do for English Language Learners?" Reconceptualizing social studies curriculum design for ELLs. *Educational Horizons, 87*(3), 182–189.

Moll, L., & Gonzalez, N. (2004). Engaging life: A funds-of-knowledge approach to multicultural education. In J. Banks & C. Banks (Eds.), *Handbook of research on multicultural education, 2nd edition.* (pp. 699–715). San Francisco, CA: Jossey-Bass.

Olmedo, I. M. (1993, Summer). Junior historians: Doing oral history with ESL and bilingual students. *TESOL Journal, 2*(4), 7–10.

Perez, D., & Holmes, M. (2010). Ensuring academic literacy for ELL students. *American Secondary Education, 38*(2), 32–43.

Perin, D., Crocco, M., Marri, A., Riccio, J., Rivet, A., & Chase, B. (2009). Integrating literacy instruction in science and social studies classrooms: Directions for teacher education. *Academic Exchange Quarterly, 13,* 97–105.

Reutebuch, C. K. (2010). *Effective social studies instruction to promote knowledge acquisition and vocabulary learning of English language learners in the middle grades.* (CREATE Brief) Washington, DC: Center for Research on the Educational Achievement and Teaching of English Language Learners.

Salazar, M., & Fránquiz, M. E. (2008). The transformation of Ms. Corazon: Creating humanizing spaces for Mexican immigrant students in secondary ESL classrooms. *Multicultural Perspectives, 10*(4), 185–191. doi:10.1080/15332860802526073

Salinas, C. (2006). Educating late arrival high school immigrant students: A call for more democratic curriculum. *Multicultural Perspectives, 8,* 20–27.

Szpara, M. Y., & Ahmad, I. (2007). Supporting English-Language Learners in social studies class: Results from a study of high school teachers. *Social Studies, 98*(5), 189–195.

Vaughn, S., Martinez, L. R., Reutebuch, C. K., Carlson, C. D., Thompson, S. L., Franci, D. J., & Society for Research on Educational Effectiveness. (2009). Enhancing social studies vocabulary and comprehension for 7th grade English Language Learners: Findings from two experimental studies. *Society for Research on Educational Effectiveness, 2*(4), 297–324.

Weisman, E. M., & Hansen, L. E. (2007). Strategies for teaching social studies to elementary level ELLs. *Education Digest, 73*(4), 61.

Weisman, E. M., & Hansen, L. E. (2007). Strategies for teaching social studies to English-Language Learners at the elementary level. *Social Studies, 98*(5), 180–184.

CHAPTER 7

TEACHING TECHNOLOGY TO ELLs

Larisa Olesova
George Mason University

Luciana C. de Oliveira
University of Miami

CASE SCENARIO

Lilly is an ELL student. Lilly and her family moved to the United States recently because Lilly's dad got a new job offer from a well-known company on the East Coast. Lilly started attending a new school. She loves her new teachers, classes, and classmates. She loves math and science classes in her new school. In addition to her favorite subjects, Lilly has to take required English classes for all ELL students. She took English classes in her home country but English classes in a new school were different. They required using computers to complete homework. Lilly has a computer at home but she usually uses it for leisure and fun. To complete homework for English class, Lilly has to do online language exercises every day. Even though she likes learning a new language, completing language exercises every day becomes a boring and difficult task. For hours she stares at the silent computer screen trying to guess the right answer. Her heart beats faster each time she clicks on the possible correct answer. She intuitively closes her eyes and when she

Teaching ELLs Across Content Areas, pages 157–185
Copyright © 2016 by Information Age Publishing
All rights of reproduction in any form reserved.

opens them to see if she did well or not, her hope is usually ruined. As a result, Lilly's grades in English went down by the end of the first semester. She lost her motivation and confidence in learning a new language.

ISSUES FOR USING TECHNOLOGY TO TEACH ELLs

English Language Learners (ELLs) in the United States represent a highly diverse group with different levels of English proficiency. Teachers who work with ELLs in elementary, middle, and high school are most often part of a non-diverse homogeneous group possessing little experience with diverse learners (Sleeter, 2001). It is in this context that some teachers could find it challenging to teach the ELLs who appear suddenly and unexpectedly in their classrooms, if they have not yet had the proper preparation and resources (Green, Tran, & Young, 2005).

There is significant diversity among students who are classified as ELL in schools. They can be divided into two main categories: ELLs who are immigrants and ELLs who are international students (or children of international students). Some immigrant ELLs and international ELLs have strong academic preparation, are at grade level, and are literate in their home languages. Some immigrant ELLs have limited formal education—or often interrupted formal education—and may not be literate in their home languages. These students often have significant gaps in their knowledge of the content areas and struggle with the expectations of school. ELLs enter U.S. schools with different English language proficiency levels, experiences with schooling, and backgrounds in subject matter knowledge. ELLs also come from a variety of language backgrounds. It is not uncommon to have ELLs representing 50 or more language backgrounds in a single school in an urban school district, for instance. Teaching these diverse learners requires a great deal of planning by the teacher to prepare meaningful lessons that are culturally and socially relevant to students' backgrounds. In addition, to help ELLs be successful academically, teachers need to create a positive school environment, combined with a meaningful and challenging curriculum based on theoretical models that include engaging activities (Genesee, Lindholm-Leary, Saunders, & Christian, 2005).

Schools may not be prepared to assist ELLs in all levels of complexity that teaching this group of students entails. Many different programs provide different types of support for ELLs. For example, ELLs may be placed in bilingual, English as a second language, or sheltered instruction programs across many states. This issue relates to the inconsistency of experiences that these students have when in U.S. schools and present a real problem for them. For example, these program models differ in terms of their emphasis on bilingualism (two-way immersion, developmental bilingual), or proficiency in English (ESL, sheltered instruction).

These issues are very complex on many levels. ELLs' limited English proficiency (LEP) can result in lower academic achievement due to the language knowledge necessary to receive high test scores in all content areas (Genesee et al., 2005; Goldenberg 2008). Some ELLs attend school exclusively in English and have immigrant parents who speak English but may still need to develop language skills in some domains. Even though there is considerable pressure for ELLs to attain literacy in English at a rapid pace, ELLs need appropriate instruction as well as time to be able to develop academic English. Everyday English, or the English language skills used to communicate in everyday life, is developed more quickly, but academic English takes many years to develop (Cummins, 2008). This language proficiency issue relates to other ELLs who could have sufficient language skills to communicate adequately in everyday situations, but have not mastered the academic language to succeed in school (Curry, 2004). ELLs are typically assessed in English after just one year in the United States and are held to the same high academic standards as native English speakers. ELLs deserve a high quality education from teachers who know ELLs' individual strengths and needs. Just good teaching is a myth about teaching ELLs (de Jong & Harper, 2005). Good instructional practices for a diverse group of students are not enough for ELLs. Teachers who are able to provide ELLs with engaging and empowering learning experiences can influence the process of successful language development, which usually happens during the first years in school (Genesee et al., 2005).

Another issue relates to ELLs' learning of multiple skills in order to participate in content area classes, as the previous chapters described. ELLs face the dual challenge of developing English language proficiency and attaining the academic skills deemed essential for school. These include their abilities to read and write in different genres of schooling, understand complex vocabulary and grammatical structures, participate and interact with others in the classroom, comprehend classroom talk, among others (Faltis, Arias, & Ramirez-Marin, 2010; Schleppegrell, 2004; Téllez & Waxman, 2006).

In addition to these skills, ELLs are required to develop excellent technological skills so they can better participate in technological environments and are expected to learn new technology quickly. Developing these technological skills, though, involves a number of challenges as well. ELLs need to have the language skills to be able to understand how to use technology or may have different levels of experience using technology and limited access to technology at home. Their schools may or may not be up-to-date with the technological advances so this presents an additional challenge for ELLs. Teachers of ELLs also need to be knowledgeable about new technologies in order to incorporate them appropriately in the classroom.

Challenges for ELLs in Classrooms

Technological skills are crucial for ELLs to be successful in school. Luckily, ELLs of the 21st century have interest in technology like other individuals of their own age. In general, young people are routinely and constantly exposed to technology from a very early age (Espinosa, Laffey, Whittaker, & Sheng, 2006). Many young individuals have their own computers, mobile phones, and tablets, making them avid users of technology (Bavelier, Green, & Dye, 2010). Frequently, they even help the adults in their lives operate their newest technological device. Young individuals between the ages of 8 to 18 years old spend more than seven hours per day using media (Rideout, Foehr, & Roberts, 2010). This higher amount of time being exposed to media has also led young individuals who in the past used to be only users to become producers of media (Graber & Mendoza, 2012). Because of the high exposure to technology, the present generation of students has been named: (a) digital natives (Prensky, 2001); (b) the videogame generation (Simpson, 2005); and (c) the iGeneration (Rosen, 2010). Even though access to and use of technology has increased significantly, schools are slow to respond to the recent digital revolution (Graber & Mendoza, 2012).

ELLs' interest in technology can help teachers create more engaging activities by integrating different technologies in their classrooms. The 2010 National Education Technology Plan states that using technology for teaching and learning is essential to engage and empower learners. Many researchers argue that technology-based activities might provide teachers an interesting way for sharing information with their students; delivering content and activities that promote deep learning; and connecting institutions, educators, learners, and their families (Barron et al., 2011; Buckingham, 2007). Previous research has consistently shown that access to technological innovations has transformed the way young children play, learn, and interact with the world (Resnick, 1998; Bavelier et al., 2010). However, while we agree that technology might benefit ELLs by keeping them engaged in the learning task, there are some challenges when ELLs use technology for their everyday life and when they use technology for educational purposes. In everyday life, some ELLs might become too addicted to technology or technology can simply create numerous distractions (Bavelier et al., 2010). In education, ELLs' technological skills rely heavily on their language skills. This close relationship between technological and language skills in education can create challenges while teaching ELLs.

Meeting Challenges and Planning to Teach

Using technology is not magically going to solve all the challenges ELLs face. But technology can definitely help teachers and learners remove barriers in language learning by providing flexibility and access to high-quality instructional materials. That is why language educators and professionals are more and more interested in evidence-based practices to use technology effectively and efficiently to enhance the language learning process. Evidence-based practices can inform language teachers of what works and what does not work when choosing the right technology in teaching ELLs. Technology tools vary greatly and have tremendous impact on education itself but need to be used properly.

Language teachers do not need to be experts when they make decisions on appropriate technology for teaching ELLs. Instead, they need to keep an open mind and be creative about technology integration into the classroom to deal with the challenges for ELLs that arise when designing learning activities (Ertmer & Ottenbreit-Leftwich, 2010). Teachers who decide to use technology in their classrooms for teaching ELLs should be aware that technology is only a tool to aid instruction. The decision on technology selection should depend on the purpose of its use not on technology itself because technology can never be a substitute for the teacher or the use of effective pedagogies. Therefore, effective integration of technology for teaching ELLs does not mean simply to add available technology to the existing curriculum for the sole purpose of entertaining students or just for the sake of using technology (Buzzetto-More & Alade, 2006; Ertmer & Ottenbreit-Leftwich, 2010). The next section will discuss different teaching strategies for effective technology integration in the classroom when teaching ELLs.

TEACHING STRATEGIES

This section discusses teaching strategies for technology integration, suggesting consideration to use the Technological Pedagogical Content Knowledge (TPACK) model by Mishra and Koehler (2006) and Compton's (2009) framework for online language teaching skills as a guide for teachers who are interested in how to enhance teaching strategies when teaching ELLs in the content areas. Teaching strategies have been found to be one of the most important factors of technology integration in teaching ELLs (Kessler, 2006). While there are many studies on teachers' technology integration in the classroom, concerns about creativity in teaching strategies for successful technology integration in the classroom are still being addressed. However, a review of selected studies has found that there is a possible gap between how technologies are presented during teacher education or professional development programs and whether teachers are able to apply their technological skills in real classrooms when they finish such programs (Guichon & Hauck, 2011). A common approach in teacher education or professional development programs is their focus and orientation on digital literacy skills and hardware/software issues, which definitely prepare teachers to use technologies but do not prepare them to integrate technologies in instruction (Compton, 2009).

To understand how to support linguistically and culturally diverse populations of ELLs in the content areas using technology, teachers can refer to the Computer Assisted Language Learning (CALL) and the TESOL (Teachers of English to Speakers of Other Languages International Association) Technology Standards (2011). The CALL and TESOL Technology Standards (2011) provide teachers with clear guidance on how to successfully integrate technology to meet the linguistic and cultural needs of ELLs in the 21st Century (Gonzalez, 2012). The CALL and TESOL Technology Standards are comprised of four goals: (a) language teachers acquire and maintain foundational knowledge and skills in technology for professional purposes; (b) language teachers integrate pedagogical knowledge and skills with technology to enhance language teaching and learning; (c) language teachers apply technology in record-keeping, feedback, and assessment; and (d) language teachers use technology to improve communication, collaboration, and efficiency. The CALL and TESOL Technology Standards (2011) clearly state the need to acquire foundational and pedagogical knowledge and skills with technology to enhance creativity of teaching strategies in language learning. This standard directly relates to language teachers' ability to select appropriate technology, make decisions when they need to integrate selected technology, and determine what relevant teaching strategies can be applied to make integration successful (Zainal, 2012). To support teachers to acquire and apply necessary foundational and pedagogical knowledge and skills in use of appropriate technology, we recommend the TPACK model by Mishra and Koehler (2006) and Compton's (2009) framework for online language teaching skills that can guide teachers in their use of technology in a classroom both online and traditional learning environments.

The TPACK model was developed by Mishra and Koehler (2006) to assist educators that were interested in using instructional technology in their classrooms. The TPACK model is composed of the following sections:

1. Content Knowledge (CK). The teachers should know the subject matter content that will be taught, including: concepts, theories, ideas, frameworks, evidence, and established practices relevant to the content.

2. Pedagogical Knowledge (PK). The teachers should have adequate knowledge about instructional methods, teaching strategies and practices for specific content and a specific target audience.
3. Technological Knowledge (TK). The teacher needs to be familiar with technology for teaching and learning, recognizing what type of technology might work better when used in the classroom.

Compton's (2009) framework for online language teaching skills includes *technology skills* in online language teaching, *pedagogical skills* of online language teaching, and evaluation skills of online language teaching. Compton (2009) modified Hampel and Stickler's (2005) "skills pyramid" and proposed a framework for novice, proficient, and expert teachers.

Content knowledge and skills is one of the most important areas because it builds a foundation for successful technology integration. Mishra and Koehler's (2006) content knowledge aligns with Compton's (2009) pedagogical skills of online language teaching. Both require teachers to adapt language learning theories and course design frameworks for second language learning in the content areas (Basharina, 2007; Compton, 2009). This relates to teachers' ability to (a) identify instructional objectives; (b) establish goals by selecting the learning environment; (c) identify characteristics of the target audience, evaluate costs; (d) calculate implementation time; (e) determine available resources, get appropriate training and preparation; and (f) test the tools ahead of time, getting pertinent school personnel involved, and guess possible barriers to find solutions (Newby, Stepich, Lehman, Russell, & Ottenbreit-Leftwich, 2010). Teacher content knowledge and skills also has direct impact on teachers' ability to select suitable technologies to meet ELLs' needs in language and culture learning. This includes teachers' familiarity with different technologies and teachers' ability to select technologies based on matching learning objectives with desired learning outcomes (Compton, 2009). To select adequate technologies, teachers need to assess the potential and limits of technologies and make a decision based on a needs analysis. The needs analysis includes alignment of selected technologies with the learning environment (online, face-to-face, hybrid, and synchronous/asynchronous), ELLs' characteristics, and learning objectives. The needs analysis requires research and selection of available technologies based on their features in order to make the learning process effective (e.g., effective instruction delivery, the ELL's engagement and interaction, and the development of the ELL's digital literacy). In addition, the needs analysis focuses on the impact of the selected technologies on interactivity, feedback, and assessment of learners' performance. This also includes an analysis of whether the desired learning outcomes are met throughout the learning process (Compton, 2009). For teachers designing online courses, knowledge of online language learning curriculum design is important, since learning language online is different from language learning in a traditional learning environment (Compton, 2009). The design principles for online learning environments are based on enhancing course communication and navigation components (Lai, Zhao, & Li, 2008).

Pedagogical knowledge and skills is another beneficial and important element in the process of technology integration when teaching ELLs in the content areas (Guichon & Hauck, 2011; Lai & Zhao, 2005). The TPACK model shows that teaching strategies is one of the most important elements for effective technology integration in teaching ELLs. Using the TPACK model for teaching ELLs means blending teaching strategies, instructional methods, and best practices with incorporation of digital instructional materials that supports language learning including vocabulary acquisition, listening, and reading skills (Koçoğlu, 2009; Zainal, 2012). For online learning, this means teachers need to be aware of different teaching strategies to promote online community building and socialization (Compton, 2009). Studies revealed that pedagogical knowledge should be accompanied by discussions of how creatively technology can be applied in specific situations (Compton, 2009; Lai & Zhao, 2005). Teachers' creativity in teaching strategies and cultural background information can help modify instruction to anticipate ELL-related challenges. The Internet and available technological tools also provide language teachers with opportunities to apply creativity in the design of stimulating and engaging activities. The issues regarding creativity of teaching strategies directly relate to teachers' competence in and attitude towards integration of technologies in teaching or technological knowledge (Hee Hong, 2010; Kessler, 2007; Olesova & Meloni, 2006).

For example, ELLs face challenges in understanding discipline-specific language because of unfamiliar vocabulary or concepts. To enhance language development, teachers can use digital games and simulations as one of the most powerful technologies for the 21st Century learners. Other examples include designing role-playing in Second Life and a 3D virtual world to help ELLs practice the second language through voice and text chat. One of the most powerful strategies to enhance learning is using multimedia environments that allow language learners to work with audio, visuals, and text (Li, 2014). When teachers select multimedia to integrate in their classrooms, they should consider connecting multimedia use to theory requirements. For example, they could consider theories such as Vygotsky's sociocultural theory, Piaget's cognitive-developmental theory, and Gardner's theory on multiple intelligences. Knowledge of how multimedia connects to various theories of learning may help minimize the barrier of not understanding the connection between the curriculum and the technology (Ntuli & Kyei-Blankson, 2011). Today teachers can easily combine video, images, and sound into engaging presentations by using different multimedia tools such as PhotoPeach (http://www.photopeach.com) or Capzles (http://www.capzles.com/).

Teachers' technological knowledge and skills is still at a low level (Guichon & Hauck, 2011; Kessler, 2007; Salaberry, 2005). According to Mishra and Koehler (2006), technological knowledge includes teacher familiarity with technology for teaching and learning and teacher ability to recognize what type of technology might work better when used in the classroom. Mishra and Koehler's (2006) interpretation of teacher technological knowledge aligns with Guichon and Hauck's (2011) understanding of teachers' techno-pedagogical competence. Teachers' techno-pedagogical competence includes the capacity to: (a) assess the potential and limits of technologies for language and culture learning; (b) carry out a needs analysis to introduce adequate technologies at appropriate moments in a pedagogical sequence; (c) handle basic tools and applications, and solve simple technical problems; (d) design appropriate tasks; (e) design for interactions within and outside the classroom in view of the technologies affordances; (f) rethink the contract with learners and colleagues; and (g) manage time and optimize the integration of technologies (Guichon & Hauck, 2011).

Basic technological skills are a necessary prerequisite for teachers to integrate technology successfully in teaching and learning in both online and traditional learning environments (Compton, 2009; Hampel & Stickler, 2005; Kessler, 2007). Basic technological skills include the ability to turn on the computer, use a mouse, and have basic knowledge of simple applications, (e.g., word processing and the Internet; Compton, 2009), keyboarding and working with menus (Kessler, 2006), and troubleshooting (Chapelle & Hegelheimer, 2004). When teaching ELLs in content areas, the basic technological skills also include the ability to use technology for communication and interaction to promote language and literacy skills of linguistically and culturally diverse ELLs (DelliCarpini, 2012). Communicative skills are some of the most important skills in second language learning, which could be effectively enhanced by technology for electronic communication. Technology helps make learning authentic by giving ELLs an opportunity to experience English communication in "the real world."

At the same time, authentic learning helps teachers engage ELLs more actively in activities as ELLs can see the relevance to their own lives. Also, ELLs benefit from this type of learning as they experience classroom interaction in real-life circumstances (Dukes, 2005). In addition, there are many benefits to incorporating communicative technology into English lessons, such as presenting new vocabulary words, providing multiple opportunities for learners to practice reading and listening skills, helping learners making connections between sounds and print, and preparing more authentic real-world activities. Perhaps the most compelling benefit is having the option to provide differentiated instruction appropriate to each learner's level of English proficiency and relevant to the learner's interests. Using communicative technology, teachers can create student-centered learning environments to differentiate among levels and to accommodate the multiple needs of their diverse ELL growing population in their classrooms. Thus, this communicative technological skill for teachers includes the ability to use and integrate Internet-based communication tools (e.g., email, electronic mailing lists, chat rooms), videoconferencing tools (e.g., Blackboard Collaborate, Yahoo Messenger, Skype, and Google Hangout), computer-mediated communication (CMC; e.g., discussion boards, forums), learning management systems (LMS; Blackboard, WebCT, and Moodle), and social networking (e.g., Facebook and Twitter). For example, teachers can use communicative tools to connect classes or give their students the opportunity to publish on the Internet for the "real-world" audience (Compton, 2009; Gonglewski, Meloni, & Brant, 2001).

Technology-mediated interactions have important implications for second language learning. Teachers have an opportunity to create a variety of interactive technology-based activities to help ELLs understand new information, express their own ideas, and interact with their classmates or real-life audiences outside of their own classroom, city, or even country (Dukes, 2005; Warschauer, 2004). This allows ELLs to practice the listening, speaking, reading, and writing skills through cooperative and collaborative activities in a safe environment. One example of how teachers can effectively promote ELLs' active participation and help them further develop second language skills in any content-based area such as math or social studies, is to give them an opportunity to collaborate with their peers. Collaboration is very effective in stimulating interest in a subject and can be facilitated in any type of learning environment (face-to-face, hybrid or asynchronous/synchronous online). For example, an online pen pal project connected classes in Croatia and Uruguay to promote cross-cultural awareness and develop second language skills. The teachers in both classes used email, Skype for videoconferencing, and Facebook private group chats for class communication (Smolcec & Carril, 2013).

Digital Storytelling

This technology application is used to take advantage of user-contributed content and to help teachers overcome some of the obstacles to productively using technology in their classroom (Robin, 2008). Teachers could request that their students create their own language-rich digital stories to express their opinions about any topic, to present their experiences about their struggles learning language, or to share their backgrounds by making a story supported with visuals. Creating a digital story provides ELLs with multiple opportunities to practice new vocabulary as well as listening and speaking skills; the task could be as simple as narrating their voice over a collection of pictures to create the story they would like to share (Hur & Suh, 2012).

Digital stories are 2–4 minute long video products which are produced by students with the help of video editing software such as Final Cut, iMovie, Windows Movie Maker, Premiere, and Photo Story. The digital stories are personal "chronological storylines, dramatic storytelling qualities, and often impressionistic or poetic forms of expression" (Vinogradova, Linville, & Bickel, 2011, p. 176) where authors usually combine verbal narratives with visual images and musical background. Digital storytelling can be used for student-centered projects (Banaszewski, 2002) and reflective practice in a community development setting (Freidus & Hlubinka, 2002). Digital storytelling can also be used as a tool to enhance students' critical thinking, as well as to engage and motivate both teachers and students (Vinogradova, 2014).

There are eight steps in the process of digital storytelling production in a language class developed by Vinogradova, Linville, and Bickel (2011) including: (a) brainstorming ideas for a digital story; (b) exchanging ideas with classmates in a story circle; (c) writing a script; (d) collecting visual images; (e) finding music to accompany the verbal and visual narrative elements; (f) creating an explicit outline of a digital story—a storyboard; (g) recording the audio narrative, and (h) producing a digital story using video-editing software. These steps can help teachers bring into the curriculum content that is both culturally and linguistically relevant to ELLs' own experiences. Teachers can use some of the extensive collections hosted by the Center for Digital Storytelling (http://storycenter.org/) and Educational Uses of Digital Storytelling Guide (http://digitalstorytelling.coe. uh.edu/).

Exploring Basics of iPad

Researchers and educators are paying more and more attention to mobile learning in language learning and content areas to support pedagogy and encourage collaboration between learners (Kukulska-Hulme & Shield, 2007; Henderson & Yeow, 2012). The majority of studies have been conducted in English, mathematics, science, and social studies (Kukulska-Hulme, 2009). Studies have found that mobile devices, such as phones, tablets, and handheld computers, that users can use anywhere and anytime through a Wi-Fi connection, have impact on improving knowledge of vocabulary (Stockwell, 2008; Zhang, Song, & Burston, 2011); reading and writing (Harmon, 2012; McClanahan, Williams, Kennedy, & Tate, 2012); and grammar, listening, and speaking (Rueckert, Kiser, & Cho, 2012).

The number of mobile device users increases every day because the users can access email, social media sites, videos, or any Internet resources. Therefore, it makes sense that teachers would take advantage of this opportunity (Kim, Rueckert, Kim, & Seo, 2013). Mobile devices, such as iPads, are becoming very popular among the young population (Lys, 2013; Sandberg, Maris, & de Geus, 2011; Tan & Liu, 2004). In language classes, students find mobile devices like iPads useful because iPads can deepen and enhance their learning experience when they use it for re-listening/re-recording or speaking. Students usually feel confident about participating in class and communicating clearly when they use iPads (Lys, 2013). Instructors can create more collaboration among students because iPads allow for a more immersive experience and engagement (Lys, 2013). One of the strategies to implement iPads for ELLs in content areas could be providing learning content with pictorial annotation for students with lower verbal and higher visual ability while providing learning content with both written and pictorial annotation can help ELLs with high verbal and visual ability (Chen, Hsieh, & Kinshuk, 2008). IPads also allow students to engage through games, such as, map-navigation or "hunting and hiding" to motivate ELLs through rewards and feedback (Schwabe & Goth, 2005).

Research has found that teachers who use mobile technologies in their classrooms should give students the length of time that need to they pass through innovation-decision process of mobile learning (Kim et al., 2013). As mobile technologies become more accessible for all students, the more learners will make use of richer learning opportunities. When teachers intend to implement mobile technologies in their future classes, they should carefully implement them taking students' perceptions into consideration. Kim et al. (2013) noted that this approach will empower ELLs by engaging them in personalized learning experiences with mobile technologies.

Learning About Apps

There are mobile applications available that are designed to teach English (see Appendix A for a list of iPhone & iPad apps to learn language). For example, English Vocabulary in Use app by Cambridge University Press available on iTunes (http://www.apple.com/itunes/) is designed for pre-intermediate and intermediate activities for those who have a basic command of English. There are applications for reading or listening skills such as Toy Story 2 Read-Along mobile app by Disney, which is fully interactive and includes games, movies, clips, coloring pages, and music to sing along. Interaction capabilities of mobile apps are very important in language learning. Mackey and Jaemyung (2007) found that interaction is helpful in the learning of lexical and grammatical target items and in oral language development. Interaction is better achieved when instructional tasks are less rigid and learners have more control of what, how, and when to learn (Johnson, 1995). Using mobile apps in language learning can increase social interaction through awareness of what to learn, learner autonomy, and task authenticity (van Lier, 1996).

Learners can also record their own voices while reading the story. Duolingo (http://www.fluentin3months.com/duolingo/) is another free mobile application in language learning. Learners have access to self-paced and self-assessed language courses. The app allows learners to re-do lessons and also provides feedback through icons to show how well learners remember what they have learned. Some learners prefer using the Duolingo website (https://www.duolingo.com/) to practice grammar while mobile app is more preferable to practice vocabulary. Duolingo app is also a great review tool once learners completed lessons on the website. Teachers can check Best Apps for English Teachers USC Rossier Online (http://rossieronline.usc.edu/best-apps-for-english-teachers/) or Free Education Apps for iPad (http://www.teachthought.com/apps-2/the-55-best-best-free-education-apps-for-ipad/) for more mobile apps.

Other Tips and Strategies

To enhance language learning in the content areas, teachers can also use digital games, virtual environments, interactive boards, podcasting, e-books, social networking, or any web 2.0 technologies to create interactive lessons (see Appendix B for a list of tools).

Digital Games are computer games, videogames, mobile games, multiuser games, or any games that are delivered electronically (Annetta, Murray, Laird, Bohr, & Park, 2006; Gros, 2007). Most elementary and secondary school students spend many hours playing digital games every week. Both boys and girls are game users (Gee 2003). Games have been used to teach English language learners in formal and informal learning situations (Zheng, Young, Wagner, & Brewer, 2009), because games provide an immersive learning environment where the user needs to solve several challenges in a certain period of time applying the game's rules that are presented to the user through text or audio (Apperley, 2010; Gee, 2003). The immersive nature of the games keeps many learners engaged in the game for hours (Prensky, 2006; Thorne & Black, 2007). Multiplayer games require several players to communicate and collaborate with each other to solve the game missions or challenges and could also be used to learn English. Playing games might benefit learners from disadvantaged backgrounds (Rosas et al., 2003). Some online games such as Free Rice might be used to practice vocabulary (http://freerice.com/#/english-vocabulary/1444).

Virtual environments are tridimensional representations of digital worlds generated by computers providing a place where the user can socialize with other users, share objects, build entire sections of their virtual word, do experiments, take courses, transport themselves to many different places, and perform virtual tasks that cannot be performed in the real world (Piccoli, Ahmad, & Ives, 2001). Users choose an avatar or virtual representation of themselves to navigate those virtual worlds and interact with other avatars (Farahmand, Yadav, & Spafford, 2013). English learners can advance their language skills when they stop to visit virtual environments where they can communicate with other users in English (Merchant, 2010; Thomas & Brown, 2009; Zheng et al., 2009). Second Life tops the list of the most widely used virtual environments and has been utilized to learn English because it allows authentic communication activities among learners (Deutschmann, Panichi, & Molka-Danielsen, 2009). However, there are some risks associated with participating in virtual environments, such as cyberbullying, cyberstalking, avatar identity theft, online privacy risks, automation and other attacks, risks for minors, and other problems (Farahmand et al., 2013). Therefore, teachers should be aware of the learning curve to contribute virtual environments.

Interactive White Boards provide teachers with the combination of a whiteboard, a computer screen, and a computer projector, allowing users to make annotations over electronic instructional materials to highlight information (Hur & Suh, 2012). Interactive boards give teachers flexibility to use them as a whiteboard by writing and erasing information, or to show digital instructional materials such as presentations, software, websites, or other interactive resources (Smith, Hardman, & Higgins, 2006). Teachers have the option of saving their lesson plans with supporting materials on a computer file that can be edited at a later time. It is possible to acquire instructional materials for a certain brand of interactive boards or to make their own materials depending on the teacher's creativity and available time. Interactive board might be a helpful tool to motivate students to learn English, but it could also be used to teach interdisciplinary lesson plans to any target audience (López, 2010). Some interactive boards are touch-sensitive while other brands use a digital pen; some boards have a mobile device that allows students to write on the interactive board from their seats on the opposite side of the classroom.

Podcasting is a type of digital media, in either audio or video format, hosted on the Internet and can be subscribed and downloaded through web feeds to personal computers or mobile devices such as iPods and listened to anytime (Amicone & Li, 2014). Podcasting can be an effective instructional tool to enhance learning and allows students to better understand classroom materials and content (Amicone & Li, 2014; Hur & Suh, 2012). For example, teachers can read books to their students via podcasting.

E-books are computer-based electronic books also known as living books, talking books, or CD-ROM storybooks. E-books may either duplicate the print version's text and illustrations or introduce new multimedia features: animation, music, sound effects, illuminated text, hot spots, and narration (Shamir & Schlafer, 2011). E-books as a digital version of print format books can be effective in promoting children's language and literacy (Park & Yang, 2013). The examples of e-books are Living Books (http://www.livingbooks.com/), Harry and the Haunted House (https://www.youtube.com/watch?v=N—rEqhLQ7E), and Just Grandma and Me (https://www.youtube.com/watch?v=q3ywkAMuE7A).

Social Networking sites are digital platforms that allow individuals to communicate and interact with each other, allowing them to share information and media (Bosch, 2009). Steadily, each user creates an individual profile and then connects with other individuals to create a network in the same social media site, where their connections can see images, videos, and information posted by the user. Users should be aware of the need to protect their privacy when using these media sites, but in general teachers should follow the rule to post information that is appropriate for the public domain. The most popular social network sites are: Facebook, Google+, Instagram, LinkedIn, Pinterest, Twitter, and YouTube. Some of these sites have a chat or video chat option that allows users to communicate in real-time, allowing them to practice written or oral communication skills. However, there are some social media sites created with the sole purpose to connect with other language learners: Live Mocha (http://livemocha.com/), Easy Language Exchange (http://www.easylanguageexchange.com/), Conversation Exchange (http://conversationexchange.com/), Busuu (http://www.busuu.com/enc/), Talk and Learn (http://www.talk-and-learn.com/), My Happy Planet (http://www.myhappyplanet.com/), Language for Exchange (http://www.languageforexchange.com/). These sites could be used for informal or formal learning (Shih, 2011).

Web2.0 is known as the read-write web (Gillmor, 2004). Web 2.0 allows two-way communication between the site and users, which encourages individuals to collaborate and contribute to the authorship of content, customize web sites for their use, and publish their thoughts (Heafner & Friedman, 2008). For example, a *blog* is an online journal that learners can frequently update online (Yang, 2009). As an educational tool, blogs can be used to publish student writing, display photos, audio, and videos. Blogs have been used in language teaching as a tutor tool when the teacher runs the blog for the class; the shared collaborative space for class where students and teacher write, discuss, and reflect; and the student blog where each student has an individual online space (Yang, 2009). However, before using blogs in classroom, the teacher must ask practical questions such as: Why do I want to use blogs?; How can blogs enhance my ability to reach curricular goals and meet content standards? (Shoffner, 2007). Teachers can easily use Blogger (http://www.blogger.com), WordPress (http://wordpress.com/), and Edublogs (http://edublogs.org/).

A wiki is an interactive webpage that allows students to read, generate, and publish content online in a collaborative environment (Wisemean & Belknap, 2013). Wikis have been used in a variety of ways including online collaborative writing, as a knowledge repository, as a presentation tool, and as a distance-learning tool (Wisemean & Belknap, 2013). Pbworks (http://pbworks.com/) and Wikispaces (http://www.wikispaces.com/) are the most popular wiki platforms among educators. These collaborative technologies can effectively impact desired learning outcomes, for example, the ELL's ability to develop second language writing, reading, and communicative skills. Teachers can design wiki-based activities in which ELLs write together to produce a collaborative product with their classmates or other ELLs outside of their own classroom, city, or even country (Warschauer, Shetzer, & Meloni, 2000; Wiseman & Belknap, 2013). Wiki-based activities help ELLs reduce their anxiety level, learn from others, and also share their own knowledge and experience with others (Meloni, Olesova, & Weasenforth, 2009).

SUMMARY

This chapter focuses on using technology to teach ELLs. The chapter provided an overview of integrating technology in teaching ELLs in the content areas. The role of the teacher is crucial for successful integration of technology into the curriculum. Teachers should design learning activities that align with academic standards, find appropriate technology tools that are available in the classroom, and tailor activities to their learners depending on the topic. This chapter reviewed a variety of instructional technologies available for getting ideas of how to make learning environments interactive and engaging to help ELLs reach their full potential. Once teacher education and professional development programs focus more on the pedagogical considerations of using technology instead of technology itself, the challenges of how to use technologies could be removed and teachers can find creative and effective ways to integrate technology in the 21st Century classroom for students who already use technology in their daily life (Anderson, 2000; Buckingham, 2007; Espinosa et al., 2006). The recommended practical ideas and tips in this chapter should be helpful for teachers to enhance learning opportunities for ELLs. Teachers cannot ignore the changes that are taking place in the classroom and need to actively incorporate technology as a tool to facilitate teaching.

APPENDIX A:
iPhone and iPad Apps for Learning Language

App	Title	Cost	Description
	ABA Flash Cards & Games– Emotions	Free	This app teaches young children over 20 different emotions via gorgeous flash cards and interactive games.
	Bluster	Free	This is a word matching game to build vocabulary and word understanding for children that includes more than 800 vocabulary words.
	Byki	$7.99	This is an app for language learning for up to 74 different languages with more than 1,000 words and phrases for each one.
	Chicktionary	Free	This is a game to unscramble a roost full of letters and create as many words as possible.
	Compare a Twist	Free	This app can be used for assessment and knowledge checks. It could also be used to create custom activities using images and text.
	Duolingo	Free	This app is designed for users to learn Spanish, English, French, Italian, German, and Portuguese.
	English Monstruo	Free	This app has eight games created to learn verb conjugation, including the ones more difficult for Spanish speakers.
	Grammar APP	$0.99	This app was designed as an interactive book with more than 200 grammar video tutorials and 1,000 exercises and questions.
	Grammaropolis	$12.99	This app uses the parts of speech as animated characters to teach grammar. Each character has personalities according to the roles they play in a sentence.
	Grammar for Kids	$1.99	This is a grammar learning game for children grades 3–7 where the dinosaur is the grammar coach. It has 1,000 sentences with unlimited questions. The first two levels are free.

(continued)

App	Title	Cost	Description
	Grammar Fun	Free	This app was developed for young children to learn grammar by matching grammatical constructs to the words in the screen.
	Grammar Dragon	$0.99	This app was developed for young children to learn grammar by matching grammatical constructs to the words in the screen.
	Grammar Jammers	Free	Developed to teach grammar to young children from Kindergarten to 5th grade using songs and rhymes. Each animation unlocks a quiz.
	Grammar Up	$4.99	Prepares users to learn English grammar. Multiple choice quizzes with more than 1,800 questions.
	Idioms	$2.99	This is a multiple choice quiz system with about 700 common idiomatic questions and explanations for each expression.
	Learn English Elementary Podcasts	Free	This is a fun app to practice language listening for English learners.
	Phrasalstein	Free	This app was designed to help students learn the meanings of phrasal verbs. The app has a practice mode and a quiz mode. Translations of the meanings are available in Spanish, German, Italian, Russian, and French.
	Scrabble	$9.99	This is a game to play with words. Available in English, French, Italian, German, Spanish, or Brazilian Portuguese.
	See.Touch. Learn.	$0.99– $3.99	This app is designed to build picture cards to replace your old flash cards. It is possible to buy up to 50 individual libraries with over 4,000 pictures and 2,200 exercises.
	Sight Words	Free	This app shows words to young children to help improve their word recognition. Select levels and words that the child needs to learn.

(continued)

App	Title	Cost	Description
	Sight Words for Reading HD	Free	This app helps students learn in context the most common words in children's literature. Words are presented in context in fun videos.
	Sounds: The Pronunciation App	Free	Learn how to pronounce words and sounds. Practice listening, writing, and reading. There are also resources for teachers to use the app in their lessons.
	Sparklefish	Free	This is a fun app that lets the users record their own voice to complete some stories. It could be used by children or adults. The first five stories are free.
	SpeakingPal	Free	This app tests your English speaking skills comparing them with a native English speaker. You can speak in English with a video character. Levels include beginners, business, and academics.
	Story Kit	Free	This creative app was designed to create electronic storybooks by: recording sounds, drawing on the screen, inserting pictures, and writing text. You can add, reorder, or delete pages.
	TapToTalk	Free	This app gives a non-verbal child or adult a voice using pictures. The user taps the screen to communicate. Each picture can lead to another screen of pictures.
	TinyVox Pro	$9.99	This app records the user's voice. It can be used in classes, meetings, or informal situations.
	Vocabology—Word of the day	$0.99	This is an app to learn vocabulary that is featured as the word of the day in several online dictionaries.

APPENDIX B
Technology Tools

Technology	Characteristics	Examples
Blogs	Online journal frequently updated	BBC Learning English Blog: http://www.bbc.co.uk/blogs/legacy/learningenglish/ Enjoy Learning English: http://enjoy-learningenglish.blogspot.com/ Learn American English: http://www.learnamericanenglishonline.com/BlogLAEO.html The English Blog: http://www.englishblog.com/learning_english/#.U31oytJdWSo Dave's ESL Café: http://www.eslcafe.com/
Digital Games	Computer games, videogames, mobile games, multi-user games, or any games delivered electronically	ESL Games: http://www.eslgamesplus.com/ Games to learn English: http://gamestolearnenglish.com/ Vocabulary Games: http://www.vocabulary.co.il/ Math Chimp: http://www.mathchimp.com/ Games for Change: http://www.gamesforchange.org/learn/game-databases/ FunBrain: http://www.funbrain.com/
Digital Storytelling	Resources for digital storytelling	Center for digital storytelling: http://storycenter.org/ Educational Uses of Digital Storytelling: http://digitalstorytelling.coe.uh.edu/ Katie Schrock's Guide To Everything: http://www.schrockguide.net/digital-storytelling.html
E-books	Electronic books also named: e-books, living books, talking books, or CD-ROM storybooks	Living Books: http://www.livingbooks.com/ Goodreads: http://www.goodreads.com/ Free Kids Books: http://freekidsbooks.org/ Free eBooks for Kids: http://www.kidsworldfun.com/ebooks.php
Interactive Boards	Interactive whiteboard to present materials and make	Smartboards: http://smarttech.com/us

(continued)

Technology	Characteristics	Examples
	annotations over digital instructional materials to highlight information for the learners	eInstruction: http://www.einstruction.com/products/interactive-whiteboards
Mobile Devices	Mobile phones, tablets, and handheld computers	Apple: http://www.apple.com/ Samsung: http://www.samsung.com/us/ Android: http://www.android.com/
Multimedia Environments	Digital tools for the creation of interactive instructional materials: audio, visuals, text, animation and others	PhotoPeach: http://www.photopeach.com Capzles: (http://www.capzles.com/ Animoto: http://animoto.com / Prezi: http://prezi.com/ Jing: http://www.techsmith.com/jing.html Youtube: https://www.youtube.com/ Quizlet: http://quizlet.com/ Audacity: http://audacity.sourceforge.net/ Audioboo: https://audioboo.fm/ Thinkglink: http://www.thinglink.com/ Glogster: http://edu.glogster.com/?ref=com Creaza: http://www.creazaeducation.com/ Mentor Mob: http://www.mentormob.com/beta/splash Timetoast: http://www.timetoast.com/ Dipity: http://www.dipity.com/ Mindmeister: http://www.mindmeister.com/ SlideShare: http://www.slideshare.net/ Aviary: https://www.aviary.com/ Creately: http://creately.com/ Popplet: http://popplet.com/

(continued)

Technology	Characteristics	Examples
Podcasting	Digital media hosted on the Internet (audio or video)	Soundcloud: https://soundcloud.com/ Screenr: http://www.screenr.com/ ESL Podcast Blog: http://www.eslpod.com/website/index_ new.html Podcasts in English: http://www.podcastsinenglish.com/ pages/levelbusiness.shtml British Council: http://learnenglish.britishcouncil.org/ en/elementary-podcasts English Pronunciation Archive: http://www.eslpod.com/website/index_ new.html
Social Networking	Digital platforms that allow individuals to communicate with each other and share information and media	Facebook: https://www.facebook.com / Twitter: https://twitter.com/ Linkedin: https://www.linkedin.com/ EdModo: https://www.edmodo.com/ Pinterest: http://www.pinterest.com/ Open Study: http://openstudy.com/
Virtual Environments	Computers simulations of digital worlds where the users can interact, share objects, build, learn and transport themselves	Second Life: http://secondlife.com/ Active Worlds: https://www.activeworlds.com/index.html Club Penguin: http://www.clubpenguin.com/
Web-Based Resources	Dictionaries, thesaurus, translator and other digital resources available with an internet connection	Multilingual Translation Dictionaries: http://www.wordreference.com/ English dictionary: http://dictionary.reference.com/ Thesaurus: http://thesaurus.com/ English dictionary & Thesaurus: http://dictionary.cambridge.org/us/ English Dictionary & Thesaurus: http://www.merriam-webster.com/ Oxford Dictionary: http://www.oxforddictionaries.com/us Google Translate: https://translate.google.com /

(continued)

Technology	Characteristics	Examples
		Bing Translator: http://www.bing.com/translator/
		TeacherTube: http://www.teachertube.com/
		Dropbox: https://www.dropbox.com/
		Box.Net: https://www.box.net/
		Google Drive: https://drive.google.com
		Evernote: https://www.evernote.com/
		Mendeley: http://www.mendeley.com/
Wikis	Interactive webpage for collaboration to generate and publish content online	Wikispaces: http://www.wikispaces.com/ Pbworks: http://pbworks.com/

REFERENCES

Amicone, J., & Li, L. (2014). Podcasting use in a junior high social studies class: A research study of impact of podcasting on student performance. In M. Searson & M. Ochoa (Eds.), *Proceedings of Society for Information Technology & Teacher Education International Conference 2014* (pp. 841–844). Chesapeake, VA: AACE. Retrieved May 12, 2014 from http://www.editlib.org/p/130868

Anderson, G. T. (2000). Computers in a developmentally appropriate curriculum. *Young Children 55*(2), 90–93.

Annetta, L. A., Murray, M. R., Laird, S. G., Bohr, S. C., & Park, J. C. (2006). Serious games: Incorporating video games in the classroom. *Educause Quarterly, 29*(3), 16–22.

Apperley, T. (2010). What games studies can teach us about videogames in the English and Literacy classroom. *Australian Journal of Language & Literacy, 33*(1), 12–23.

Banaszewski, T. (2002, January/February). Digital storytelling finds its place in the classroom. Retrieved from http://www.infotoday.com/MMSchools/jan02/banaszewski.htm

Barron, B. G., Cayton-Hodges, L., Bofferding, C., Copple, L., Darling-Hammond, L., & Levine, M. (2011). *Take a giant step: A blueprint for teaching children in a digital age.* New York, NY: The Joan Ganz Cooney Center at Sesame Workshop. Retrieved online on March 10, 2013 from: www.joanganzcooneycenter.org/Reports-31.html.

Basharina, O. (2007). An activity theory perspective on student-reported contradictions in international telecollaboration. *Language Learning & Technology, 11*(2), 82–103.

Bavelier, D., Green, C. S., & Dye, M. W. (2010). Children, wired: For better and for worse. *Neuron, 67*(5), 692–701.

Bosch, T. E. (2009). Using online social networking for teaching and learning: Facebook use at the University of Cape Town. *Communication: South African Journal for Communication Theory and Research, 35*(2), 185–200.

Buckingham, D. (2007). *Beyond technology: Children's learning in the age of digital culture.* Cambridge, England: Polity.

Buzzetto-More, N. A., & Alade, A. J. (2006). Best Practices in e-Assessment. *Journal of Information Technology Education, 5*, 251–269.

Chapelle, C. A., & Hegelheimer, V. (2004). The language teacher in the 21st century. In S. Fotos & C. M. Browne (Eds.), *New perspectives on CALL for second language classrooms* (pp. 299–316). Mahwah, NJ: Lawrence Erlbaum Associates.

Chen, N.-S., Hsieh, S. W., & Kinshuk. (2008). Effects of short-term memory and content representation type on mobile language learning. *Language Learning & Technology, 12*(3), 93–113.

Compton, L. (2009). Preparing language teachers to teach language online: A look at skills, roles, and responsibilities. *Computer Assisted Language Learning, 22*(1), 73–99. doi: 10.1080/09588220802613831

Cummins, J. (2008). BICS and CALP: Empirical and theoretical status of the distinction. In B. Street, & N. H. Hornberger (Eds.), *Encyclopedia of Language and*

Education (2nd Edition, Literacy) (pp. 71–83). New York, NY: Springer Science & Business Media.

Curry, M. J. (2004). UCLA community college review: Academic literacy for English language learners. *Community College Review, 32*(2), 51–68.

de Jong, E., & Harper, C. (2005). Preparing mainstream teachers for English language learners: Is being a good teacher good enough? *Teacher Education Quarterly, 32*(2), 101–124.

DelliCarpini, M. (2012). Building computer technology skills in TESOL teacher education. *Language Learning & Technology, 16*(2), 14–23.

Deutschmann, M., Panichi, L., & Molka-Danielsen, J. (2009). Designing oral participation in Second Life—a comparative study of two language proficiency courses. *ReCALL, 21*(2), 206–226.

Dukes, C. (2005). Best practices for integrating technology into English language instruction. *SouthEast Initiative Regional Technology in Education Consortium, 7*(1), 3–7.

Ertmer, P. A., & Ottenbreit-Leftwich, A. T. (2010). Teacher technology change: How knowledge, confidence, beliefs, and culture intersect. *Journal of Research on Technology in Education, 42*(3), 255–284.

Espinosa, L. M., Laffey, J. M., Whittaker, T., & Sheng, Y. (2006). Technology in the home and the achievement of young children: Findings from the early childhood longitudinal study. *Early Education and Development, 17*(3), 421–441.

Faltis, C., Arias, M. B., & Ramirez-Marin, F. (2010). Identifying relevant competencies for secondary teachers of English learners. *Bilingual Research Journal, 33,* 307–328.

Farahmand, F., Yadav, A., & Spafford, E. H. (2013). Risks and uncertainties in virtual worlds: An educators' perspective. *Journal of Computing in Higher Education, 25*(2), 49–67.

Freidus, N., & Hlubinka, M. (2002). Digital storytelling for reflective practice in communities of learners. *SIGGROUP Bulletin, 23*(2), 24–26.

Gee, J. P. (2003). What video games have to teach us about learning and literacy. *Computers in Entertainment (CIE), 1*(1), 1–4.

Genesee, F., Lindholm-Leary, K., Saunders, W., & Christian, D. (2005). English language learners in US schools: An overview of research findings. *Journal of Education for Students Placed at Risk, 10*(4), 363–385.

Gillmor, D. (2004). We the media: Grassroots journalism by the people, for the people. Sebastopol, CA: O'Reilly Media.

Goldenberg, C. (2008). Teaching English language learners. *American Educator, 32*(2), 8–44.

Gonglewski, M., Meloni, C., & Brant, J. (2001). Using e-mail in foreign language teaching: Rationale and suggestions. *The Internet TESL Journal, 7*(3). Retrieved from: http://iteslj.org/Techniques/Meloni-Email.html.

Gonzalez, D. (2012). Review of TESOL technology standards: Description, implementation, integration. *Language Learning & Technology, 16*(2), 31–34.

Graber, D., & Mendoza, K. (2012). New media literacy education (NMLE): A developmental approach. *Journal of Media Literacy Education, 4*(1), 82–92.

Green, T. D., Tran, M., & Young, R. (2005). The impact of ethnicity, socioeconomic status, language, and training program on teaching choice among new teachers in California. *Bilingual Research Journal, 29(3)*, 583–598.

Gros, B. (2007). Digital games in education: The design of game-based learning. *Journal of Research on Technology in Education, 40(1)*, 23–38.

Guichon, N., & Hauck, M. (2011). Editorial: Teacher education research in CALL and CMC: more in demand than ever. *ReCALL, 23*, 187–199. doi: 10.1017/S0958344011000139

Hampel, R., & Stickler, U. (2005). New skills for new classrooms: Training tutors to teach languages online. *Computer Assisted Language Learning, 18(4)*, 311–326.

Harmon, J. (2012). Unlock literacy with iPads. *Learning and Leading with Technology, 39(8)*, 30–31.

Heafner, T. L., & Friedman, A. M. (2008). Wikis and constructivism in secondary social studies: Fostering a deeper understanding. *Computers in the Schools, 25*, 288–302.

Hee Hong, K. (2010). CALL teacher education as an impetus for L2 teachers in integrating technology. *ReCALL, 22*, 53–69. doi: 10.1017/SO95834400999019X

Henderson, S., & Yeow, J. (2012). IPad in education: A case study of iPad adoption and use in a primary school. Proceedings of the 45th Annual Hawaii International Conference on System Sciences, January 4–7, 2012., Computer Society Press, 2012 (78–87). Retrieved from http://www.computer.org/csdl/proceedings/hicss/2012/4525/00/4525a078.pdf.

Hur, J. W., & Suh, S. (2012). Making learning active with interactive whiteboards, podcasts, and digital storytelling in ELL classrooms. *Computers in the Schools, 29(4)*, 320–338.

Johnson, K. (1995). *Understanding communication in second language classrooms.* Cambridge, England: Cambridge University Press.

Kim, D., Rueckert, D., Kim, D.-J., & Seo, D. (2013). Students' perceptions and experiences of mobile learning. *Language Learning & Technology, 17(3)*, 52–73. Retrieved from http://llt.msu.edu/issues/october2013/kimetal.pdf.

Kessler, G. (2006). Assessing CALL teacher training: What are we doing and what could we do better? In P. Hubbard & M. Levy (Eds.), *Teacher Education in CALL* (pp. 22–42). Amsterdam, Netherlands: John Benjamins.

Kessler, G. (2007). Formal and informal CALL preparation and teacher attitude toward technology. *Computer Assisted Language Learning, 20(2)*, 173–188. doi: 10.1080/09588220701331394

Koçoğlu, Z. (2009). Exploring the technological pedagogical content knowledge of pre-service teachers in language education. Procedia-Social and Behavioral Sciences, 1(1), 2734–2737.

Kukulska-Hulme, A. (2009). Will mobile learning change language learning? ReCALL, 21(2), 157–165.

Kukulska-Hulme, A., & Shield, L. (2007). An overview of mobile assisted language learning; can mobile devices support collaborative practice in speaking and listening? Paper presented at EuroCALL 2007, September, Conference Virtual Strand. Retrieved from http://citeseerx.ist.psu.edu/viewdoc/download?doi=10.1.1.84.1398&rep=rep1&type=pdf.

Lai, C., & Zhao, Y. (2005). The essence of second language education and technology integration. In Y. Zhao (Ed.), Research in technology and second language learning: Development and directions (pp. 401–408). IAP.

Lai, C., Zhao, Y., & Li, N. (2008). Designing a distance foreign language learning environment. In S. Goertler & P. Winke (Eds.), *Opening doors through distance language education: principles, perspectives, and practices.* (CALICO Monograph Series, Vol. 7, pp. 85–108). San Marcos, TX: Computer Assisted Language Instruction Consortium (CALICO).

Li, C. H. (2014). An alternative to language learner dependence on L2 caption-reading input for comprehension of sitcoms in a multimedia learning environment. Journal of Computer Assisted Learning, 30(1), 17–29.

López, O. S. (2010). The digital learning classroom: Improving English language learners' academic success in mathematics and reading using interactive whiteboard technology. Computers & Education, 54(4), 901–915.

Lys, F. (2013). The development of advanced learner oral proficiency using iPads. Language Learning & Technology, 17(3), 94–116. Retrieved from http://llt.msu.edu/issues/october2013/lys.pdf.

Mackey, A., & Jaemyung, G. (2007). Interaction research in SLA: A meta-analysis and research synthesis. In A. Mackey (Ed.), Conversational interaction in second language acquisition (pp. 409–452). Oxford, England: Oxford University Press.

Meloni, C., Olesova, L., & Weasenforth, D. (2009, April). Addressing global problems and improving language skills with integrated technologies. Teachers of English to Speakers of Other Languages (TESOL) Annual Convention, Denver, CO.

Merchant, G. (2010). 3D virtual worlds as environments for literacy learning. *Educational Research, 52*(2), 135–150.

Mishra, P., & Koehler, M. (2006). Technological pedagogical content knowledge: A framework for teacher knowledge. *The Teachers College Record, 108*(6), 1017–1054.

McClanahan, B., Williams, K., Kennedy, E., & Tate, S. (2012). A breakthrough for Josh: How use of an iPad facilitated reading improvement. *Tech Trends: Linking Research and Practice to Improve Learning, 56,* 20–28.

Newby, T. J., Stepich, D., Lehman, J., Russell, J., & Ottenbreit-Leftwich, A. (2010). *Educational technology for teaching and learning,* 4th Edition. Boston, MA: Pearson.

Ntuli, E., & Kyei-Blankson, L. (2011). Teacher criteria for evaluating and selecting developmentally appropriate computer software. *Journal of Educational Multimedia and Hypermedia, 20*(2), 179–193.

Olesova, L., & Meloni, C. (2006). Designing and implementing collaborative internet projects in Siberia. In P. Hubbard & M. Levy (Eds.), *Teacher Education in CALL* (pp. 237–249). Amsterdam, Netherlands: John Benjamins.

Park, Y. J., & Yang, Y. (2013). Pre-Service teachers' perception of and technology competency at creating and using e-picture books. *International Education Studies, 6*(4), 124–133.

Piccoli, G., Ahmad, R., & Ives, B. (2001). Web-based virtual learning environments: A research framework and a preliminary assessment of effectiveness in basic IT skills training. *MIS Quarterly, 25*(4), 401–426.

Prensky, M. (2001). Digital natives, digital immigrants part 1. *On the Horizon, 9*(5), 1–6.

Prensky, M. (2006). *Don't bother me, mom, I'm learning!: How computer and video games are preparing your kids for 21st century success and how you can help!*. St. Paul, MN: Paragon House.

Resnick, M. (1998). Technologies for lifelong kindergarten. *Educational Technology Research and Development, 46*(4), 43–55.

Rideout, V. J., Foehr, U. G., & Roberts, D. F. (2010). *Generation M [superscript 2]: Media in the lives of 8-to 18-year-olds* (Publication No. 8010). Menlo Park, CA: The Henry J. Kaiser Family Foundation.

Robin, B. R. (2008). Digital storytelling: A powerful technology tool for the 21st century classroom. *Theory into Practice, 47*(3), 220–228.

Rosas, R., Nussbaum, M., Cumsille, P., Marianov, V., Correa, M., Flores, P., & López, V. (2003). Beyond Nintendo: design and assessment of educational video games for first and second grade students. *Computers & Education, 40*(1), 71–94.

Rosen, L. D. (2010). *Rewired: Understanding the iGeneration and the way they learn.* New York, NY: Macmillan.

Rueckert, D., Kiser, R., & Cho, M. (2012, March). "Oral language assessment made easy via VoiceThread!" *TESOL International Convention and English Language Expo*, Philadelphia, PA, March 28–31.

Salaberry, M. R. (2005). The use of technology for second language learning and teaching: A retrospective. In Y. Zhao (Ed.), *Research in technology and second language learning: Development and directions* (pp. 61–91). IAP.

Sandberg, J., Maris, M., & de Geus, K. (2011). Mobile English learning: An evidence-based study with fifth graders. *Computers & Education, 57*(1), 1334–1347.

Schleppegrell, M. J. (2004). The language of schooling: A functional linguistics perspective. Mahwah, NJ: Lawrence Erlbaum.

Schwabe, G., & Goth, C. (2005). Mobile learning with a mobile game: Design and motivational effects. *Journal of Computer Assisted Learning, 21*(3), 204–216.

Shamir, A., & Shlafer, I. (2011). E-books effectiveness in promoting phonological awareness and concept about print: A comparison between children at risk for learning disabilities and typically developing kindergarteners. *Computers & Education, 57*(3), 1989–1997.

Shih, R. C. (2011). Can web 2.0 technology assist college students in learning English writing? Integrating Facebook and peer assessment with blended learning. *Australasian Journal of Educational Technology, 27*(5), 829–845.

Shoffner, M. (2007). Pre-service English teachers and technology: a consideration of weblogs for the English classroom. *Contemporary Issues in Technology and Teacher Education, 7*(4), 245–255.

Simpson, E. S. (2005). Evolution in the classroom: What teachers need to know about the video game generation. *TechTrends, 49*(5), 17–22.

Sleeter, C. E. (2001). Preparing teachers for culturally diverse schools research and the overwhelming presence of whiteness. *Journal of Teacher Education, 52*(2), 94–106.

Smith, F., Hardman, F., & Higgins, S. (2006). The impact of interactive whiteboards on teacher–pupil interaction in the National Literacy and Numeracy Strategies. *British Educational Research Journal, 32*(3), 443–457.

Smolcec, M., & Carril, C. (2013). *Developing an online project.* Retrieved from http://www.slideshare.net/msmolcec/developing-and-online-project-tm2013.

Stockwell, G. (2008). Vocabulary on the move: Investigating an intelligent mobile phone-based vocabulary tutor. *Computer Assisted Language Learning, 20*(4), 365–383. doi:10.1080/09588220701745817

Tan, T. H., & Liu, T. Y. (2004, August). The mobile-based interactive learning environment (MOBILE) and a case study for assisting elementary school English learning. In *Advanced Learning Technologies, 2004. Proceedings. IEEE International Conference* (pp. 530–534). IEEE.

Téllez, K., & Waxman, H. (2006). (Eds.), *Preparing quality educators for English language learners: Research, policy, and practice.* Mahwah, NJ: Erlbaum.

Thomas, D., & Brown, J. S. (2009). Why virtual worlds matter. *International Journal of Learning and Media, 1*(1), 37–49.

Thorne, S. L., & Black, R. W. (2007). Language and literacy development in computer-mediated contexts and communities. *Annual Review of Applied Linguistics, 27,* 133–160.

van Lier, L. (1996). Interaction in the language curriculum: Awareness, autonomy and authenticity. London, England: Longman.

Vinogradova, P. (2014). Digital stores in heritage language education: Empowering heritage language learners through a pedagogy of multiliteracies. In T. Wiley, D. Christian, J. K. Peyton, S. Moore, and N. Liu (Eds.), Handbook of heritage, community, and Native American languages in the United States: Research, educational practice, and policy (pp. 314–323). Routledge.

Vinogradova, P., Linville, H., & Bickel, B. (2011). "Listen to my story and you will know me": Digital stories as student-centered collaborative projects. TESOL Journal, 2(2), 173–202.

Warschauer, M. (2004). Technology and social inclusion: Rethinking the digital divide. Cambridge, MA: Massachusetts Institute of Technology.

Warschauer, M., Shetzer, H., & Meloni, C. (2000). Internet for English Teaching. Alexandria, VA: TESOL Publications.

Wisemean, C., & Belknap, J. (2013). Wikis: A knowledge platform for collaborative learning in ESL reading. TESOL Journal. 4(2), 360–369.

Yang, S. H. (2009). Using blogs to enhance critical reflection and community of practice. Educational Technology & Society, 12(2), 11–21.

Zainal, A. (2012). ESL teachers' use of ICT in teaching English literature: An analysis of teachers' TPCK. Procedia-Social and Behavioral Sciences, 34, 234–237.

Zhang, H., Song, W., Burston, J. (2011). Reexamining the effectiveness of vocabulary learning via mobile phones. TOJET: The Turkish Online Journal of Educational technology, 10(3), 203–214. Retrieved from http://files.eric.ed.gov/fulltext/EJ944968.pdf.

Zheng, D., Young, M. F., Wagner, M., & Brewer, R. A. (2009). Negotiation for action: English Language Learning in game-based virtual worlds. The Modern Language Journal, 93(4), 489–511.

CHAPTER 8

TEACHING ARTS TO ENGLISH LANGUAGE LEARNERS

Frank C. Martin, II and Tolulope Filani
South Carolina State University

CASE SCENARIO

Tobi is 11 years old and has recently moved to the United States with his Nigerian immigrant parents. His father works three jobs to support his family. Tobi's mother stays at home taking care of him and his two siblings. Although English is the official language of Nigeria, it remains a second language in many homes. At home, Tobi speaks the Queen's Anglo-phone (British) English and *Yoruba*, an indigenous language associated with his family's Nigerian ethnicity. Tobi has difficulty communicating in his new 5th grade American classroom due to his accent, which is his main problem to slowly transit, understand, and pronounce the standard American English. This problem is further exacerbated when he is often made fun of by his peers for his "British accent." Consequently, Tobi becomes withdrawn in his classes and discouraged in many class activities. His academic performance is thus affected significantly. In a meeting with Tobi's parents, his teacher recommended that Tobi be placed in an ESOL class where ELLs are provided with extra support to improve English. The parents were concerned because prior to immigrating to America, Tobi was a brilliant and well-rounded child with a passion for school. At home after the meeting, Tobi's parents asked

Teaching ELLs Across Content Areas, pages 187–208
Copyright © 2016 by Information Age Publishing
All rights of reproduction in any form reserved.

him what his problems were and how he could be helped. His parents were surprised by his response. He simply answered that it was in the art classes or with art activities that he could find a means to express himself without being intimidated and laughed at by his peers due to his not being able to speak English in the American way. The teacher also observed that Tobi was almost a transformed child with much interest in the arts lessons (i.e., visual, music, dance, and theatre).

ISSUES FOR USING ARTS TO TEACH ELLs

The lesson from the case scenario described above is a strong advocacy for the exploration of the power of the arts as tools for enhancing learning for ELLs and even for all students. Research supports the importance in education through the arts. The idea of using arts as an education archetype is clearly articulated in The Power of the Arts in the book, *Integrating the Arts Elementary School Curriculum,* written by Phyllis Gelineau (2004):

> The arts have been a part of us from the very beginning. Since nomadic peoples first sang and danced for their ancestors, since hunters first painted their quarry on the walls of caves, since parents first acted out the stories of heroes for their children, the arts have described, defined, and deepened the human experience. All peoples, everywhere, have an abiding need for meaning to connect time and space, experience an event, body and spirit, intellect and emotion. People create art to make these connections, to express the otherwise inexpressible. A society and a people without the arts are unimaginable. Such a society and people could not long survive. (p. 3)

Prior to planning to teach and engage ELLs through the arts, the teacher should first of all examine his or her fundamental concept of teaching. This is necessary because how we conceptualize our activity of teaching will directly affect what choices we make when interacting with our students and in designing the activities intended to support them when engaging with new ideas (Hyman, 1974). Hyman describes teaching as "an intentional, deliberate family of logical and strategic acts aimed at inducing learning of skills, knowledge, and values" (p. 35). Hyman further discusses a triadic character of teaching with the major element being the "teacher, student, and subject matter." Yet, the learning environment is often seen as an inextricable component of this association. Thus, it is also important to construct that environment that is healthy and supportive for student learning.

As a pedagogical paradigm, the arts-integrated curriculum should be grounded in Howard Gardner's multiple intelligences theory, in which intelligence is described as an adaptation and life is "a continuous creation of increasingly complex forms and a progressive balancing of these forms with the environment" (Campbell & Campbell, 1999, p. 3). Gardner further posits that all humans are inherently created with multiple forms of intelligence in varied degrees, and that competence in one is not a sine-qua-non for competence in the others (Gardner, 1993). In addition, Gardner describes intelligence as an *ability* "to solve problems, or to fashion a product, to make something that is valued in at least one culture" (p. 16). He identified nine forms of intelligence, which are: linguistic, logical-mathematical, visual-spatial, body-kinesthetic, musical, interpersonal, intrapersonal, naturalist, and existential.

When using arts, visual literacy forms an important component of what a teacher can do to help students understand concepts and learning objectives. Most educational projects incorporate powerful visual elements. ELLs may not be familiar with some learning concepts because of language and cultural difference. Thus, the use of visual prompts is a good strategy to enhance their understanding when they see concrete examples of visual arts.

It is important that the teachers of ELLs can conduct an interview with the purpose of assessing each ELL student in order to gain insight into the level of each learner's understanding. Some difficulty with ELLs may be due to the cultural differences and misunderstanding of contexts. The use of idiomatic speech is another way for the teacher to provide a means for translating information regarding projects to be completed for evaluation and grading, and some understanding of the criteria by which grades will be assigned.

Teachers should also pay attention to making the ELLs feel welcomed and supported in classrooms so that they are more engaged. For example, teachers can review all art vocabulary with the ELLs and all students by category (i.e., names of various art media and art processes) and employ a planned interview with each ELL in order to make sure that the ELL has understood the application of the terminology in differing contexts.

A more specific example would be, when studying the art application and learning the terminology, such as "value," the teacher can make the connection by discussing cultural *value,* market *value,* or historical *value,* all of which are connected with *value* in differing contexts. Then, the teacher can discuss value as an *element of art,* which is a specific visual and visible property regarding the transition of light to dark and dark to light within a given visual work. Otherwise, this terminology can be confusing to even native English speakers. Thus, using the different contexts of each application of this word, the teacher helps ELLs' better understanding with concrete examples and this even helps all the students understand the word in contexts.

Challenges for ELLs in Classrooms

Using arts as a tool, the teacher needs to have information about the ELL's background so that a work of art from the ELL's home country can be incorporated. This can be a stimulus of discussion for the ELL to offer more insight than peers who may not understand. For example, showing diverse forms of the piñada as an example of entertainment sculpture, the teacher can consider establishing group projects around seeking to create *papiér maché piñadas.* Visual tools are crucial to illustrate the topic and help with the need to comprehend verbal cues, which may be difficult for an ELL to hear accurately and to understand.

The ELLs at the different levels of learning academic content and second language development may face different challenges. Teachers need to differentiate instruction to meet their needs at different levels. The following discussion focuses on these different levels.

ELLs at the Elementary School Level

ELLs at this level are likely to have limited vocabulary. Yet, ELLs in this age group are likely to be more manageable and to catch on to linguistic cues more quickly because they have fewer inhibitions due to their young ages. In such instances, devising appropriate activities by using visual props are essential components of the planning lessons. Visual props, such as actual art objects, illustrations in texts, and power point slides, will help students who do not have the cognitive sophistication to better understand verbal abstractions. Illustrated demonstration will be the good strategy. For example, if the lesson is on color, using paints or crayons, the teacher should clearly pronounce each color and demonstrate the use of the medium and then ask students to do the same.

ELLs at the Middle School Level

This age group is usually between 12 and 14 years old. The ELLs should have more cognitive understanding. Demonstration at this stage is still a valuable tool; yet, due to intellectual development, the students should be engaged to describe in simple terms an idea for a project as an opportunity to use an artwork to express. Clear direction for the desired exercise to be undertaken is essential. Illustrations of specific experiences, recreations of views from home, outside of the window, of spaces in the art making area are all excellent activities. Clearly establishing goals will help the students reach the desired outcome. The clearer instruction is provided, the better understanding they will have.

ELLs at the High School Level

By ages 15–17, students should have an individualized, sophisticated view of the world. At this stage, the ELLs can work on art projects that they wish to initiate as a form of self-expression. Even if the ELLs at this stage may have limited English proficiency, the teachers can try to reinforce the student's sense of autonomy and encourage their originality in creating visual works of arts. Collaborative projects designed to be completed by ELLs with peers should be encouraged. Teachers should be aware and accept the students' own ideas and intentions toward increasing self-direction. Introducing the idea of images inspired by music, popular culture, entertainment, or popular media and literature may create a space for students to express their own individual interests. In the process of generating visual images, teachers can also reinforce new vocabulary and stimulate the exchange of ideas with peers in the classrooms. The main goal is to allow opportunities for ELLs to work with peers and use visual art works as a venue for the ELLs to integrate their culture as an incentive.

When teaching Art Appreciation, for example, teachers can try to approach the topic by addressing the entire class as if the entire class were all learning a new language. This can put ELLs at ease. Vocabulary sheets should be provided and a review of correct pronunciation of all significant terminology should be provided for the entire class, because English speakers may also have trouble pronouncing art terms, such as, *chiaroscuro, sfumato, pentimenti,* or *contrapposto.* In terms of learning content, these older ELLs are perhaps the most challenging due to the fact that they must learn academic content and at the same time they must also learn English as the second language. Yet, these ELLs are usually sophisticated, engaged, and involved learners. Their inner motivations can create a wonderful asset in finding ways to offer creative assessment of and incorporation of art materials.

When engaging ELLs of all groups in art activities, teachers must be sensitive. It is important that teachers facilitate ELLs' understanding of concepts while not making ELLs feel to *lose face* before their peers. For this reason, advice and correction can occur in one-on-one sessions, at the after-class meetings, or during teacher–student conferences. In addition, teachers can also devise other means that protect an ELL's dignity and privacy. Permitting ELLs to submit questions in written form or allowing time for additional instruction through peer tutoring is another good tip. It is also important that teachers are supportive and understanding in helping their students, maintaining a healthy and respectful relationship between teacher–students and students–students. Having mutual respect is an initial step in making ELLs feel comfortable to learn.

Meeting Challenges and Planning to Teach

According to the Socratic Method, teaching must draw from the students' experiences, awareness, and understanding. The content and knowledge may already be in their possession, but the learners may not yet have been made fully aware. This method may not be effective for every learner, especially young ELLs. Therefore, teachers must try to devise a strategy based on the developmental level of the ELL students with a variety of approaches. Some suggestions for meeting the challenges by using differing methods and communications for presenting information to students at differing levels are provided below.

Demonstration Methods

Demonstration is a valuable tool for visual arts. The teacher must provide clear, appropriate examples to the concepts under discussion. Arts lesson demonstration may fall into three categories: *in-class demonstration* completed in situ in a studio space; off-site demonstration in a gallery of museum, and *deferred demonstration* by using electronic means to present visual representation of concepts or information. All of these methods may be used for ELLs and all students with studio activities.

In-class demonstration.   Demonstration *in situ* by the teachers using tools, art materials, or drawings and diagrams is one of the effective means to present visual materials. Figure 8.1 is an example of a 12-year-old, 6th grade student's *I, Eye, Aye* exercise, using an automatic drawing technique to discover forms. The demonstration of this exercise led by her teacher is included in Figure 8.2. When demonstrating the expressive power of *line*, the basic elements of art, the teacher might use serene, undulating, sinuous line contrasted with erratic, irregular, jagged lines, contrasted with directional, straight, angular lines, each inhering different properties and each implying a certain emotive content. Another example is the illusion of shading and volume incorporating hatching or cross-hatching, using short, straight, parallel lines placed in close proximity, following the contours of a shape to create the illusion of a three-dimensional form. Such demonstrations may be used to illustrate the differences between the terms *shape* and *form* while simultaneously offering examples of useful techniques to achieve certain effects in recording representational images and demonstrating different methods of drawing. In in-class demonstrations, teachers must pay attention to allowing students time to absorb the material and to ask questions. Demonstrating the same problem with variations is a good strategy, especially for ELLs who may have difficulty in the initial demonstration to better grasp the concept.

Off-site demonstration.   Teachers can take students to visit an off-site location. For example, it may include visiting a gallery of museum relevant

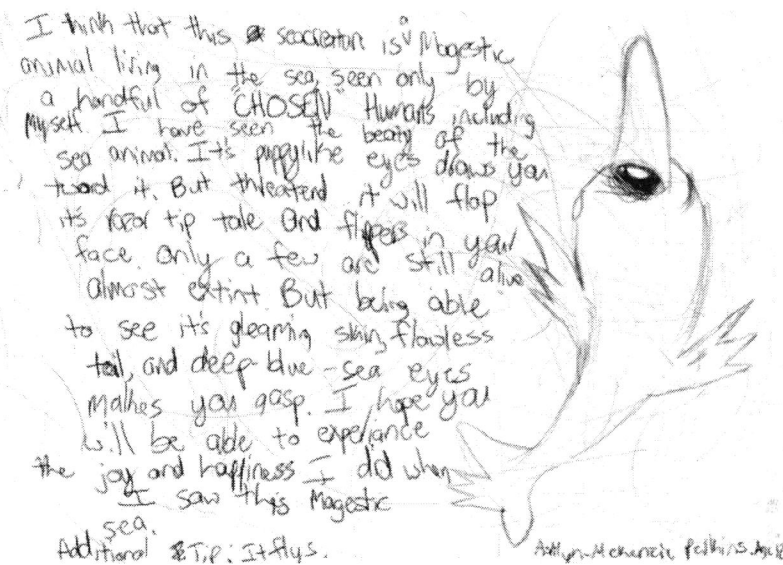

Figure 8.1 Student drawing from Ms. Gwendolyn Sewer's art class (6th grade, age 12). Felton Laboratory Charter School, Orangeburg, SC. Using the "I, Eye, Aye Essay": An exercise intended to help ELL students discover English homonyms. *Note:* A translation of the "I, Eye, Aye" essay text reads: "I think that this sea creature is a majestic animal living in the sea, seen only by a handful of "chosen" humans including myself. I have seen the bea[u]ty of the sea animal. It[']s puppy-like eyes draw[s] you t[o]ward it. But threatened it will flap it[']s razor tip[ped] ta[i]l[e] and flippers in your face. Only a few are still alive—almost extin[c]t. But being able to see it[']s gleaming skin, flawless tail, and deep-blue sea eyes makes you gasp. I hope you will be able to experience the joy and happiness I did when I saw this majestic sea [animal]. Additional tip; it fl[y]ie[s]." —Ashlyn McKenzie Perkins

to the lesson topic about history and culture or visit the festival of arts to meet artists, ask questions, understand how masterpieces are created, or watch artists work in a variety of mediums (e.g., oils and watercolors, ceramics, sculpture, jewelry, mixed media). Following the off-site visit, teachers can organize the student-led demonstration, in which the teacher facilitates and a student performs the demonstration involved in the visual work creation process. It can also involve photography or printmaking. For example, the students take the initiative to demonstrate concepts while the teacher facilitates process related to topics after off-site visits. The benefit of this method is that the students are more engaged and often take initiative in their work with better understanding of the subject. Teachers can also organize students into teams allowing socialization as a tool in structured small cooperative group projects. Peer-teaching and student engagement is

Figure 8.2 Ms. Gwendolyn Sewer's teacher demonstration drawing for the "I, Eye, Aye" exercise (6th grade art class). Felton Laboratory School, Orangeburg, SC.

one of the effective weapons in the arsenal. Allowing ELLs to provide leadership in groups and collaborative demonstrations will build confidence, enhance mastery of vocabulary, and contribute to overall integration within the learning community and increased student confidence.

Deferred demonstrations. This demonstration can be using films, video, electronic representations, and the incorporation of technology (e.g., power points and graphic presentation). If a computer device is available, teachers can actually encourage the students to incorporate contemporary technology to allow students to better understand information translated via demonstrations. Students may also be encouraged to learn how to operate power-point programs, and to search for related examples of deferred demonstrations, which may be shared with the class, especially if the demonstrations may be found in various languages, in which the translation of concepts may be additionally highlighted by the instructor. ELLs would benefit in incorporated new vocabulary by searching online demonstrations in a first language that may be compared to the translations of the same activity or idea into English. Such analogous searches not only help ELLs build vocabulary and enrich concept growth, but this method can be used to help other students better understand the basics of a process or an idea.

When teaching concepts, additional explanation and activities should be provided. However, the demonstration will be more helpful after establishing basic parameters for what is to be learned and how the new concept is to be applied with an example. Learning becomes exciting when students discover new potential applications for ideas or images in context, which they may creatively transfer to a new, unique application.

Discussion Methods

Discussion helps students better understand concepts and gives them the opportunities to test their ideas and opinions against that of their peers. Good discussion is like art and needs to be well organized to engage all students in discussing concepts, innovative ideas, or any relevant topics. Yet, discussions need to avoid going off topic and miss the pedagogical aim. ELLs with a limited vocabulary may have difficulty in understanding concepts due to cultural differences and language barrier. Discussion thus may be challenging; yet, it can be an opportunity for them to interact with peers. Also due to limited vocabulary, ELLs may not be fully engaged in discussion. Thus, teachers should organize the discussion by arranging the ELLs with the peers at the level that they feel comfortable. If necessary, teachers can devise an individual plan for each ELL. If the size of the class allows, peer tutoring provides opportunities for the ELLs to discuss relevant topics. The essence of using the various discussion methods is the idea that, when knowledge emerges from the experiences of the individuals that are engaged with those experiences in a meaningful way, the individuals can have opportunities to articulate their insights, feelings, and responses to stimuli in order to draw upon internal resources that help process external events.

Active Participation

In order to make learning meaningful and to achieve the desired results, teachers must engage students in active participation. Teachers can use cooperative learning for students to be engaged in active learning. This may be difficult for ELLs initially. However, it is a long-term goal for ELLs to grasp the concepts and information and feel comfortable learning the subject matter so that they become increasingly successful in schools. To achieve this goal, ELLs must develop proficiency and an enhanced command of vocabulary to better understand the subject matter. Thus, it is necessary for teachers to find ways to engage ELLs by actively observing the ELLs' needs to avoid producing anxiety. Teachers must establish the necessary rapport for the students in class to be actively engaged and strategies for their active participation in the classroom to ensure student learning success. Teachers can devise active engagement strategies by developing personal connections with their students to help students develop an intrinsic desire to succeed. When all students are engaged in their own learning, learning becomes fun and productive. For example, *covert active engagement* strategies are, as the name suggests, unseen by the teacher; yet, the teacher can hold students accountable for their learning. Using this type of strategies, students are imagining, thinking, picturing, remembering, visualizing, reflecting, pondering, or even creating a mind movie. Although covert active participation strategies are not observable, they are essential to any given lesson because they give students time to *think* about questions elicited by the teacher before they are prompted to *perform* an overt activity. On the other hand, *overt active engagement* strategies are observable and measurable by the teacher. This type of active participation can also be used as an informal, formative assessment because it provides the teacher with immediate feedback on the students' understanding of a given lesson.

The Socratic Method

This method is based on the teacher directed employment of deductive and inductive reasoning to prompt students' responses to questions. This is a method created by the ancient Greek philosopher, Socrates. It is a form of inquiry and discussion between individuals based on asking and answering questions to stimulate critical thinking and to illuminate ideas. By systematically using simple questions, the teacher allows the students to search their own ideas, responses, awareness, knowledge, and understanding in order to increase engagement regarding an idea or issue. In the visual arts, this technique is an excellent introduction to difficult or obscure artworks, which students may not be familiar with. An important component is encouraging students to offer a well-reasoned defense of his or her position with regard to equivocal issues such as "taste." If or when challenged to offer reasons for liking or disliking an artwork in a style or created by a method that is unfamiliar, students may be encouraged to move out of the safety zone with their preconceived ideas regarding art and meaning. The effect of the Socratic Method is generally slow but once the technique is introduced, its positive results will be observed after consistent practice. The best approach is to make gradual progress, that is, to move from simple questions (e.g., Where do you think the artist is using line in this work?) to increasingly advanced questions (e.g., How does the presence of a simple painted mark symbolize the human presence itself?).

For ELL students, it is helpful to provide simple explanations of terminology in advance, or initiating a preliminary demonstration of questions and answers to show ELLs and allow them time to anticipate questions and formulate answers. Teachers may also ask students for suggestions of model questions to relevant or difficult to understand works of art so that the class may discover the process of seeking answers collectively and collaboratively.

By seeking students' opinions regarding aesthetic issues, teachers can engage students in *valuative discussion*. For example, the teacher can raise questions on an artwork that may generate controversial debate. A sample question can be: Is the Mona Lisa by Leonardo da Vinci beautiful or merely famous? Of course, there is no final answer to such a debatable question. The interest stems from how and what students may choose to cite as their justifications for their own responses. ELLs can be encouraged to express their unique ideas before and with their class peers, should be given adequate support, resources, and teachers should show sincere interest in their opinions and observations. The discussion method is an entry level tool for devising enhanced awareness and understanding of concepts. The instructor should help all students understand the differences between statements of facts and help students become aware of the value of critical assessment and its stages of careful observation, thoughtful evaluation, reflective judgment, formulation of an opinion, and expression or discussion of that opinion based on its relationship to the object assessed. Practicing these processes will help ELL students with self-expression, vocabulary mastery, and social skills development.

Aesthetics and culture may overlap and thus teachers must be aware of the cultural backgrounds of their students in order to appropriately engage ELLs for aesthetic responses, and teachers also must be attentive to students' articulation of their ideas and beliefs. For example, the teacher should pay attention to what students say about what is *beautiful* or *not beautiful* in order to gain context clues for topics discussed by the ELLs. The teacher must also seek to provide a learning atmosphere of psychological safety and maintain appropriate language and references to support the development of student expressiveness when using the arts as a means of instruction to facilitate the ELLs' learning. In addition to the challenges, in the sections followed, we will provide tips and strategies to better work with ELLs.

TEACHING STRATEGIES

There are many different teaching strategies that teachers can use by incorporating arts as a tool to facilitate the ELLs' learning and to enhance their participation and expression. The following are such tips and strategies, which include Using Visual Arts & Projects, Incorporating Performance Tasks, and many Other Tips and Strategies.

Using Visual Arts & Projects

Explaining Art Vocabulary in Context

In using the visual arts, teachers must carefully review vocabulary and terms in context. For example, in math or physics class, the term *line* applies to the shortest distance between two points. Teachers can employ that definition into visual art to help ELLs better understand. In arts, the word *line* is in fact a physical gesture made into a visible permanent form through use of some tool or device to record the gesture's action. This can easily be demonstrated by simply holding a pencil or a white board marker, or even the stylus of an electronic tablet and making a gesture that is immediately recorded and shown to the class. Thus, while art uses many terms that we may encounter in everyday experience, the art-specific contexts are often at odds with the popular associations with certain terms. For that reason, when teaching ELLs, the teacher needs to explain the terminology in the context to avoid misunderstanding and confusion. Teachers may help students understand the basic components of art vocabulary (e.g., line, shape, form, texture, color, mass, space, size, scale), and then progress to introduce the principles of arts (e.g., unity, variety, balance, proportion, emphasis, rhythm), or the conceptual rules that make works of art discernable.

Using Afterschool Time

It is helpful that teachers can take advantage of afterschool time to engage students with art projects or acuities, such as organizing the afterschool art clubs to enhance not only arts appreciation, but learning. The activities without the pressure allow students the opportunity to talk more freely regarding concerns, and challenges, which the teacher may offer support and resources to the ELLs in a combined endeavor to master the subject matter and obtain enhanced communications skills.

Using Visual Cues

In order to effectively guide ELLs toward enhanced verbal and written communications skills for language development, teachers can use their own aesthetic awareness to draw upon visual cues shown by ELLs that indicate comprehension or evidence of confusion or not understanding. Using visual cues is a useful tool in the arsenal of possible methods of approaching transfer of concepts concerning the visual and fine arts to ELLs. The visible demeanor of many ELLs, due to students' respect for the teacher, may not be seen. However, this skill becomes important for the teacher of the ELLs who are challenged in their endeavor in learning a new language in an unfamiliar culture. Empathy for the learner is an important point for teachers to develop skilled observation of their ELLs, followed by careful listening, and offering clear, non-intrusive and sympathetic corrections needed. Yet, it is NOT necessary to correct every word or every error made by an ELL student every time. Indeed, such a reminder seems to be necessary for teachers. It is also important to create a classroom culture in which all students, especially the ELL student, feels comfortable expressing his or her ideas without extraneous prejudgment or intervention.

Developing the Observing Skills

Our human brains are pre-programed to seek, appreciate, and even enjoy pattern recognition in many differing forms. Not only do we take pleasure in looking at the repeated elliptical forms of the petals of a daisy, or the fractal patterns of the veins of a leaf, we enjoy arranging the furniture in our homes in harmonious, often symmetrical ways. This innate ability is important for developing skill in looking, and through looking, enhancing our learning. An excellent performance-based activity is to offer ELLs the opportunity to observe and look carefully at any designed work, even a chair or the cover of a book (or more grandiose things as each teacher may determine at his or her own discretion), and use that opportunity to inventory and record all of the details of the thing observed, developing both skills in observation and concentration. The skill of observation can be extended into learning activities, such as an exercise to orally describe or write down what has been observed.

Valuing Creativity

In the visual arts, creativity is highly valued. Indeed, one of the most important justifications for the inclusion of the arts in school curricula is their value in fostering and applying human creative abilities. Creativity is understood in this context as a capacity to assimilate traditional or conventional behaviors, rules, relationships, patterns, or ideas and other concrete or conceptual entities, and transform them into new, innovative applications that generate enhanced value. Students who are ELL are already placed in a position of having a potentially innovative way of understanding concepts and ideas being expressed to them in a new language. Encouraging ELL students to be uninhibited in their application of concepts learned, and suggesting that they draw upon all of their experiences as a source of inspiration is likely to cause such participants in your classrooms to enliven and enrich the experiences of all students due to the added diversity, cultural complexity, and new ideas and ways of understanding reality that such students inherently provide. Teachers can also encourage students to look at photos or paintings and make up stories about them orally or in writing.

Using Descriptive Language

When describing artworks, several categories of descriptive language may be used to describe and explain the art objects. First, is description without content interpretation, in which the observer simply takes a survey of what an image may represent. Second, involves specific colors and then it evolves to representations of objects in a naturalistic, mimetic style and to representations of objects in a subjective manner. Deciphering an artwork or a lack of objects (in abstract works) is a first level of learning by both looking at carefully and actually seeing what is given in the work of art. Describing at the second level requires a use of detached, objective, descriptive language without adding the formulation of opinions concerning the content or meaning of the image or abstractions perceived. The interpretation is the third level of description with awareness following the initial phase of grasp, the second phase of formal analysis, and the final phase of interpretation of meaning. Descriptive language at this level is simple and direct, a factual report on what has been perceived. This stage of viewing may result in reporting the number of figures (if figures are shown), positions on the picture plane (center, right, or left), the gender of subjects (male, female, or other), colors used, and other straightforward information at the most basic level.

Incorporating Performance Tasks

Studio activities are an excellent means through which teachers can help ELLs understand concepts and apply concepts to contextual usage. This is because a studio activity is a form of extended demonstration and it can help make an abstract concept concrete. It is the principle-based learning necessary for art appreciation.

Writing With I, Eye, Aye

To use this strategy, the teacher should engage students in imagining a scene or object, writing down a description, and then drawing, painting, or sculpting the imagined scene; then, guide the students to do it reversely (i.e., drawing, painting, or sculpting a scene and then completing a written description of what was seen). This activity is intended as a means to show the different sounds of letters in English and the different contexts of their use. The first person pronoun "I" involves demonstration of the student as both artist and subject, the noun "eye" emphasizes the visual tools and the importance of careful observation, and the affirmation "aye" says "yes" to discovering pattern, texture, shape, and form within our environment and transforming these varying levels of recognition into creative works that distill experience, awareness, vision, and aesthetics through verbalized descriptions.

Combining Arts With Language

This is an exercise that combines the arts and language. This strategy is more effective with the students from the upper elementary-school grades to middle school grades. The concept is that students create a drawing, painting, sculpture, or print of something to the interest of the students; after this work has been completed, which generally requires three or four class periods to finalize such an artwork with detail, the student is then asked to write first a detailed description of the work created, and then an interpretation of its "meaning" and iconography. This exercise will help ELLs with clarity of expression, articulation of interior narratives, and mastery of descriptive language and terminology (see two drawings from an ELL in Figure 8.3 and Figure 8.4).

Incorporating the ELLs' Cultural Heritage

The ELLs are likely to learn and function in a bewildering and different culture from their own. Teachers should not take any aspect of learning for granted. This may require interrogating some of the usual methods and approaches. Teachers should also be cautious to not alienate the ELLs due to a failure and be considerate of his or her contextual challenges. Teachers should also find ways to learn about culture and even

Figure 8.3 Drawing from Ms. Alethea Bryant's Class (4th grade student, age 10). Marshall Elementary School, Orangeburg, SC. Fire Cracker Festival memory drawing by student from Amdabad, India.

Figure 8.4 Drawing from Ms. Alethea Bryant's class (5th grade student, age 12). Marshall Elementary School, Orangeburg, SC. Apartment dwellings ("flats") memory drawing by a student from Amadavad, India.

basic indigenous language of your ELLs and know their families. Allowing all students to discuss the home environment through an art project or assignment may give your ELLs an opportunity to offer an introduction to the class of his or her cultural richness. For example, a teacher had an ELL, Diop from Mali, who participated in an art appreciation class. When the topic involved indigenous tribal art forms from diverse African ethnicities, Diop was extremely pleased to volunteer to wear his most pristine Woloof fashions to class and explain many details regarding the symbolic importance of each component of his traditional garb. This was fascinating to the other students and to the teacher. It also gave Diop an opportunity to demonstrate the tradition and complexity of his African ethnicity. It became a lesson in texture, color, design, originality, textiles, and dress as a form of cultural expression.

Using Drawing and Images as Phonetic Tools

For this exercise, teachers should encourage students to offer ideas regarding how to facilitate pronunciation of art terminology. One example is the use of an illustrated pronunciation key, which helps with retaining vocabulary and supports phonetic spelling: An example is

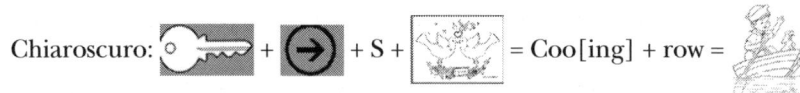

or

Pentimenti: the instructor may use an image of a pen (ink pen) + cup of tea + 2 Men + Tee (golf ball support) to provide pictorgraphs for this term.

Pictographs aligned into "terms" may serve as clues to memory and as identifiers of objects to enhance concept recognition in addition to being an innovative and fun idea for ELL students and all other learners. Students may model their combination of pictographs on an interpolation of Egyptian hieroglyphs.

Other Tips and Strategies

Arranging Classroom Seating for Attentiveness

To improve the ELLs' language skills, teachers must find ways to engage ELLs so that the academic tasks can be accomplished. Classroom seating is one of the things teachers should pay attention to. By appropriately arranging seating, teachers can facilitate ELLs' learning and increase their attentiveness. This can enhance their participation in learning the subject matter. Specifically, the following tips are provided regarding how to facilitate their learning by arranging seating.

Elementary School Seating. Pre-School, kindergarten, and elementary teachers may have more freedom in structuring the seating of their young charges, and thus are in a position to easily place ELL students near the front of the classroom. This placement allows ELL students to see the instructor with ease, hear all terms used (increasing their accuracy of understanding), and encourages active participation and sustained awareness and attentiveness—all of which are tools which may help increase linguistic fluency and understanding. This level is the easiest to address with simple placement strategies, and is likely to offer significant results in a short time frame.

Middle School Seating. Beginning at the Middle School level students are likely to begin to select their own seats according to their social preferences, however, if ELLs are a minority in such classrooms, they may not have communication skills in English sufficient to help. A class seating chart could be created to intentionally situate ELL students near the front of the classroom. Seating ELL students where they may be able to see the instructor easily, and take visual cues on pronunciation will help facilitate language learning.

High School Seating. The growing emotional sophistication of high school aged students implies that it is always best to try and form some consensus with them in terms of offering structured seating plans, giving a rationale. Most likely, the best argument is to suggest placement based on instructor needs for communicating rather than noting the potential challenges to the students. Some strategic thinking may be required here to both protect the ELL students from isolation and the peculiarities of adolescent logic. Simply be aware of the dynamics in your own classroom and arrange accordingly. If a seating plan is not feasible, default to after class support and strategies employing additional instruction.

Using Interpretive Analysis

Interpretation is a challenging aspect of teaching and learning about artworks. Interpretations of art objects have relevance for both artists and their audiences, and complications pertaining to signification and meaning can be very difficult to address with coherence in all categories of art. Interpretation is the activity of translating the significations of an art object or event into meanings that may not be obvious from initial participation or encounter of the art object. Like language, art requires interpretation and understanding of a message embedded within the art object; a message which may not be made available to the observer of the artwork based on many factors (frame of reference, exposures, experience, familiarity with the subject matter, context, or culture and a host of other factors). Interpretation of artworks may operate on very different levels. For example, two people looking at two perpendicular lines (+) as a work of art may understand entirely differently. One person may signify the letter after "s" as in "short;" yet, the other may signify an addition sign, signaling the compounding of two quantities ($5 + 4 = 9$) or it could be interpreted as a religious symbol (e.g., a cross). In order to understand how a sign signifies, we often need a cultural context for clues. For ELLs there is often a dualistic difficulty, the barrier of language and linguistic use, and the barrier of culture and contextual use for signs and symbols used in art objects. Interpretation may use many differing approaches. When addressing the challenges of discussing visual symbolic traditions, teachers must take time to ask questions to help ELLs.

Using Deductive/Inductive Reasoning

Artists often think both through symbols and with an idea other than what it may be shown through reasoning deductively or inductively. For example, two perpendicular lines may indicate a cross, a plus sign, or a directional sign. The potential meaning of artworks is interpreted through the use of context and linguistic, signifying implications. For example, if we were to observe a painting with a male figure holding an object composed of two perpendicular lines, and if this image of a male figure was represented with a golden circle painted around his head, and from which an eerie yellow glow seemed to emanate, we might conclude that such an image has some relationship with the Divine Powers art. An ELL unfamiliar with the Western tradition might not come to such conclusions concerning meaning. Thus, it is important to guide ELLs with valuable resources using deductive and inductive reasoning methods. However, the difficulty may be with translation. To translate these meaning-specific visual tools and cues is a learning challenge because they were developed over the history of centuries' tradition, with an emphasis upon visual assessment, into other areas of learning with fundamental connections to linguistic and symbolic expressiveness.

Making Connections Between Seen and Unseen

Art often communicates messages through our associations of ideas with symbols and images. An important tool in the art repertoire is the use of implication and association. For example, a teacher might show a flag of the "Stars and Stripes" as an image of the political idea of American identity, or an egg may be a suggestion or the idea of "fertility" or "propagation." By making a connection between the seen and unseen in the fine arts will provide teachers with opportunities to discuss diverse concepts such as implicature, art symbolism, inference, iconography, and iconology. Having clear examples of artists using these conversational tools will help ELL learners clarify these complex concepts, and will enrich the expressive range of all student works.

Breaking Down Barriers for Expression

A principal role of the instructor in the visual arts as well as teachers in many other areas of academic endeavor is to help destabilize barriers to the externalization of inner expressiveness. While teachers need to organize the class and offer a semblance of orderly environment, students are intended to have creative impulses and they must be given a sense of freedom to generate original, interesting artworks. This is a challenge that each teacher must face. For teachers, creating a healthy, inquisitive atmosphere that maximizes student learning is an important part of fostering a positive school environment. Feed your students a diet of inspirational images, ideas, and discourse to see what exciting surprises they may produce using the power of arts with their imaginations.

Creating an Environment to Value Diverse Culture

One of the challenges for ELLs is to feel comfortable and encouraged to ask questions about unfamiliar images or artworks. An interesting *ice-breaker* is to search for films in diverse languages about art topics, which may have subtitles in English. Using films in languages spoken by ELLs, can be used as a strategy to make ELLs more comfortable because their language is used as an asset for learning. For example, an ELL enrolled in an Art Appreciation class was from Serbia, who spoke English, Serbian, Croatian, and Italian with some fluency. When showed a subtitled film made in Italy pertaining to the restoration of the Sistine Chapel, the teacher asked him to help explain to the entire class the different ways in which what was shown as English text in the film may have varied from the translated text of the subtitles. This made him an instant art historical authority for his peers, and many students quickly learned that Sergei (not his actual name) could be a great benefit to them in helping to decipher the rather obscure foreign sources for some of their research work. This greatly increased his popularity and helped enhance his English language vocabulary due to the increased demand for his willing services as a translator.

Finally, in seeking to devise a teaching strategy within the disciplines of the visual arts for ELLs, Judie Haynes and Debbie Zacarian (2010) offer a strategy with several key points, which are an excellent way to begin engaging ELLs. According to Haynes and Zacarian, this strategy is designed to help teachers meet the needs of ELLs and all students as follows:

- *Make lessons visual.* Use visual art representations to explain new vocabulary and also use graphs, maps, photographs, drawings, and charts to introduce new vocabulary and concepts. Tell a story about information in the textbook using visual arts or art objects. Create semantic and story maps—graphic organizers to teach students how to organize information.
- *Link new information to prior knowledge.* Teachers need to consider what schema ELL students bring to the classroom and to link instruction to the students' personal, cultural, and world experiences. Teachers also need to know what their students do not know. They must understand how culture impacts learning in their classroom.
- *Determine key concepts for each lesson.* Teachers write the key concept for a unit of study in student-friendly language and post it in the room. New learning should be tied to this concept. Additionally, teachers should begin each lesson by writing a content objective on the board. At the end of the lesson, students should be asked if the objective was met. Classroom teachers also need to set language objectives for the ELLs in their class. A language objective might be to learn new vocabulary, find the nouns in a lesson, or apply a grammar rule.

Modify Vocabulary for ELLs

ELLs require direct instruction of new vocabulary. Teachers should also provide practice in pronouncing new words. ELLs need much more exposure to new terms, words, idioms, and phrases than do English fluent peers. Teachers need to tie new vocabulary to prior learning and use visual to reinforce meaning. Content area teachers should teach new vocabulary words that occur in the text as well as those related to the subject matter. Word wall should be used at all grade levels.

Use Cooperative Learning Strategies

Lecture style teaching excludes ELLs from the learning in a classroom. We don't want to relegate ELLs to the fringes of the classroom doing a separate lesson with a classroom aide or ESL teacher. Working in small groups is especially beneficial to ELLs who have an authentic reason to use academic vocabulary and real reasons to discuss key concepts. ELLs benefit from cooperative learning structures. Give students a job in a group. Monitor that they are participating.

Modify Testing and Homework for ELLs

Content area homework and assessments needs to be differentiated for ELLs. Teachers should allow alternative types of assessment: oral, drawings, physical response (e.g., act-it-out), and manipulatives as well as modification to the test. Homework and assessment should be directly linked to classroom instruction and students should be provided with study guides so that they know what to study. The ELLs in your class may not be able to take notes (Haynes and Zacarian, 2010).

SUMMARY

This chapter focused on using arts as a tool to teach ELLs. The visual arts are an excellent vehicle to help ELLs gain access to concepts, ideas, vocabulary applications, and new linguistic contexts. Developing visual literacy and learning to articulate inner narratives can be achieved by using visual materials that provide ELLs with unique learning opportunities. Clear instructions and guidelines for art projects allow the students to develop creative skills and apply challenging new conceptual information. Teachers must pay attention to conciseness and clarity for project guidelines. Differentiated strategies depending upon the ELL's individual language level is important. A quiet interview is a good strategy through which the instructor will be able to make an adequate assessment of an ELL's vocabulary range, contextual grasp, and language skill mastery. Teachers must also provide a safe environment for questions, consider the possibility of different cultural contexts and acculturation process for ELL students, and offer modifications as needed to help ELL students integrate into the cultures of the school and classrooms as well as the society as a holistic institution. Teachers in the art classes must support ELLs in the translation of the art tools into other areas of learning with linguistic expressiveness and enhanced self-expression via the fabrication of arts objects.

REFERENCES

Campbell, L., & Campbell, B. (1999). *Multiple intelligences and student achievement: Success stories from six schools.* Alexandria, VA: Association for Supervision and Curriculum Development.

Gelineau, R. P. (2004). *Integrating the arts across the elementary school curriculum.* Belmont, CA: Wadsworth/Thompson Learning.

Gardner, H. (1993). *Multiple intelligences: The theory in practice—A reader.* New York, NY: Basic Books.

Haynes, J., & Zacarian, D. (2010). *Teaching English language learners across the content areas.* Retrieved from: http://www.everythingesl.net/inservices/seven_teaching_strategies_clas_06140.php

Hyman, R. T. (1974). *Ways of teaching* (2nd ed.). Philadelphia, PA: J. B. Lippincott.

PART III

OTHER ISSUES ON TEACHING ELLs

CHAPTER 9

INCREASING ACADEMIC VOCABULARY FOR ELLs

Angela Crespo Cozart
College of Charleston

CASE SCENARIO

Juan, a gregarious student, has been in the United States for almost two years. He is from Ecuador. He is talkative in both English and Spanish. His grades from Ecuador show he was an above-average student. He understands and speaks English without an accent. Juan is especially talkative during recess and lunchtime. At first, Juan's teachers were pleased with his love of conversation. Juan gave them plenty of opportunities to give him feedback so he could improve his English. They were pleased with his spoken English, but they soon became frustrated with Juan for his lack of academic progress, especially his grasp of academic, content-based vocabulary. As far as they were concerned, there was an obvious disconnect with his spoken English and his academic progress. Unfortunately for Juan, some of his teachers thought that he was lazy. How could a child who speaks English so well not be able to understand basic concepts and academic vocabulary? In their minds, he must be "playing" them and trying to get away with not doing his work. Other teachers are convinced that Juan has a learning disability and have requested the special education teacher test him. Is Juan lazy and trying to manipulate his teachers in an attempt to get away from doing his work? Or is he having a disability issue?

Teaching ELLs Across Content Areas, pages 211–235
Copyright © 2016 by Information Age Publishing
All rights of reproduction in any form reserved.

IMPORTANCE OF ACADEMIC VOCABULARY

In the scenario above, we were introduced to Juan, a gregarious elementary school student who could not, or would not, apply himself to do his schoolwork. What was Juan's problem and what should teachers know and do in order to help him? Juan is learning a new language; central to language and being able to learn and communicate is being able to increase his vocabulary so he can develop new "conceptual frameworks" and "understand...increasingly more sophisticated ideas" (Blachowicz, Fisher, & Watts-Taffe, 2006, p. 2).

When students are in the process of learning a new language, they seek to increase their vocabulary. A common phrase usually uttered by language learners is, "How do you say...?" They are looking for how to say something in the new language. They start with simple, concrete words and then try to learn how to convey abstract and complete thoughts along with complex ideas—words, though, are the building blocks from which they start. These learners understand that "vocabulary is central to English language [or any other language]...[learning] because without sufficient vocabulary, students cannot understand others or express their own ideas" (Lessard-Clouston, 2013, p. 2).

Individuals in the early stages of learning another language are usually thinking about conveying basic ideas; they often wish to learn how to say words that surround them or words that are necessary for survival. Travelers usually want to know how to say *bathroom*; young adults want to learn how to say *beer*; teachers want to learn how to say *parents*. Teachers, on the other hand, are looking to have their learners go beyond that; they are looking to improve their students' "reading comprehension and overall academic success," and research has shown that "vocabulary knowledge relates strongly to" both (Lehr, Osborn, & Pacific Resources for Education and Learning, 2005, p. 6).

Nuclear physicists cannot express ideas about their field of study if they use their elementary school vocabulary; complex ideas are expressed with more developed, specific vocabulary. This is expected of native-English speakers, and it is just as important for English Language Learners (ELLs). Nuclear scientists are explicitly taught their vocabulary. They do not learn to speak the language of nuclear scientists, write like them, and increase their knowledge of the subject by just associating with individuals in their field. In the case of nuclear physicists, it takes years of study.

One of the first things Juan's teachers should learn is the basic principles of second language acquisition, specifically Basic Interpersonal Communicative Skills (BICS), or surface fluency, and Cognitive Academic Language Proficiency (CALP), or academic proficiency; these two terms were coined by Cummins in 1979 (Cummins & Ontario Institution for Studies in Education, 1979; Cummins, 1981), and are covered in Chapter 2 of this book. An understanding of BICS and CALP will help teachers develop patience with, and empathy for, their English learners and the struggles they face in academic classes.

We cannot expect English learners to be academically on par with their native-English counterparts if they have been in this country for only a few years. (See Chapter 2 for information about length of time needed for BICS and CALP development). Native-English speakers often have a vocabulary of between 5,000 to 7,000 words when they enter school, but some non-native English speakers enter their first classroom with no knowledge of English whatsoever (Chung, 2012). According to the American Community Survey of the 2010 U.S. Census Bureau, 59.5 million people spoke a language other than English at home (Ryan, 2013). Teachers must be patient and realize that their students are coming from homes where English is seldom, if ever, spoken. After a few years, these students may sound like fluent English speakers, but they have not learned academic vocabulary or the strategies needed to be academically successful (see Chapter 2). In order to impress upon my college students, all of whom are future teachers, how words are at the core of understanding academic content and higher-level ideas, I do the following activity with them.

Can You Guess?

1. Ask for 4 volunteers and divide them into pairs.
2. Their task is to communicate to their partners what is written on one of two pieces of paper.
3. One piece of paper says, "I love you," and the other piece says, "The quantum state of a spatially closed universe can be described by a wave function which is a functional on the geometries of compact three-manifolds and on the values of the matter fields on these manifolds." (Hartle & Hawking, 1983, p. 2960)

The student who receives the first piece of paper ("I love you.") is able to get his/her partner to guess those words in usually less than 10 seconds. They usually point to themselves, form a heart with the fingers of both hands, and then point to the other student. The second pair is always completely stumped. They think they are also going to be asked to act out something as simple as "I love you." Even with the help of the rest of the class, they cannot guess what is on the second sheet of paper. After they realize they are not going to figure out what is written on the second piece of paper, I ask them the following question: Why was statement number one so much easier to state than statement number two? We then discuss the length of the statements, the complexity of the ideas, and the fact that most of us do not have the vocabulary needed to express ideas in this subject area, words such as *spatially closed universe, wave function,* and *compact three-manifolds.* I use this short activity to help students understand the importance of vocabulary development.

As teachers, we wish for students to learn academic vocabulary, but what exactly is academic vocabulary? According to Baumann and Graves (2010),

> Researchers, writers, and theorists tend to define academic vocabulary in one of two ways: (1) as domain-specific academic vocabulary, or the content-specific words used in disciplines like biology, geometry, civics, and geography; or (2) as general academic vocabulary, or the broad, all-purpose terms that appear across content areas but that may vary in meaning because of the discipline itself. (p. 6)

Domain-specific academic vocabulary "refers to the content-specific terms and expressions found in content area textbooks and other technical writing" (p. 6). Table 9.1 includes examples of various subjects and their domain specific vocabulary words. These are just a few words that students must understand in order to grasp the information in those particular content areas.

I often have teachers ask me to share with them *the* strategy they need to use in order to help their English learners, especially in the area of vocabulary development. I tell them that learning English is like losing weight; no magic weight-loss pill exists, just like there is no magic English for Speakers of Other Languages (ESOL) strategy that will help students attain CALP as quickly as they gain BICS. Losing weight calls for the deliberate implementation of strategies for weeks, months, and sometimes even years; gaining CALP takes years of explicit teaching and the use of many deliberate strategies. That explicit instruction must include the teaching of general vocabulary and in the higher grades, the teaching of domain-specific academic vocabulary.

If the prospective nuclear physicists mentioned above associated with nuclear scientists but never actually studied the content, they might sound proficient. They would have probably learned the jargon, or technical

TABLE 9.1   Domain-Specific Academic Vocabulary

Social Studies	Science	Math	Music
civilization	conduction	quotient	decrescendo
colony	species	polynomial	chromatic scale
dynasty	theory	exponent	staccato
empire	bacteria	theorem	treble clef
feudalism	constellation	median	major scale
migration	photosynthesis	obtuse	tempo

language of their subject area, but they would not be able to fully understand the concepts of their field and could not conduct research and write like true scientists. They would "sound" proficient, like English learners with a good grasp of BICS, but they would not have a strong understanding of the cognitive academic language needed in their field. Likewise with ELLs; if the specific vocabulary of a discipline is not explicitly taught, students will continue sounding like native speakers—their BICS will be excellent—but their CALP will not develop.

Learning vocabulary is much more than memorizing a list of words. Some students may recognize a word and even be able to pronounce it, but in order to help ELLs, teachers have to go beyond teaching students to be able to recognize and pronounce words.

A few years ago, a colleague informed me that we had a four-year-old in our lab school who could read at the college level. I wanted to see this for myself, so one day I made an appointment to visit this child while in school. I selected a college-level science textbook and asked the young boy to read it for me. To my surprise, he was able to correctly pronounce about 95–98 percent of the words. I then asked the young boy to explain to me what he read. I received a blank stare. The ability for this very young child to utter upper-level, difficult-words-for-his-age, or hyperlexia, did not mean he could read or understand the words he was seeing on the page. Reading requires understanding, (Ramirez, Chen, & Pasquarella, 2013; McKenna & Robinson, 2014) and this child did not understand the words he pronounced.

Being able to verbalize what is on the page without being able to decode its meaning is not the ability we wish to develop in our ELLs. Students need to learn to pronounce words, understand their meanings, how they are used, when they are used, and the importance of context and/or content area (Blachowicz et al., 2006). They should also have multiple exposures, time to discuss the new vocabulary words, and time to practice (Townsend & Kiernan, 2015). When teaching vocabulary, three important words to keep in mind are *form, meaning,* and *use* (see Figure 9.1).

- *Form* includes a word's spelling and pronunciation—this is sometimes the easy part. Form calls for students to learn syntax, spelling, phonemes, syllable stress, root meanings, prefixes, and suffixes. When teaching high school English, I could always tell which of my students had or were taking Latin. Whenever those students faced a new word in their readings, they always looked for the root word and dissected the word according to root, prefix, and suffix. Their study of Latin had taught them the role that Latin plays in English and thus they knew how to go about figuring out the meaning of a new word on their own. Students of Latin do not learn how to do

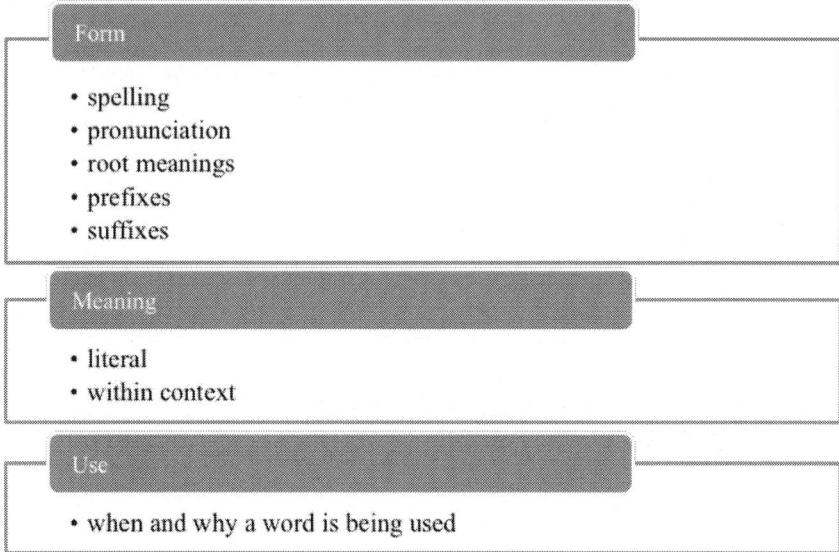

Form

- spelling
- pronunciation
- root meanings
- prefixes
- suffixes

Meaning

- literal
- within context

Use

- when and why a word is being used

Figure 9.1 Form, meaning, and use.

this by themselves; they are explicitly taught the skill. This is what we should do with ELLs—teach them this skill explicitly.

- "*Meaning* encompasses the way that form and meaning work together, in other words, the concept and what items it refers to, and the associations that come to mind when people think about a specific word or expression" or words' connotations (Lessard-Clouston, 2013, p. 3). In other words, meaning refers to two things: first, the literal meaning of a word, and second, the meaning of a word within the reading's context. Example: *The blue sky is beautiful.* The word "blue" refers to the literal color of the sky. *Jim is feeling blue.* Jim is not literally blue; he is feeling sad.
- *Use* refers to when and why a word is being used—the situation in which the word or phrase is being employed. For example: "Shut up" has become an exclamatory term. Young people use it to show they are excited about something. They may not want to say "Shut up" to a police officer who surprises them with a speeding ticket.

As mentioned, most children enter school with a vocabulary of 5,000 words; this means they can pronounce the words and comprehend the words' meanings. Non-native English speakers may enter school with a large vocabulary also, but not necessarily in English. If the home language is the one that is used exclusively in the home, the child may enter school with a very limited number of English vocabulary words. This means the ELL has many more words to learn in order to reach the same level as their native-English speaking peers. According to Peregoy and Boyle (2012), native-English speakers acquire approximately 1,000 words per year up until they enter college. After that, they acquire up to 2,000 words per year. "On the other hand, for language learners, the studying time for vocabulary acquisition and/or learning must be doubled, especially for academic purposes" (Alharbi, 2015; p. 502).

While native speakers may be focusing on increasing their academic vocabulary, English learners have to focus on both general words and academic vocabulary. More strategies are discussed in the following sections. In general, to help the ELLs build vocabulary, teachers should pay attention to two things:

- explicit teaching during which time students learn English "syntax, grammar, vocabulary, pronunciation, and norms of social usage," when they learn form, meaning, and use; and
- opportunities to use the vocabulary they are learning within a meaningful context (Goldenberg, 2008, p. 13).

This whole first section above needs to be broken down into maybe two or three sections. The first section should be introducing the problem. Right now, your problem is only mentioned in about one or two sentences. You need to expand the problem and make that the first section of your paper. It should only be about 3 or 4 paragraphs. You should end the first section with a sentence or two with what you are planning to include in this chapter (purpose).

Then the rest of your above section can be explaining the main ideas of language acquisition and what entails reading (phonemic awareness, semantics, syntax, and pragmatics). You should never finish a paragraph or a section with a quotation as you do above. Also, you can include the form, use, etc. in the second or third section too. As it stands now, the above section needs major structure changes.

STRATEGIES FOR BUILDING VOCABULARY

ELLs need intensive, continuous help with their English, and they need specific strategies and feedback that native-English speakers may not need. For example, being aware of cognates (to be discussed below) is beneficial for all students, but cognate awareness is especially useful to ELLs. Following are several strategies that will benefit ELLs.

Scaling Words

Imagine you are taking a cooking class and the instructor tells you that you should truss the duck, meunière the aubergine, and then deglaze the frying pan with vegetable stock. What would you do? Depending on the class and your knowledge of cooking terms, you might ask your peers or the instructor what truss, meunière, aubergine, and deglaze mean. Your understanding these terms is crucial to your being able to complete the task at hand. The instructor could very well take a hands-off approach and let you figure out the meaning of the terms yourself. An effective instructor, though, would make sure you knew the meaning of the terms before you started. This instructor would help you make a connection between what you already know about cooking and the new terms you are learning. The instructor would also give you an opportunity to pronounce the words and put them into practice. One way the instructor can find out what you already know about cooking terms is by providing you time and showing you how to scale, or rate, cooking vocabulary words (see Table 9.2).

In your own class, you can learn what students already know by having them scale the upcoming lesson's vocabulary. Notice: the teacher does not scale the words or tell the students which words they should know or do not know. Students come to class with different backgrounds and schooling experiences; some students may know all the words you may have selected and some may know none of them. Students do the scaling, but the teacher selects key words and models the strategy first. The National Behavior Support Service (n.d.) recommends these steps for creating a rating table: Steps for Scaling Activities:

1. The teacher selects the scaling strategy to be used, models it, and explains its purpose.
2. The teacher selects the vocabulary words he/she thinks are key to understanding the lesson and provides them to the students.
    a. Students work in pairs and rate the words by placing a checkmark in the box that applies.
    b. The teacher may ask the students to write a sentence for each word for which the students know the meaning.
3. Students discuss the terms, especially those with which the students are not very familiar and then the students predict the meaning of those words.
    a. The teacher explains the meanings of unfamiliar words.
    b. The teacher draws attention to the unfamiliar words every time they are found during the lesson.
4. Collect rating scales for future use. The teacher can keep track of the students' progress (p. 1)

TABLE 9.2   Cooking Class Scaling Table

Consider the words below. Place a checkmark in the box that best describes your familiarity with it.

Cooking Words/Terms	I Have Implemented the Strategy or Cooked the Item	I Have Observed Someone Use the Strategy or Cook the Item	I Have Heard the Word	I Have Never Heard the Word and Have No Idea What It Means
truss				
meunière				
aubergine				
deglaze				
vegetable stock				

If every person in the cooking class placed the checkmark in the first box, the instructor would know that the class has a rather informed group of students. The instructor could move on to other techniques. On the other hand, if most of the students in the class check off the second and third boxes, the instructor knows that he/she must cover the material and give students an opportunity to practice using the words.

Instead of a cooking class, Table 9.3 includes vocabulary words for a high school English class getting ready to read "Richard Cory," the narrative poem by Edwin Arlington Robinson. Notice how the scaling strategy is a little different.

Having students fill out vocabulary scales can save much time and frustration. Imagine you are the instructor in the English class mentioned above. If every student placed a checkmark in the last column or box, you would pay particular attention to that word. If, on the other hand, no one placed a checkmark in that column or box, you would know you need not pay special attention to that word. Rating scales can be used for any subject area and grade level. Teachers adapt or create scales according to their students' needs.

TABLE 9.3   "Richard Cory" Academic Word Scaling Table

Place a checkmark in the box that best describes your familiarity with the word.

Words/Terms	Know It Well	Have Seen/Heard It	No Clue
pavement			
sole			
clean-favored			
imperially			
arrayed			
fluttered			
admirably			
grace			

Making Cognate Connection

What is a cognate and how do they help English learners? "Cognates are words that are orthographically, semantically, and syntactically similar in two languages because of a shared etymology," or history (Montelongo, Hernández, Herter, & Cuello, 2011, p. 429). Most native-English speakers who have not been made aware of them cannot identify or define the word cognate. However, if they have come in contact with Spanish speakers (or a number of other languages)—in classrooms, supermarkets, restaurants, or even just walking down the street—they have more than likely heard several cognates. Following are a few examples of Spanish/English cognates: *patio*/patio, *rancho*/ranch, *emergencia*/emergency, *café*/coffee, *restaurante*/restaurant.

In fact, there are over 20,000 Spanish/English cognates (Montelongo, Hernández, & Herter, 2011, p. 161). Yet, many teachers are not aware of the words and their connection to English, and they are not aware of how identifying those words can help their Spanish acquisition. Once native-English speakers are aware of the different kinds of cognates and how these English words can be used as a tool to help them learn Spanish, they start making connections between the two languages; they start using cognates as a bridge to second language acquisition (Colorín Colorado, 2007). Key here though, is that they need cognate awareness. This is also what English learners need. They need to know what cognates are, and they need explicit instruction in learning to identify them while they listen and read. This explicit instruction is important, even if students are already strong readers in their native language.

Students who are strong readers in their first language will be stronger readers of English as compared to readers who struggle to read in their first language. In other words, there is a correlation between first-language and second-language reading. Students are able to generalize the strategies they learned in their first language to learning the second (Nagy, 2005). An analogy to help understand this phenomenon is cooking. A cooking instructor has set up a class to teach students how to cook Cajun cuisine. The class will meet one day a week for four weeks and two students are enrolled in the small class. One student is from Germany and has been cooking German food for years. The other student is from France and does not know how to boil water. Both students know nothing about Cajun cuisine except the fact that they enjoy eating it. In the short amount of time the instructor has to work with them, what person will make the better student? Which student will more than likely learn how to cook Cajun foods quicker and better? Although both know little to nothing about Cajun foods, the student with some kind of background in cooking—the German student—will more than likely learn how to cook Cajun food better and quicker. Why?

This student already knows the basic principles of cooking and can transfer those skills to this new arena. The second student will struggle because he/she does not know the basics of how to boil water, how to hold a knife when chopping or dicing, or how to measure dry and wet ingredients.

Just like the cooking instructor mentioned above will take advantage of the students' prior knowledge about cooking, teachers should take advantage of students' knowledge of their first language—spoken and written. We should teach students that what they know in their first language can help them in learning their second language. This teaching has to be explicit. We need to teach them what to look for. They know their first language and maybe how to read and write it, but this does not mean they know what cognates are or that they know how to listen or look for them. Being able to look for cognates and recognize them is important because, according to Ramirez et al., "Findings suggest that knowledge of cognates facilitates the transfer of Spanish derivational awareness to English vocabulary and reading comprehension" (2013, p. 73).

Following is an activity I've often used with my Spanish- and French-speaking students to help them become aware of the ubiquity of cognates. I ask students to summarize the following sentences; they are to identify the words they can understand.

1. Teacher reads the following: Yesterday my family and I visited the zoological park. We saw crocodiles, incredible elephants, coyotes, a group of gorillas, and an interesting baby leopard. Unfortunately, on my way home, I had an accident. I was riding my bicycle and I slipped on a banana and hit my head on a rock. It was a catastrophe. I ripped my pants and hurt my head.
2. As the teacher reads the passage, students write down the words they recognize.
3. Students work in pairs, compare their words, and write the gist of the short narrative.
4. Students share their work with the rest of the class. To make the exercise even more fun, some of the students are allowed to act out the story.

Most French- and Spanish-speaking students should be able to identify the cognates mentioned in the story above. Some of those cognates are found in Table 9.4.

Once students learn what cognates are, they start listening for them. A fun homework assignment to give ELLs, no matter what their grade level, is to ask them to make a list of all the words they hear that they think are cognates. They can listen for them in their content classes, the hallways in school, when they visit the mall, when they watch television, or when

TABLE 9.4   English/Spanish/French Cognates

English	Spanish	French
family	familia	famille
zoological	zoológico	zoologique
park	parque	parc
crocodiles	cocodrilos	crocodiles
incredible	increíble	incrédíble
elephants	elefantes	éléphant
coyotes	coyotes	coyote
group	groupo	groupe
gorilla	gorila	gorille

they listen to the radio. Sometimes students even involve their siblings and parents in the quest for cognates. This kind of assignment has two goals; it helps students increase their vocabulary, but it also helps them to view learning English differently: It becomes doable. If students involve their parents, there is the added benefit of having the family working together towards English acquisition. Students must be informed though that not all words that sound alike are cognates.

Some words may sound alike and may be spelled almost the same, but they are not cognates; these words are called false cognates. Confusing them with real cognates can put students in positions where they are passing along false information or putting themselves in a difficult situation. One of my students found this out when she tried to inform her Spanish-speaking friends that her boyfriend liked to joke and embarrass her. She told them that her boyfriend would *embarazada* her often. She could not understand why the entire family looked surprised. They were shocked because she did *not* tell them that her boyfriend embarrassed her often; she told them that her boyfriend kept impregnating her. *Embarazada* does not mean embarrassment; it means pregnancy. Table 9.5 includes a few additional false Spanish cognates we should teach students so they do not embarrass themselves.

The cognate examples mentioned above are English/Spanish ones. Teaching Spanish speakers English/Spanish cognates is relatively easy because of the number of English/Spanish cognates, and in U.S. Schools "by far, the majority of ELLs—80 %—are Spanish speakers" (Goldenberg, 2008, p. 10). What about other languages? U.S. schools have students who speak over 400 different languages (Goldenberg, 2008, p. 10). How can we use cognates when teaching Chinese students? Unfortunately, Mandarin comes from a completely different language branch. It has very few things in common with English. We have some loan or borrowed words in the

TABLE 9.5 False Cognates

Spanish	Does Not Mean	Spanish Meaning
molestar	to molest	to bother
recordar	to record	to remember
contestar	to contest	to answer
éxito	exit	success
asistir	to assist	to attend
carpeta	carpet	folder
emocionante	emotional	exciting
once	once (the measurement)	eleven
revolver	gun	to turn over or return
Vaso	vase	glass or tumbler

areas of food and technology, but there are no Mandarin or Cantonese/English cognates (Pavlik, 2012). Although the majority of students in many of our classes are native-Spanish speakers, teachers must do due diligence and research cognates for other languages.

The most attractive thing I have found with cognates is that they have a positive impact on content learning even before students start learning the cognates. Students are usually delighted to find out they already "know" some English words, and when they find out the list of cognates is so exhaustive, they are even happier. When they realize they already know so many words, learning English is no longer viewed as daunting; they come to realize that they are not learning English from "scratch," or from zero. They know that if they start looking for cognates, their English vocabulary list of words will grow rapidly.

Using Semantic Features and Graphic Organizers

Semantic feature analysis is an excellent visual strategy used to help students learn the relationship between words while drawing upon students' prior knowledge. This strategy allows students to observe and learn how sets of things are related and also how they are different. When can semantic feature analysis be used, in what content areas classes and with what kinds of groups? Semantic feature analysis can be used in social studies, English, music, math, science—in just about any content area class; before, during, and after reading; elementary through high school; and individually, with small groups, and with a whole class. Following are instructions for creating a semantic feature analysis.

- Select a category or topic for the semantic feature analysis.

- Provide students with key vocabulary words and important features related to the topic.
- Vocabulary words should be listed down the left hand column and the features of the topic across the top row of the chart.
- Have students place a + sign in the matrix when a vocabulary word aligns with a particular feature of the topic. If the word does not align, students may put a – in the grid. If students are unable to determine a relationship they may leave it blank.

Table 9.6 is an example of a semantic feature analysis (and directions) for use with the poem "Richard Cory." This analysis can be used to go over parts of speech. Table 9.7 is an example of a social studies semantic feature analysis, but the focus on this grid is on cultural features.

Graphic Organizers

According to Gallavan and Kottler (2007), "Graphic organizers offer visual models that equip teachers and students with tools, concepts, and language to organize, understand, and apply information" (p. 117). In other words, graphic organizers are visual tools with content-embedded information; they help students understand and organize information because they have to organize the information to fit into the visual. As they fill in their graphic organizers, they are also making connections between what they already know and the new information they are learning. This process helps students integrate their new knowledge into their existing schema to make the information better understood and retained.

Following a lecture or keeping up with all the activities that are going on in a class can be difficult for a non-English speaker. When it comes to note taking, how can they decide what is important enough to write down?

Table 9.6 "Richard Corey" Semantic Feature Analysis

Directions: On the left-hand side are vocabulary words found in "Richard Cory." The first column includes the vocabulary words; the other columns include features that vocabulary word may or may not possess. Place a plus sign (+) if the word has the feature and a minus (–) if it does not have the feature. The first one has been completed for you.

Vocabulary Words	Features			
	Noun	Verb	Adjective	Adverb
pavement	+	–	–	–
sole				
clean-favored				
imperial				
fluttered				
admirably				
grace				

TABLE 9.7   Social Studies Feature Analysis

Place a checkmark in the box if the word has the feature indicated by the column heading, place a zero in the box if the word does not have the feature indicated by the column heading.

Culture/ Kingdom	Features/Properties				
	Traded Goods/ Resources With Other Cultures	Practiced Uniform Religion	Had a Written Language	Erected Public Monuments and Architecture	Used a Tribute/Taxation System
Maya					
Inca					
Aztec					
Ghana					
Mali					
Songhai					

Some ELLs may try to write down everything they hear and become frustrated because they cannot keep up with the class discussion or lecture; some may become completely bewildered and write nothing down because all the information becomes a blur to them—content overload. When they do not take notes, ELLs will not have the information they need in order to study at a later date. In addition, they will not be able to avail themselves of "the taking of notes [that] seems to ease the load on the working memory and thereby helps people resolve complex problems" (Boch & Piolat, 2005, p. 104). Because graphic organizers are filled in by the students, often with teacher and peer collaboration, they are an excellent way to get students to take notes without becoming frustrated or overwhelmed. Graphic organizers call for key words and concepts, thus limiting the amount of information that needs to be included. In addition, because they are visual, graphic organizers provide a guide as to what to look for and where to include the information. This is very important for ELLs because they are learning both the content and the language.

A plethora of graphic organizers exist and are available online, many of them for free. Following are three of the many kinds of graphic organizers available:

- *Venn Diagram.* Good for comparing and contrasting ideas, character traits, and concepts. The diagram can be used to compare vocabulary words (see Figure 9.2).
- *Alpha Boxes.* Good for activating prior knowledge. Give students at the start of a lesson or unit and have them fill in the words with which they are familiar. Have them add new words as they go through the lesson. The chart can be used as a formative assessment (see Figure 9.3).

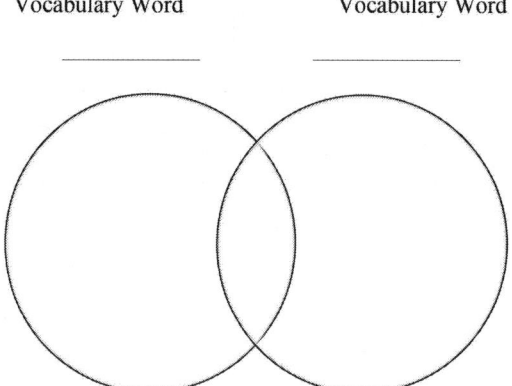

Vocabulary Word   Vocabulary Word

_____   _____

Figure 9.2   Venn diagram.

A	B	C	D
E	F	G	H
I	J	K	L
M	N	O	P
Q	R	S	T
U	VW	XY	Z

Figure 9.3   Alpha boxes.

- *Form, Meaning, and Use.* This is an example of a graphic organizer for high-level ELLs that can be used to help them with form, meaning, and use (see Figure 9.4).

Creating Comprehensive Word Lists

Teachers should select the appropriate words to be taught for a particular lesson. Baumann and Graves (2010) recommend several questions teachers should ask when thinking about what vocabulary to teach:

1. What words are "essential for the understanding of the lesson"?

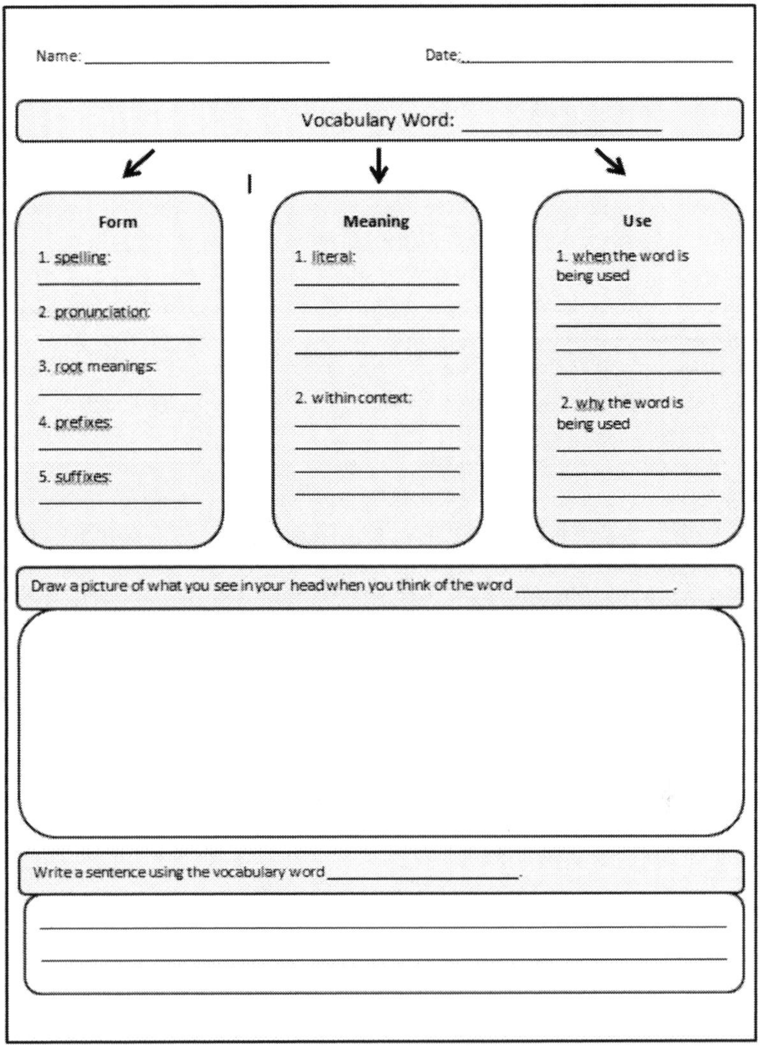
Name: ______ Date: ______

Vocabulary Word: ______

Form
1. spelling: ______
2. pronunciation: ______
3. root meanings: ______
4. prefixes: ______
5. suffixes: ______

Meaning
1. literal: ______
2. within context: ______

Use
1. when the word is being used ______
2. why the word is being used ______

Draw a picture of what you see in your head when you think of the word ______.

Write a sentence using the vocabulary word ______.

Figure 9.4 Form, meaning, and use graphic organizer.

2. What words are "important for developing a broader reading and writing vocabulary"?
3. What words are "common, but not likely to be known by the students"?
4. What words are "not in the selection but represent themes in narrative or key concepts in informational texts" (Baumann & Graves, 2010, p. 8)?

At some point, teachers should address all of the above questions, but helping students understand the lesson should be central to what they do. Although we would like to think that the learning that occurs in our classrooms is all that should concern us, we need to keep in mind the reality of standardized tests. In order to do well on them, students not only need to learn the daily lessons, but develop a broad reading and writing vocabulary, along with common words and words that represent themes in narrative texts and key concepts in informational texts.

In order to truly meet the needs of students, teachers need to know their students. Are their students at the beginner level, intermediate, or are they advanced learners? Did they attend schools in their home countries? Can they read and write in their home language, and at what level? All activities should be completed with an eye towards assessment so that subsequent lessons can be created to meet the students' needs. Who should, though, be creating word lists for students?

Teachers are taught to teach vocabulary, but students are the ones who know if they understand a word or not. For this reason, teachers should sometimes let students decide what it is that they need to learn. If students are allowed to designate what words they want and desire to learn, they may be more motivated to learn the words. An easy assignment for students is to ask them to look over a reading assignment and select the words on which they want to focus. Of course, teachers are the ones in the classroom with a true understanding of the content, so they cannot always relinquish the creating of word lists to the students.

Still, the following question remains: What words should be selected? Sweeny and Mason (2011) recommend teachers should follow these steps when selecting vocabulary:

1. Read text selection(s) in advance to determine instructional purpose.
2. Identify words or concepts students need to know.
3. Identify connections and relationships between words or concepts chosen for instruction.
4. Choose words students must know prior to reading.
5. Decide which words students only need to know incidentally and therefore do not require direct teaching.
6. Determine what you want the children to learn (p. 3).

Basic Academic Words in Classrooms

At the start of this chapter, you were given a definition of academic vocabulary words. Following is another definition. Townsend and Kiernan (2015) define academic vocabulary words as:

Words that appear with much greater frequency in academic texts than in other types of texts, such as literacy texts or popular media. In addition, academic vocabulary words are typically abstract, technical, nuanced, and/or densely packed with meaning. (p. 113)

While researching the definition of academic vocabulary, Baumann and Graves (2010) found a plethora of terms: "general academic vocabulary, academic literacy, academic background, general academic words, domain knowledge," (p. 4) to name just a few. Some of the terms have the same meaning and some of them have several definitions (Baumann & Graves, 2010).

Baumann and Graves developed a classification scheme with five types of "academic words and conceptual representations" (2010 p. 9) that could be of benefit to teachers. Table 9.8 includes Baumann's and Graves types, definitions, and examples.

Researchers have created various lists of words. For example, there is the 220 word Dolch list (Pressley, 2005) of most frequently used words, or basic sight words for pre-primer to second graders. Burke (2015) has created an

TABLE 9.8   Baumann and Graves' Academic Vocabulary Classification

Types and Definitions	Definition	Examples
Domain-specific academic vocabulary	The relatively low-frequency, content-specific words and phrases that appear in content area textbooks and other technical writing materials.	Math: apex, bisect, geometry, polyhedron, Pythagorean theorem, scalene triangle
General Academic vocabulary	Words that appear reasonably frequently within and across academic domains. The words may be polysemous, with different definitions being relevant to different domains.	Analyze, assume, code, conduct, context, document, error, link, minor, period, project, range, register, role, sum (all selected from Coxhead's 2000 list)
Literary vocabulary	Words that authors of literature use to describe characters, settings, and characters' problems and actions.	Awkward, chortled, diffident, haphazardly, hyperbolic, mellow, sun-drenched, serene, stern, suavely, tornadic, torrid.
Metalanguage	Terms used to describe the language of literacy and literacy instruction and words used to describe processes, structures, or concepts commonly included in content area texts.	Language of Literacy and Instruction: epic, genre, glossary, idiom, infer. Processes in Content Area Texts: calculate, compare, estimate, explain
Symbols	Icons, emoticons, graphics, mathematical notations, electronic symbols, and so forth that are not conventional words.	$X-24, >, a2 + b2 = c2$, %, ¶, ;-), ™, 5, $, &

Academic Vocabulary List with words that have been "categorized by parts of speech" (p. 3). This list also includes nouns, adjectives, verbs, and adverb suffixes. An example of how the suffixes appear on the Burke list (2015) is found below in Table 9.9.

Burke's list (2015) also includes common prefixes and their meanings. Table 9.10 shows an example of how three of them are presented and defined.

Other Tips and Strategies

This section of the chapter will offer additional strategies to help students build their academic vocabulary. Teachers often encourage students, both in ESOL and regular classes, to look up words in the dictionary. What usually happens, though, is that students look up the words and then have to look up additional words because the words used to define the original words are unknown to them. This usually leads to frustration. Dictionaries should not be banned, but Sibold (2011, p. 26) offers a strategy that reduces the kind of frustration often encountered with dictionaries.

Presenting a New Word

1. Introduce the word.
2. Provide synonyms.
3. Describe or explain the word.
4. Use the word in a sentence.

TABLE 9.9 Burke Suffixes

Noun Suffixes	Adjective Suffixes	Verb Suffixes	Adverb Suffixes
-ability	-able	-ate	-ly
-ant	-ed	-fy	-fully
-ar	-er	-iate	-iately

TABLE 9.10 Burke Prefixes

Prefix	Meaning(s)
ant-	against, opposite, opposing
auto-	self
dys-	bad

When possible, a visual should be introduced along with the introduction of the word. Students should then be encouraged to repeat the words and create additional sentences.

Word Cards

Students can be encouraged to keep tract of their academic vocabulary on word cards (see Figure 9.5). As words are introduced in a lesson, students write the word on one side of a card; index cards with a punched hole held together with a metal ring work well. On the flip side of the card, the student should draw a picture or cut out an image from a magazine or newspaper. If it is of help, the student can write the following on the back of the card:

- a sentence using the word
- synonyms
- the word in the home language

Students should be encouraged to make cards for words they hear outside of the classroom also: television, radio, hallway, movies, playground, and so forth.

Music

Using music is a great strategy for teaching and learning English. They can be used to understand culture, values, and beliefs, but they can also be used to teach and learn vocabulary. Songs can be used for pronunciation. Most students like to find out the meanings of the words they are singing.

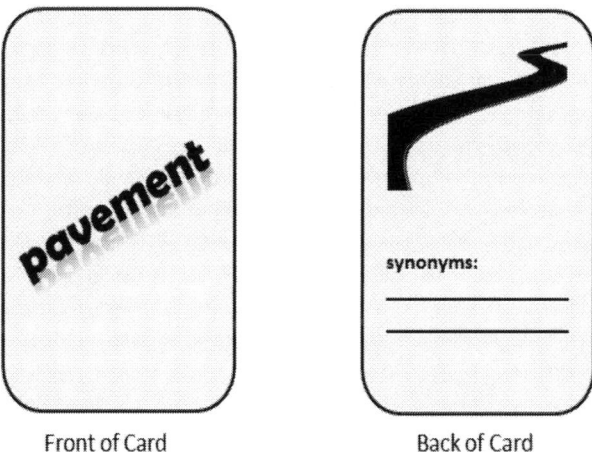

Front of Card   Back of Card

Figure 9.5 Flashcards.

Billy Joel's *We Didn't Start the Fire,* with all of its references to historical figures and facts is a great song to use in high school history courses.

> Little Rock, Pasternak, Mickey Mantle, Kerouac
> Sputnik, Chou En-Lai, "Bridge on the River Kwai"...
>
> Lebanon, Charles de Gaulle, California baseball
> Starkweather, homicide, children of thalidomide...
>
> "Wheel of Fortune," Sally Ride, heavy metal, suicide
> Foreign debts, homeless vets, AIDS, crack, Bernie Goetz
> Hypodermics on the shores, China's under martial law
> Rock and roller cola wars, I can't take it anymore

Embedded in the song are historical figures and facts, but also regular vocabulary words. Billy Joel's song is a fast paced one, but most pop songs have the features that lend themselves to learning English. They

- contain many personal pronouns and short, common, short words;
- are written at the fifth-grade level;
- contain language that is conversational;
- are sung at a slower pace than regular, spoken English;
- contain more pauses; and
- are very repetitive.

A cloze activity can be used with a song's lyrics to see if the students' words come close semantically. Songs can be used to highlight and explain difficult-to-understand idioms. Students can also be asked to "rewrite" some of the lyrics using synonyms.

Read Aloud

Are read alouds only for the lower grades? Definitely not! Many students, including high schoolers, enjoy listening to a teacher read, especially if the teacher reads with emphasis and passion. I can still see the faces of my students when we read "Sinners in the Hands of an Angry God," by Cotton Mather. I had a fellow teacher who had what we call a "radio" voice. He had a powerful, articulate, passionate voice. When he walked into our classroom wearing an academic robe, we knew we were in for a treat; we felt we were transported back to Mather's church and that his angry, pleading voice was reverberating from the classroom walls. My high school students were transfixed!

When using the Read Aloud strategy, all words in the text should not be treated the same. The teacher needs to identify which words will receive extra emphasis and the words should be "infused into instruction and practice...before, during, and after the...[selection] has been read to students"

(Sweeny & Mason, 2011, p. 5). If the teacher has the students revisit the words throughout the day or at another time during the week, students come to see learning vocabulary should not be done in a vacuum—increasing vocabulary should be part of what they should be doing on a regular basis.

Reading, Grammar, and Writing (RGW)—An Integrated Approach

I've never seen a student become excited when told, "We are now going to do some vocabulary work." Very often, students are taught new vocabulary by (a) hearing the new word, (b) writing the word, (c) looking up the words in a dictionary, (d) writing the word's definition, and (e) writing a sentence to demonstrate they understand the word's meaning.

If they go through this activity every week with several new words, no wonder they become bored with vocabulary development. Learning new academic vocabulary words, though, does not have to be boring. Below you will find a way of integrating vocabulary words, literature, and grammar that is not boring because long periods of time are not spent on any one activity, and students get the opportunity to use the words shortly after learning them. This strategy can be used with any grade level.

1. Select a reading passage (short story, novel chapter, or even poem).
2. Have students read along with the teacher.
3. As they read, have them write down whatever words they do not understand.
4. Once the passage has been read, the class has a discussion about the topic first and then they review the vocabulary words the students wrote down.
5. Students work to determine the meaning of the words by looking for prefixes, suffixes, root words, and context.
6. The class as a whole, with the teacher's help, determines the meanings of the words.
7. The students are then given a writing assignment to demonstrate they understand the words. Students should be given a writing prompt that calls upon their creativity—one that is fun to address yet meets the lesson's requirements.

When using this strategy, the class focuses on three areas: literature, vocabulary development, and writing. The students hear the words, deconstruct the vocabulary words by looking for roots, prefixes, and suffixes, and then they use the words in their writing. By the end of the class, students have heard and written the words several times. This kind of activity breaks up a class so that students do not get bored doing only one thing during a full period. Students also come to realize the interconnectedness of vocabulary, grammar, and writing.

SUMMARY

This chapter focuses on teaching academic vocabulary words to ELLs. The chapter begins with a case scenario about Juan, a gregarious ELL from Ecuador to indicate the importance of vocabulary. The chapter then discusses the importance of building academic vocabulary. The chapter discusses how learning vocabulary is much more than recognizing, memorizing, and being able to pronounce a list of words. In order to help ELLs, teachers have to help students go beyond this and learn how to decode words. Students should have multiple exposures to the new vocabulary words, with adequate time to discuss and practice them. Teachers need to keep in mind form (word's spelling and pronunciation), meaning (the literal meaning of a word and the meaning of a word within the reading's context), and use (when and why a word is being used). The chapter continues with several strategies, such as scaling words, making cognate connections, using semantic features and graphic organizers, creating comprehensive word lists, and including music in the classroom. It ends with RGW—An integrated approach to learning vocabulary.

REFERENCES

Alharbi, A. M. (2015). Building vocabulary for language learning: Approach for ESL learners to study new vocabulary. *Journal Of International Students, 5*(4), 501–511.

Baumann, J. F., & Graves, M. F. (2010). What is academic vocabulary? *Journal of Adolescent & Adult Literacy,* (1), 4–12.

Blachowicz, C. L. Z., Fisher, P., & Watts-Taffe, S. (2006). *Integrated vocabulary instruction: meeting the needs of diverse learners in grades 1–5.* Naperville, IL: Learning Point Associates.

Boch, F., & Piolat, A. (2005). Note taking and learning: A summary of research. *WAC Journal, 16,* 101–113.

Burke, J. (2015) *Academic vocabulary list.* West Virginia Department of Education website. *Retrieved* from http://www.englishcompanion.com/pdfDocs/acvocabulary2.pdf

Chung, S. F. (2012). Research-based vocabulary instruction for English Language Learners. *Reading Matrix: An International Online Journal, 12*(2), 105–120.

Colorín Colorado. (2007). *Using cognates to develop comprehension in English.* Retrieved from http://www.colorincolorado.org/article/14307/

Coxhead, A. (2000). A new academic word list. *TESOL Quarterly, 34*(2), 213–238.

Cummins, J. (1981). Age on arrival and immigrant second language learning in Canada: A reassessment. *Applied Linguistics, 1,* 132–149.

Cummins, J., & Ontario Inst. for Studies in Education, T. P. (1979). Cognitive/Academic Language Proficiency, Linguistic Interdependence, the Optimum Age Question and Some Other Matters. *Working Papers on Bilingualism,* No. 19.

Gallavan, N. P., & Kottler, E. (2007). Eight types of graphic organizers for empowering social studies students and teachers. *Social Studies, 98*(3), 117–128.

Goldenberg, C. (2008, Summer). Teaching English Language Learners: What the research does—and does not—say. *American Educator, 32*, 8–44.

Hartle, J. B., & Hawking, S. W. (1983). Wave function of the universe. *Physical Review D, 28*(12), 2960.

Lehr, F., & Osborn J. (2005). *A focus on professional development: research-based practices in early reading series*. Honolulu, HI: Pacific Resources for Education and Learning.

Lessard-Clouston, M. (2013). *Teaching vocabulary*. Alexandria, VA: TESOL International Association.

McKenna, M. C., & Robinson, R. D. (2014). Teaching through text: Reading and writing in the content areas (2nd ed.). New York, NY: Pearson.

Montelongo, J. A., Hernández, A. C., Herter, R. J., & Cuello, J. (2011). Using cognates to scaffold context clue strategies for Latino ELs. *The Reading Teacher, 6*, 429.

Montelongo, J. J., Hernández, A., & Herter, R. J. (2011). Identifying Spanish-English cognates to scaffold instruction for Latino ELLs. *Reading Teacher, 65*(2), 161–164.

Nagy, W. E. (2005). Why vocabulary instruction needs to be long-term and comprehensive. In E. H. Hiebert and M. L. Kamil (Eds.), *Teaching and learning vocabulary: Bringing research to practice* (pp. 27–44). Mahwah, NJ: Lawrence Erlbaum.

National Behavior Support Service (NBSS). (n.d.). Vocabulary/knowledge rating comprehension and learning strategy. *Navan Education Centre*. Retrieved from http://education.ky.gov/curriculum/lit/Documents/kclm/vocabulary_rating_comprehension_strategy_teaching%20tools.pdf.

Pavlik, A. (2012). *Teaching English language learners from China* (Honors Thesis). Retrieved from http://scholars.unh.edu/cgi/viewcontent.cgi?article=1068&context=honors

Peregoy, S., & Boyle, O. (2012). *Reading, writing, and learning in ESL: A resource book for teaching K–12 English learners* (6th ed.). Boston, MA: Pearson.

Pressley, M. (2005). *Dolch 220 basic word: Dolch professional development guide*. Columbus, OH: SRA.

Ramirez, G., Chen, X., & Pasquarella, A. (2013). Cross-linguistic transfer of morphological awareness in Spanish-speaking English Language Learners: The facilitating effect of cognate knowledge. *Topics in Language Disorders, 33*(1), 73–92.

Ryan, C. (2013). Language use in the United States: 2011. American Community Survey. US Census Bureau. Accessed 26 August 2015 at https://www.census.gov/prod/2013pubs/acs-22.pdf

Sibold, C. (2011). Building English language learners' academic vocabulary: Strategies and tips. *Multicultural Education, 18*(2), 24–28.

Sweeny, S. M., & Mason, P. A. (2011, August). Research-based practices in vocabulary instruction: An analysis of what works in grades PreK–12. Prepared by the Studies & Research Committee of the Massachusetts Reading Association, Boston, MA.

Townsend, D., & Kiernan, D. (2015). Selecting academic vocabulary words worth learning. *The Reading Teacher*, (1), 113.

CHAPTER 10

INCREASING CULTURAL AWARENESS FOR TEACHERS

Cristina Alfaro
San Diego State University

CASE SCENARIO

I began my educational journey as a runaway kindergartener on the first day of school. I entered school as a fluent Spanish speaker with a teacher whose first classroom rule stated, "English Only"; if you want to speak, you must speak English only. Since I did not speak English, I did not understand this rule. As the teacher was explaining an art project that we were going to do in a partner activity, I was excited and enthusiastic about it. I wanted to understand what she was saying, so I then asked my friend, who was somewhat bilingual, "¿Qué dijo la maestra?" ("What did the teacher say?"). At that moment, Mrs. Paulson walked up to me and said here is an example of breaking rule #1. All eyes were on me as Mrs. Paulson walked me over to the other side of the room, she told me to go sit at a desk positioned in the corner of the room, next to the door; she directed me to put on the "donkey ears" placed on that desk—this was the consequence for speaking Spanish in the classroom. I saw the donkey ears, I saw my peers staring at me, I saw the door. At that moment I saw my only way out of this humiliation was to run out the door and away from school! Years later, I received my Bilingual Teaching Credential and I contacted Mrs. Paulson and asked if she would

Teaching ELLs Across Content Areas, pages 237–259
Copyright © 2016 by Information Age Publishing
All rights of reproduction in any form reserved.   **237**

like to meet with me for coffee. She accepted my invitation. She thought I was going to thank her for making a positive impact in my life. By this time, she was retired and was happy to see one of her former students. In our meeting, I shared with her my feeling of despair, humiliation, and cognitive dissonance that her "English Only" rule caused me due to her disregard for an ELL's culture and linguistic background. With tears in her eyes she responded: "I was sincerely wrong; it was my belief that the sooner my students stopped speaking Spanish, the better their chance of learning English and becoming successful."

Mrs. Paulson was not an evil person wishing to inflict harm on her students with this English hegemonic unjust practice. The reality is that she had been colonized by society, as many teachers are, believing that there is no time to be spent on engaging a student's funds of knowledge (Gándara & Hopkins, 2010; Moll, Amanti, Neff, & Gonzalez, 1992) in the English-only classroom, and that there was no place in her classroom for her students' Spanish native language, even if this was at the cost of her students' cognitive and socio-psychological development (Garcia & Sylvan, 2011). Despite no definitive research that links teachers' ideological stances with instructional practices, many scholars suggest that a teacher's ideological orientation is often reflected in her or his beliefs and attitudes about English Language Learners (ELLs) and their families and are therefore, consequently reflected in the manner she or he teaches students (Alfaro, 2008; Alfaro, Durán, Hunt, & Aragón, 2014; Macedo, 2000; Sleeter, 2001). The extremely rapid growth of linguistically and culturally diverse students in today's classrooms has elevated the pressing need for culturally and linguistically competent EL teachers (Bartolomé, 2010; Gándara & Hopkins, 2010; Garcia, 2014).

ROLE OF CULTURALLY, LINGUISTICALLY COMPETENT EDUCATORS

In today's culturally and linguistically diverse society, all teachers teach or will teach ELLs. However, many practicing mainstream teachers have not been adequately prepared to engage ELLs in their classrooms through a cultural wealth model. Yosso (2005) identifies seven forms of cultural wealth; given the focus in this chapter, the focus is on linguistic, social, and familial capital.

Teachers must become researchers of their students and communities to engage the ELLs in significant learning. Recent research studies framed using the cultural wealth model have begun identifying the characteristics of linguistic cultural wealth to better prepare teachers to work with ELLs and their communities (Gonzalez, et al., 2005; Olivos, Jiménez-Castellanos, & Ochoa, 2011; Valdez, 1996). Given what we know about the importance of teacher knowledge regarding the community they serve, it is critical that teachers engage in the process of gaining community knowledge to enrich their instruction and to provide a framework for teaching in a relevant, purposeful, respectful, and powerful manner.

Community School Scan Process

The reality is that teachers of ELLs will most likely teach in communities where classrooms are made up of culturally and linguistically diverse learners. Hence, culturally and linguistically competent teachers must have the vision of working and learning from their ELLs' community context; this prepares them to effectively support their students' learning, as well as provide an infrastructure for students to support one another's thinking and learning. The Community School Scan Process (CSSP) developed by Ochoa (2012) is the initial foundational activity to prepare teachers to acquire cultural and linguistic competence to enrich the curricula and the strategies they use with the community's funds of knowledge (Moll et al., 1992). The CSSP prepares teachers to reach beyond knowing about the general and many times superficial cultural events, holidays, traditions, sayings, and beliefs; it delves into the contextual reality of their ELLs real-time life experiences.

Actualizing the CSSP Steps

CSSP guides the work of teaching and learning in linguistically and culturally diverse communities, more significantly it assists teachers in developing relevant, purposeful, and powerful lessons as they prepare to teach ELLs.

Step I. Teachers individually or with a grade level CSSP Team review the five components of the CSSP: (a) demographic characteristics, (b) cultural characteristics, (c) associational patterns, (d) patterns of influence, and (e) socio-psychological attitudes and conditions, further described below.

Step II. Teachers enter into a critical dialogue with regard to answering the following questions about what constitutes a school community.

- How is the community a mosaic of the cultural diversity and complexity?
- How does one identify the needs and concerns of the community?
- How does one use the community resources to benefit children/youth/families?
- How does one incorporate the community assets and resources (funds of knowledge) of the school community in the school's curriculum?

Step III. Teachers engage a participatory action research approach suggested by Stringer (2009), who describes the practitioner inquiry process as a "Look, Think, Act" cycle. The "Look" phase is the process of examining the physical geography, the sociocultural and linguistic spaces, and the sociopolitical influences of the community, using available data, people, observations, and analyzing its sources. The "Think" phase refers to the reflection process and/or critique of the sources collected on the school community, as well as the social, educational, economic, and political implications of the patterns found under each of the five components. The "Act" phase begins with identifying the sociocultural assets and resources of the community that can be incorporated into the school curriculum and the strategies teachers use to contextualize concepts and multiple meaning for ELLs. I view this challenge as a fundamental matter of equity that teachers can either announce or denounce dimensions of equitable classroom practices (Alfaro, et al., 2015) and can thus affect the equality or inequality of ELLs' education experience.

Formulating the CSSP Questions

To actualize the CSSP, teachers are provided with a bank of questions that correspond to five specific components. Questions are meant to provoke inquiry to begin the work in designing, conceptualizing, and actualizing the CSSP to study the selected EL school community. The following subsections provide a selected number of sample questions that serve as a representative sample of an extensive bank of questions developed by Ochoa (2012).

Demographic questions. This first component examines the geography and physical characteristics of the school community.

- What is the ethnic diversity of the community and how has it changed overtime?
- What are the patterns of achievement by the ethnic group over the years? Dropouts? Special education? Gifted?
- What is the income distribution by ethnicity? Housing patterns? What type of industry or economic sectors is present in the community?
- What hospitals, clinics, and social services are accessible to the community?
- What types of jobs are available for your students' families and caretakers?

Cultural questions. This second component examines the sociocultural characteristics of the school community. As one walks through the main streets of the community, what are the (a) images, (b) sounds, (c) smells and tastes, (d) modes of interactions, and (e) sense of belongingness?

- What is the history of the community? How was the community started? What are major historical events? Holidays? Important traditions? Important sayings?
- What is the history of ethnically diverse groups in the school community?
- Cross-culturally, how are families organized (i.e., what is the father role, mother role, child role)? Are families nuclear or extended? What ties are there to relatives?
- What recreational activities do families prefer?
- What are the food preferences and eating habits? What do they normally eat for breakfast, lunch, or dinner?
- What holidays are considered important to the cultural groups in the community?
- What TV programs do they watch? Do they listen to radio or television programs in languages other than English?
- What newspapers or magazines do people read?
- What music is popular?
- Who are the apparent heroes, sports figures, politicians, and movie stars, social activists, others?
- What is the folklore of the community?

Socio-attitudinal questions. This fifth component examines the explicit and implicit linguistic and cultural dynamics and tensions in the school community.

- What is the community social climate towards ethnically diverse immigrants?
- How do interethnic and interracial marriages shape the identities of children, couples, families, and communities?
- How do the different cultural groups in the community see social and economic status? Sexual orientation? Marital status? Racial academic ability? Religious practices? Cultural heritage?
- What is the perceived dominant culture in the community? What are the perceived subordinate cultures in the community? Who feels powerless?
- What dominant stereotypes exist in the community? How are they stumbling blocks for communication? Pre-conceptions of how people view other people?
- What anxiety, fears, tension exit in the community that skew perceptions? Withdrawal, or hostility?

- What people or groups are considered agitators, radicals, trouble-makers, etc. Why?

The breadth of cultural, linguistic, and familial wealth data collected in each of the five areas described above becomes the descriptive community profile to be used by teachers for reflection and development of curriculum that is guided by socio-constructivist principles (Kincheloe, 2008).

There is no magic bullet of how to teach linguistically and culturally diverse students; teachers that sincerely desire to learn how to connect to their students' *funds of knowledge* and want to make a positive difference in teaching ELLs can use the CSSP to help guide their work in teaching and learning, even if it means that it will require additional time and effort. Teachers that engage in the CSSP have the potential to experience a great deal of satisfaction and confidence when they realize that the initial steps to developing cultural and community knowledge will pay off for them, and their students, in the long run because they will be able to teach in more meaningful and powerful ways that positively impact their students' education and life chances.

Once teachers have gone through the process of obtaining a solid knowledge base of their students' contextual reality and use of effective EL teaching strategies; they must also engage in the process of developing a clear understanding of how the ideology that informs their pedagogy determines the level of EL curriculum access and equitable spaces in their classroom.

Ideology. What and How to Think About ELLs.—It is essential for teachers to gain a firm understanding of dominant ideologies and develop useful counterhegemonic discourses that can resist and transform oppressive practices in today's culturally and linguistically diverse classrooms (Darder, 2015). The process of critical dialogue, continuous self-questioning, and reflection emanates the evolution of an awaking to critical consciousness (*conscientizacao*) that beacons teachers toward ideological clarity (Freire, 1993). A teacher's well-articulated ideological clarity is the beacon that will empower her/him to navigate through, with, and around the sociopolitical-restrictive language policy agendas and standards waves. It is important for teachers to arrive at the realization that it is their ideology that "announces or denounces" teaching for equity and social justice. Bartolomé (2010) explains that ideological clarity requires that teachers' individual explanations be continually compared and contrasted with those propagated by the dominant society. It is to be hoped that the juxtaposing of ideologies forces teachers to better understand if, when, and how their belief systems uncritically reflect those of the dominant society and support unfair and inequitable conditions (p. 168). Additionally, Freire (1993) reminds us that teaching and learning in schools constitutes a political act tied to the ideological forces that operate on behalf of the dominant class. Education never is, has been, or will be a neutral enterprise (p. 127). In order for teachers to experience a breakthrough to epistemological solidarity in their classroom practice with ELLs, they must work diligently to become ideologically clear—They must ask themselves: What beliefs, values, and epistemological theories inform my thinking about teaching ELLs? Do I sincerely believe that all children have the potential to learn and be great contributors to society? Do I honestly value my ELLs' *funds of knowledge?* Have I made an effort to learn about my students' community, culture, and language? What are the political, social, cultural, linguistic, gendered, and emotional circumstances in which I have learned? What kind of teacher do I want to be? What do I want my students to know and do well? How do I want my students to remember what we learned together? What kind of changes do I need to make to my teaching that will enhance my students' bi-cultural/multicultural identity and literacy development?

Engaging ELL Parents

ELL parents are primarily engaged in their child's education at home and out of the schools (Moreno & Lopez, 1999). Given this view, teachers can mistake that parents are not engaged and/or do not care about their child's school socialization and academic progress. The challenge then becomes the act of breaking down these silos informed by deficit views and creates communication barriers. Current research informs us that the more parents are engaged in their child's education the better their child will perform academically. This is especially true when it comes to the education of ELLs, where their parents play a unique and critical role in their child's school socialization and academic success.

Olivos et al. (2011) argue that the ideal relationship between parents and schools is one of mutual trust, respect, and reciprocity. It is important to recognize the incredible power and force that is held in the hands of parents, if and when teachers extend the opportunity and support for them to participate in their child's academic journey in relevant, meaningful, and purposeful ways. Creating equitable spaces for parent engagement requires a triangular partnership between family, school, and community to better support ELL's academic success. This triangular partnership is intended to break down the silos that exist between the critical stakeholders. The degree of intersections of this triangular partnership can potentially enrich student learning. It is imperative that teachers make it a point to look for and recognize the nonstandard ways that parents partake in their child's school socialization and academic support. Consider the *consejos* (advice) that Latino parents provide their children as well as the support they provide in their native language; these are just a couple of the invisible processes that take place in the home that go unnoticed, devalued, and/or unrecognized by mainstream parent involvement typologies.

Therefore, it is imperative for teachers to not underestimate or under-utilize ELLs parents' ability and willingness to assist in their child's academic success (Rodríguez-Brown, 2010). In order to shift the deficit view of EL parents, especially in low status communities, teachers need to embrace a cultural wealth model where families, and what happens in their home and community, are viewed from a strength-based perspective. The CSSP presented at the beginning of this chapter is an authentic manner for teachers to authentically get acquainted with their students, families, and community hopes, struggles, and dreams. Through this process teachers can begin to develop their unique and authentic relationship with parents through an assets based perspective—where every teacher is a learner and every learner is a teacher (Freire, 1993).

ELL parents appreciate it when a teacher takes the initiative to gain knowledge about their students' culture and learn a little Spanish vocabulary to facilitate the communication between the individuals that most care about a child's school socialization and academic success.

BASIC HISPANIC TRADITIONS, FOODS, HOLIDAYS

The section that follows includes some basic information generated from students and teachers who teach in communities with students of mostly Mexican decent. I have included this section to serve as a basic tool for the non-Spanish speaking teacher to initiate basic communication, in Spanish, with students and their family about their family members, traditions, holidays, and *consejos* (parental/family advice). The intent is that a teachers' cultural, linguistic, and familial knowledge base will continue to evolve and that each individual teachers' cultural wealth bank will take on its unique shape while using this information as a starting point for connecting with their ELLs and their families in more intentional and powerful ways.

The information in Tables 10.1–10.6 regarding basic Hispanic words, vocabulary, traditions, food, holidays, and *consejos* (advice) are only a starting point for teachers; the goal is for teachers to continue their cultural and linguistic quest for knowledge in order to continue to authentically and strategically reach out to students, parents, and their community. It is important to know that other national origin Latino/Hispanic communities throughout the United States will have a different set of traditions, holidays, foods, and even vocabulary words. These Latino/Hispanic cultures might be from the Caribbean, South America, Central America, or even Spain.

I often wonder how different my kindergarten experience could have been if Mrs. Paulson would have known about the cultural wealth model, engaged in the CSSP, and interrogated how her ideology informed her classroom practice which, in her case, negated to create access to the

TABLE 10.1   Basic Language About Family and Cultural Traditions: What Teachers of Latino English Learners Should Know

Family Members	Miembros de Familia
Father	Padre
Mother	Madre
Dad	Papá
Mom	Mamá
Daughter	Hija
Son	Hijo
Sister	Hermana
Brother	Hermano
Grandmother	Abuela
Grandfather	Abuelo
Cousin	Prima (Female)
	Primo (Male)
Uncle	Tio
Aunt	Tia
Godmother	Madrina (niña)
Godfather	Padrino (niño)
Goddaughter	Ahijada
Godson	Ahijado
Relationship between the parents and godparents (no existing word)	Comadre (Female)
	Compadre (Male)
Great grandfather	Bisabuelo
Great grandmother	Bisabuela
Great great grandfather	Tatarabuelo
Great great grandmother	Tatarabuela

curriculum and did not provide an equitable and safe learning space for ELLs, "*como yo*" (like me).

It is important to point out that much of the literature on the preparation of EL teachers focuses on imparting technical knowledge such as the various methodologies that will help them develop expertise in a range of content areas for teaching in language settings where the majority of students are ELLs or Emergent Bilinguals (Wright, Boun, & Garcia, 2015). It is imperative to recognize that equally as important to teachers' knowledge of these technical/EL strategies and methodological skills is a teacher's knowledge of how a well-developed ideology informs a teachers' pedagogy that creates access to a rigorous curriculum as well as equity in the EL classroom. Teachers must subscribe to a framework that challenges the notion of English language development as a monolithic construct; on the contrary they must view it as the balancing of asymmetric powers embedded in the complexity of cultural wealth and asset-based approaches and relations.

TABLE 10.2   Basic Language About Family and Cultural Traditions: What Teachers of Latino English Learners Should Know

Basic Greetings	Saludos Básicos
Hi	Hola
Hello	Hola
Good morning	Buenos días
Good afternoon	Buenas tardes
Good evening	Buenas noches
Goodnight	Buenas noches
How are you?	¿Cómo estás? ¿Cómo te va?
Brother	Hermano
Nice to see you	Gusto en saludarte
See you soon	Hasta pronto
See you later	Hasta luego
See you tomorrow	Hasta mañana
Welcome	Bienvenido
Goodbye	Adios
How is your family doing?	¿Cómo está tu familia?
Thank you	Gracias
Thank you very much	Muchas gracias
A thousand thank yous	Mil gracias
We are so glad you came to visit	Estamos tan contentos que nos visita
Please let me know	Por favor, hágamelo saber
I need your help	Necesito su ayuda
We are here to serve you	Estamos aqui para servirle
Please feel free to visit our classroom	Por favor, siéntase libre de visitar nuestro salón de clases

Educational practices that unite students, family, and educators as partners in learning can create pedagogical spaces where teachers have the cultural and linguistic competence necessary to examine further their perceptions about their students and their practice (Flores, 2005). If including students and families in conversations about instruction can change students' attitudes and perceptions of teachers, the same might hold true as a way to increase the sociocultural awareness that shift teachers' attitudes about students and families (Bartolomé, 2010; Stringer, 2009). If teachers are better able to understand the rich experiences of students as learners, it could transform their teaching (Shor, 1992).

In conclusion, teachers working ELLs must develop ideological clarity with respect to their personal and professional beliefs and core values, particularly when it comes to working with ELLs from low-status communities (Alfaro, 2008). Teachers must embrace ELLs from a socio-constructivist

TABLE 10.3 Consejos, Dichos, y Proverbios (Advice, Sayings, and Proverbs)

Spanish Consejos, Dichos, y Proverbios	English Translation/Meaning
Dime con quién andas y te diré quién eres.	Tell me who you walk with and I'll tell you who you are: If you spend a lot of time with a certain type of person(s), you'll start to become more like them. English versions of this saying are "hunt with cats and you catch only rats" and "Birds of a feather flock together."
Dime de que presumes y te diré de qué careces.	Tell me what you boast about and I'll tell you what you lack.
Luz de la calle oscuridad de la casa.	In Spanish there is this saying "Candil de la calle, oscuridad de tu casa." Which is essentially told to people who do good outside (e.g., at work or school), but does nothing good at home for his or her family. A literal translation to English would be something like "A light in the street, but darkness at home."
Camarón que se duerme se lo lleva la corriente.	The shrimp that falls asleep is swept away by the current. Meaning/English equivalent: You snooze, you lose.
Cría cuervos y te sacarán los ojos.	Raise crows and they will peck your eyes out. Meaning/English equivalent: If you take care of indecent people, they will take advantage of you in the end.
Cuando el río suena, agua lleva.	When the river makes noise, it's carrying water. Meaning/English equivalent: Where there's smoke, there's fire.
De tal palo, tal astilla.	Such is the stick, such is the chip. Meaning/English equivalent: Like father, like son.
No hay mal que por bien no venga.	There's no bad from which something good doesn't come. Meaning/English equivalent: Every cloud has a silver lining.
Cuentas claras amistades largas	Clear agreements and long friendship. Meaning: Take of what you owe your friend, otherwise it can potentially lead you to a bad or end of a relationship.
Del dicho al hecho hay mucho trecho.	Meaning: saying is one thing, doing it is another or all talk and no action.
No hay que llegar primero sino hay que saber llegar.	You don't have to arrive first, but you have to know to arrive. Meaning: Don't worry about being the first one to get things done, but instead make sure you know how to do things well.
Hablando del rey de Roma ...	Speaking of the king of Rome ... Meaning/English equivalent: Speak of the Devil ...
Al mal tiempo, buena cara.	Put a good face to bad times. Meaning/English equivalent: Be positive even in bad situations.
Barriga llena, corazón contento.	Full stomach, happy heart.
Ojos que no ven, corazón que no siente.	Eyes that don't see, heart that doesn't feel. Meaning/English equivalent: Out of sight, out of mind.

TABLE 10.4   Traditional Mexican Food/Comida Típica Mexicana

Name and Description	Visual Representation
Tamales/ Tamales are packets of corn dough with a savory or sweet filling and typically wrapped in corn husks or banana leaves. As with most Mexican foods each region of Mexico has its own specialties.	
Mole is the generic name for a number of sauces originally used in Mexican cuisine, as well as for dishes based on these sauces. Outside Mexico, it often refers specifically to mole poblano. In contemporary Mexico, the term is used for a number of sauces, some quite dissimilar, including black, red, yellow, colorado (another name for red), green, almendrado, de olla, huaxmole, and pipián.	
Menudo is a traditional Mexican soup (also known as pancita) made with beef stomach (tripe) in broth with a red chili pepper base. Usually, lime, chopped onions, and chopped cilantro are added, as well as crushed oregano and crushed red chili peppers. Menudo is usually eaten with corn tortillas or other breads, such as bolillo.	
Pozole/posole is made from nixtamalized cacahuazintle maize, with meat, usually pork, chicken, turkey, pork rinds, chili peppers, and other seasonings and garnish such as cabbage, salsa, and limes and/or lemons. Pozole is served in Mexican restaurants worldwide.	
Tacos are flour or corn tortillas topped with traditional roasted meats such as carne asada (beef). Other popular meats are chorizo, a spicy sausage, grilled chicken, fish, or roasted pork. Many tacos use various other parts of the animal. Tacos are served with salsa, guacamole, and other veggies.	
Flautas are a Mexican food dish most often consisting of a small rolled-up tortilla and some type of filling, including beef, cheese, or chicken. The filled tortilla is crisp-fried. The dish is often topped with condiments such as salsa and guacamole.	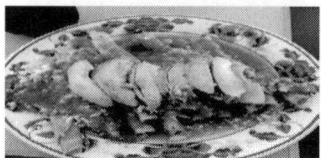

(continued)

TABLE 10.4   Traditional Mexican Food/Comida Típica Mexicana (cont.)

Name and Description	Visual Representation

Sopes originated in the central and southern parts of Mexico, where it was sometimes first known as pellizcadas. It is an antojito which at first sight looks like an unusually thick tortilla with vegetables and meat toppings. The base is made from a circle of fried masa of ground maize in lime (also used as the basis for tamales and tortillas) with pinched sides. This is then topped with refried black beans and crumbled cheese, lettuce, onions, acidified cream, red or green salsa. The salsa is made with chiles or tomatillos, respectively).

Caldo de Res/Beef Soup allows so many variations; from the most simple broth with two or three vegetables and some herbs. It includes different cuts of meat and a great selection of vegetables that can be savored as a main dish or as an entrée dish. The vegetables vary depending on the region of México. It is usually served with rice and in some regions the meat and vegetables are served on a separate plate.

Elote/Corn on the Cob is a popular street food in Mexico, although it is frequently served at home and prepared in the same way (boiled or grilled in husk). In Mexico, Chicago, and the southern United States, it is customary to consume elotes on a stick or by grasping the husk of the cob that has been pulled down to form a "handle." Condiments such as salt, chilli powder, butter, cheese, lemon juice, mayonnaise, and sour cream (or crema) are usually added to the elote. Lemon pepper seasoning is popular as a condiment in Texas. Another way of presenting elotes is by serving the cut kernels in a bowl.

Torta is a Mexican Sandwich filled with meats and vegetables on a special bread.

(continued)

TABLE 10.4 Traditional Mexican Food/Comida Típica Mexicana (cont.)

Name and Description	Visual Representation

Nopales are a common ingredient in numerous Mexican cuisine dishes. The nopal pads can be eaten raw or cooked, used in marmalades, soups, stews, and salads, as well as used for traditional medicine or as fodder for animals.

Frijoles charros/cowboy beans is a traditional Mexican dish. It is named after the traditional Mexican horsemen, or charros. The dish is characterized by pinto beans stewed with onion, garlic, and bacon. Other common ingredients include chili peppers, tomatoes, cilantro, ham, sausage, pork, and chorizo. It is served warm and is usually of a soupy consistency.

Salsa/sauce is often a tomato based sauce or dip which is heterogeneous and includes additional components such as (but not limited to) onions, peppers, beans, corn, and various spices. They are typically piquant, ranging from mild to extremely hot.

Aguas frescas/Cool waters are a combination of fruits, cereals, flowers, or seeds blended with sugar and water to make light nonalcoholic beverages. They are popular in Mexico, Central America, the Caribbean, and the United States. Some of the more common flavors include tamarind, hibiscus, and agua de horchata.

Atole is a traditional hot corn- and masa-based beverage of Mexican, Guatemalan, Honduran, and Salvadoran origin. Chocolate atole is known as champurrado or atole. It is typically accompanied with tamales, and very popular during the Christmas holiday season (Las Posadas).

(continued)

TABLE 10.4   Traditional Mexican Food/Comida Típica Mexicana (cont.)

Name and Description	Visual Representation
Champurrado is a chocolate-based atole, a warm and thick Mexican drink, prepared with either masa de maíz (lime-treated-corn dough), masa harina (a dried version of this dough), or corn flour (simply very finely ground dried corn), panela; water or milk, and occasionally cinnamon, anise seed and or vanilla, ground nuts, orange zest, and egg can also be employed to thicken and enrich the drink. Champurrado is also very popular during Dia de Los Muertos (Day of the Dead in Spanish) and at Las Posadas (the Christmas Season) where it is served alongside tamales. An instant mix for champurrado is available in Mexican grocery stores.	

TABLE 10.5   Traditional South American Food Comida Típica de Sur América

Name and Description	Country	Visual Representation
Ceviche is a seafood dish of fresh fish served in a zesty marinade of lime juice and chili. It is a cold dish, where the acidity of the marinade is what "cooks" the fish from raw.	Peru	
Empanadas are filled with all kinds of flavors and fillings, from the standard beef and cheese fillings, to creamy sweet corn and veggie spinach and ricotta. Across the border you will find regional variations, with meaty salteñas in Bolivia and deep fried Pastels in Brazil. Empanadas will be your South American comfort food.	Argentina Bolivia Brazil	
Chimichurri is a green sauce used for grilled meat, originally from the Rio de la Plata, Argentina. It is made of finely-chopped parsley, minced garlic, olive oil, oregano, and white vinegar. In Uruguay, the dominant flavoring is parsley, garlic, red pepper flakes, and fresh oregano.	Argentina Uruguay	

(continued)

TABLE 10.5 Traditional South American Food Comida Típica de Sur América (continued)

Name and Description	Country	Visual Representation
Coxinhas are chicken drumstick-shaped treats. In this recipe, chicken and cheese are encased in a delicious dough which is covered in breadcrumbs then deep fried until they are golden brown and crispy. They are equally delicious eaten hot or cold and can be served as a snack or as part of a main meal with salad.	Brazil	
Aji Amarillo is a yellow chili pepper used in all sorts of Peruvian dishes. This hot yellow chili pepper has a very distinct taste and gives traditional Peruvian dishes such as aji gallina (hen curry) and papa a la huancaína (potatoes in a spicy cheese sauce) their color and flavor.	Peru	
Arepas are little corn flatbreads are served with cheese, avocado, egg, or jam. They can be eaten for breakfast or an afternoon snack.	Venezuela	
Feijoada is a meaty black bean stew often considered as Brazil's national dish. It is made with various trimmings of salted pork and beef. This hearty chili is cooked in a thick clay pot and served with a variety of sides or alone.	Brazil	
Picarones are doughnuts found in street stalls and food markets. They have their distinctive orange color from the sweet potato and/or pumpkin in the ingredients. They are sweet and sticky, rolled in cinnamon and sugar.	Peru	

(continued)

TABLE 10.5   Traditional South American Food Comida Típica de Sur América (continued)

Name and Description	Country	Visual Representation
Pupusa is a traditional Salvadoran dish made of a thick, handmade corn tortilla (made using masa de maíz, a cornmeal dough used in Mesoamerican cuisine) that is usually filled with cheese, seasoned pork meat, or refried beans.	El Salvador	

TABLE 10.6   Holidays/Dias Festivos

Month	Holiday	Description
January/ Enero	1st Año Nuevo	Celebrates the arrival of the New Year and (la Nochevieja-old night or old year) says goodbye to the old. In much of the Spanish-speaking world, traditions include making a toast, exchanging a kiss or hug, or eating twelve grapes—one for each stroke of midnight—to ensure your wishes come true for the New Year. To wish someone a happy New Year, say ¡Feliz año nuevo! or ¡Próspero año nuevo!
	6th Dia de Reyes	Most of the Hispanic world celebrates El Dia De Reyes, the Epiphany, remembering the day when the three wise men following the star to Bethlehem, arrived bearing their treasured gifts of gold, frankincense, and myrrh for the baby Jesus.
February/ Febrero	2nd Dia de la constitución Mexicana	The Constitution of Mexico (Spanish: Constitución Política de los Estados Unidos Mexicanos) is the current constitution of Mexico. It was drafted in Santiago de Querétaro, in the State of Querétaro, by a constitutional convention, during the Mexican Revolution. It was approved by the Constitutional Congress on February 5, 1917. It is the successor to the Constitution of 1857, and earlier Mexican constitutions.
	14th Día de San Valentin/ Día del Amor y la Amistad	Valentine's Day

(continued)

TABLE 10.6   Holidays/Dias Festivos (continued)

Month	Holiday	Description
March/ Marzo	16th Día Natalicio de Benito Juarez	Was a Mexican lawyer and politician of Zapotec origin from Oaxaca who served as the president of Mexico for five terms; he resisted the French occupation of Mexico, overthrew the second Mexican Empire, restored the Republic, and used liberal measures to modernize the country.
April/Abril	Semana Santa: Jueves Santo, Viernes Santo, y Domingo de resureccion	Is Mexico's second most important holiday season of the year, behind only Christmas, and runs from Palm Sunday to Easter Sunday. In addition to attending mass on Good Friday and Easter Sunday, many Mexicans will also take advantage of the holiday to go on vacation. Holy Week, celebrates the Christian holiday of Easter. Mexico is nearly 90 percent Catholic, so this religious holiday takes on a special meaning that the entire community shares and participates in.
	30th Dia del Niño	Children's Day has been celebrated annually in Mexico since 1925. Children are recognized as an important part of society so the day focuses on the importance of loving, accepting, and appreciating children. Schools host special events inviting parents to celebrate and share Children's Day with students. Parties are held and children take part in activities like face painting, story-telling, art workshops, and plays.
May/Mayo	1st Dia del trabajo	International Workers' Day, also known as Labor Day in some places, is a celebration of laborers and the working classes.
	10th Dia de las Madres	Mothers' Day (El Dia de la Madre) is a popular celebration for mothers and mother figures across Mexico. Mothers and mother figures are given flowers, cards, candy, and other gifts that symbolize appreciation, respect, and love. Mothers' Day is an observance and not a public holiday in Mexico. However, some public offices have been known to close early in the afternoon so employees can spend some of the day with their mothers.
September/ Septiembre	16th Dia de la Independencia/ Día del Grito	Mexicans celebrate their country's Independence Day with fireworks, parties (fiestas), food, dance, and music on September 16. Flags, flowers, and decorations in the colors of the Mexican flag—red, white, and green—are seen in public areas in cities and towns in Mexico. Whistles and horns are blown and confetti is thrown to celebrate this festive occasion. "Viva Mexico" or "Viva la independencia" are shouted amidst the crowds on this day.
November/ Noviembre	2nd Día de los Muertos	El Dia de los Muertos (the Day of the Dead), a Mexican celebration, is a day to celebrate, remember, and

(continued)

TABLE 10.6   Holidays/Dias Festivos (continued)

Month	Holiday	Description
		prepare special foods in honor of those who have departed. On this day in Mexico, the streets near the cemeteries are filled with decorations of papel picado, flowers, candy calaveras (skeletons and skulls), and parades. It is believed that the spirit of the dead visit their families on October 31 and leave on November 2. In order to celebrate, the families make altars and place ofrendas (offerings) of food such as pan de muertos baked in shapes of skulls and figures, candles, incense, yellow marigolds known as cempazuchitl (also spelled zempasuchil), and most importantly a photo of the departed soul is placed on the altar.
	16th Revolucion Mexicana	The Mexican Revolution was a major armed struggle ca. 1910–1920 that radically transformed Mexican politics and society. Although recent research has focused on local and regional aspects of the Revolution, it was a "genuinely national revolution."
December/ Diciembre	12th Día de la Virgen	The Day of the Virgin of Guadalupe (Día de la Virgen de Guadalupe) is a popular Catholic feast that celebrates the belief that a man encountered the Virgin Mary, Mexico's patron saint, in Mexico City on December 9 and 12, 1531. Public celebrations, or fiestas, are held in honor of Mary, the Virgin of Guadalupe, on December 12. Catholics from across Mexico and other countries pay pilgrimage to see an image of Mary (Virgen Morena), believed to be authentic, in the Basilica of Guadalupe in Mexico City. Children are dressed in traditional costumes and are blessed in churches. Thousands of people come to church to pray.
	16th–24th Posadas	Posadas are an important part of Mexican Christmas celebrations. The word posada means "inn" or "shelter" in Spanish, and this tradition reenacts Mary and Joseph's search for a place to stay in Bethlehem. Posadas are held in Mexico on each of the nine nights leading up to Christmas, from December 16–24. Posada parties are not only marked by traditional rituals but are also filled with cheerful socializing, authentic food, and fun for the entire family, including a special Christmas drink and a piñata filled with candy. Mexican piñatas are designed in the shape of a seven-point star, created with cardboard and paper mache, and decorated with crepe paper. The seven points represent the seven deadly sins that need to be destroyed by the "sinner" who is blindfolded (signifying blind faith). Hoping to conquer sin, he attempts to hit the swaying piñata with a stick and break open the center, which bestows him with "blessings" (candy).

(continued)

TABLE 10.6   Holidays/Dias Festivos (continued)

Month	Holiday	Description
	24th Noche Buena	Frequently called Christmas Eve, is a night of celebration within Latino households. While most Americans sit in anticipation of Christmas day, Latinos celebrate early, gathering family and friends for a big dinner; an evening that also has plenty of music and gifts. From household to household traditions may vary, but generally the celebration that begins on the eve of Christmas bleeds into the next day, and Christmas morning is used as a time for rest. Misa de Gallo (Midnight Mass) occurs on the eve of Christmas to commemorate the birth of Jesus, which took place at midnight. Many mass-goers attend service with a baby Jesus figurine so that it can be blessed before placing it back in their nativity. Misa de Gallo, which translates to Mass of Roosters, grew from a legend about a rooster who witnessed and announced the birth of Jesus to the world. It is now a mainstay tradition in many Latino households, and usually led by a feast.
	25th Navidad	Celebrations are held throughout Mexico on Christmas Day (Navidad) each year to commemorate the birth of Jesus, whom many Christians believe is the son of God. It is also a worldwide celebration in most Christian churches on December 25. Christmas Day is often spent as a day to rest after festivities. People wish each other Merry Christmas (Feliz Navidad). It is common to relax, catch up with family and friends, and eat leftovers (recalentado) from Christmas Eve (Noche Buena) dinner.

perspective that views their *funds of knowledge* as assets and strengths upon which to build (Quezada & Alfaro, 2012). As our educational system becomes more culturally responsive to EL school communities it needs to be inclusive of the ideological shifts proposed by Quezada and Alfaro (2012): First, in the development of culturally and linguistically proficient teachers. For urban communities, this means shifting from being a traditional teacher to a *culturally proficient teacher* whose belief system will hold students' cultural backgrounds of language, race, gender, and socioeconomic status as assets on which to construct their educational experiences. Second, teachers as researchers, a shift in the teacher's role from the technician who follows a one-size-fits-all curriculum to a researcher of students' EL background where teachers engage deeply in their understanding of the complexities of school communities. Third, teachers as guides, shift their role from depositors of knowledge to facilitators of knowledge as it relates to ELLs learning the academic and social literacies in their second language simultaneously to access the core curriculum. Fourth, teachers as students and students as teachers, this requires a shift to creating interactive relationships between student and teacher. The teacher creates a constructivist classroom environment in which the learning is reciprocal based on an authentic dialogical process. Fifth, teachers as collaborators must shift from working in isolation to working collaboratively with teachers, students, parents, and community.

English is perceived as the *language of power*. This perception translates into Standard English as the status language for social and economic communication (Baker, 2011; Callahan & Gandara, 2014). Given historical and deeply engrained English monolingual, assimilationist, and deficit ideologies regarding linguistic minority students, I maintain that teacher professional development must explicitly address the role of ideological clarity, pedagogical clarity, access for all, and equity in shaping the curriculum and classroom space.

SUMMARY

This chapter began with a personal vignette that illustrates the need for ideological clarity of teachers of ELLs to work toward continually developing an elevated critical consciousness of their students' linguistic, social, and familial capital (Yosso, 2005). Although, the vignette depicts an incident that occurred many decades ago, current research informs us that history continues to repeat itself. Thus, teachers must have the courage to intervene strategically, forcefully, purposefully, and consistently to dismantle discriminatory hegemonic ideologies and practices. The chapter discusses the role of culturally, linguistically competent educators; the CSSP and steps for actualizing it. The chapter discusses the important issue and strategies of engaging ELL parents. The chapter also introduces basic Spanish vocabulary and Mexican/Mexica-American traditions, food, and holidays, serving as a starting point for teachers to continue their cultural and linguistic quest for knowledge in order to continue reaching out to students, parents, and their community. Teachers must become skilled at using "cultural wealth" pedagogical approaches when teaching linguistic minority students so they can ultimately appropriate new language varieties in an additive and self-empowering fashion. Teaching standard academic discourse in English cannot be adequately accomplished without taking a detour through the richness of students' cultural wealth and funds of knowledge.

REFERENCES

Alfaro, C., Durán, R., Hunt, A., & Aragón, M. J. (2015). Steps toward unifying dual language programs, Common Core State Standards, and critical pedagogy. *Association of Mexican American Educators Open Issue, 8*(2), 17–30.

Alfaro, C. (2008). Teacher education examining beliefs, orientations, ideologies & practices. In L. Bartolome (Ed.), *Ideologies in education: Unmasking the trap of teacher neutrality* (pp. 231–241). New York, NY: Peter Lang.

Baker, C. (2011). *Foundations of bilingual education and bilingualism.* Buffalo, NY: Multicultural Matters.

Bartolomé, L. (2010). Daring to infuse ideology into language-teacher education. In S. May & C. Sleeter (Eds.), *Critical multiculturalism: From theory to practice* (pp. 47–60). New York, NY: Routledge.

Callahan, R. M., & Gandara, P.C. (2014). *The bilingualism advantage: Language, literacy, and labor market.* Clevedon, Bristol: Multicultural Matters.

Darder, A. (2015). *Freire and education.* New York, NY: Routledge.

Flores, B. M. (2005). The intellectual presence of the deficit view of Spanish-speaking children in the educational literature during the 20th century. In P. Pedraza & M. Rivera (Eds.), *Latino education: An agenda for community action research* (pp. 75–98). Mahwah, NJ: Lawrence Erlbaum Associates.

Freire, P. (1993). *Pedagogy of the city.* New York, NY: Continuum.

Gándara, P., & Hopkins, M. (2010). *Forbidden languages: English learners and restrictive language policies.* New York, NY: Teachers College Press.

Garcia, O. (2014). U.S. Spanish and education: Global and local intersections. In K. M. Borman, T. G. Wiley, D. R. Garcia, & A. B. Danzig (Eds.), *Review of Research in Education: Language Policy, Politics, and Diversity in Education, 38*(1), 58–80.

Garcia, O., & Sylvan, C. E. (2011). Pedagogies and practices in multilingual classrooms: Singularities in pluralities. *The Modern Language Journal, 95*(3), 385–400.

Gonzalez, J. M., Jurado, V., Laiz, L., Zimmermann, J., Hermosin, B. & Saiz-Jimenez, C. (2005). *Pectinatus portalensis sp. nov.* In Validation of publication of new names and new combinations previously effectively published outside the IJSEM, List no. 102. *International Journal of Systematic and Evolutionary Microbiology, 55,* 547–549.

Kincheloe, J. (2008). *Critical pedagogy.* New York, NY: Peter Lang.

Macedo, D. (2000). The colonialism of the English only movement. *Educational Researcher, 29*(3), 15–24.

Moll, L. C., Amanti, C., Neff, D., & González, N. (1992). Funds of knowledge for teaching: Using a qualitative approach to connect homes and classrooms. *Theory into Practice, 31*(2), 132–141.

Moreno, R. P., & Lopez, J. A. (1999). *Latina mothers' involvement in their children's schooling: The role of maternal education and acculturation.* Julian Samora Research Institute. Working Paper Series.

Ochoa, A. (2012). *Guidelines and bank of questions for community environmental scan.* Dual Language and English Learner Department, DLE 515 Foundations of Bilingual Education, San Diego State University, San Diego, CA. Course Syllabus Spring.

Olivos, E., Jiménez-Castellanos, O., & Ochoa, A. (2011). *Bicultural parent engagement: Advocacy and empowerment.* New York, NY: Teachers' College.

Quezada, R., & Alfaro, C. (2012, August). Cutting to the common core moving pedagogic mountains. *Language Magazine, 11*(12), 19–22.

Rodríguez-Brown, F. (2010). A research perspective on the involvement of linguistic-minority families on their children's learning. In E. Garcia & E. Frede (Eds.), *Developing the research agenda for young English language learners* (pp. 100–118). New York, NY: Teachers College Press.

Shor, I. (1992). *Empowering education: Critical teaching for social change.* Chicago, IL: University of Chicago Press.

Sleeter, C. E. (2001). Preparing teachers for culturally diverse schools: Research and the overwhelming presence of whiteness. *Journal of Teacher Education, 52*(2), 94–106.

Stringer, E. T. (2009). *Action research.* Thousand Oaks, CA: Sage.

Wright, W. E., Boun, S., & Garcia, O. (2015). *The handbook of bilingual and multilingual education.* Hoboken, NJ: Wiley.

Yosso, T. J. (2005). Whose culture has capital? A critical race theory discussion of community cultural wealth. *Race, Ethnicity, and Education, 8*(1), 69–91.

Valdez, G. (1996). *Con respect: Building the bridges between culturally diverse families and schools.* New York, NY: Teachers College Press.

CHAPTER 11

MOTIVATING ELLs USING A PSYCHOLOGICAL APPROACH

Ron Collins
Mars Hill University

CASE SCENARIO

Ricardo is an 18-year-old Latin male. He has recently immigrated to the United States from Bogota, Columbia. He quit school to support his mother and younger brother. He tried to apply for a number of jobs but because of his poor English language skills he failed to secure one. His lack of proficiency also caused him difficulty interacting with non-Hispanic people. His mother cannot speak English either and they communicate entirely in Spanish at home. Ricardo has dreamt of getting a good job and helping his family move to a better neighborhood. Yet, being unable to speak English has been a major issue. Therefore, Ricardo has decided to return to school and take the English as a second language class. Yet, Ricardo fears that he will not be able to master English because he has been out of school and lacks confidence in his ability. In class he is having difficulty understanding the lessons that are explained in English by his teacher. The situation in the classroom is starting to affect his motivation to continue in the class. His teacher believes Ricardo is not motivated enough to study and that is why he is not doing well in class. Ricardo senses that his teacher does not think highly of him and this has added to his fear of communicating with her about his learning difficulty. He is now thinking about dropping the class altogether.

Teaching ELLs Across Content Areas, pages 261–286
Copyright © 2016 by Information Age Publishing

In the above scenario, we see that motivation can be affected by the perceptions that the students have of their success rate in trying to reach their goals. This may become an obstacle for the English Language Learners (ELLs) having success in the pursuit of learning English. It is the teacher's responsibility to facilitate a learning environment. As each student is different, finding out about their individual situations and needs might facilitate a richer learning environment. To motivate ELLs achieving learning success is especially important for the K–12 teachers in classrooms. This is because the ELL school population has increased at a higher rate, reaching 5.3 million, and every teacher is confronted with the issues of working with ELLs today (Li, 2015).

MOTIVATING ELLs FOR SUCCESS

One way for a teacher to help ELLs in the K–12 classroom become successful in their endeavor to learn a new language would be to try and understand what the individual learner's needs happen to be. The teacher also needs to know how those needs can be used to motivate the student to achieve success. From a psychological perspective, a need is a psychological feature that could arouse an organism to action toward a goal. It gives purpose and direction to an individual's behavior. It would be beneficial for teachers who work with ELLs in the classroom to review some of the needs theories of psychology in order to learn more about their students' needs and how to motivate them to learn.

There are a number of differing schools of thought in the field of psychology and those schools of thought view motivation differently. Here are some of the major schools and how they differ.

Psychodynamic Perspective

This approach is popular with a number of psychiatrists. It was founded by Sigmund Freud at the end of the 19th century. This psychological model believes that human behavior is controlled by inner forces that the individual has only a little power or awareness about. This school of thought places emphasis on the influence of the unconscious mind on a person's behavior. One of the central tenants of contemporary psychodynamic theory rests on a series of propositions that deal with an individual's unconscious cognitive processes, their affective state, and motivational processes. Freud felt that individuals were motivated by libidinal influences that drove them to pursue certain goals. He felt these were unconscious processes that influence both motivation and persistence of effort (Bauer, 1994).

Biological Perspective

The biological school of thought looks at human behavior as a dynamic of the internal chemistry of the body. A biological psychologist considers changes in motivation levels as a derivative of the changes in levels of neuro-transmitters. This can be seen in the "bio-psychological" theory of personality that was proposed by Jeffrey Alan Gray (1981). Adherents of this approach look at the changes in a behavior as a reaction to the level of neurotransmitters, or other bodily functions. Instinct theories and drive theories draw heavily from the biological perspective.

Motivation from the perspective of the biological approach to psychology is a function of physiological regulation. This term refers to the activation of motivation by certain portions of the nervous system. The idea is that motivation is mainly regulated by an individual's brain, particularly by the hypothalamus. The mechanisms that help regulate motivation include such things as blood-sugar level during eating and the central nervous system mechanisms which function to maintain a steady state of physiological maintenance (Maarten, Boksema, Meijmana, & Lorista, 2006). Trait theorists also fall under this approach as they look at personality.

Behavioral Perspective

The behavioral model starts in the late 19th century and was forwarded by theorists like John Watson. Behaviorism was concerned with motivation primarily from the observable and measurable aspects of human behavior. They believed that the external surroundings and environmental causes were the major factors in shaping the behavior of an individual. Their main focus was on stimulus and response. They did not feel what a person thought or felt was important. Behaviorists felt that only the response to a stimulus was important to study. B. F. Skinner was among the greatest proponents of behaviorism during the 20th century. He looked at the learning process and motivation in a different way. Skinner was basically concerned with how learning was affected by stimuli presented after the act was actually performed. According to Skinner certain stimuli caused the organism to repeat an act more frequently. He called those stimuli that created this effect "reinforcers" (Komaki, Coombs, & Schepman, 1996). The behavioral school of thought was the dominant philosophy in the psychology through the 1950s. ESOL teachers can benefit from Skinner's work in operant conditioning and reinforcement as a means of controlling and motivating their student's classroom behavior. Variations of his approach have been utilized in the classroom since the 1950s in what has become known as "behavior modification." This is a technique/tool for improving both learning and behavior of students.

Cognitive Perspective

This school of thought in psychology arose as a reaction against behaviorism's rejection of an individual's personal experiences. The approach is based on the notion that behavior is controlled by the way we know, comprehend, and reflect the world. This approach to psychology studies mental processes including how people think, recognize, remember, and learn. From the cognitive school of thought, motivation can be seen as a state or a process in someone's mind that stimulates, promotes, or controls some action toward a goal. The idea of motivation, in this approach, is based on two fundamental elements: What information is available to the individual at the time and what are their personal past experiences?

Cognition is a thought. This thought becomes the means by which our minds obtain knowledge and relate it to our thinking processes and perceptions of our environment. The cognitive approach to psychology explains motivation as a behavior that is activated by our examination and consideration of incoming environmental stimuli or information. This view of past experiences and thought processes is completely opposite the behaviorist point of view in which we respond out of received conditioning to some stimuli that will control our responses in various situations from some type of programmed training (Nevid, 2012).

Humanistic/Existential Perspective

This arose mainly as a counter response to psychoanalysis, behaviorism, and cognitivism. Carl Rogers, Abraham Maslow, and Rollo May were among the pioneers and leaders in this perspective. Humanists believe people have full control over their lives and are solely accountable for shaping their thoughts, ideas, behavior, and attitude.

The idea of motivation from the humanistic/existential perspective can be seen in the research of Gagne and Deci (2005). Their research comes as a response against what they felt were inconsistencies of the extrinsic motivational theory. This gave rise to self-determination theory (Gagne & Deci, 2005). They noted that people felt the highest levels of intrinsic motivation when they were allowed to feel autonomy and were recognized for their competence in different situations. They found that factors that diminish feelings of autonomy or competence gave rise to lowered levels of intrinsic motivation. The more individuals were allowed to have a say in what they did or how they did it, the more something gave rise to feelings of empowerment, which in turn elevated feelings of motivation.

From the humanistic school of thought in psychology we find one of the oldest and most prevalent of the needs theories of motivation, which comes from Abraham Maslow. Abraham Maslow (1954) believed that psychological forces drive human behavior. The theory postulated a graduated scale of human needs ranging from basic, physical ones such as hunger and thirst to higher level ones such as the need to be loved and the need for self-fulfillment. Though developed for organizations, it has relevance for school systems as well.

Maslow believed supervisors would see more success in their employees' endeavors if they recognized the various needs of individual subordinates and if they varied the rewards that they were going to offer to them.

In his approach, Maslow (1954) uses a pyramid of needs beginning with lower ordered needs and moving up to higher ordered or growth needs. The first level of needs, according to Maslow, are the physiological needs of individuals; these include bodily needs such as food, water, and air. If these needs are not met, there can be no progression upward. The second level of needs includes security and safety needs such as shelter, clothing, and the ability to feel safe in one's environment. According to this theory, if these needs can be achieved and maintained, the individual can progress to higher ordered needs of social relationships, belongingness, acceptance, and emotions. The fourth level of the pyramid deals with internal factors such as self-respect, autonomy, and achievement and external factors such as status, recognition, and self-esteem. Individuals must feel good about themselves and what they are trying to do. The fifth and highest level is self-actualization. Here the individual attempts to become the best person they are capable of being in achieving their potential and fulfillment (Kendrick, Griskevicius, Neuberg, & Schaller, 2010). See Figure 11.1 for the pyramid of needs.

Even though the needs of each ELL are different, Maslow's needs theory gives us an understanding of why students may undertake the rigors of learning a new language.

From the cognitive theory of human behavior, we have another theory of motivation. Victor Vroom (1964) addressed motivation by what the individual thought about the reward. He argued that the strength of our tendency to act in a certain way depends on the strength of our expectation of a given outcome and its importance to us. Applying this to the ELLs' learning situation, if the learner feels that they can accomplish the tasks of learning the second language, that they will be rewarded for doing so, and that the value of the reward for learning the language is important to them, then they will work that much harder to achieve it. Vroom explained this approach with the equation seen in Figure 11.2.

In his famous equation, M = Motivation; E = expectancy (the belief that they can learn English), I = instrumentality (that by learning English they will be rewarded in some way), and V = valence or value (i.e., that the reward will be something that they personally think is valuable) (Vroom,

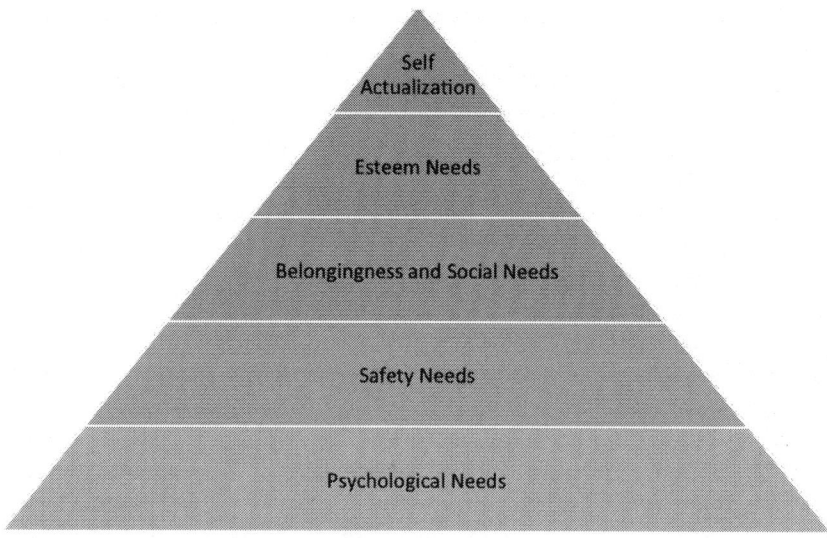

Figure 11.1 Hierarchy of needs. *Source:* Adapted from Maslow (1954).

Figure 11.2 Motivation equation (Vroom, 1964). Vroom introduces the model and its concepts of valence, expectancy, and force.

1964). From the Behavioral school of thought, we find that B. F. Skinner holds that motivation is the product of providing the right stimulus and conditioning the students need to study in a manner that will bring them success. To emphasize the conditioning process, he coined the term operant conditioning or changing of behavior by the use of reinforcement, which is given after the desired response.

According to Saul McLeod (2015), Skinner identified three main types of behavioral responses or what he called operants. They included: (a) neutral operants, these were responses, which neither increased nor decreased the probability of a particular behavior being repeated; (b) reinforcers, which were responses that increased the probability of a behavior being repeated (it should be noted that, he identified two types of reinforcers, positive reinforcers and negative reinforcers); and (c) punishers, which were responses that actually decreased the likelihood of a behavior being repeated.

According to McLeod (2015), any teacher in the classroom can offer positive reinforcement that will help lead toward behavior modification for a student by providing compliments, approval, encouragement, or affirmation. McLeod suggests a ratio of about five compliments for every one criticism should prove to be a very effective proportion to help alter a student's behavior toward the desired state. I agree with McLeod that these types of reinforcements increase the likelihood of students doing better. I have used these in my own classes and have found them to be of great benefit, especially with students who may have a diminished sense of self-efficacy. The important thing to remember for the teacher is that the student's sense of self-esteem needs to be bolstered.

From the cognitive school of thought, we also have social learning theory's perspective on how to increase motivation. Bandura (1977) postulated that people can learn to modify their behavior by watching others achieve success doing things. Bandura cautions that although people can learn through observation, an essential part of the whole process is their internal mental states at the time of the observation.

According to Bandura (1977) observational learning can occur in three basic contexts. The first being that the person modeling a desired behavior is physically present, or represented in some form, such as a video where they demonstrate the behavior. The second may involve some form of verbal instruction that can be oral or written that explains the desired behavior. The third type may take the form of a "symbolic model." Here a real or fictional character is able to display the desired behaviors. This type of modeling can occur in almost any form of media.

When considering an observational learning approach, Cherry (2014) cautions that an important point for a teacher to be mindful of is that in order for observational learning to be successful for the student in the classroom, the teacher needs to ensure that the students are properly motivated to imitate the behavior that was modeled. This means the teacher needs to set the stage for learning to occur. This point is especially true if the students tend to be marginal.

Cherry (2014) suggests that using either reinforcements or punishment or both may have to play some major role in the motivation. These motivators, she notes, can be highly effective if the student is observing others experiencing some type of reinforcement or punishment. She provides an example: If a student sees another student being rewarded with extra credit for being in class on time, they may start coming a few minutes early each day to class too.

So how can a teacher of ELLs identify some of the needs of her students? As a psychologist I suggest that one way for the teacher to achieve this would be to engage the students in conversation. Talk to them between lessons and between classes. During the teacher's conversations with students, they need to be mindful of "I" statements. "I" statements can reveal how a person derives their identity. They can be strong indicators of what a person thinks about themselves. Statements about sense of abilities and interests are strong indicators of a student's feelings of self-efficacy.

WHAT IS MOTIVATION?

How can the teacher apply these needs theory elements to help the ELLs achieve success? After determining what the needs of the learner might actually be, the teacher can then guide the student to initiate and maintain goal-oriented behaviors toward their goal. Motivation has been explained as the processes that cause people to act to achieve a goal. Motivation can involve the cognitive, biological, emotional, or social forces that activate people's behavior. According to Jeffrey Nevid (2012) in his explanation about motivation, it becomes the "why" in relation to our behavior. He suggests that motivation is the phenomena that directs and maintains our goal directed behaviors to meet the needs or wants that drive us and explain why we do what we do. For Nevid, motivation is the why we as humans persist through obstacles and endure the frustrations when we are tested to our limits.

In a study by Collins and McCarty (2008) that looked at intelligence and other factors related to success in business, the researchers were able to identify motivation out of a number of considerations as one of the strongest factors that allowed individuals to be successful in business. It is the same for students in the classroom. Motivation is the factor that can account for the intensity and duration of an individual's effort to achieve a goal. And, as Bandura (1997) has pointed out, the best way to motivate someone is to increase and maintain their self-efficacy.

According to Pinder (2008) there are three major components to motivation. They include direction, intensity, and persistence. The direction deals with the focus of their motivation, the intensity deals with how hard an individual wants to try to achieve their goal, and the persistence measures how long that individual can maintain their efforts.

For the ELLs, the direction involves making the decision to enroll in an ESOL class in the first place. The intensity is seen in the concentration and determination exhibited by the ELLs as they study to pursue their goal. Finally, persistence is seen in the effort expended to stay on target toward achieving the goal. According to Collins and DeSantis (2008), individual motivation can begin to drive certain people due to a number of factors that include negative environmental factors. There are cases where after individuals were told they would not succeed in some endeavor, they redoubled their efforts and began to push even harder to achieve their goals. In cases such as these, the people's persistence was increased by being told they could not attain their goal. This is especially true of motivation when it relates to creative thinking.

General Theories of Motivation

There are a number of general theories of motivation that span the main schools of thought in psychology. Some of these include drive theories, instinct theories, and incentive theories that explain why people are motivated to do certain things. See Figure 11.3 for the general theories of motivation.

Drive Theory

This theory proposes that all organisms are driven by the need for survival. Drive theories can be explained by internal motivation or fulfillment of needs. According to the drive theory of motivation, as put forward by Clark Hull (1943), Abraham Maslow (1954), and other theorists later, people are motivated to take certain actions in order to reduce the internal tension that is caused by unmet needs. For example, you might be motivated to eat something in order to reduce the internal state of hunger (Kenrick et al., 2010).

An early pioneer in the field of drive theory was Clark Hull. As for motivation, Hull explained motivation in terms of unmet needs (see Figure 11.4). Hull noted that individuals in the course of life may suffer some type of deprivation during their life and that their deprivation would then create a need in them. Once this feeling of need was created, it would then activate some type of drive and the drive in turn would activate a behavior. The behavior would be goal directed. According to Hull, the drive to succeed

Theories of Motivation

Figure 11.3 Theories of motivation.

Theory of Motivation

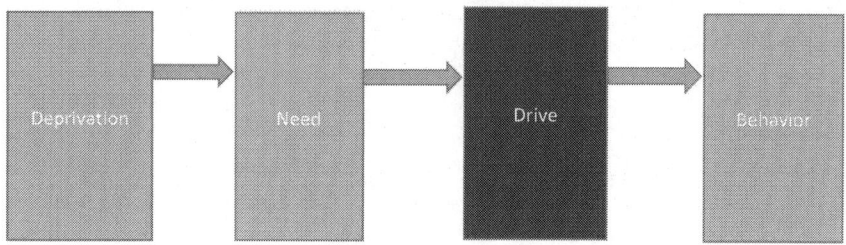

Figure 11.4 Drive theory of motivation. *Source:* Hull (1943).

in achieving the goal would probably have survival value as the compelling feature (Complete Dictionary of Scientific Biography, 2008).

Instinct Theory

This theory deals with natural instincts of all animals. As Nancy Melucci (2010) notes, instinct theory proposes that all organisms tend to engage in certain behaviors that will lead them to success in terms of issues like natural selection. She suggests that instinct theory defines motivation as being essentially intrinsic in nature and is based on the biological psychology approach. Melucci in her text provides examples of natural animal behaviors that include migration patterns of different species as well as mate selection processes as prime representations of instinctually motivated behaviors in all animals. It should be noted that although instinct theories tend to derive their strength of reason from the natural environment, they also tend to have less strength in their explanatory ability dealing with human needs. This has caused controversy and criticism of the theory (Maarten et al., 2006; Melucci, 2010).

Incentive Theory

This theory suggests that people are motivated to do things because of either internal needs or external reinforcements (see Figure 11.5). Numerous theorists from different schools of thought in psychology have addressed this general category. It is explained as the pull toward certain behaviors that might offer a more positive incentive than those offering negative outcomes. Several theorists that address incentive motivation through external rewards include B. F. Skinner and Victor Vroom. B. F. Skinner (circa 1950s) from the behavioral school of psychology developed his theory of operant conditioning and contingencies, known as contingency theory. While from the cognitive approach in 1964, Victor Vroom developed the expectancy theory through his study of the motivations behind decision making. Each of these theories postulates what they feel motivates individuals and how they believe we can sustain the individual's drive and intensity through rewards (Komaki et al., 1996; McLeod, 2015; Van Eerde & Thierry, 1996).

In these models, they address the issues of *extrinsic motivation*. Here the motivation is influenced by external factors that exist outside of the individual. The subject's performance of some desired activity occurs to attain a reward, such as grades for students or money for workers. It could also be threats or punishment of some type (Ryan & Deci, 2000a).

Some psychologists argue that incentive motivation or doing some activity or task for the pure enjoyment of it may become reduced if external rewards are then introduced to continue the activity. This might be seen in a person who loves to play the piano for fun and is very good at it. Then, once they begin to be paid to perform, they may not want to do it so much as they did before being paid to perform. This could cause reduction in the drive motivation. In other words, as Bernstein (2011) suggests, the differences in motivation from one individual to another or situation to situation may be traced to the type of incentives being used or presented as well as the value that a particular person places on the incentives at a specific time.

The phenomenon of *intrinsic motivation* can be explained as the self-desire to seek out new things and new challenges, to analyze one's capacity, to observe and to gain knowledge (Ryan & Deci, 2000b). It is driven by a type of interest or enjoyment in the task itself, and it exists within the individual rather than relying on any external pressures or any desire for

Types of Motivation

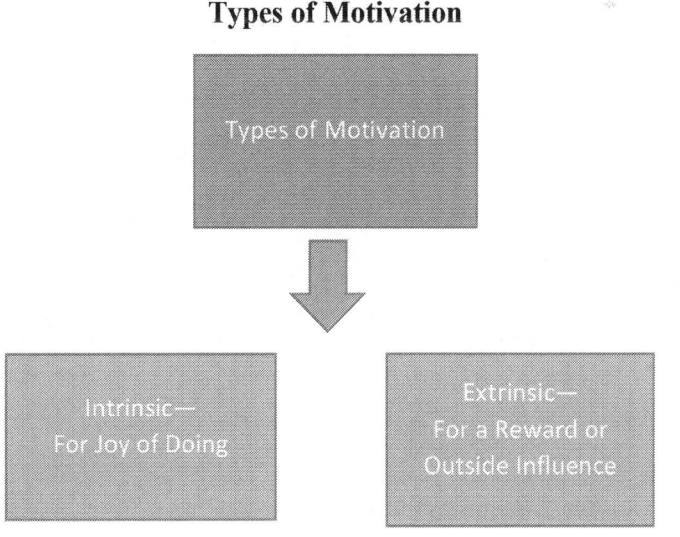

Figure 11.5 Two major types of motivation.

reward. Studies have revealed that subjects who have an internal motivation will engage in activities out of curiosity driven behaviors even with an absence of rewards. ELLs who are intrinsically motivated will more likely be engaged in the task of learning more willingly as well as working to improve their skills, which in turn will increase their capabilities (Bandura, 1997).

Students who have confidence in themselves are likely to be intrinsically motivated, especially if they attribute their educational results to factors under their own control, also known as autonomy or locus of control. Here they believe they have the skills to be effective agents in reaching their desired goals, also known as self-efficacy beliefs (Bandura, 1997), and are interested in mastering a topic, not just in achieving good grades.

Intrinsic motivation has the advantage over external motivation of being longer lasting and self-sustaining. Efforts to build intrinsic motivation are typical in promoting student learning. With intrinsic motivation, efforts focus on the subject rather than external reinforcements or punishments. A disadvantage to establish intrinsic motivation is that it takes a longer time to foster and may require intricate and lengthy preparations (Ryan & Deci, 2000b).

It must be remembered when discussing ELLs in general, that they are individuals, so a variety of approaches may be needed to motivate different students. It is often helpful to know what interests one's students in order to connect these interests with the subject matter. This requires getting to know one's students.

Among the theories that address motivation and success in achieving one's goals from the social cognitive school of thought, is self-efficacy theory formulated by Albert Bandura. Bandura (1997) postulates in his theory that how a person feels about themselves can affect their motivation and in turn their performance in completing tasks. Self-efficacy is defined as an individual's belief that they are capable of performing some type of task.

Bandura (1997) suggests that the more confidence you have in your ability to succeed, the better you will do in achieving it. He goes on to suggest that people with low self-efficacy are more likely to lessen their effort or give up trying to achieve their goals. He further suggests that the more positive a person's self-efficacy the more they will be engaged in their tasks and the higher their performance will be in turn. He indicates that a person with a high self-efficacy will take creative criticism by increasing their efforts and motivation. While people with low self-efficacy will more than likely lesson their efforts.

According to Bandura (1997) there are four ways that self-efficacy can be increased in individuals: *enactive mastery* (actually performing the task), *vicarious modeling* (watching someone else who is similar to you perform the task), *verbal persuasion* (being coached and convinced by someone who is trusted), and *arousal* (working up to an emotional feeling of exhilaration, like a sports performer). He indicates that enactive mastery may be the most important way to increase self-efficacy.

How can the teachers of ELLs utilize this understanding of psychological concepts and aspects of motivation to facilitate a stronger commitment from their students toward achieving success in the classroom? One of the simplest ways is for the teacher to start out with the easiest of tasks and utilize praise to bolster the ELL's confidence. This may assure the students of enactive mastery as they perform the tasks assigned. Here they gain relevant experience with the task and are shown to have accomplished it successfully. This will help them in their beliefs in their own ability when they attempt to do the assignments at home. As these students are seen getting praise and acceptance from their classmates, a sense of vicarious learning is also occurring. Not only does the student performing the task do something, but the others in the class will also become more confident in their own ability to do the task.

As Bandura (1997) points out, continue telling the students how well they are doing. This provides verbal persuasion that they will succeed in accomplishing the task. This reinforcement of their belief in themselves should bolster their confidence and give them the needed energy to move through the lessons. Finally, the teacher can use the tactics of a sports coach by getting the students "psyched up" for presentations of their ability in class. Numerous studies in the field of sports psychology have addressed the issue of getting athletes emotionally exhilarated or aroused as Bandura (1997) explains. Bandura argues that arousal increases self-efficacy, which in turn increases performance.

Another point that a teacher of ELLs needs to consider is that the level of arousal may influence the amount of information processing students are able to do. According to Atherton (2013), there is a curvilinear relationship between motivation and anxiety. He points out that a sense of well-being is related to performance in learning and that this is achieved at a moderate level of arousal. Atherton points out that "too little arousal leads to boredom, and too much to anxiety." He cautions that both boredom and or anxiety can have the effect of inhibiting effective performance.

An earlier study by Gardnera, Day, and MacIntyrea (1992) revealed a relationship between motivation, anxiety, and performance. In their study, they looked at the effects of both integrative motivation and anxiety on computerized vocabulary acquisition. The study established a protocol to use a simulated analog procedure as a type of second language learning task. They also wanted to study the effects of induced anxiety on the participants. To do this, they introduced the element of videotaping one group of the participants while they were in the process of learning and not the other group. In their findings, they reported a curvilinear relationship between motivation and anxiety. They also reported that the participants in the study who scored higher on their scale of "integrative motivation" tended to have higher vocabulary acquisition and were able to initiate their translations faster than participants who had lower scores on the scale. Additionally, they found that individuals with more positive attitudes tended to respond faster and more consistently to the attitude items for which they tested.

This would tend to indicate that the ELLs teacher should establish a moderate level of arousal in students. This may be achieved through the use of small competitions in class, say in the form of extra points for presenting material in class. This would also suggest that too much pressure on the students, especially for something like grades, will have a detrimental effect on their motivation.

HOW TO MOTIVATE ELLs IN THE CLASSROOM?

As almost every teacher can attest, one of the more difficult components of teaching is motivating and maintaining goal-directed behaviors in students. It is also one of the most important things. If a student loses their motivation they fail to learn effectively. This can affect their ability to comprehend, retain, and utilize new information.

Motivation can also affect the student's attitude, which will in turn affect the willingness to meet the rigors of learning new material. The components of attitude, which include cognitive, emotional, and behavioral elements, can impede the ELLs from maintaining their *intensity* and *persistence.* Theorists give us a number of ways to effectively counter the distractions of external forces. These include providing positive reinforcement (Komaki et al., 1996). Both positive and negative reinforcement increases the likelihood of goal-directed behaviors being repeated. An example of a positive reinforcement would be when you receive something, such as a reward, for a certain type of behavior. A negative reinforcement would be when you are allowed not to have to do something you dislike doing. Shaping behaviors can also aid students to become more enthusiastic about learning and recognizing the value of their work. This can be accomplished through praise for incremental increases in behavior that lead to accomplishing achievement toward larger goals.

Another way to motivate the student is through valued rewards. As Victor Vroom (1964) points out in *expectancy theory,* the learner must feel that they have the ability and that their performance will be rewarded. They also must feel that the reward is of value to them. Offering a reward to one person might not have the same value to a second person, especially if the second person already has that reward item.

Another method to engage the ELLs students in goal-directed behaviors comes from the participative leadership style as put forward by Peter

Drucker (management by objectives). This theory reveals that people become more involved if they have some say in the outcomes. Here goals are set by supervisors (teachers) and subordinates (learners); they are agreed upon by both parties, and timetables are established for achieving these goals by both teachers and students working together. It is a collaborative approach (Rogers & Hunter, 1991).

Still another approach to increase motivation comes from studies on memory and recall. Students will learn material faster and recall it more accurately if they can associate the material with something they already know. This increases their mastery of the subject matter and increases motivation. The *laws of association*, of which there are three basic laws, (law of contiguity, law of similarity, and law of contrast), date back to Aristotle in the third century B.C. These laws, which are the basis for modern day learning theory, reveal that individuals retain material faster and better when they can associate it with something they have already learned. Using examples from their lives can also help in this approach.

Mintz (2015) suggests placing students in structured learning categories, since research indicates that most students tend to learn best in multiple ways it would be more appropriate to present information in multiple ways. Mintz further suggests that in a learning environment, the peer group of the students may be the single most important source of influence on the individual students' development. He suggests that the degree to which a teacher is student oriented can also be an important source of influence on their development. Mintz believes that students learn in multiple ways and the learning is usually reflected in multiple ways. Teachers can use rubrics in classes to present material, some from lecture, some from PowerPoints, and some from outside speakers. The students' assignments likewise are also done in multiple ways, quizzes, tests, research papers, individual or group, oral presentations or debates.

Other methods to motivate the ELLs in the classroom include making the class interactive. Keep the tempo upbeat and as light as possible. Among some techniques suggested by busyteacher.org (2015), are to use references to "pop" culture in class activities allowing the students to connect with the lessons. They also suggest integrating technology into the lessons as much as possible. According to busyteacher.org (2015), a little friendly competition may foster learning. I do this in my psychology classes by dividing the students into groups and having group debates to earn extra credit points on approved topics. Readings should always be age appropriate for the ELL students (busyteacher.org, 2015).

In motivating ELLs, the teacher must also be mindful of the students' learning styles. For the styles of learning the English as a second language, teachers need a varied approach. This is sometimes referred to as a rubric of lessons covering similar material. This should help address the various learning styles of the students. Some may be auditory learners; some may learn better using visual or tactile aids to assist in the learning process while still others may learn best by "manipulating objects or engaging in projects," these students are known as "kinesthetic learners." As I stated previously, I have used this same approach for a number of years. In the rubric approach, students are graded on quizzes, tests, readings, written papers, and oral presentations that allow them all to do well in at least one area.

According to an article published by the British Counsel, London in July 2009, motivating students is a problem that has been around for a long time, especially in language classes. The article (British Counsel, 2009) stresses that there are a number of ways to motivate students in the classroom. Among a number of methods they describe are several I feel are of specific interest. The first is the "paired work or group work" approach. Here, students can help each other out while working on the tasks of learning. I have found this to be exceptionally good for students who might be marginal if they were working on their own but bring their work up to acceptable standards with the help of other students. This approach can also reinforce learning with the more gifted students by providing them the time to explain it to someone else. The second approach to motivate students according to the article was in the "seating of students." They prefer the "horseshoe" or curved seating arrangement. This, they point out can maximize eye contact for both the students with the instructor as well as the students with each other. Finally, the British Counsel article (2009) describes a technique I think is especially useful, that of "role playing." Using this approach I have found that even students that have marginal skills in test taking or report writing can excel. This reinforces learning with all levels of students.

Ken Bain (2004) states that teachers need to distinguish between the learning styles of *deep learners, strategic learners,* and *surface learners.* Each of these styles presents different challenges for the ELLs' teacher. According to Bain, deep learners enjoy the challenge of mastering a difficult and complex subject. This type of student tends to be intrinsically motivated. Teaching them can be an enjoyable experience for the teacher. Bain then identifies the styles of the other two types. He reports that the strategic learners tend to be primarily motivated by reinforcements or rewards. This type of student will react well to competition along with the opportunity do better than others. They are usually among your better students, often making grades well above average. The problem he identifies with this type of student is that they tend not to want to become engaged deeply with any subject unless there is some type of specified reward attached to the assignment. Bain notes that this type of learner is sometimes referred to as a "bulimic learner," that is, they tend to learn as much as is needed to do well on some type of scored test, then quickly forget all that they studied once the test is over.

According to Bain, if a teacher is faced with this type of learner, the teacher should avoid any of their appeals for some form of competition. Instead he suggests that the teacher's responsibility is to determine if the student has any interest in the subject and then try to appeal to whatever intrinsic interest that they might have with the subject. Assignments, according to Bain, should require strategic learners to have a "deep engagement" with a topic to be able to successfully complete their assignments.

The third type of learner Bain identifies is the surface learner. These learners tend to be motivated by the fear of failure and a desire to avoid it. According to Bain, the surface learner will typically try to avoid any type of deep learning. This learner may view deep learning as an inherently risky endeavor, probably out of their fear of failure. They instead will do whatever it takes to pass a test or an assignment, but usually will not go beyond the minimum. He cautions that the teacher faced with surface learners needs to try and instill and increase their levels of self-confidence. This should in turn increase their feelings of self-efficacy (Bain, 2004).

Bain also suggests a method made popular by Lev Vygotsky (1962), a Russian teacher, psychologist, and educational theorist, using the scaffolding approach. In this method the teacher needs to "scaffold" their learning material and assignments. Bain (2004) feels that by designing a series of activities or assignments that follow one another and increase in complexity over time will help bolster the surface learners' confidence as they reflect on what has been learned and accomplished (Vygotsky, 1962, cited in Bain [2004]; Bandura, 1997; Bain, 2004).

According to James Middleton (1995), an educational psychologist at Arizona State University developing methodologies for educational technology in mathematics learning, teachers need to understand the importance of engaging their students to determine their interests so they can adjust their activities and assignments to be of interest to the ELLs. Middleton (1995) suggests that allowing the student to have some say in the selection of assignments aids motivation in several ways. First, it stimulates them through their involvement of creation and provides them some element of free choice in the selection of what they are doing.

According to Middleton, if the student perceives the assignment or activity as both stimulating and controllable, then they will in turn think of it as interesting and engage in the assignment. He cautions that if either of these conditions becomes insufficient or lacking, then the student may disengage themselves from the activity. If this happens, according to Middleton, the teacher may need to introduce an extrinsic motivator in order to influence the ELLs to continue with the assignment. Therefore, under the idea of best practices for the ELL teacher, it would be important to provide teaching and learning activities that are both stimulating and offer their students some degree of personal control in developing the assignment.

Issues for Teachers to Be Aware

There are a number of issues that teachers need to be aware of in dealing with motivating their ELLs. First, an important issue for teachers to know is to avoid having their students deal with the pressure of grades. As Davis (2009) suggested, many teachers tend to place too much pressure on students relative to grades that they will receive. Her suggestion was that by taking the pressure off students to have to achieve a certain grade, they will actually do better. She recommended de-emphasizing grades in the classroom as a way of diminishing arousal. This would agree with what Atherton (2013) as well as Gardnera et al. (1992) pointed out as the curvilinear relationship between motivation and anxiety. Motivation is related to a person's sense of performance and is achieved at a moderate level of arousal. As Atherton succinctly pointed out, too little arousal or too much anxiety inhibit performance.

Secondly, an important issue is that of structure. Structure helps build and maintain motivation. Students who know what they need to do as well as when tasks are needed to be completed can maintain self-efficacy and feelings of accomplishment in completing the tasks on time. As Davis (2009) points out, students love structure and will respond well to knowing what they need to do to be successful. Providing students with an instructional outline on the first day of class, or even before the class, helps let them know what they need to do and when they need to do it. This can also add to their understanding of what is needed and if the material has value to them (Komaki et al., 1996; Bain, 2004; Davis, 2009). I have used this approach with students and feel that it is a fundamental component of success in class.

Thirdly, allowing students to see other students successfully complete the tasks is another way that a number of the theorists feel will add to the students' feelings of self-efficacy. As Bandura (1977) indicated, students can learn through watching others successfully perform a task. However, the teacher should be mindful, as Cherry (2014) cautions, to remember that for observational learning to be successful in the classroom, teachers must insure that students are properly motivated to imitate the behavior being modeled. This means setting the stage for learning to occur. As was stated earlier, this is especially evident if the students tend to be borderline. Cherry (2014) suggests that including the use of reinforcements and or punishment will allow the teacher to shape the behavior modification of the students toward the desired outcome. This is especially true if other students witness their classmates experiencing some type of reinforcement or punishment (Komaki et al., 1996; Bandura, 1997; Davis, 2009; Cherry, 2014; McLeod, 2015).

Finally, one more important issue that a number of the theorists refer for teachers to be aware of includes allowing the students to achieve a sense of competence. This can be accomplished in a number of methods, one being as Bain (2004) suggested scaffold the material, another as Posamentier (2013) suggested by using sequential forms of achievement or connectedness so students can see how one point ties in with another. Or as the dean of students (Allegheny College, 2015) points out, a strategy the student can delineate between realistic and achievable goals would help them feel "smart." These strategies will help to create the comfort zone for students when tackling new material. They all are in agreement with Albert Bandura's (1997) theory of self-efficacy. Once students can start feeling comfortable with learning, this will be directly related to their self-esteem, and self-efficacy and these will be directly related to their level of motivation they can achieve (Bain, 2004; Bandura, 1997; Davis, 2009; Allegheny College, 2015; Posamentier, 2013; Van Eerde & Thierry, 1996).

Strategies for Teachers to Motivate ELLs

Strategies for teachers to motivate ELLs include a host of low risk strategies that may insure good overall participation. Using these strategies or variations on them can ensure that you'll hold your students' attention in class and hopefully throughout the semester.

The Introduction/Ice Breaker Strategy

One of the first things teachers can do is have students introduce themselves and their goals. This is sometimes also referred to as the "ice breaker strategy." It involves getting the students talking about themselves. Here is an example. I would ask the students to tell us something about themselves, who they are, where they come from, how long they have lived in the area or at the school, if they have any personal goals, fears, and expectations for the class. I also like to place them in groups as soon as possible to start them on some type of a project that they can work on together. This allows the students to feel comfortable with their peer group and learn that they are not alone in what they do not know about the subject.

I have found that students enjoy structure. They like to know what assignments are coming and when they are coming. I try to provide a syllabus on the first day of class that will cover all of my expectations for the class. From this the student will know what to expect as well as find out about the material we are covering.

Pairing Students Up Strategy

Another motivational teaching strategy that I have used and that is successful in the classroom is to pair students up on occasion to see if they understand the reading assignments or lecture material that I have covered. After the first or second assigned reading, I pair the students and have them answer specific questions regarding the material. This should aid in helping the students to understand the material that was assigned as well as serve as an analysis of the readings. It should also increase their understanding of any new concepts that were covered. Students can be paired up at the time the readings were assigned. This will allow them time to prepare analysis together and come up with answers that will reflect their understandings of the material. I also like them to prepare several questions that they may have thought of from the readings. In the discussion with the students about the topic, others can learn by listening to the students discuss their findings.

Problem-Based Group Learning

Another strategy I suggest for teachers to help build students motivation, especially in more advanced classes, is the "problem-based learning strategy." First, the teacher can break the ELLs with other students up into small groups, unless they have already been assigned to a group for the entire class. Then, the teacher can present a problem that the students may encounter in a real life situation. Once the problem has been specified, the students need to gather in their groups to work on the problem. Each group is to work separately on the situation, analyze the problem, and attempt to identify any possible causative factors and how they would handle the situation. They have the class period to complete the assignment. At the end of the class or the beginning of the next class, the groups must each present their findings.

Personalize the New Material Strategy

Another good strategy that teachers can use in the classroom includes attempting to personalize the new material that they will be presenting to the students and put it into familiar types of settings so that students can better associate the learning topic or concept with something they are already familiar with. The more the students feel they are familiar with the new topic, the more comfortable they will be handling the assignments.

Incorporate Visual Aids

I also like to use videos embedded into my PowerPoints from YouTube and other multi-media sources. This enables the students to hear the information presented in a different way and from a different person or perspective. The videos also allow for them to visualize the accompanying new information. Sometime I use comic strip characters' discussion to cover the new material. Repetition is always helpful in allowing students to learn new information. The more they feel they are learning the material the greater the increase in their feelings of self-efficacy and hence their motivation to work harder.

Give Homework Assignment

Another strategy that teachers can find helpful is to assign the students a homework assignment that consists of having to analyze a problem, write up their analysis, and turn it in on the next class as homework. I have found that the more analysis they put forward, the better their comprehension of the subject matter.

Other Tips and Strategies

According to Barbara Gross Davis (2009) in her book *Tools for Teaching*, there are a number of ways for the ESOL teacher to increase student motivation in their classroom. Davis begins by suggesting that teachers usually place way too much pressure on students relative to grades that they will receive. She suggests that by taking the pressure off students to have to achieve a certain grade they will actually do better. She recommends de-emphasizing grades in the classroom. Another of her salient points is that students tend to love structure and will respond well to knowing what they need to do to be successful. Providing students with an instructional syllabus helps let them know what they need to do and when they need to do it. According to Davis (2009) all students tend to require early and frequent feedback on how they are doing. This feedback will help bolster their morale by encouraging them to finish assignments, and it helps reinforce the idea that they can do it. They can develop self-efficacy that the assignment is not beyond their ability to do (Davis, 2009; Bandura, 1997). Davis suggests that the teacher push their students to finish all assigned readings; this should help keep them current with the assignments and tasks they will face.

Another strategy that Davis (2009) suggests will bolster morale, increase motivation, and should ensure some type of opportunity for the students to be successful is by assigning tasks and giving assignments that are achievable (Bain, 2004; Bandura, 1997; Davis, 2009). These tasks should be neither too easy nor too difficult. It is suggested that the teacher create an environment that is positive and a feeling of openness for the students. The thought is that this will make the students more comfortable in working on their tasks. This is also a key element of what Bandura explained as the way to build self-efficacy (Bandura, 1997).

Yet another strategy that Davis (2009) points out will help build motivation in students is to aid them in finding out about any possible personal meaning that they can derive from the material being studied as well as any value that they may obtain from it. This will enable the student to form associations with the new material and help place it more securely in their memories.

Some additional strategies to motivate students come from the Allegheny College website (2015) specified by the dean of students. These strategies include some common sense issues that students need to be reminded about.

One strategy they delineate is the setting of realistic and achievable goals. This approach would enable students to be able to feel "smart." This will help create their comfort zone while taking on new material. This would be in agreement with Albert Bandura's (1997) theory of self-efficacy. A student's feeling of comfort with learning is directly related to their self-esteem, and self-efficacy and these are directly related to motivation. A second strategy the dean proposed was to try establishing the use of reinforcements for any progress toward the students' goals. This would help shape their behaviors toward a desired state or goal. This goes along with the thinking from B. F. Skinner's contingency theory (Allegheny College, 2015; Komaki et al., 1996).

In the dean's report on strategies the point is made that students need to be prepared for the eventual "set-backs" that can happen to anyone. Once they realize this they will be able to redirect and reenergize themselves back toward their goals. Also, teachers should encourage the students not to give up on their goal. Teachers should encourage their students to try and think positively about everything. The students should be persuaded to believe in the "power of positive thinking" (Allegheny College, 2015).

Teachers should also encourage their students to seek out support systems. Remind the students to let others be aware of their goals. Friends and loved ones can usually supply needed support and comfort when tasks become difficult. Students could learn to try and spend some time reflecting or talking to others about obstacles they have encountered that have deterred them from achieving their goals in the past (Allegheny College, 2015).

Students should also learn that they can say no to outside distractions that deter them from their goals. That they need to stay focused on what is important to them and build on it. Another strategy that the dean of students (Allegheny College, 2015) offered was for teachers to have their students try to establish some type of routine for study and regular exercise. They could include in their routine time for meditation, prayer or yoga. The report suggests that this may help cultivate discipline in the students.

Other helpful strategies suggested in this website include the use of positive imagery to give students a better feeling about themselves and the topics being learned, the use of inspirational quotes to bolster their morale, and letting the students know that it is ok to seek out counseling or mentoring when roadblocks, either physical or mental, were encountered (Allegheny College, 2015). Finally, the report suggested that the students practice good self-care.

One strategy for students to learn faster and improve their motivation according to Collins (1990) is for the teacher to make sure that there is some relatedness between lessons. Collins reports that the more related new material is to material already assimilated, the easier the new material will be to learn and the quicker students will be ready for additional material.

Another strategy Collins (1990) provides is that combining visual aids along with semantic information helps students to assimilate and learn faster and more efficiently than providing them semantic only information. The faster the students can learn the new material, the more motivated they will be to learn additional information.

Some additional helpful strategies have been outlined by Alfred Posamentier, Dean and professor of mathematics education at Mercy College, New York. In November of 2013 he posted nine strategies for motivating students in mathematics. Many of these strategies are useful no matter what the discipline. He reminds all of us in education that motivating students is one of the most important tasks we have during instruction. He suggests that effective teachers need to focus their attention not only on the self-directed learners but also on the less interested students.

The first strategy that Posamentier (2013) puts forward for the teacher, once they have identified a void in the student's base of knowledge, is to point out to the student that there is a void and try to inspire them to learn what it is they did not know. He suggests using exercises that put the student in familiar situations as well as unfamiliar situations with the material.

Another strategy that Posamentier suggests is to use sequential forms of achievement or connectedness. Show students how one point ties in with another allowing them to follow a chain of events that makes logical sense to them. Using this strategy can also lead the students to identify patterns. He suggests that discovering patterns can create motivation as students take pleasure in "owning an idea."

Motivation can also arise when students are shown the usefulness of a new topic, Posamentier (2013) advises. He suggests that the teacher, at the beginning of the class when a new topic is going to be discussed, shows the students some form of practical application of the topic. This, he states, will activate genuine interest on the part of the students that can lead to increased motivation to apply the new information.

Posamentier (2013) suggests that the teacher uses a story telling approach to bolster motivation. The teacher can tell a story, maybe about an historical or current event. The story can be either real or contrived using the new information. This will allow the students to hear about the topic and visualize it in the story setting. The story telling strategy is an interesting approach that could pay dividends for the students trying to learn new material.

Another helpful strategy that several of these theorists have alluded to includes the fact that students, as well as people in general, tend to require feedback on how they are doing. This should be done fairly soon after a task has been attempted and as frequently as possible. This feedback allows individuals to know how they are doing as well as helps to bolster their morale when they see how much they have accomplished. Feedback can help motivate and encourage students to finish assignments. This strategy can also act as a reinforcement to shape their behaviors toward the desired outcome. Seeing that they are achieving success on a task allows students to build self-efficacy. As has been pointed out, the achievement of success can increase motivation (Bandura, 1997; Komaki et al., 1996; Ryan & Deci, 2000a; Bain, 2004; Davis, 2009).

Finally, a strategy that seems to work well to motivate individuals, whether it is with ELLs or employees in a work situation, is to engage them in goal-directed behaviors through what is known as "a participative leadership style" (Peter Drucker's management by objectives approach) or self-determination theory of the humanistic school of thought. According to both of these approaches people become more involved if they have some say in the outcomes. Goals in this strategy are set by teachers and learners together; they are agreed upon by both parties and they work together to establish timetables for achieving those goals. Research tends to support this method, as it allows people to feel high levels of intrinsic motivation when they feel autonomy and empowerment. According to research in this area, the more individuals were allowed to have a say in what they do or how they do it, gives rise to feelings of elevated empowerment, which in turn elevates feelings of motivation (Rogers & Hunter, 1991; Ryan & Deci, 2000a; Gagne & Deci, 2005).

Any of these strategies may work for the teacher in the classroom, but it is important to make sure that the students feel they are among the valued members of the class and that the teacher is student oriented toward helping them achieve their goals.

SUMMARY

This chapter discussed how to motivate ELLs from a number of psychological perspectives. We discussed the theories on motivation. We reviewed some of the best strategies and approaches to motivate ELLs in our classrooms. One of the first strategies we may want to employ is to make the students feel comfortable in the classroom setting. This can be thought of as inclusion. An inclusive teaching strategy can refer to any teaching approach that addresses the needs of the individual students. This would include their different backgrounds, varied learning styles, and differing abilities. This can also allow the students to feel valued. Feeling valued will increase one's feelings of self-efficacy. Teachers need to insure that their lesson material has content relevance for the students. This can facilitate a healthy learning environment. There should be continuity between lessons, with relatedness from one topic to the next. ELLs need to see the value of the new information being presented. The material should be challenging and thought provoking. The teacher needs to be able to aid the students in finding out about any possible personal meaning they can derive from the material being studied. Finally, structure will help provide a strong base from which students can feel comfortable in their lessons.

REFERENCES

Allegheny College [Dean of Students]. (2015). *12 Strategies for motivation that work.* Meadville, PA: Retrieved from: www.12 strategies for motivation that work@ allegheny.edu.

Atherton, J. S. (2013). *Learning and teaching; Motivation and anxiety* [On-line: UK]. Retrieved June 19, 2015 from http://www.learningandteaching.info/learning/motivanx.htm

Bain, K. (2004). *What the best college teachers do.* Cambridge, MA: Harvard University Press.

Bandura, A. (1977). *Social learning theory.* Englewood Cliffs, NJ: Prentice Hall.

Bandura, A. (1997). *Self-efficacy: The exercise of control.* New York, NY: Freeman Press.

Bauer, G. (Ed.). (1994). *The essential papers on transference analysis.* Northvale, NJ: Jason Aronson.

Bernstein, D. A. (2011). *Essentials of psychology.* Belmont, CA: Wadsworth.

British Council, London (July, 2009). *Ways of motivating EFL/ESL students in the classroom.* London, England: BBC. Retrieved from http://www.teachingenglish.org.uk/blogs

Cherry, K. (2014). *Social learning theory.* Retrieved from: http://psychology.about.com/od/developmentalpsychology/a/sociallearning.htm

Collins, R. W. (1990). *Transfer of learning between related and less related tasks using content specific and content general learning strategies.* Miami: Florida International University.

Collins, R., & DeSantis, M. L. (2008). Creativity and intelligence. *Mensa Research Journal, 39*(3), 57–59.

Collins, R., & McCarty, V. (2008, Summer). Intelligence and other factors related to success in business. *Mensa Research Journal, 39*(2), 6–8.

Complete Dictionary of Scientific Biography. (2008). *Clark Leonard Hull.* Encyclopedia.com. Accessed November 11, 2013. Retrieved from: http://www.encyclopedia.com/doc/1G2-2830905773.html

Davis, B. G. (2009). *Tool for teaching* (2nd ed.). San-Francisco, CA: Jossey-Bass/Wiley.

Gagne, M., & Deci, E. (2005). Self-determination theory and motivation. *Journal of Organizational Behavior, 26,* 331–362. Retrieved from: www.Wileyinterscience.com

Gardnera, R. C., Day, J. B., & MacIntyrea, P. D. (1992). Integrative motivation, induced anxiety, and language learning in a controlled environment. *Studies in Second Language Acquisition, 14,* 197–214.

Gray, J. A. (1981). A critique of Eysenck's theory of personality. In H. J. Eysenck (Ed.), *A model for personality* (pp. 246–276). Berlin, Germany: Springer.

Hull, C. L. (1943). *Principles of behavior: An introduction to behavior theory.* New York, NY: Appleton-Century-Crofts.

Kenrick, D. T., Griskevicius, V., Neuberg, S. L., & Schaller, M. (2010). Renovating the pyramid of needs: Contemporary extensions build on ancient foundations. *Perspectives on Psychological Science, 5*(3), 292–314.

Komaki, J. L., Coombs, T., & Schepman, S. (1996). Motivational implications of reinforcement Theory. In R. M. Steers, L. W. Porter, & G. Bigley (Eds.), *Motivation and work behavior* (6th ed., pp. 87–107). New York, NY: McGraw Hill.

Li, N. (2015). *A book for every teacher: Teaching to English Language Learners.* Charlotte, NC: Information Age.

Maarten A. S., Boksema, T. F., Meijmana, M., & Lorista, M. (2006, May). Mental fatigue, motivation, and action monitoring. *Biological Psychology, 72*(2), 123–132.

Maslow, A. (1954). *Motivation and personality.* New York, NY: Harper & Row.

McLeod, S. (2007, updated 2015). *Skinner operant conditioning.* Retrieved from http://www.simplypsychology.org/operant-conditioning.html

Melucci, N. (2010). *E-z psychology.* New York, NY: Barron's Educational Series.

Middleton, J. A. (1995, May). A study of intrinsic motivation in the mathematics classroom: A personal constructs approach. *Journal for Research in Mathematics Education, 26*(3), 255–257.

Mintz, S. (2015). *The psychology of learning and the art of teaching.* Columbia University, Graduate School of Arts & Sciences, Teaching Center. Retrieved from http://www.columbia.edu/cu/tat/pdfs/psych_learning.pdf

Nevid, J. S. (2012). *Essentials of psychology: Concepts and applications* (3rd ed.). Belmont, CA: Cengage Learning.

Pesce, C. (2015). *How to motivate ESL students: The 10 best ways to increase teenage student motivation.* Retrieved from Busyteacher.org

Pinder, C. C. (2008). *Work motivation in organizational behavior* (2nd ed.). London, England: Psychology Press.

Posamentier, A. S. (2013, November), *9 Strategies for motivating students in mathematics.* Mercy College, NY. Retrieved from: http://www.edutopia.org/blog/9-strategies-motivating-students-mathematics-alfred-posamentier

Rogers, R., & Hunter, J. E. (1991). Impact of management by objectives on organizational productivity. *Journal of Applied Psychology, 76*(2), 322–336.

Ryan, R. M., & Deci, E. L. (2000a). Self-determination theory and the facilitation of intrinsic motivation, social development, and well-being. *American Psychologist, 55*(1), 68–78.

Ryan, R., & Deci, E. L. (2000b). Intrinsic and extrinsic motivations: Classic definitions and new directions. *Contemporary Educational Psychology, 25*(1), 54–67.

Van Eerde, W., & Thierry, H. (1996). Vroom's expectancy model and work related criteria: A meta-analysis. *Journal of Applied Psychology, 81*(5), 575–586.

Vroom, V. H. (1964). *Work and motivation.* Hoboken, NJ: John Wiley & Sons.

CHAPTER 12

INFORMATION
FOR PROFESSIONALS

Nan Li
Claflin University

Barbara Ragin
Summerton Early Childhood Center

CASE SCENARIO

Westside Elementary School is an inner-city school. One hundred Sixty-seven ELLs from Grade PreK–5 makes up almost one fifth of the school population. Two ESOL teachers who have an ESOL endorsement serve in the pullout ESOL program for the entire school. Most classroom teachers do not have training related to working with English Language Learners (ELLs). Therefore, they rely on the ESOL teacher to provide ELL-related instruction support. They also rely on her to have communication with the ELLs' parents if needed. When an ELL who does not speak any English is enrolled, the classroom teachers are usually in panics because they do not know where to start or what to do with their ELLs and often ask the ESOL teacher to keep the students in the ESOL classroom most of time. It is believed if a student does not know any English, it is better for the student to learn the English language first in the ESOL room before the student can be mainstreamed. However,

Teaching ELLs Across Content Areas, pages 287–319
Copyright © 2016 by Information Age Publishing
All rights of reproduction in any form reserved.

due to the fact that the ESOL teacher also has to work with her ELLs at the beginning level and intermediate level across all the PreK–5 grade levels, it is almost impossible for the ESOL teacher to teach different subjects to the new ELL student. Thus, the students without English proficiency miss the instruction in math, social studies, and science from their mainstream classrooms. Gradually the classroom teacher loses the ownership of the ELLs because the students do not benefit from instruction from the content classrooms.

The above case scenario is a commonly-observed phenomenon. ESOL teachers are often overloaded with teaching ELLs and coordinating with the teachers in content areas. In order to respond to the rapid increase of the ELL school population in the K–12 classrooms, teaching ELLs is no longer the sole responsibility of the ESOL teachers but a collective effort and work between ESOL teachers and teachers in mainstream classrooms, which make it possible that ELLs succeed in schools. Professional training and credentials to in-service teachers on teaching ELLs are necessary. However, the requirements for having a credential related to teaching ELLs vary from state to state. Some states offer initial teaching license in K–12 TESOL, whereas other states offers ESOL endorsement to those who have already held an initial teaching license in other subject areas. According to Education Week (2009), during the 2008–2009 school year, 33 states have teacher standards for ELL instruction, and 11 states offer incentives to earn an ESOL license and/or endorsement. Three states (Arizona, Florida, and New York) require perspective mainstream teachers to demonstrate competence in ELL instruction.

ELL RELATED PROFESSIONAL STANDARDS

TESOL-CAEP Standards

The Council for the Accreditation of Educator Preparation (CAEP) is the new accrediting body for educator preparation. On July 1, 2013, the NCATE (National Council of Accreditation for Teacher Education) and Teacher Education Accreditation Council (TEAC) consolidated into CAEP. CAEP goals are to raise the performance of candidates as practitioners in the nation's P–12 schools and to raise standards for the evidence the field relies on to support its claims of quality. CAEP and Teachers of English to Speakers of Other Languages (TESOL) provide a framework for P–12 ESOL teacher standards and preparation (TESOL, 2010). The standards include five domains that exemplify the interdisciplinary characteristics of teaching ELLs as a profession: (a) language; (b) culture; (c) planning,

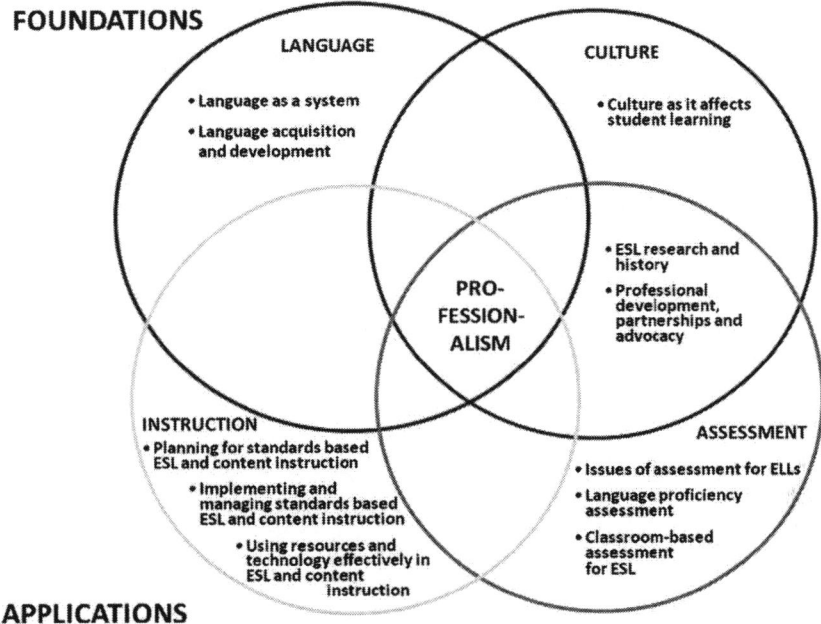

FOUNDATIONS

LANGUAGE
• Language as a system
• Language acquisition and development

CULTURE
• Culture as it affects student learning

PRO-FESSION-ALISM

• ESL research and history
• Professional development, partnerships and advocacy

INSTRUCTION
• Planning for standards based ESL and content instruction
• Implementing and managing standards based ESL and content instruction
• Using resources and technology effectively in ESL and content instruction

ASSESSMENT
• Issues of assessment for ELLs
• Language proficiency assessment
• Classroom-based assessment for ESL

APPLICATIONS

Figure 12.1 TESOL P-12 Standards (p. 19, TESOL, 2010). Used with permission from TESOL International Association. The figure is intended for personal use and not allowed for reproduction and distribution.

implementing, and managing instruction; (d) assessment; and (e) professionalism. Figure 12.1 illustrates the interrelationship among the five domains. As depicted in the figure, the knowledge of language and culture serves as the foundation in the profession; also, instruction and assessment play a key role at the application level. Overlapping of each domain reinforces the professional competence in linguistics knowledge, culturally responsive teaching, instruction, and assessment.

In this book, the standards for five domains and their performance indicators in rubrics are cited. Performance indicators are not necessarily set in stone. In the rubrics for standards under each of the five domains, there are approach standard, meets standards, and exceeds standards. ESOL teacher candidates are expected to meet the criteria under approach standard and meets standards before they meet the criteria under exceeds standards. The original document has 105 pages and it can be located at the TESOL official website at http://www.tesol.org/docs/books/the-revised-tesol-ncate-standards-for-the-recognition-of-initial-tesol-programs-in-p-12-ESOL-teacher-education-(2010-pdf).pdf?sfvrsn=2

Domain 1: Language

Domain 1 includes standards covering language as a system and language acquisition and development. Language is a system of communication, which involves listening, speaking, reading, and writing skills. However, when it is used in different contexts, different forms of language are put to use. As stated in Chapter 2, there is a distinctive difference between the Basic Interpersonal Communicative Skills (BICS) and Cognitive Academic Language Proficiency (CALP) (Cummins, 1999). A person who is fluent in restaurant English might not have the proficiency level to solve a math word problem. Genesee (1993) points out that historically teaching language to ELLs is the major focus of educational programs, and the other aspects such as their cognitive and social development are excluded, but the constructivist view of learning and teaching supports that language is integrated into academic instruction in a meaningful context (Kaufman, 2004). Hence, TESOL requires ESOL teacher candidates to "demonstrate understanding of language as a system, including phonology, morphology, syntax, pragmatics and semantics, and support ELLs as they acquire English language and literacy in order to achieve in the content areas" (TESOL, 2010, p. 23). In addition, ESOL teacher candidates need to have an understanding of the effect the first language has on the second language acquisition. Moreover, ESOL teachers "understand and apply theories and research in language acquisition and development to support ELLs' English language and literacy learning and content-area achievement" (TESOL, 2010, p. 32). Candidates are familiar with different views on language development, the stages of language acquisition, the role of first language transfer, and errors as the signs of language learning. The performance indicators for this domain include:

- knowledge of the components of language and language as an integrative system;
- application of knowledge of phonology, morphology, syntax, semantics, and pragmatics;
- knowledge of rhetorical and discourse structures as applied to ESOL learning;
- proficiency in English and serves as a model for students;
- understanding of current and historical theories and research in language and research in language acquisition as applied to ELLs;
- understanding of theories and research that explain how L1 literacy development differs from L2 literacy development;
- recognition of the importance of ELLs' L1s and language varieties; and
- understanding and application of the role of individual learner variables in the process of learning English.

Domain 2: Culture
Two standards are under this domain: (a) culture as it affects student learning and (b) culture as it affects English language learning. It is imperative for ESOL teacher candidates to understand the role of the ELLs' home cultures and "involve ESOL families and community members in student's learning" (TESOL, 2010, p. 38). In order for ESOL teacher candidates to choose appropriate and effective teaching techniques, they need to understand how to use information to connect to their ELLs backgrounds. The performance indicators include:

- understanding and application of knowledge about cultural values and beliefs in the context of teaching and learning;
- understanding and application of knowledge about the effects of racism, stereotyping, and discrimination to teaching and learning;
- understanding and application of knowledge about cultural conflicts and home events that can have an impact on ELLs' learning;
- understanding and application of knowledge about communication between home and school to enhance ESOL teaching and build partnerships with ESOL families;
- understanding and application of concepts about the interrelationship between language and culture;
- employment of a range of resources, including the internet, to learn about world cultures and specifically the cultures of students in their classrooms and apply that learning to instruction; and
- understanding and application of concepts of cultural competence, particularly knowledge about how an individual's cultural indent affects their learning and academic progress and how levels of cultural identity will vary widely among students.

Domain 3: Planning, Implementing, and Managing Instruction
Three standards are related to this domain: (a) planning for standard-based ESOL and content instruction; (b) implementing and managing standards-based ESOL and content instruction; and (c) using resources and technology effectively in ESOL and content instruction.
Providing research-based best practices and creating a supportive learning environment can enhance ELLs' learning. Thus, TESOL standards requires ESOL professionals to "know, understand, and use evidence-based practices and strategies related to planning, implementing, and managing standards-based ESOL and content instruction" and to be "knowledgeable about program models and skilled in teaching strategies for developing and integrating language skills" (TESOL, 2010, p. 43). Incorporating technology into instruction and choosing appropriate resources are required as well. The performance indicators are:

- Planning standards-based ESOL and content instruction.
- Creating supportive, accepting, classroom environments.
- Planning differentiated learning experiences based on assessment of students' English and L1 proficiency, learning styles, and prior formal educational experiences and knowledge.
- Providing for particular needs of students with interrupted formal education (SIFE).
- Planning for instruction that embeds assessment, includes scaffolding, and provides re-teaching when necessary for students to successfully meet learning objectives.
- Organizing learning around standard-based subject matter and language learning objectives.
- Incorporating activities, tasks, and assignments that develop authentic uses of language as students learn academic vocabulary and content-area material.
- Providing activities and materials that integrates listening, speaking, reading, and writing.
- Developing students' listening skills for a variety of academic and social purposes.
- Developing students' speaking skills for a variety of academic and social purposes.
- Providing standards-based instruction that builds on students' oral English to support learning to read and write.
- Providing standards-based reading instruction adapted to ELLs.
- Providing standards-based writing instruction adapted to ELLs. Develop students' writing through a range of activities, from sentence formation to expository writing.
- Selecting, adapting, and using culturally responsive, age-appropriate, and linguistically accessible materials.
- Selecting materials and other resources that are appropriate to students' developing language and content-area abilities, including appropriate use of L1.
- Employing a variety of materials for language learning, including books, visual aids, props, and realia.
- Using technological resources (e.g., Web, software, computers, and related devices) to enhance language and content-area instruction for ELLs.

Domain 4: Assessment

There are three standards under this domain: (a) issues of assessment for English language learners, (b) language proficiency assessment, and (c) classroom-based assessment for ESOL. Specifically, these assessment standards require that the ESOL teacher candidates, first of all, must "demonstrate understanding of various assessment issues as they affect ELLs, such as accountability, bias, special education testing, language proficiency, and accommodations in formal testing situations" (TESOL, 2010, p. 56). Then, they are required to "know and use a variety of standard-based language proficiency instruments to show language growth and to inform their instruction" (TESOL, 2010, p. 61), and use the testing results for "identification, placement, and reclassification of ELLs" (TESOL, 2010, p. 61). Finally, they are required to "know and use a variety of performance-based assessment tools and techniques" (TESOL, 2010, p. 64) to guide their instruction. The related performance indicator given in the program standards include:

- understanding of the purpose of assessment as they relate to ELLs and use results appropriately;
- being knowledgeable about and able to use a variety of assessment procedures for ELLs;
- understanding of key indicators of good assessment instruments;
- distinguishing among ELLs' language differences, giftedness, and special education needs;
- understanding and implementing national and state requirements for identification, reclassification, and exit for ELLs from language support program;
- understanding the appropriate use of norm-referenced assessments with ELLs;
- assessing ELLs' language skills and communicative competence using multiple sources of information;
- using performance-based assessment tools and tasks that measure ELLs' progress;
- understanding and using criterion-referenced assessments appropriately with ELLs;
- using various instruments and techniques to assess content-area learning such as math, science, social studies for ELLs at varying levels of language and literacy development;
- preparing ELLs to use self–and peer-assessment techniques when appropriate; and
- using a variety of rubrics to assess ELLs' language development in classroom setting.

Domain 5: Professionalism

Two standards support this domain: (a) ESOL research and history and (b) professional development, partnership, and advocacy. ESOL professionals are expected to "keep current with new instructional techniques, research results, advances in the ESOL field, and education policy issues, and demonstrate knowledge of the history of ESOL teaching" (TESOL, 2010, p. 68). Additionally, they "take advantages of professional growth opportunities and demonstrate the ability to build partnerships with colleagues and students' families, serve as community resources, and advocate for ELLs" (TESOL, 2010, p. 71). The performance indicators include

- knowledge of language teaching methods in their historical context;
- knowledge of the evolution of laws and policy in the ESOL profession;
- ability to read and conduct classroom research;
- participating in professional growth opportunities;
- establishing professional goals;
- working with other teachers and staff to provide comprehensive, challenging educational opportunities for ELLs in the school;
- engaging in collaborative teaching in general education, content-area, special education, and gifted classrooms;
- advocating for ELLs' access to academic classes, resource, and instructional technology;
- supporting ELL families; and
- serving as professional resource personnel in their educational communities.

The Common Core State Standards and TESOL Standards

Common Core State Standards (CCSS) refers to a U.S. education initiative that seeks to bring diverse state curricula into alignment with each other by following the principles of standards-based education reform (Wikipedia, 2013). For example, it details what K–12 students should know in English language arts and mathematics at the end of each grade. The standards are designed to be robust and relevant to the real world, reflecting the knowledge and skills that students need for success in college and careers (Common Core State Standards Initiative, 2012). The goal of the CCSS is to provide students with high quality education. Currently, forty-five states, the District of Columbia, four territories, and the Department of Defense Education Activity have adopted the CCSS. Yet, some questions remain. For example, how the CCSS will have an impact on English language learners has not been addressed and questions about the role of ESOL teachers remain unanswered (Staehr Fenner, 2013).

However, the CCSS initiative is sponsored and supported by the National Governors Association (NGA) and the Council of Chief State School Officers (CCSSO) to seek ways to establish consistent educational standards across the states as well as ensure that students graduating from high school are prepared to enter credit-bearing courses at two- or four-year college programs or to enter the workforce (Wikipedia, 2013). Teachers need to know the three components of the CCSS initiative. These components are: Content-area and ESOL teachers; content-area and English Language Proficiency (ELP) and English Language Development (ELD) standards; content-area and ELP/ELD assessment. These three critical components are important for both content-area teachers, the ESOL teachers, policy makers, and administrators to understand in order to provide effective education to ELLs (Staehr Fenner & Segota, 2012). The interaction of the three components leads to ELLs' academic achievement. In addition, if one component is not fully developed, the other two cannot serve well to help ELLs learn the contents defined in CCSS and the English language, simultaneously.

On February 14, 2013, TESOL International Association gathered 30 ESOL teachers and administrators, education experts, researchers, and thought leaders to start a conversation about how CCSS would change the roles of ESOL teachers (Staehr Fenner, 2013). The findings from the dialogue indicate that due to the fact that CCSS places an emphasis on developing academic language for all students, both content-area and ESOL teachers face the challenges of teaching academic language and cognitively demanding content at the same time. In addition, the findings signify that ESOL teachers have had substantial training in language learning theories, linguistics, language pedagogy, and literacy development, but most content-area teachers have not received sufficient training in those areas. ESOL teachers are usually aware of the community multicultural resources. Thus, content-area teachers need some guidance from ESOL teachers in order to provide effective instruction to ELLs. Furthermore, implementing CCSS takes a collaborative effort. Therefore, it is the responsibilities of both content-area and ESOL teachers to provide quality education to ELLs.

As a result, the dialogue also proposed that new instructional strategies were needed in order to meet the rigorous CCSS standards. "ESOL curriculum should focus on depth and rigor and not rush through the materials" (Staehr Fenner, 2013, p. 13). Additionally, based on the ELLs' language proficiency levels, authentic lessons that are grounded in the CCSS should be implemented. The contents and goals need to be differentiated according to the ELLs' language level. Moreover, the mainstream teachers need to have guidance to "teach grammatical structures and academic languages" (Staehr Fenner, 2013, p. 13) in the lessons.

With the change of the educational landscape, the role of ESOL resource teachers are not limited to teaching English only, but advocating for ELLs and actively collaborating with the mainstream teachers to provide the academic language needed for ELLs while implementing the CCSS process.

The ESOL teachers should be encouraged to participate in the process of decision making and their voice needs to be heard.

TRENDS AND PROGRAMS IN L2 TEACHING

The debate continues on second language (L2) teaching that began in the 1990s focusing on how and what L2 teaching and learning is. In the past 15 years, several crucially combined factors have affected current perspectives on the teaching of English as L2 worldwide: (a) the decline of methods, (b) a growing emphasis on the bottom-up and top-down skills, (c) the creation of new knowledge about English, and (d) integrated and contextualized teaching of multiple language skills (Hinkel, 2006). Indeed, a constant heated discussion has been focused on how the ELLs should be served across the country. We have the CCSS and TESOL standards, but there is no set curriculum for ESOLs. Through our connection with ESOL resource teachers in different school districts, we know that the ESOL curriculum framework emphasizes the development of the four language skills. Many ESOL teachers develop their own materials to work with ELLs on math, science, and social studies. Time management was always a challenge because too many areas needed to be covered in a short period of time, especially in a pull-out program. Today, the ESOL teachers acknowledge that they must develop their own materials and tie them into CCSS at the K–12 schools (Staehr Fenner, 2013).

According to Gottlieb (2006), in the last decades, a shift has taken place in teachers' instructional practices in serving the English language learners. Traditionally, the language instruction at K–12 schools and adult education originated from the linguistic field. Starting from the 1980s, with the introduction of the integration of educational theories and linguistics knowledge, the correlation between the content of subject matter and students' language development has been recognized.

Cummins' (1999) research on BICS and CALPS provides a theoretical foundation for the critical need to develop ELLs' academic language in content areas. Historically, ESOL teachers have focused on ESOL and teaching ELLs on these areas: listening, speaking, reading, writing, and language arts at their language proficiency levels. The ELLs are usually served in the ESOL resource classrooms. When ELLs return to their mainstream classroom, they struggle in math, science, and social studies because the textbooks are written at their grade levels. As a result, there is a gap between the ESOL language education and the content knowledge. If the ELL population is not large enough at one school, the ESOL teacher needs to travel among several schools to provide the services, which makes it more challenging for ESOL teachers to meet the needs of the ELLs on a daily basis.

Hence, the collaboration between the ESOL teachers and the mainstream classroom teachers (Honigsfeld & Dove, 2010) has been highly proposed to solve the problem of curriculum misalignment. However, every school is different and every district has its own policy related to ELL service. In this section, we will introduce the types of ESOL programs that are commonly implemented in American schools.

Different Types of Programs for ELLs

Across the United States, ELLs are placed in different educational programs. In this book, we introduce only the most commonly implemented programs. These ELL-related programs include: *pullout program, inclusion program, sheltered instruction, bilingual program,* and *self-contained ESOL program.* Generally speaking, pullout programs have been used for many years to serve struggling ELLs. The Council of the Great City Schools (CGCS) is an organization that focuses on urban education. The CGCS investigated the characteristics of ELLs in 58 member school districts (Antunez, 2003). The responses from 36 districts (62%) indicated the number of ELLs was increasing with the CGCS school districts. The study also showed that sheltered instruction was identified as the most commonly offered program for ELLs and the pullout program was the second for the member districts. Inclusion programs have gradually begun to replace pullout programs in some states (Byrnes, Kiger, & Manning, 1997). Zehr (2006) also reported that inclusion programs replaced the pullout programs at all elementary schools in St. Paul, Minnesota. These are some trends related to teaching ELLs. More details about the ELL-related programs will be discussed in the following section.

Pullout Program

The pullout program for ELLs refers to the program in which ELLs receive assistance for a portion of the day through the pull-out component. When pulling-out, they go to the ESOL resource classroom for intensive instruction in English and also receive language support within each content area while the ELL students spend the majority of their day in classrooms with English speaking peers. This allows them to be a part of the student body within their school. Pullout programs involve instruction that is provided outside the regular classroom (Passow, 1989). Pullout programs have been adopted to serve children from African American families as well as children from other minority groups, especially from inner-city areas since the Elementary and Secondary Education Act of 1965 was passed (Van Loenen & Haley, 1994). It has been used as a popular instructional delivery model for ELLs. The ESOL teacher pulls ELLs out of the regular classrooms to provide a 30 to 60 minute long instruction on language arts, reading, and writing in the ESOL room. The length of time depends on the number of ELLs and the language proficiency level of ELLs. The ELLs meet the ESOL teacher in the resource room on a daily basis, but sometimes twice or three times a week.

The effectiveness of the pullout program has been argued because the findings have remained inconclusive. However, Carter (1984) points out some disadvantages of a pullout model: (a) the shortened instructional time due to being in and out the classrooms; (b) hard time for students to connect the contents in the regular room to that at the pullout setting; (c) lower expectation and easier assignment from the regular teachers; and (d) ELLs served in a segregated pullout program. In addition, scheduling is not easy for the ESOL resource teacher because ELLs are pulled out from more than one classroom (Ovando & Collier, 1998). Finally, pullout ESOL teachers find it hard to communicate with the mainstream teachers (Cook & Zhao, 2011).

In spite of the disadvantages, advantages of a pullout program are identified by research (Ovando, Collier, & Combs, 2005; Cook & Zhao, 2011). First, students can get one-on-one help in a small group setting. Second, the pullout program provides an environment for ELLs to rely on. It is easy for ELLs to build a relationship with the ESOL resource teacher in a small group setting. In addition, usually, ELLs verbalizes their ideas in the resource room more than in the big group. Finally, ELLs feel safe and comfortable in small groups. Although the research findings about the effectiveness of pullout programs reveal both advantages and disadvantages, and both positive and negative responses toward pullout programs are found in research, the pullout program has been implemented across the United States in schools where other programs cannot be implemented due to the small size of the ELL population. The pullout model provides a supportive learning environment for ELLs to learn the language and culture.

Inclusion Program

Inclusion has been the practice of serving students with special needs within the general education setting (Ferguson, 1995; Stainback & Stainback, 1984; Turnbull, Turnbull, Shank, & Leal, 1995). Aldridge and Goldman (2002) explained that inclusion was "a movement that was designed to bring special education services into the general classroom" (p. 134). Inclusion programs for ELLs is in-class ESOL instruction that is provided by mainstream classroom teachers (Wright, 2015). Due to the negative responses toward pullout programs, inclusion programs for ELLs to have in-class instruction started to develop since 1995 assisted by Chapter 1 programs (Anstrom, 1995; Ovando & Collier, 1998). Chapter 1 of the

Elementary and Secondary Education Act of 1965 is the major federal program to improve the education of disadvantaged children. There are pros and cons for inclusion programs.

ELLs typically need additional resources and support to adjust to the various linguistic complications of learning a new language. Thus, ELLs immersed in a regular paced English class with students who are fluent in English do not have the benefits of learning as in the ESOL room. Some concerns for inclusion programs include the fact that full inclusion does not usually take into consideration the ELL students' needs, especially if an ELL child does not know English. It is also a concern that teachers of the full inclusion model are not prepared to successfully help ELL students acquire a new language. Wright (2015) suggests that classroom teachers in the inclusion model need to meet the state certification requirements to work with ELLs if it is available in that state. In addition, curriculum and materials for ELLs should be provided to the classroom teachers. Furthermore, the classroom teacher should provide the same kind of instruction that an ESOL teacher does in a pullout program.

However, the types of curriculum and instruction that should be used for ELLs in inclusion programs have remained a focused discussion for teacher educators and researchers for many years to come. Stainback and Stainback (1984) remarked that, in the mainstream classroom, curricula needed to be accommodating, flexible, and challenging to all students. Watts-Taffe and Truscott (2000) mentioned the importance of scaffolding, strong discussion, and vocabulary discussion in helping the language development of ELL students in an inclusive setting in addition to agreeing with Stainback and Stainback. Though inclusive models have been suggested to serve ELLs, how to implement the inclusive model at a school setting has been an issue. Every school district has a different situation. Findings from the previous research (Cook & Zhao, 2011; Honigsfeld & Dove, 2010) suggested that collaboration and co-teaching between the classroom teachers and the ESOL resource teachers is the key to successfully implement the inclusion models. We hope the examples of inclusive models and debates that are provided in the following resources will help teachers and their schools develop some ideas about the implementation of an inclusive model.

1. Honigsfeld, A., & Dove, M. (2010). *Collaboration and co-teaching: Strategies for English Learners*. Newbury Park, CA: Corwin.
2. *English as a Second Language: Inclusion or Separation for English Language Learners*. Retrieved from: http://esoledu.blogspot.com/2011/06/inclusion-or-separation.html or *TESOL Quarterly* (2003).
3. Conversations about Inclusion: Connecting Mainstream and ESL by Lisa Simons. Retrieved from: http://minnetesol.org/blog1/

minnetesol-2008-journal/2008-journal/conversations-about-inclu-
sion-connecting-mainstream-and-esl/

Sheltered Instruction

Sheltered Instruction refers to grade-level content instruction in which the classroom teacher provides modified instruction by using the grade-level content objectives so that the content will be meaningful and comprehensible to English language learners (Echevarria, Vogt, & Short, 2013). ELLs will learn the content knowledge at their grade level and at the same time develop academic English language. As described in Chapter 3, the Sheltered Instruction Observation Protocol (SIOP) model offers guidelines to teachers about how to prepare and develop a SIOP lesson.

One of the important characteristics of the SIOP model is to include both content objectives and language objectives. When classroom teachers write lesson objectives, the objectives related to the development of a concept, an idea, or a skill that reflects the grade-level curriculum standards should be clearly stated. When adding language objectives, teachers need to consider what language piece is needed in order to support ELLs and for all students to have access to the content knowledge. Therefore, teachers should be mindful when integrating the need of language development into every lesson. An effective lesson does not happen without good strategies. Echevarria et al. (2013) suggest the following effective strategies in the SIOP model: modeling, helping students make connection between the content and personal experiences or existing schemas, differentiated instruction, writer's workshop, cooperative learning, high level of students' engagements, supplementary materials, technology integration, and so on. Consistently weaving language objectives into content objectives helps students develop both content knowledge and academic language proficiency. The resources related to SIOP can be found at: http://www.cal.org/siop/about/index.html

Bilingual Program

Bilingual Program usually refers to the program in an English-language school system in which students with little fluency in English are taught in both their native language and English. The purpose of the program is to build a bridge that helps students become proficient in their native language and English. Since the passing of the Bilingual Education Act of 1968, the bilingual program, also called the transitional bilingual education program, has received much government support. Students speak the same primary language and are taught by bilingual teachers. The program is to gradually transit the bilingual students to English speaking only classrooms. The model is usually found at the elementary school level, and the typical grade span is K–3 (Wright, 2015). To meet linguistic, academic, and cultural needs of ELLs, the bilingual program is often intended to accomplish three goals: (a) to help ELLs transition to mainstream classrooms; (b) to have access to the grade-level content areas and move to the English-only mainstream classroom as soon as possible; and (c) to adapt to the mainstream cultural and school community (Ovando et al., 2005; Wright, 2015).

The bilingual education model offers bilingual instruction in content areas at grade levels for students coming from the two language backgrounds. Using the native language to provide instruction in content areas will ensure that the ELLs have access to the grade level content areas. At the beginning stage of the early grades, the use of the first language can be as much as 90% of the instruction time; as the students move to higher grade level, English and the first language are separated for instruction, and the instruction in the first language is as much as 50% (Thomas & Collier, 2002). Some advantages of bilingual model include: (a) students are exposed to the grade level; (b) the native language skills are maintained; and (c) students have an equal opportunity to have access to education. However, due to the span of the program, many students are not ready for the mainstream classroom when they are dismissed from the bilingual education program. Reaching the proficiency level of English development takes a longer time. In addition, many ELLs do not begin school in kindergarten and the age at the time of their arrival in America varies (Ovando & Collier, 1998; Wright, 2015).

Self-Contained ESOL Program

In the self-contained program model, ELLs are placed with other ELLs for the entire day where they receive sheltered instruction from teachers trained in sheltering techniques (Wikipedia, 2013). In the self-contained ESOL program, ELL students are grouped together in one classroom to receive instruction at their language proficiency level. Usually, only the district with a large population of ELL students offer self-contained ESOL programs. For example, Tungate (2012) reports that the Warren County School District in Kentucky offers a self-contained ESOL program, which is called Intensive Language Classrooms, to the large number of refugees from Burma and Central Africa. Sometimes, students' math might be on grade level, but they struggle with the language used in math. Sometimes, their instructional levels are below their grade levels. Boyson and Short (2003) report that 196 schools located in 30 states offer 115 newcomer programs at the middle and high school levels. In terms of adopting a program for a school, there is no perfect program or one formula to follow. Implementing an ESOL program depends on the number of ELL students at the school district. However, what works best for the students should be the first concern.

ASSESSMENT AND RELATED ISSUES

As classroom teachers, we constantly face the challenge of assessing our ELLs' academic performance. How do we decide whether an ELL's performance is related to the language barrier or to a lack of the academic knowledge? We gather different kinds of data related to ELLs to help us make decisions about our academic plan for them. All we try to do is have a picture of where the student's instruction level is through assessing the data. We might get data about the language background of the family, the literacy level of the first language, the parents' educational level in the first language, and the benchmark score of the student's language proficiency level. Not every piece of information we collect is directly from a testing instrument. Gottlieb points out the variables in assessing ELLs:

- Language(s) and culture(s) of everyday interaction
- The exposure to academic language outside school
- Educational experiences outside and in the United States
- Continuity of educational experiences (mobility, interruption of schooling)
- Proficiency (including literacy) in the native language (L1)
- Academic achievement in the native language (L1)
- Proficiency (including literacy) in English (L2)
- Academic achievement in English
- Allotment of time per day for educational support services
- Amount and type of sustained support across years—stability of instructional program and language(s) of delivery
- Socioeconomic status in the United States, including access to resources and opportunities for learning (Gottlieb, 2006, p. 6)

In the next section, we will discuss the purpose of assessment, the type of assessments, the characteristics of each stage of ELLs' language development, and some strategies to assess ELLs.

Purpose of Assessment

Very often, when *assessment* is mentioned, we immediately think about standardized testing such as English Language Development Assessment (ELDA), or other state required tests at the end of the school year. Assessment is appraising or estimating the level of magnitude of some attribute of a person (Cook & Zhao, 2011; Mousavi, 2009). Without assessment, neither ESOL resource teachers nor classroom teachers have a benchmark to guide their instruction. The following are several types of assessment used for assessing the ELLs.

Initial Assessment

When a new ELL arrives, the first assessment tool many school districts give is the *Home Language Survey.* The survey usually contains questions about language(s) spoken at home. If the student speaks another language other than English, further testing should be given. Different states give different initial benchmark test. Some states use ELDA, some states use Wisconsin Language Development Assessment (WLDA), and other states use Language Assessment Battery (LAB). The test results will reflect the language proficiency level of the student and help ESOL resource teachers make decisions about placing the student at an appropriate language level.

Ongoing Formative Assessment

Formative assessment refers to a process used by teachers and students during instruction that provides feedback to adjust ongoing teaching and learning to improve students' achievement of intended instructional outcomes (Wikipedia, 2013). They are generally low stakes because formative assessments have low or no point value. Examples may include asking students to: draw a concept map in class to represent their understanding of a topic, submit one or two sentences identifying the main point of a lecture, or turn in a research proposal for early feedback. The purpose of the ongoing formative assessment is to monitor the ELL students' language development and academic progress. After an ELL is placed at the appropriate language level, formative classroom assessment will begin to take place. ELLs' language level can fluctuate within a short period of time. Therefore, ongoing assessment is needed through teacher observations, assignments, and portfolios. Teachers need to adjust the instructional level according to the students' needs. At this stage, it is critical that both ESOL resource teachers and classroom teachers work together to fill in the gap of the students' academic achievements. For example, an ELL's math might be on grade level, but due to the language barrier, the student cannot comprehend the math language. In a case like this, scaffolding strategies such as modeling and modifying the English language is needed in order for the student to have access to the grade level content.

End of the School-Year Summative Assessment

Summative assessment refers to the assessments used to evaluate student learning, skill acquisition, and academic achievement at the conclusion of a defined instructional period (Wikipedia, 2013). It is different from the initial or on-going assessment because the summative assessment is to provide the evaluation of the final quality of teaching and learning with an overall grade or score. At the end of the school year, standardized testing and standardized language testing usually take place. Along with the recommendations of the ESOL resource teacher and the classroom teacher, the summative assessment also serves as one of the indicators when a decision is made to exit an ELL from the ESOL program service. If the ELL stays in the same school district, the assessment data can be used as the benchmark at the beginning of the new school year. However, research findings indicate that ELLs' language proficiency level regress during the summer break (Cook & Zhao, 2011). Hence, at the beginning of the new school year, assessing returning ELLs' language proficiency level will help ESOL teachers identify the gap.

Stages of ELLs' Language Development

After ELLs have the initial placement test, their language proficiency levels marked as "Level 1," "Level 2," "Level 3," or "Level 4" will be put on their files and their files will be sent to the classroom teachers. Very often, classroom teachers do not know what ELLs can do at each level. Here we will discuss the characteristics of five stages of language acquisition.

Stage 1: Preproduction Stage
L2 students at this stage:
- are in a "silent period."
- respond to oral communication cues, and can respond in one or two word phrases, but cannot verbalize their ideas.
- know basic greeting and vocabulary words.
- write alphabet or single words.

Stage 2: Early Production
L2 students at this stage:
- respond in simple sentences or phrases.
- repeat and memorize words, phrases, or short sentences.
- can carry simple conversation in a contextualized learning environment.
- understand the meaning through listening, but not able to communicate their thoughts or ideas in complete sentences.
- can read with support, but not independently.
- write short sentences or short paragraph with simple grammatical structures.

Stage 3: Speech Emergence
L2 students at this stage:
- can produce long sentences though grammatical mistakes occur.
- verbalize thoughts and ideas in complete sentences though grammatical mistakes occur.

- use new words and phrases in oral language and written language.
- can write sentences with complex grammatical structures with inaccurate grammatical structure.
- read independently.
- write short paragraphs for different purposes.

Stage 4: Intermediate Fluency
    L2 students at this stage:
- comprehend ideas and thoughts in most contexts.
- communicate ideas and thoughts with few grammatical mistakes.
- understand abstract concepts with support.
- write 3 paragraph long essays.

Stage 5: Fluency
    L2 students at this stage:
- function appropriately in mainstream classrooms.
- understand and use idioms, slangs, and proverbs appropriately.
- read academic related materials independently.
- write in different genres.

Strategies for Assessing ELLs

Two kinds of assessment are usually provided to ELLs: standardized assessment and ongoing classroom assessment. All students are required to take standardized testing. There is no exception for ELLs even though their language proficiency level is at level one or two. When giving standardized testing, accommodations can be made for ELLs. In order to lower ELLs' testing anxiety, giving them the test in a small group in a separate room or extending the testing time are helpful tips. ELLs might be able to answer questions but might not be able to understand the directions and some school districts allow teachers to read the directions to ELLs so that they will understand what they are expected to do.

Ongoing classroom assessment takes place on a daily basis in classrooms. Teacher observations, ELLs' assignments and work samples, quizzes, conversations, portfolios, and class activities can all serve as ongoing assessment tools. Here are some strategies to assess the four language domains: listening, speaking, reading, and writing.

Listening
Listening is a receptive skill. It is hard to assess whether an ELL understands the discourse unless there is a productive skill such as speaking or

writing to go along with it. Hence, in a classroom setting, assessing listening skills takes place in a natural environment. If a student can respond appropriately by following your directions to write a summary of what you just taught, you can identify whether the student understands or not. The following activities can be used as reference for assessing ELLs' listening skills:

- dictation;
- matching game;
- respond to teachers' directions;
- label a map after listening to a short story or a short lecture;
- "thumb up" or "thumb down";
- take class notes; and
- respond to teachers' directions by writing, drawing, or repeating.

Speaking

Speaking is a productive skill. Every language is made up of phonemes, morphemes, syntax, and semantics. Speaking a language that can be understood involves skills in appropriately articulating the sounds (pronunciation), using grammatical structures, and interpreting meaning in context. Speaking involves two parties in an interactive process in which a message is conveyed, listened, interpreted, and responded to (Underhill, 1987). Therefore, speaking cannot be separated from listening. Here are some suggested activities to assess ELLs speaking skills: role playing, a skit, retell a story, presentations, interview with guided questions and topics, and explain the process of an experiment, etc. Depending on the language proficiency level, cues can be given to ELLs. For example, the following can be used:

- I like this story because...
- I would like to have a new ending of the story...
- My favorite character in the story is...because...
- The story reminds me of my experiences in...
- I wish I could be the character in the story...
- From the cover of the book, I predict the story is about...
- Based on the discussion in our group, we come up with the conclusion that...
- If I were the character in the story, I would...
- Three new things I have learned from today's social studies...
- The life cycle of a caterpillar is...

Reading

Reading is a receptive skill. Reading is a complex cognitive process. Children learn to read before they reach the third grade, but they read to learn after they are in the third grade. Decoding skills such as phonemic awareness and phonic skills are fundamental in learning to read. Comprehension plays a significant role in the process of reading. Without comprehension, students might be able to "read" but do not understand what they are reading about. ELLs need to develop reading strategies that help them develop both comprehension and linguistic knowledge. In standardized testing, students are required to read a paragraph, and then they are required to answer multiple choice questions and answer some short questions. In order to prepare them for taking standardized test, reading strategies need to be developed. Therefore, the following reading activities can be used for classroom assessment:

- Guided reading (it requires ongoing assessment): http://teacher. scholastic.com/products/guidedreading/pdfs/whatis.pdf
- Shared reading: http://www.eduplace.com/rdg/res/literacy/ em_lit4.html
- Read aloud: http://www.readaloud.org/
- Independent reading: http://www.eduplace.com/rdg/res/literacy/ in_read1.html
- Literacy circle: http://www.readwritethink.org/classroom-resources/lesson-plans/literature-circles-getting-started-19.html
- Using vocabulary strategies such as identifying prefix, suffix, root, synonym, antonym, meaning in the context to interpreter the meaning of new words : http://www.pinterest.com/lisaflorenz/prefix-suffix-antonym-synonym/
- Interpreting new meaning of familiar words in the new context

Writing

Writing is a productive skill. Writing is a process that involves students' prior knowledge and background and their interpretation of the world to make meaning by communicating in writing (Peregoy & Boyle, 1993). The purpose of writing is to communicate ideas of the writer's worldview about a topic. When ELLs communicate in writing, we can see the influence of their first languages as well as the cultural backgrounds they grow up with. The suggested assessment activities are as follows:

- Interactive writing: http://www.readwritethink.org/classroom-resources/lesson-plans/teaching-audience-through-interactive-242.html
- Writer's workshop: http://en.wikipedia.org/wiki/Writing_Workshop; http://www.busyteacherscafe.com/literacy/writing_workshop.html
- Use story maps and graphic organizers: http://www.cobbk12.org/ Cheathamhill/LFS%20Update/Graphic%20Organizers.htm; http:// www.educationoasis.com/curriculum/GO/character_story.htm
- Write summary

- Dictation
- Cloze test
- Short answer
- Essays (start with 3 paragraph essay, then gradually move to 5 paragraph essay)
- Narrative writing about an event, an experience, or an activity
- Write critique about a story
- Write about the character traits of a character in a story
- Write book report
- Write a new ending of the story

When a writing assignment is given, a rubric should be given to the ELLs as well. ELLs need to know what they are expected to do and what the final writing product should be like. Rubrics should be designed in a way that is easy to read, easy to understand, and easy to follow.

To conclude the part of classroom assessment for the four language domains, we have covered a lot of activities that can be used as formative assessment tools. As you can see, it is almost impossible to separate the four domains of the language skills. Therefore, assessing ELLs' integrated language skills and content knowledge is imperative. For example, when using a K-W-L graphic organizer, we can identify what students know, what kind of existing schema students have, what they want to learn, and what they have learned. When we encourage students to complete the chart in complete sentences, we identify ELLs' writing skills by diagnosing the linguistic gap that ELLs may have. If we ask ELLs to share their writing with a partner or in a group, we can assess the student's speaking skills. It depends how we would like to use a K-W-L chart, we can assess their listening, speaking, reading, and writing skills.

ELL POPULATION DATA AND STATISTICS

In the last 30 years, the demographic of the U.S. population has changed dramatically. More than 30 million immigrants including both authorized and unauthorized have moved to the United States (Migrant Policy Institute, 2010a), which resulted in a shift in the landscaping of educational demographics. More than 150 languages are spoken by ELLs in the United States. About one in four children in America from an immigrant family speaks another language other than English at home (Mather, 2009). Followed by Chinese, Vietnamese, and French/Haitian Creole, Spanish is the most commonly spoken home language by ELLs. Spanish speaking school-aged children make up about 66% of the ELL population. Spanish is spoken by two-third of ELLs in 28 states within the United States.

Based on the statistics the U.S. population will continue to be more racially and ethnically diverse. In 2013, American children's population (0–17 years old) was made up of 53% Caucasians, 24% Hispanic, 14% Black, and 5% Asian (childstats.gov, 2013). The other races make up the other 5%. The population of Hispanic people has increased significantly from 9% of the child population in 1980 to 24% in 2013. By 2015, it is projected that 32% of American children will be Hispanic. According to the National Clearing House for English Language Acquisition (NCELA, 2011), in the U.S. public school enrollment of ELLs from PreK through Grade 12 increased 51% over a 10-year period from the 1998–1999 school year to the 2008–2009 school year. The reported enrollment of ELLs from PreK–12 for the 1998–1999 school year was 3,540,673, whereas there were 5,345,673 ELLs enrolled in the 2008–2009 school year. The number of ELLs in 2008–2009 was 11% of the total enrollment in public schools.

In the 2007–2008 school year, the top 12 states that had a high number of ELL enrollment were Nevada, California, New Mexico, Arizona, Texas, Alaska, Oregon, Colorado, Hawaii, Utah, Washington, and Florida (see Table 12.1). In addition, about one fourth of ELL enrollment in the United States is found in 25 districts. Of the 25 districts, 13 are located in California, four in Florida, four in Texas, and the rest are in New York City, Illinois, Nevada, and Colorado (Migrant Policy Institute, 2010b). The states that had more than 100,000 ELLs enrolled in the year of 2007–2008 are California, Nevada, Arizona, Texas, and Florida. While the total K–12 enrollment remains stable and relatively unchanged, the ELL population increased from 13.5% in 1990 to 25% in 2010. With the ELL population growth rate of 800% (3,077 to 28,548), South Carolina ranked number 1 between the school year of 1997–1998 and 2007–2008. Indiana State followed by growing 400% (Migrant Policy Institute, 2010c).

The ELL population will continue to grow in the next 40 years. Sooner or later, teachers will have ELLs in their classrooms. Therefore, ESOL teachers will not be the only ones in a school district who provide language acquisition class to ELLs. Classroom teachers need to have training in working with students from diverse cultural and linguistic backgrounds so they can better serve ELLs in the mainstream classrooms. In addition, "ESOL teachers and mainstream teachers need to team up to teach common core" (Education Week, 2013).

SUGGESTIONS FOR TEACHER EDUCATION PROGRAMS

Teacher education generally refers to the procedures of preparing prospective teachers with the knowledge, attitudes, and skills needed to perform their tasks in the classroom, school, and community. Teacher education is

TABLE 12.1   ELL Population Growth Rate by State and by District

The Growth Rate of ELL Population by State (1998–2008)

Over 400%	South Carolina, Indiana
Over 300%	Nevada
Over 200%	Arkansas, North Carolina, Virginia, Delaware, Georgia, Alabama, Kentucky, Tennessee

ELL Population Over 100,000 by State (2007–2008)

California:	1,562,036 = 24.3% of Pre-K–12 enrollment
Texas:	701,799 = 15% of Pre-K–12 enrollment
Florida:	234,934 = 8.8% of Pre-K–12 enrollment
Arizona:	166,572 = 15.3% of Pre-K–12 enrollment
Nevada:	134,377 = 31.3% of Pre-K–12 enrollment

ELL Population by Top School Districts (2007–2008)

Santa Ana, CA:	36,807 (62.1%)
Campton, CA:	17,496 (57.9%)
Garden Grove, CA:	23,698 (47.8%)
Pomona, CA:	15,826 (47.5%)
Los Angeles, CA:	328,684 (44%)
Fontana, CA:	16,587 (39.6%)
Dallas, TX:	51,328 (32%)
Fresno, CA:	25,233 (31%)
Sacramento, CA:	15,382 (30%)
Oakland, CA:	15,010 (30%)

Source: Migrant Policy Institute, 2010b & 2010c.

often divided into these stages: initial teacher training education (i.e., pre-service courses) before entering the classroom as a fully responsible teacher; induction, the procedure of accepting into the program after the first few years of training or the first year in a particular school; teacher development or continuing professional development for an in-service process for practicing teachers (Wikipedia, 2013). According to Education Week (2009), in the school year of 2008 to 2009, 33 states have teacher standards for ELL instruction, but only 3 states (Arizona, Florida, and New York) requires all perspective teachers to demonstrate competence in ELL instruction. The following states offer incentives to in-service teachers to earn ESOL license and/or endorsement: Arizona, Arkansas, Delaware, Florida, Idaho, Iowa, Kansas, Maryland, New York, Washington, and West Virginia. Of the 50 states, 46 states provide ESOL instruction in English only while 33 states provide ESOL instruction in both English and other languages. Seven states (Arizona, Arkansas, California, Connecticut, Massachusetts, New Hampshire, Wisconsin) ban or restrict native language instruction. In the school year of 2006–2007, in Title III language education program, the average ratio of certified teachers in ESOL and the number of ELLs is

1:19. However, the ratio varies from state to state, in some states the ratio is as high as 1:466 (Oklahoma) and 1:372 (Missouri), but in some other states the ratio is as low as 1:3 (Florida, Kentucky) and 1:7 (New Mexico). With the rapid growth in the ELL school population, the need for certified teachers in Title III continues to increase. Yet, the adequate growth of teacher effectiveness to educate ELLs has not been investigated (Cook & Zhao, 2011; Lewis et al., 1999).

It is true that each school district has ESOL specialists that support the needs of ELLs, but it is also true that most classroom teachers have the responsibilities also and need sufficient training to work with ELLs effectively. In most U.S. schools, ESOL teachers or specialists serve ELLs in a separate resource room and provide instruction in English language development and literacy for 40 minutes to one hour every day if the ESOL teacher does not need to travel to another school. ELLs spend the majority of the instruction time with the mainstream teachers who have not been trained to work with them effectively. Research (Cummins, 1999) indicates that ELLs need to develop both BICS and CALP. In order for ELLs to succeed, they need to develop the academic language needed in math, science, and social studies. Very often, there is no collaboration between the classroom teachers and ESOL resource teachers due to busy schedules. Historically, compared with their English peers, ELL students' academic achievement has been correlated to low performance. Though ELLs have been served in different program models such as inclusive models, pullout models, push-in models, bilingual education model, sheltered instruction model, or English-only model, etc., teachers are the ones to make a model or a program work and to empower their students to produce positive outcomes.

By law, ELLs are required to take standardized tests and teachers are being held accountable for their students' progress. To be able to meet the needs of ELLs, teachers need the professional development training to understand ELLs' leaning and language needs and to foster their growth academically, but most teachers do not have this kind of training (Gándara, Maxwell-Jolly, & Driscoll, 2005). With the adoption of common core standards and the high stake of teachers' evaluations, improving teaching practices to meet the needs of ELLs, which make up 11% of the total Pre-K–12 population, should be addressed.

Pre-Service Teacher Education Program

State Requirements for Pre-Service Teachers to Work With ELLs

A pre-service teacher generally refers to a college student in a teacher education program who is in the process of being prepared to be a teacher through education and training provided before they undertake teaching.

In terms of knowledge and skills pre-service teachers should have to serve ELLs as part of initial certification or endorsement, inconsistencies have been observed from state to state. States with specific coursework or certification can be classified into five categories (see Table 12.2)

The requirements in the four states that require all teachers (pre-service and in-service) to have training in working with ELLs vary. Implemented in 2005, Arizona requires ESOL endorsement for all the certified teachers, administrators, and superintendents. The provisional endorsement requires 3 semester hours. While in New York, all pre-service teachers are required to take 6 semester hours in language acquisition and literacy development, in Florida, 3 semester hour are required for training in TESOL for all pre-service and in-service teachers, but 15 hours are required for teachers who provide primary literacy instruction.

Pre-service teachers need to be prepared for diverse classrooms. Though some states have taken the initiatives to add the TESOL components to the teacher education programs, the requirement is at the minimal level. The focus needs to be on the development of their oral language skills and the academic language proficiency as well as culturally responsive teaching practices (Francis, Rivera, Lesaux, Kieffer, & Rivera, 2006).

Samson and Collins (2012) point out three essential areas where teachers of ELLs need to develop knowledge and skills: Supporting oral language development, explicitly teaching academic English, and valuing cultural diversity. First, oral language proficiency lends ELLs the opportunities to

TABLE 12.2 Variation of State Requirements for Pre-Service Teachers of ELLs

State Requirements	States
Required for all teachers	Arizona, California, Florida, New York (4 states)
Include a general reference to the special needs of ELLs	Alabama, Colorado, Idaho, Illinois, Iowa, Louisiana, Maryland, Massachusetts, Michigan, Minnesota, Nevada, New Jersey, North Dakota, Rhode Island, Tennessee, Vermont, Virginia (17 states)
Implement NCATE standards containing references to ELLs (pending)	Alaska, Connecticut, Delaware, Georgia, Kansas, Mississippi, South Carolina (7 states)
In teacher standards, contain "language" as an example of diversity	Arkansas, Montana, New Mexico, North Carolina, Ohio, Oregon, West Virginia, Wyoming (8 states)
No requirements	District of Columbia, Hawaii, Indiana, Kentucky, Maine, Missouri, Nebraska, New Hampshire, Oklahoma, Pennsylvania, South Dakota, Texas, Utah, Washington, Wisconsin (15 states)

Source: Adapted from Ballantyne, Sanderman, & Levy (2008).

participate in class activities such as discussions. Thus, explicitly teaching vocabulary words and grammatical structures is needed to foster ELLs' oral language development. Second, teachers need to have knowledge to differentiate social language and academic language. Teachers need to expose students to complicated use of words and language structures in different contexts. Moreover, helping ELLs cope with the challenge of transitioning from home culture to the school culture is critical. Accepting students' cultural perspectives and embracing them in a safe school environment can be reflected in teaching practices such as inclusive practices and multicultural reading materials.

Using the state teacher-certification examinations and subtests for California, Florida, Massachusetts, New York, and Texas, evidence of oral language, academic language, and cultural diversity (Samson & Collins, 2012) is not found in all of the five states. Some states mention one or two areas specifically and some states partially mention one area and ignore the other areas. For example, California demonstrates specific evidence in the areas of oral language and cultural diversity, and Florida does not mention academic language at all.

Knowing the rapid change in demographics in the American schools and adequately preparing our pre-service teachers who can provide effective instructional practices to ELLs is imperative. Teacher education programs need to take the lead to incorporate the three areas of oral language development, academic language development, and cultural diversity into teacher education programs in order to produce quality future teachers to improve ELLs learning outcomes. As Samson and Collins (2012) state, "we cannot stress enough just how vital it is to articulate the need for teacher-education programs to prepare teachers for all of the students they will encounter in the schools" (p. 21).

Clair (1993), Williams (2001), and Youngs & Youngs (2001) state that the curricula of the teacher preparation programs at the college level needs to incorporate the needs of the public schools in their mandatory courses. In this book, based on research findings, we propose the following recommendation for teacher education programs:

1. Require courses to develop the understanding of oral language development, academic language development, and cultural diversity.
2. Align with the state requirements and provide strong evidence to help pre-service teachers meet the requirements.
3. Add the component of collaboration and team teaching at different phases of the teacher education program.
4. During the student internship, pre-service teachers need to have the exposure of working with students from diverse linguistic and

cultural backgrounds and demonstrate competence in design lessons for all students.

5. Aggressively recruit and retain professors from diverse linguistic and cultural backgrounds.

Professional Development for In-Service Teachers

In general, professional development refers to ongoing learning and or formal training opportunities available to teachers and other education personnel through their schools and districts with the purpose for teachers to upgrade the content knowledge and pedagogical skills (Wikipedia, 2013). With the ELLs growing faster in the public schools, the challenge for the mainstream in-service teachers to serve the ELLs has become even greater. As Montgomery, Roberts, & Growe (2003) stated, the teachers must be ready to deliver an education for ELLs that is equivalent to the education offered to the native speakers across the school curricular. However, ESOL has not been made a priority in teacher education programs in the states in which historically ELLs are not a substantial part of the school population (Cook & Zhao, 2011; Giambo & Szecsi, 2005). Lue (2003) points out that some states with a long history of serving ELLs might have modified their curriculum in their teacher education program to meet the challenges of understanding the needs of ELLs, but other states, where serving ELLs is considerably new, realize that simple modification might not be sufficient. Moreover, the program modification might be carefully designed, but the current in-service teachers might not be prepared to carry out the changes in the current curricular. Therefore, to respond to the needs of the ELLs at school, professional development is a great means to prepare in-service classroom teachers to work effectively with ELLs in mainstream classrooms.

The four states that require pre-service teachers to have ESOL training also require in- service teachers to develop the knowledge and skills to work with ELLs through professional development trainings (Ballantyne, Sanderman, & Levy, 2008). In the state of Arizona, provisional endorsement in ESOL requires in-service teachers to have one semester or 15 credit hours of professional development in developing instructional strategies, teaching with the state proficiency standards, and employing different assessment tools to monitor ELLs' academic progress. The provisional endorsement expires three years later, after which teachers need to take another 15 credit hours of professional development in order to get the endorsement. In California, out-of-state teachers are required to complete Cross-Culture Language and Academic Development credential or equivalent if they wish to have a teaching license in California. In Florida, in-service teachers need to take either 3 semester hours in ESOL or in-service training in order to get ESOL provisional endorsement. In New York, all teachers graduating from accredited teacher education programs need to have 6 hours in language acquisition and language development.

As we can see, some states require in-service teachers to have professional development in instructional practices, language acquisition, language development, and cultural diversity to work with ELLs. Yet, many other states have not put these requirements on their agenda for the mainstream teachers at large. Therefore, preparing our in-service teachers to work with ELLs is as critically important as preparing our pre-service teachers because in-service teachers are the ones who work directly with the ELLs now in classrooms today.

Providing in-service training is much needed. It is a joint effort to prepare in-service teachers. There are different federal and state grant programs available for training mainstream teachers to work with ELLs. University teacher education programs need to work with the local school districts closely to meet the needs of the increasing demand of working with ELLs. In addition, teacher effectiveness needs to demonstrate competence in the three areas of oral language development, academic language development, and cultural diversity. Finally, the school vision, mission, and expectation should be clearly communicated with teachers.

In order to better prepare both pre-service and in-service teachers to work with ELLs effectively, the suggestions in this book serves as a reference for teachers, administrators, superintendents, and university professors. We provide a lens for administrators in school districts and teacher education programs to see the urgent need of training teachers to have the necessary knowledge and skills to work with ELLs and all students.

SUMMARY

This chapter focused on professional standards, requirements, and information. It first introduced the framework for the P-12 CAEP/ESOL standards, common core standards and then discusses trends and programs in teaching ELLs, and assessment and related issues. The chapter also provided ELL-related data and statistics, and suggestions for teacher education programs. In order to prepare a TESOL professional, competence in five domains that lead to the profession were discussed. The five domains that are interrelated and support each other are: language, culture, instruction, assessment, and professionalism. Thirteen standards that support the five domains are introduced as well. Examples of suggested performance indicators for each standard are presented. With the implementation of the CCSS, the role of ESOL teachers are not limited to teaching English, but advocating for ELLs and actively collaborating with the mainstream teachers to provide the academic language needed for ELLs to succeed. The shift from teaching the four language skills only to incorporating content knowledge, academic language, and assessment in ESOL into teaching ELLs has taken place. Different types of programs for ELLs were discussed as well. This chapter also discussed assessment, the purpose and types of assessments, the characteristics of each stage of ELLs' language development as well as strategies to assess ELLs. Finally, suggestions for teacher education programs to effectively prepare for teachers to work with ELLs are discussed.

REFERENCES

Aldridge, J., & Goldman, R. (2002). *Current issues and trends in education.* Boston, MA: Allyn & Bacon.

Anstrom, K. (1995). New directions for chapter 1/title 1. *Directions in Language and Education, 1*(7), 3–14.

Antunez, B. (2003). *English language learners in the great city schools: Survey results on students, language and programs.* Washington, DC: Council of the Great City Schools. (ERIC Document Reproduction Service No. ED 479473).

Ballantyne, K. G., Sanderman, A. R., & Levy, J. (2008). *Educating English language learners: Building teacher capacity.* Washington, DC: National Clearinghouse for English Language Acquisition. Retrieved from http://www.ncela.us/files/uploads/3/EducatingELLsBuildingTeacherCapacityVol3.pdf

Boyson, B. A., & Short, D. J. (2003). *Secondary school newcomer programs in the United States.* Wahsington, DC: Center for Research on Education, Diversity, and Excellence. Retrieved from http://www.cal.org/crede/pdfs/rr12.pdf

Byrnes, D. H., Kiger, G., & Manning, M. L. (1997). Teachers' attitudes about language diversity. *Teaching and Teacher Education, 13*(6), 637–644.

Carter, L. F. (1984). The sustaining effects: Study of compensatory and elementary education. *Education Researcher, 13*(7), 4–13.

Childstats.gov. (2013). America's children: Key national indicators of well-being. Retrieved from http://www.childstats.gov/americaschildren/demo.asp#pop1

Clair, N. (1993). *ESOL teacher educators and teachers: Insights from classroom teachers with language-minority students.* Paper presented at the 27th annual meeting of the Teachers of English to Speakers of Other Languages, Atlanta, GA.

Common Core State Standards Initiative. (2012). *Mission statement.* Retrieved from http://www.corestandards.org/

Cook, H. G. & Zhao, Y. (2011, April). *How English language proficiency assessments manifest growth: An examination of language proficiency growth in a WIDA state.* Paper presented at the annual meeting of the AERA, New Orleans, LA.

Cummins, J. (1999). *Enrichment in dual language Spanish/English programs.* Leadership Letters: Issues and Trends in Bilingual Education. Glenview, IL: Scott Foreman.

Echevarria, J., Vogt, M., & Short, D. (2013). *Making content comprehensible for English learners: The SIOP model.* Upper Saddle River, NJ: Pearson.

Education Week. (2009). Teaching ELL students. Retrieved from http://edweek.
org/media/ew/qc/2009/17teachingell.hon28.pdf

Education Week. (2013). *ESOL and classroom teachers team up to teach common core.*
Retrieved from http://www.edweek.org/ew/articles/2013/10/30/10cc-ES-
OLteachers.h33.html

Elementary and Secondary Education act of 1965. Public law 89-10. Congress of
the U.S., Washington, DC: House. Retrieved from: http://eric.ed.gov/
?id=ED017539.

Ferguson, D. L. (1995). The real challenge of inclusion. *Phi Delta Kappan, 77*(4),
281–287.

Francis D., Rivera M., Lesaux N., Kieffer M. & Rivera H. (2006). *Practical guidelines for the Education of language learners: Researched-based recommendations for
instruction and academic intervention.* Retrieved from http://www.centeronin-
struction.org/files/ELL1-Interventions.pdf

Gándara, P., Maxwell-Jolly, J., & Driscoll, A. (2005). Listening to teachers of English
learners. Retrieved from http://www.cftl.org/documents/2005/listeningfor-
web.pdf

Genesee, F. (1993). All teachers are second language teachers. *The Canadian Modern
Language Review, 50,* 47–53.

Giambo D., & Szecsi, T. (2005). Opening up the issues: Preparing preserice teachers
to work effectively with English language learners. *Childhood Education, 82*(2),
267–277.

Gottlieb, M. (2006). *Assessing English language learners: Bridges from language proficiency to academic achievement.* Thousand, CA: Corwin Press.

Hinkel, E. (2006). Current perspectives on teaching the four skills. *TESOL Quarterly, 40*(1), 109–131.

Honigsfeld A., & Dove, M. (2010). *Collaboration and co-teaching: Strategies for English
Learners.* Thousand Oaks, CA: Corwin.

Kaufman, D. (2004). Issues in constructivist pedagogy for L2 learning and teaching.
Annual Review of Applied Linguistics, 24, 303–319.

Lewis, L., Parsad, B., Carey, N., Bartfai, N., Westat, E. F., & Smerdon, W. (1999).
Teacher quality: A report of the preparation and qualification of public
school teachers. Retrieved from http://nces.ed.gov/pubs99/1999080.pdf

Lue, M. (2003). A coat of many colors: Preparing teachers to meet the needs of learners
in inclusive settings. *Reports Descriptive.* Retrieved from http://www.eric.ed.gov/
ERICDocs/data.ericdocs2/content_storage_01/0000000b/80/28/0b/ 04.pdf

Mather, M. (2009). Reports on America: Children in immigrant families chat new
path. http://www.prb.org/pdf09/immigrantchildren.pdf

MigrantPolicyInstitute (2010a). ToplanguagesspokenbyEnglishlanguagelearnersna-
tionallyandbystate.Retrievedfromhttp://www.migrationpolicy.org/research/
top-languages-spoken-english-language- learners-nationally-and-state

Migrant Policy Institute (2010b). *States and districts with the highest number and share
of English language learners.* Retrieved from file:///C:/Users/Sung/Down-
loads/FactSheet_ELL2%20(1).pdf

Migrant Policy Institute (2010c). Number and growth of students in US schools in
need of English instruction. Retrieved from file:///C:/Users/Sung/Down-
loads/FactSheet%20ELL1%20-%20FINAL.pdf

Montgomery, P., Roberts, M., & Growe, R. (2003). English language learners: An issue of educational equality. *Reports-Descriptive.* Retrieved from http://files.eric.ed.gov/fulltext/ED482753.pdf

Mousavi, S. A. (2009). *An encyclopedic dictionary of language testing* (3rd ed.). Taiwan, China: Tung Hua Book Company.

National Clearinghouse for English Language Acquisition. (2011). The growing numbers of English learners students. Retrieved from http://www.ncela.gwu.edu/files/uploads/9/growingLEP_0809.pdf

Ovando, C. J., & Collier, V. P. (1998). Bilingual and ESL classrooms: Teaching in multicultural contexts (2nd ed.). Boston, MA: McGraw-Hill.

Ovando, C. J., Collier, V. P., & Combs, M. C. (2005). *Bilingual & ESL classrooms: Teaching in multicultural contexts.* New York, NY: McGraw Hill.

Passow, A. H. (1989). *Curriculum and instruction in chapter 1 programs: A look back and a look ahead.* Washington, DC: Office of Educational Research and Improvement (ED). (ERIC Document Reproduction Service No. ED 306346).

Peregoy, S., & Boyle, O. (1993). *Reading, writing, and learning in ESOL: A resource book for teachers.* White Plains, NY: Longman.

Samson, J. & Colllins, B. (2012). Preparing all teachers to meet the needs of English language learners: Applying research to policy and practice for teacher effectiveness. Retrieved from http://files.eric.ed.gov/fulltext/ED535608.pdf

Staehr Fenner, D. S. (2013). *Implementing the common core state standards for English learners: The changing role of the ESOL teacher.* A Summary of TESOL International Association Convention. Alexandra, VA: TESOL International Association Press.

Staehr Fenner, D., & Segota, J. (2012). *Standards that impact English language learners.* Washington, DC: Colorin Colorado. Retrieved from http://www.colorincolorado.org/article/50848/#proficiency.

Stainback, W., & Stainback, S. (1984). A rationale for the merger of special and regular education. *Exceptional Children, 51*(2), 102–111.

TESOL. (2010). Standards for the recognition of initial TESOL programs in P-12 teacher education. Retrieved from http://www.tesol.org/docs/books/the-revised-tesol-ncate-standards-for-the-recognition-of-initial-tesol-programs-in-p-12-ESOL-teacher-education-%282010-pdf%29.pdf?sfvrsn=0

Thomas, W. P., & Collier, V. P. (2002). *A national study of school effectiveness for language minority students' long-term academic achievement. Final report: Project 1.1.* Washington, DC, and Santa Cruz, CA: Center for Research on Education, Diversity & Excellence.

Tungate, M. (2012). Self-contained classes help English learners learn English. Retrieved from http://www.kentuckyteacher.org/features/2012/11/self-contained-classes-help-english-learners-learn-in-english/

Turnbull, A. P., Turnbull, H. R., Shank, M., & Leal, D. (1995). *Exceptional lives: Special education in today's schools.* Upper Saddle River, NJ: Merrill/Prentice Hall.

Underhill, N. (1987). *Testing spoken language.* Cambridge, England: Cambridge University Press.

Van Loenen, R., & Haley, P. K. (1994). *Consultation and collaboration: English as a second language regular classroom teachers working together.* Washington, DC:

Languages and Linguistics. Retrieved from ERIC Document Reproduction Service No. ED372645.

Watts-Taffe, S., & Truscott, D. M. (2000). Using what we know about language and literacy development for ESOL students in the mainstream classroom. *Language Arts, 77*(3), 258–265.

Wikipedia. (2013). Difference between formative and summative assessment in education. Retrieved from: http://en.wikipedia.org/wiki/Formative_assessment

Williams, J. (2001). Classroom conversations: Opportunities to learn for ESOL students in mainstream classrooms. *Reading Teacher, 54*(8), 750–757.

Wright, W. E. (2015). *Foundations for teaching English language learners: Research, policy, and practice.* Philadelphia, PA: Caslon.

Youngs, G. S. & Youngs, G. A., Jr. (2001). Predicators of mainstream teachers' attitudes toward ESOL students. *TESOL Quarterly, 35*(1), 97–120.

Zehr, M. (2006). Team-teaching helps close language gap. *Education Week.* 26(14), 26–29.

APPENDIX A

Index for Subject Glossary

Academic Attainments: Learning achievements or accomplishments. ELLs' academic attainments continue to be the concern of many educators. Achievement data suggest that ELLs in general lag behind their English-speaking peers and the performance gap between ELLs and their English-speaking peers (non-ELLs) is persistent. For example, the National Center for Educational Statistics on student achievement reveals that the students of the nation's second largest ethnic group (i.e., the Hispanic students) are consistently underperforming their Caucasian peers (NCES, 2012). (Chapter 1)

Active Learning: A methodological approach to teaching based in student participation with regard to pro-actively engaging with materials that are to be mastered by reading about, discussing, and identifying concepts or problems within the established discourse. (Chapter 8)

Active Observation: A methodology based in aesthetic education in which the observer is proactively aware of his or her own distinctive processes of engagement and observation, using phenomenological awareness and perceptive and perceptual tools, fully engaging behavior, experience, and environment in a dialogic model. (Chapter 8)

Affective Filter Hypothesis: Explains how emotional factors can affect the ELLs to learn the English language skills. If the ELLs are nervous,

Teaching ELLs Across Content Areas, pages 321–337
Copyright © 2016 by Information Age Publishing
All rights of reproduction in any form reserved.

unmotivated, bored, frustrated, or stressed, they may not be receptive to language input and thus they may filter the input. (Chapter 2)

Academic Language: Complex language that is used for learning cognitively abstract content and engaging in demanding academic reading, writing, speaking, and listening. It is noted for having abstract, higher level vocabulary and complex sentence structures, as well as demanding deeper thinking than everyday conversational language. (Chapter 3)

Aesthetics: From the Greek Αισθητική or "Aisthētiké." Thus, the English term is derived from the Greek word for sensory input and inner response and cognition-based evaluation of every description. Aesthetics, a branch of the philosophical field of Axiology, or the study of evaluation and application of judgment, is studied philosophically as the awareness, assessment, and formation of discourse on beauty. (Chapter 8)

Alpha Boxes: A graphic organizer that helps activate prior knowledge and build vocabulary by helping students make connections before, during, and after reading a new selection. (Chapter 9)

Aporetic: Derives from the ancient Greek word πορία and refers to philosophical situations in which two opposing options serve to cancel each other in a form of impasse. In making aesthetic decisions, for example different cultures may operate based in differing concepts of what is or is not beautiful with neither being either "right" or "wrong," but merely "different." (Chapter 8)

Arousal: Albert Bandura (1997) explains that there are four ways to increase self-efficacy in individuals: enactive mastery, vicarious modeling, verbal persuasion, and arousal. Arousal is working up to an emotional feeling of exhilaration, like a sports performer. (Chapter 11)

Art Appreciation: The study of the diverse applications and aspects of the arts including but not limited to who may operate in the world of art, how and why cultural decisions are undertaken in differing global contexts, awareness of art vocabulary, assessment of differing art media, art forms, and the transitions of art history as well as how various societies value and engage with the diverse art forms. (Chapter 8)

Basic Interpersonal Communication Skills (BICS): Refers to the social language in everyday life or the oral English needed and used mostly in conversational contexts. BICS is gained through communication and interaction (Cummins, 1999). (Chapter 2)

Backwards Planning: Refers to designing instruction with the needs of students first concerning skills, content, and knowledge, and then focusing on the end product and assessment. (Chapter 6)

Bilingual Program: Refers usually to the education program in an English-language school system in which students with little fluency in English are taught in both their native language and English. The purpose is to build a bridge that helps students become proficient in their native language and English. (Chapter 12)

Biological Perspective: A psychological approach that holds that human behavior is a dynamic of the internal chemistry of the body. Biological psychology considers changes in motivation levels as a derivative of changes in levels of neuro-transmitters. (Chapter 11)

Chiaroscuro: An Italian term that literally means "light (*chiaro*) dark (*oscuro*)"; an artistic technique in which subtle gradations of light to dark or dark to light values create the volumetric illusion of rounded three-dimensional forms in space; also sometimes termed *modeling*. (Chapter 8)

Cognitive Academic Language Proficiency (CALP): Refers to the academic language that is specifically related to the subject content areas, in which cognitively demanding language skills are required (Cummins, 1999). (Chapter 2)

Bottom-Up Processing: The process by which the reader or listener focuses on bits and pieces of language, such as sound segments, words, and phrases to interpret a text or oral utterance. (Chapter 3)

Cognate: Words in different languages that have similar meanings and sounds. (Chapter 9)

Cognition: Cognition is a thought. This thought becomes the means by which our minds obtain knowledge and relate it to our thinking processes and perceptions of our environment. In other words, it is the mental action or process of acquiring knowledge and understanding through thought, experience, and the senses. (Chapter 11)

Cognitive Perspective: A psychological approach that holds a person's behavior is a reaction to their individual personal experiences. The approach is based on the notion that behavior is controlled by the way we think, comprehend, and reflect on the world. (Chapter 11)

Cohesion Devices: Language elements that signal grammatical and/or lexical relationships across sentences or clauses. Examples of cohesion devices are pronouns and transitional words to explicitly link different parts of the text. Examples of transitional words that help to provide coherence in a text are: in addition, furthermore, therefore, and as a result. (Chapter 3)

Common Core State Standards: A U.S. education initiative that seeks to bring diverse state curricula into alignment with each other by following the principles of standards-based education reform (Wikipedia, 2013). For example, it details what K–12 students should know in English language arts and mathematics at the end of each grade. The initiative is sponsored and supported by the National Governors Association (NGA) and the Council of Chief State School Officers (CCSSO) that seek to establish consistent educational standards across the states and ensure that students graduating from high school are prepared to enter credit-bearing courses at two- or four-year college programs or to enter the workforce. (Chapter 12)

Communicative Competence: The ability to use oral and written language appropriately with a variety of different speakers. It includes grammatical competence, sociolinguistic competence, strategic competence, and discourse competence. (Chapter 3)

Communicative Technological Skills: To build upon teachers' ability to promote successful socialization of students and to provide practice opportunities for communicative encounters via web-based communicative tools (e.g., Skype) and social networks (e.g., Facebook), and CALL software. (Chapter 7)

Communities of Learners: Refers to small or larger groups of learners engaging in discussion openly. Learners both speak and listen. (Chapter 5)

Comprehensible Input: Krashen (1982) believes that the best ways to learn a second language is to supply *comprehensible input* in low anxiety situations. In other words, the language message input conveyed to the ELLs must be comprehensible. (Chapter 2)

Computer Assisted Language Learning (CALL): The field of second language learning that encompasses any use of computer technology in the domain of language learning. (Chapter 7)

Content Objectives: Those objectives students need to know and be able to do in content areas for a particular lesson. (Chapter 6)

Contextual Support: Assistance provided to the learner to help him or her understand. Examples of contextual support are the use of visuals, demonstrations, graphic organizers, and drawing or writing on the board to make a concept or task clearer. Using an example that is familiar to the student is another way to provide assistance. (Chapter 3)

Contrapposto: A natural action position as if walking in which a figure is shown with most of the weight placed on one leg while the other remains disengaged, resulting in being obliquely balanced around a central vertical axis. It also refers to a weight-shift principle. This shifting of weight results in a diagonal balancing of tension and relaxation. (Chapter 8)

Critical Pedagogy: Refers to helping students question and then develop their own understanding and meaning of what they learn and how they view the world in instances of domination and oppression. (Chapter 6)

Culturally Relevant Pedagogy (CRP): Refers to a theoretical framework for teaching students from diverse racial, social, ethic, and language backgrounds in a way that incorporates experiences, backgrounds, and perspectives into the curriculum. (Chapter 6)

Deep Learners: The first type of learners that Bain (2004) identifies. According to Bain, deep learners enjoy the challenge of mastering a difficult and complex subject. This type of student tends to be intrinsically motivated. Teaching them can be an enjoyable experience for the teacher. Bain then identifies the styles of the other two types. (Chapter 11)

Deep Processing Theory: Craik & Lockhart (1972) believe that the depth of mental processing affects memory. Memories that are deeply processed, at the semantic level, lead to longer lasting memories while shallow processing leads to memories that decay easily. (Chapter 2)

Differentiated Instruction: The accommodations made to curriculum and instruction for learners of differing learning styles, proficiency levels, and background experiences. (Chapter 5)

Discourse Communities: Groups of learners that have developed ways of communicating and interacting. Learners may have learned words, values, and practices that are specific to their group and that they all understand. (Chapter 5)

Domain-Specific Academic Vocabulary: Words that are specific to certain content areas, such as science, math, geography, music, and art. (Chapter 9)

Draw-a-Scientist Test: An instructional activity that can be used to determine students' perceptions of scientists. Developed in 1983 by David Wade Chambers, the activity requires students to draw a scientist. The drawings usually include many stereotypical "mad scientist" images such as lab coats, messy hair, Caucasian men, glasses, and flames. Teachers can use this activity understand students' ideas of diversity and culture in science, as well as their attitudes toward science. (Chapter 4)

Drive Theory: Proposes that all organisms are driven by the need for survival. Drive theories are those that can be explained by internal motivation or fulfillment of needs. According to the drive theory of motivation—as put forward by Clark Hull (1943), Abraham Maslow (1954) and other theorists later—people are motivated to take certain actions in order to reduce the internal tension that is caused by unmet needs. (Chapter 11)

5E Instructional Model: Used commonly during science inquiry but also supports ELLs. Coined by Bass et al. (2009), it is named after its five phases: engage, explore, explain, elaborate, and evaluate. In this model, teachers sequence the lesson so that students can build conceptual understanding on their prior knowledge and experiences. (Chapter 4)

Elements and Principles of Art: The elements of art consist of all fundamental components that may be observed as basic units of any work of art such as line, shape, form, mass, space, size, scale, texture, or any palpable physical and observable properties of an art object or event. The principles of art, in contrast, consist of abstractions based in guidelines that may be intuitively applied in the arrangement of the physical elements. Principles include ideas such as unity, variety, balance, rhythm, proportion, and emphasis. The principles are conceptual properties while the elements tend to be immediately observable material realities. (Chapter 8)

Enactive Mastery: Refers to gaining relevant experience with the task or job. If an individual has been able to do a job successfully in the past, then he or she will be more confident to be able to do it in the future. According to Albert Bandura (1997), there are four ways that self-efficacy can be increased in individuals: enactive mastery, vicarious modeling, verbal persuasion, and arousal. *Enactive mastery* (i.e., actually performing the task) may be the most important way to increase self-efficacy. In other words, Enactive mastery is the highest form of self-efficacy attained through successful achievement of tasks. (Chapter 11)

English Learner (EL): Refers to a student who is in the process of learning English. This term is exchangeable with the term ELLs. In recent years, this term has been used (e.g., by U.S. Department of Education) to substitute for the previous term LEP. (Chapter 1)

English Language Learner (ELL): Refers to a student who is in the process of acquiring English; whose primary language is not English. This term is used more frequently in recent years to substitute other terms (e.g., LEP or ESL students). (Chapter 1)

English as a Second Language (ESL): Refers to the fact that English is taught by teachers whose native language is English. An ESL student is now a less common term than the ELL and ESL is more often used as an educational approach to support ELLs to learn English. (Chapter 1)

English as a Foreign Language (EFL): Refers to English being taught by teachers whose native language is not English. An EFL program is for students who learn English as a foreign language in a country where English is not the L1. (Chapter 1)

English for Speakers of Other Languages (ESOL): Refers to the program in which English is taught by teachers whose native language is English. It is also referred to as ENL, English as a New Language. The ESOL program offered in public schools often pulls ELLs out of regular classes to learn English. (Chapter 1)

Evaluation Skills: Relates to teachers' ability to conduct three levels of analysis including software, tasks, and learner performance. This helps to derive conclusions regarding CALL tasks benefits; software impact on control, interactivity, and feedback; and course effectiveness on whether learning outcomes are met through using technology. (Chapter 7)

Evidence-Based Practice: Based on the conscientious, explicit, and judicious use of current research findings and research-based theory as evidence in making decisions. (Chapter 7)

Mobile Applications: A type of software designed to run on a mobile device, such as a smartphone or tablet computer. They are generally small, individual software units with limited function. (Chapter 5)

Extrinsic Motivation: Motivation that is influenced by external factors that exist outside of the individual. The subject's performance of some desired activity occurs to attain a reward, such as grades for students or money for workers. It could also be threats or punishment of some type (Ryan and Deci, 2000a). (Chapter 11)

False Cognate: Words from two different languages that have similar sounds but actually have different meanings. (Chapter 9)

Fluency: Ability to speak, read, or write easily, smoothly, and with expression using correct prosody. It varies according to the task, text, topic, and the learner's age and second language proficiency. (Chapter 3)

Formal Analysis: An analysis of an artwork, predicated upon assessment of how an artist has employed use of the elements and principles of art; the analysis of physical and conceptual properties in art. (Chapter 8)

Formative Assessment: Refers to a process used by teachers and students during instruction that provides feedback to adjust ongoing teaching and learning to improve students' achievement of intended instructional outcomes by ongoing feedback. They are generally low stakes because of low or no point value. Examples include asking students to: draw a concept map in class to represent their understanding of a topic, submit one or two sentences identifying the main point of a lecture, or turn in a research proposal for early feedback. (Chapter 12)

Generation 1.5 Students: Refers to those ELLs who are U.S. educated but who may not be proficient in academic language related to school achievement; yet, they may have strong L2 oral stills. They are caught between generations (i.e., belong to neither Generation 1 nor Generation 2) of immigrants. Thus, they may also have limited L1 skills. (Chapter 1)

Genre: A goal-oriented activity for a particular cultural purpose that creates a text with certain grammatical and lexical features according to Systemic Functional Linguistics. These features specify the text, or make it the certain type of text. For example, certain features make the text a poem, a persuasive article, or a picture book. Teachers familiar with the grammatical and lexical features of a particular genre can help their ELLs become familiar with those features and thus improve their learning of the genre. For example, if teachers point out examples of figurative language in poems, students are more likely to notice figurative language in poetry they read and attempt to include this feature in their own poems. (Chapter 3)

Gradual Release of Responsibility: An instructional model in which teachers introduce a new concept or skill by modeling and demonstrating what should be done, provide students with substantial support as they practice the new concept or skill with peers, and then gradually decrease the amount of support as students become more proficient and are able to apply what they have learned independently. (Chapter 3)

Graphic Organizers: Visual learning strategies that guide students' thinking as they fill in maps and diagrams. Students are able to learn relationships between facts, concepts, and/or ideas. (Chapter 9)

Incentive Theory: Suggests that people are motivated to do things because of either internal needs or external reinforcements. It is explained as the pull toward certain behaviors that might offer a more positive incentive than those offering negative outcomes. (Chapter 11)

Inclusion Program: Inclusion programs for ELLs is in-class ESOL instruction that is provided by mainstream classroom teachers (Wright, 2010). However, there is debate as to the benefits of the inclusion program for ELLs. ELLs typically need additional resources and support to adjust to the various linguistic complications of learning a new language. Although some schools and states have adopted mandatory full inclusion programs, educators argue that ELLs immersed in a regular paced English class with students who are fluent in English does do not have benefits although the inclusion program for ELLs saves costs, such as the cost of hiring ESL specialists for ELL students in an ESOL atmosphere for learning. (Chapter 12)

Initial Assessment: Assessment that is usually carried out at the beginning of a program to identify learners' strengths and weaknesses but can also take place at any stage, even before the program has begun. The assessment may be a specific check on a particular skill, understanding, or aptitude, or it may be a broad indicator of general areas that need attention to identify a learner's needs and strengths. (Chapter 12)

Inquiry: Also called science inquiry or scientific inquiry. Refers to the many ways scientists study and explain the natural world. Inquiry involves active learning, a process that may be uncomfortable for students with experience in passive learning environments. Students in an inquiry-based science classroom learn to ask questions, conduct investigations, and use evidence from multiple sources to answer those questions. They also learn to substantiate their explanations and defend their conclusions. Inquiry lessons are characterized by discovery, collaboration, and discourse. (Chapter 4)

In-Service Teacher: In-service means something that happens while someone is a full-time employee. Therefore, *in-service teachers* are the ones who have a teaching license and are teaching in their own classrooms. (Chapter 12)

Instinct Theory: Looks at the natural instincts of all animals. As Nancy Melucci (2010) notes, instinct theory proposes that all organisms tend to engage in certain behaviors that will lead them to success in terms of issues like natural selection. (Chapter 11)

In Situ Demonstrations: A demonstration on the site, as in the case of demonstrations of painting within the classroom, in a space perhaps not specified as an art room; or any demonstration provided on site. (Chapter 8)

Intrinsic Motivation: This can be explained as the self-desire to seek out new things and new challenges, to analyze one's capacity, to observe and to gain knowledge (Ryan and Deci, 2000b). It is performing an action or behavior because you enjoy the activity itself. Whereas acting on extrinsic motivation is done for the sake of some external outcome. (Chapter 11)

Interaction Hypothesis: Long (1983) advances two major claims about the role of interaction in L2 acquisition: (a) comprehensible input is necessary for L2 acquisition; and (b) modifications to conversations that take place in the process of negotiating a communication problem help make input comprehensible to a second language learner. (Chapter 2)

Interactive Processes: Processes the mind engages in while listening and reading to make meaning of and interpret the linguistic clues it receives. During listening, the brain goes through seven different processes to comprehend what is heard (Brown, 2015). To be an effective reader, the reader needs to engage in both top-down and bottom-up processing. This combination of top-down processing and bottom-up processing is called interactive reading. (Chapter 3)

Intonation: A pitch change over an entire sentence. In English, pitch falls on declarative sentences and "wh" interrogatives, but rises in yes–no interrogatives. (Chapter 3)

Language Development: Refers to the process of L2 development and includes these stages in the process of L2 development: preproduction stage, early production, speech emergence, intermediate fluency, fluency. (Chapter 12)

Language Objectives: Refers to those objectives that include language functions, academic vocabulary, and language structures that English language learners need to understand and know for a particular lesson. (Chapter 6)

Language Proficiency: Includes knowledge of the structural rules guiding sounds (phonology), word forms (morphology), and word order (syntax). These structural rules work together with word choices (vocabulary) to make meaning (semantics). Language proficiency also includes knowledge about how to use language in socially and culturally appropriate ways (pragmatics). (Chapter 3)

Lau v. Nichols Decision: A civil rights case that was brought by Chinese American students in San Francisco, CA. The students were not receiving special help in school despite their inability to speak English. The Civil Rights Act of 1964 bans discrimination on the basis of national origin. The U.S. Supreme Court in 1974 ruled in favor of the students, thus expanding rights of students nationwide with limited English proficiency for instructional support. Lau remains an important decision on the fourteenth amendment. (Chapter 1)

Limited English Proficiency (LEP): Refers to the ELLs who have a lower level of the English language skills. Yet, many educators believe that this term has a connotation that focuses on limitation. It is thus substituted with other terms (e.g., ELs or ELLs in recent years). (Chapter 1)

Linguistically and Culturally Responsive: An environment created in the classroom that takes into account learners' culture and language backgrounds and practices. (Chapter 5)

Mediational Tools: Any type of resource used for learning. This includes concrete resources, such as technology, and abstract resources, such as different languages. (Chapter 5)

Metacognitive Awareness: Awareness of one's own thinking processes as one engages in a task or simply means being aware of how you think. Developing metacognitive awareness is an important part of helping ELLs become more effective. If students are conscious of how they learn, they can identify the most effective ways of doing so. (Chapter3)

Metacognitive Strategies: Learning strategies that are used to plan, monitor, and evaluate a learning task, such as, checking one's comprehension when listening or reading. (Chapter 3)

Mobile Technologies: Refer to smart phones and tablets that can store, access, create, allow modifying, transferring, and organizing a wide range of data in various forms. They can also remote-connect to databases, fit in your pocket, and run on rechargeable batteries. (Chapter 7)

Modifying Speech: Ways that one can change the way they speak and write in order to become more understandable to learners. (Chapter 5)

Morphology: The study of words and word formation, including the structure of words, their inflections, derivations, and how they are formed. An example of inflectional morphology is "s" for regular plurals; an example of derivational morphology is adding the affix -able to the word change (verb) to become changeable (adj.). Derivational morphology usually deals with affixes that change the part of speech of a word. (Chapter 3)

Motivation: Has been explained as the processes that cause people to act to achieve a goal. Motivation can involve the cognitive, biological, emotional, or social forces that activate people's behavior. It is the general desire or willingness of someone to do something. (Chapter 11)

Multi-Modal: When the curriculum and instruction in the classroom taps into the reading, writing, speaking, and listening skills of learners. (Chapter 5)

Multi-Sensory: When the curriculum and instruction in the classroom taps into a number of sensory modes of learners—sight, sound, touch, smell, and taste. (Chapter 5)

Next Generation Science Standards (NGSS): A set of evidence-based curriculum standards that detail the science knowledge and skills all K–12 students should know. Rather than focusing on many discrete facts, NGSS emphasizes (a) deep understanding of core concepts, (b) the process of developing and testing ideas, and (c) evaluating scientific evidence. NGSS also addresses the habits of mind and practices of scientists and engineers. NGSS is the result of a large-scale collaboration involving the National Research Council, National Science Teachers Association, American Association for the Advancement of Science, and Achieve. These standards were approved in April 2013 and have since been fully adopted by 14 states. (Chapter 4)

Nonverbal Responses: A response by the learner that does not rely on the oral production of language. This response should demonstrate the learners' knowledge and understanding. (Chapter 5)

Organization of Learning: The way the classroom space is organized both socially and physically. This includes a seating chart, learner roles, and classroom norms and procedures. (Chapter 5)

Papiér Maché: A French term (literally signifying "chewed" paper) indicating a combination of paper and glue (generally wheat paste, or flour and water) which begins in a malleable state but dries to a hard, very solid finish, which is commonly used as an additive or modeling technique for creating light-weight sculptural works. (Chapter 8)

Pedagogical Skills: Refers to teachers' ability to convey knowledge and skills of language learning theories, strategies for language assessment, and language learning curriculum design in order to facilitate student's communicative competence and online interaction in technology-based instruction. In addition, pedagogical skills include skills to choose suitable materials and tasks for technology-based instruction. (Chapter 7)

Pentimenti/Pentimento: Derived from an Italian term indicating the idea of "change" or "repentance," which is generally applied to painting and describing a part of an image that has been over-painted by the artist, but which has become visible again (often as a ghostly outline) because the upper layer of pigment has become more transparent through age (generally in reference to oil painting). The presence of *pentimenti* is often used as an argument in matters of attribution and may be investigated to better understand an artist's thought and creative processes, as it is felt that such evidence of an artist's second thoughts is much more likely to occur in an original painting than in a copy. (Chapter 8)

Phonology: The study of the sound systems of languages, including the inventory of sounds of a language, how they are combined to form syllables and words, and how sounds can have variants depending on the context in which they occur. For instance, English allows the consonant clusters in streets, but disallows the opening sequence of *mblink*. (Chapter 3)

Piñatas: A kind of sculptural "container," often made of papiér maché and cardboard, or light-weight ceramic, and sometimes cloth, which is hollow, decorated with paint and other materials, then, is filled with toys or treats and is broken open as part of a celebration or ceremony. (Chapter 8)

Pre-Service Teacher: Someone who is in the process of receiving education and training to become a teacher. Usually it refers to someone who is a part of a teacher education program at an accredited college or university. (Chapter 5)

Professional Development: Generally refers to ongoing learning and training opportunities available to teachers and other education personnel through their schools and districts. The purpose of such formal in-service training for teachers is to upgrade the content knowledge and pedagogical skills of the teachers. (Chapter 12)

Psychodynamic Perspective: A psychological approach that is popular with a number of psychiatrists. It was founded by Sigmund Freud at the end of the 19th century. This psychological model believes that human behavior is controlled by inner forces that the individual has only a little power or awareness about. This school of thought places emphasis on the influence of the unconscious mind on a person's behavior. (Chapter 11)

Pullout Program: Refers to ELLs who are taken out of the mainstream classroom for a part of the day and receive language support from an ESL teacher and assistance during the portion of the day through the pull-out component. When pulling-out, they go to the ESOL classroom for intensive instruction in English and also receive language support within each content area while the ELL students spend the majority of their day in classrooms with English speaking peers. This allows them to be a part of the student body within their school. (Chapter 12)

Realia: Refers to objects and materials found in everyday life that can be used as teaching aides. (Chapter 6)

Scaling: An activity that evaluates students' prior knowledge. Before reading a selection, students are given a list of words related to the topic and they rate how well they know those words. (Chapter 9)

Science Demonstration: A teaching method of modeling a particular science concept or process. Demonstrations can be suitable when dangerous, expensive, or scarce materials are involved, but also when the goal is to focus students' observations on a particular scientific phenomenon. Good science demonstrations engage students in observing and explaining. A demonstration should include three steps that help teachers: (a) activate students' prior knowledge, (b) focus students' observations, and (c) engage students to explain the concept. (Chapter 4)

Self-Contained ESOL Program: In the self-contained program model, ELLs are placed with other ELLs for the entire day where they receive sheltered instruction from teachers trained in sheltering techniques. The ELL students in such programs are grouped together in one classroom to receive instruction at their language proficiency level. Usually, only the district with a large population of ELL students offer self-contained ESOL program. (Chapter 12)

Self-Efficacy: One's beliefs in one's ability to produce designated levels of performance that exercise influence over events that affect one's life. This belief determines how you feel, think, motivate yourself, and behave to produce diverse effects through four major processes: cognitive, motivational, affective, and selection processes (Bandura, 1997). Thus, self-efficacy is the belief you have ability to accomplish a task in a way to achieve a desired result. It is having faith in yourself, which is different than a feeling of confidence. (Chapter 11)

Semantic Feature Analysis: A strategy, using a matrix, that encourages students to determine how terms are alike and different. Via this activity, students analyze relationships among vocabulary words and concepts. (Chapter 9)

Sentence Frames/Stems/Starters: A teaching tool that makes up part of a learners' oral or written response to a question. Frames are more structured, while stems and starters only provide the beginning part of a response for learners. (Chapter 5)

SIOP Lesson Model: Refers to Sheltered Instruction Observation Protocol. It is an empirically-tested approach that helps teachers prepare all students, especially English language learners, to become college and career ready (Person, 2013). In a SIOP lesson, teachers adjust the language demands of the lesson in many ways, such as modifying speech rate and tone, using context clues and models extensively, relating instruction to student experience, adapting the language of texts or tasks, and using certain methods familiar to language teachers (e.g., demonstrations, visuals, graphic organizers, or cooperative work) to make academic instruction more accessible to students of different English proficiency levels. (Chapter 2)

Sfumato: Meaning "smoky" or "smudged"—A shading technique in drawing and painting best exemplified by the emergence from shadow demonstrated in works by Leonardo da Vinci, where darkness is used to enhance the illusory perception of three-dimensional depth projection in a two-dimensional artwork in which lines/strokes are blended to smoothness. (Chapter 8)

Sheltered Instruction: Refers to an approach to teaching English language learners which integrates language and content instruction. It consists of a set of teaching strategies, designed for teachers of academic content, that lower the linguistic demand of the lesson without compromising the integrity or rigor of the subject matter. It was originally designed for content and classroom teachers who teach in English. See more on SIOP model. (Chapter 12)

Sociopolitical Consciousness: Refers to understanding one's roles, rights, and responsibilities in society. (Chapter 6)

Socratic Pedagogical Method: A teaching or pedagogical method that employs a dialogic interactive device described by the classical Greek philosopher, Plato, in his writings pertaining to his mentor, the philosopher, Socrates, who was well-known for subjecting his students and his acquaintances to an extended and carefully crafted process of questioning and response described as the "elenchus," or in ancient Greek, λεγχος. This process of questioning and listening carefully to student responses was intended to allow students to discover knowledge and answers within their existing awareness, based in their own processes of cognition and understanding while examining the logic and clarity of the reasoning supporting their claims regarding what they considered was or was not true. (Chapter 8)

Space: An element of art, the actual emptiness that surrounds objects or the void inside of hollow objects, or the symbolic representation of such a void. Artists use various forms of perspective to manipulate the viewer's perception of space. Relevant perspective terms are: aerial perspective, linear perspective, isometric perspective, and Eastern perspective. (Chapter 8)

Strategic Learners: Second type of learners that Bain identifies. The strategic learners tend to be primarily motivated by reinforcements or rewards. This type of students will react well to competition along with the opportunity do better than others. They are usually among your better students, often making grades well above average. (Chapter 11)

Stress: Relative prominence a syllable receives. A stressed syllable is longer, louder, and has a higher pitch, as how the first syllable in the word _prominence_ sounds. However, not every word in a sentence will be stressed. The words that are stressed in a sentence are usually content words, such as nouns, verbs (excluding auxiliary verbs), adjectives, and adverbs. (Chapter 3)

Stress-Timed Languages: Languages that organize the rhythm of an utterance around stressed words and syllables. For instance, when we say the sentence, English is a stress-timed language, we tend to divide the sentence into four equally-timed units around the underlined stressed words by assigning one beat to each unit: _English_/is a _stress_/-_timed_/'_language_/. (Chapter 3)

Summative Assessment: Refers to the assessments used to evaluate student learning, skill acquisition, and academic achievement at the conclusion of a defined instructional period and it summarizes achievement at a particular time. It is different from the initial or on-going assessment because the summative assessment is to provide the evaluation of the final quality with an overall grade or score. (Chapter 12)

Surface Learner: Third type of learners that Bain identifies. These learners tend to be motivated by the fear of failure and a desire to avoid it. According to Bain the surface learner will typically try to avoid any type of deep learning. This learner may view deep learning as an inherently risky endeavor, probably out of their fear of failure. These learners tend to be motivated by the fear of failure and a desire to avoid it. (Chapter 11)

Syllable-Timed Languages: Languages that assign almost equal stress to each syllable or word in an utterance. A sentence such as _Chinese is a syllable-timed language_, will assign equal stress to each word. If one beat is assigned to each word, the sentence will be said as follows: *Chinese/ is / a / syllable/ -timed/ language/*. (Chapter 3)

Teacher Education: Refers to the procedures of preparing prospective teachers with the knowledge, attitudes, and skills needed to perform their tasks in the classroom, school, and community. Teacher education is often divided into these stages: initial teacher training education (i.e., pre-service courses) before entering the classroom as a fully responsible teacher; induction, the procedure of accepting into the program after the first few years of training or the first year in a particular school; and teacher development or continuing professional development for an in-service process for practicing teachers. (Chapter 12)

Teaching English to Speakers of Other Languages (TESOL): Refers to teaching English to speakers whose L1 is not English. TESOL is also the term referring to an international association with the mission to advance professional expertise in English language teaching and learning for the students of other languages than English. (Chapter 1)

Technology Integration: Using technologies effectively and efficiently both online and offline to enhance ELLs' language learning development in different content areas in meaningful ways. (Chapter 7)

Technology-Mediated Interactions: Related to teachers' knowledge of what communicative technology they should use, and how they should use this technology to create learning environment for shared understanding on the content, the procedure, and each other. (Chapter 7)

Technological Pedagogical Content Knowledge (TPACK) Model: A framework that identifies the knowledge teachers need to teach effectively with technology. (Chapter 7)

Technological Skills: Related to teachers' ability to make use of technology, to become familiar with a range of technology, to effectively judge different technologies, and to choose the most appropriate technology for teaching purposes. (Chapter 7)

TESOL-CAEP Standards: CAEP refers to Council for the Accreditation of Education Preparation (CAEP) and TESOL refers to Teachers of English to Speakers of Other Languages (TESOL). The TESOL-CAEP Standards provide a framework for P-12 ESOL teacher standards and preparation. The standards include five domains that exemplify the interdisciplinary characteristics of teaching English language learners as a profession. (Chapter 12)

Texture: An art element referring to either the tactile representation of a surface or the representation or invention of the appearance of such a surface quality, or the actual surface quality of an object or artwork. (Chapter 8)

Total Physical Response: An approach to teaching a second language that is based on the coordination of language and physical movement. In TPR, instructors give commands to students in the target language, and students respond with whole-body actions. The method is an example of the comprehension approach to language teaching (1965). (Chapter 2)

Trends in L2 Teaching: Refers to the development of language (L2) teaching debates that began in the 1990s on how L2 teaching and learning should constitute and the debates continue. In the past 15 years, several crucial factors have combined to affect current perspectives on the teaching of English worldwide: (a) the decline of methods, (b) a growing emphasis on both bottom-up and top-down skills, (c) the creation of new knowledge about English, and (d) integrated and contextualized teaching of multiple language skills (Hinkel, 2006). (Chapter 12)

Value: As an element of art, it refers to the relative lightness and darkness of surfaces. Value may range from white through various grays to black or it may be considered a property of color. Subtle relationships between light and dark areas (shadow) determine how things may appear. A gradual shift from lighter to darker tones can give the illusion of a curving surface, while an abrupt value change usually indicates an abrupt change in surface direction. (Chapter 8)

Verbal Persuasion: Bandura (1997) explains that there are four ways to increase self-efficacy in individuals: enactive mastery, vicarious modeling, verbal persuasion, and arousal. Verbal persuasion is being coached and convinced by someone who is trusted. (Chapter 11)

Vicarious Modeling: Bandura (1997) explains four ways to increase self-efficacy in individuals: enactive mastery, vicarious modeling, verbal persuasion, and arousal. Vicarious modeling is watching someone else who is similar to you perform the task. (Chapter 11)

Visual Literacy: Visual literacy is a term applied to instances concerning an individual's ability to interpret and decipher the cultural, aesthetic, and implied meanings within artworks or with regard to the phenomenal world of experience. (Chapter 9)

Vocabulary Banks: The display of frequently used vocabulary words that learners need to know in order to understand the mathematics concept introduced. (Chapter 5)

World Class Instructional Design and Assessment (WIDA): A language standards framework that helps English learners understand language use in academic contexts. In other words, this is the language that ELLs need acquire and negotiate in order to participate successfully in school. (Chapter 2)

ABOUT THE CONTRIBUTORS

Dr. Nan Li, Editor, is a professor, researcher, and writer with over 20 publications. Dr. Li is Director of the projects funded by the U.S. Department of Education and by the South Carolina Commission on Higher Education. Dr. Li plays a key role in preparing teachers to work with ELLs. Dr. Li is the recipient of the South Carolina Governor's Distinguished Professor Award and Exemplary Service to the Teaching Profession, along with several other distinguished awards. Dr. Li has also received multiple grant awards, totaling $3.2 million of external funding for professional development to prepare the K–12 teachers and pre-service teachers to work effectively with the ELLs in classrooms. Her grant programs also received the prestigious Rose-Duhon-Sells Multicultural Program Award (2014) by the National Association for Multicultural Education (NAME) and the Innovation in Teacher Education Award (2014) by the Southeastern Association for Teacher Educators (SRATE). Dr. Li has served on the Executive Board of the South Carolina Association of Teacher Educators (SCATE) and on the ATE and NAME Committees. Graduating from Indiana University of Pennsylvania, Dr. Li's dissertation research was conducted on the learning experiences of English language learners. Since then, her teaching, research, and service has been on ELLs, L2 education, and teaching diversity. Dr. Li has presented at over 50 professional conferences, such as American Educational Research Association and Association for Teacher Educators. Her review appears on Teacher College Records, published by Teacher College, Columbia University.

Teaching ELLs Across Content Areas, pages 339–346
Copyright © 2016 by Information Age Publishing
All rights of reproduction in any form reserved.

Dr. Li's recent book, *A Book for Every Teacher: Teaching English Language Learners*, published by Information Age Publishing, provides helpful teaching tips and information for K–12 teachers to successfully work with ELLs, such as vocabulary words, basic L2 theories, other useful information and strategies. See this book at: http://www.amazon.com/Book-For-Every-Teacher-Teaching/dp/168123050X

Dr. Cristina Alfaro is Associate Professor of English language and Bi-literacy development at San Diego State University (SDSU), where Dr. Alfaro also serves as Chair in the Department of Policy Studies in Language and Culture. She earned her doctorate degree, in Teacher Preparation for Multilingual Learners, from the Claremont and San Diego State University joint graduate program. Dr. Alfaro teaches credential and graduate level courses where her work focuses on preparing teachers in the area of English language and Bi-literacy development with a global perspective. She has two decades of experience in directing both local and international teacher education programs in California, Mexico, and Europe. Dr. Alfaro is the recipient of the College of Education 2010 Excellence in Teaching Award. Her background as an elementary bi-literacy teacher in ethno and linguistically diverse communities, has served her well in preparing teachers to teach students how to critically read the word and the world.

Dr. Ronald Collins is Associate Professor of Psychology at Mars Hill University in North Carolina and also a renowned clinic psychologist. Dr. Collins holds two doctorates in clinical psychology and in adult education and human development. He has taught courses in forensic psychology, learning theories, theories of personality, statistics, research methods, abnormal psychology, counseling methods, organizational behavior, decision making, business ethics, and human resource management. Dr. Collins is a former associate editor for education with the *Mensa Research Journal*. He is a licensed clinical and forensic psychologist. He is a member of the American College of Forensic Examiners and holds diplomat status in that organization. His work experience includes both a psychologist and a special agent with 30 years in law enforcement, which includes the United States Secret Service (i.e., Central Intelligence Agency), the office of the Florida Attorney General, and the Colorado Department of Corrections. He has also worked as a court psychological examiner for the Department of Family and Children, and as both a professor of psychology and a professor of business. Dr. Collins has held membership in a number of professional organizations including the American Psychological Association, Fraternal Order of Police, The American College of Forensic Examiners, The Association of Former Agents of the United States Secret Service, and The American Educational Research Association. He is the author of the *Kabiroff Papers*

(1988), *Transfer of learning* (1990), *Psychological Perspectives on Security Issues* (2000, 2013). He has published numerous articles in the field of psychology, motivation, intelligence, and business for professional peer reviewed journals that include the *Journal of Human Resource Management, Journal of Employee Assistance Research, The Mensa Research Journal,* and the *Journal of Human Service Education.* His biography was selected for inclusion in the Who's Who in America (1998).

Dr. Angela Crespo Cozart is an associate professor in the School of Education, Health, and Human Performance at the College of Charleston, Charleston, South Carolina. She earned her PhD degree in Foreign Language Methodology with an emphasis in ESL from the University of Tennessee, Knoxville, Tennessee. Dr. Cozart is currently the program director for the Department of Teacher Education's Master of Arts in Teaching Programs: Early Childhood, Elementary, Middle Grades, and Special Education. She is also the director for the department's Certificates: ESOL and Special Education. Dr. Cozart is a former secondary English teacher. She currently teaches graduate online ESOL courses, the first of their kind in South Carolina. She also teaches literacy for math, science, English, and history pre-service teachers. She is a native-Spanish speaker and learned English upon entering U.S. schools. Her passion is helping service and pre-service teachers understand the role of culture and language in the classroom. She has delivered workshops on vocabulary building in the science classroom for ELLs, culture, second-language acquisition, and ESOL principles and strategies.

Dr. Thomas Destino is Professor of Education and Director of the ESL (English as Second Language) Program at Mars Hill University in North Carolina. Dr. Destino received his PhD from The Ohio State University in Second and Foreign Language Education and his Post-Doctoral Research Fellowship from University of California, Santa Cruz. Dr. Destino also served as Director of Special Projects and teaching ESL courses at The University of California, Riverside in the Extension, International Education Programs. His research interests include English Language Learner education, literacy development in content areas in particular. Dr. Destino's publications focus on the teaching and learning of science in a second language, the politics of bilingual education, and second language learning theories. He also works in the area of language policy and politics. For example, his publication, English Language Development Standard Course of Study appears in North Carolina Department of Public Instruction. His article, Science and second language development, appears in The Ernesto Galarza Public Policy and Humanities Research Bureau by University of California Press. His teaching responsibilities include second language and literacy development, issues in teaching English learners, and race and cultural studies. He is currently director of Teaching with Primary Sources, a grant through the Library of Congress. He is a strong proponent of primary source teaching and learning and has been active in professional development for teachers throughout his career.

Dr. Tolulope O. Filani is Professor of Art and Art Education and Chair of the Visual and Performing Arts Department at South Carolina State University. Dr. Filani earned PhD, MEd, and BEd degrees in Art Education and Visual Arts from the University of Missouri at Columbia. In addition, he holds the Higher National Diploma in Sculpture from Yaba College of Technology, also in Lagos. Dr. Filani is listed in *Who's Who of the French Association Dialogue Entrée Les Cultures, Paris, France* and the *Who's Who in Art in Nigeria* by the Smithsonian Institution's Library Museum of African Art, Washington, DC. His awards include the 2010 South Carolina State Academic Affairs Extra Mile Award; the Donald K. Anderson Graduate Student Teaching Award, University of Missouri; Superior Graduate Achievement Award, University of Missouri; and, the UNESCO prize for promotion of the arts in Nigeria. Dr. Filani has published and presented extensively in the areas of art therapy, arts integration, and program assessment in the arts. He has exhibited internationally, showing works in London, Paris and across Nigeria in addition to executing a number of major public and privately commissioned works of sculpture throughout Nigeria, Europe, and in the United States. Filani's artworks embody a synergy of classical Euro-centrist humanism, tempered by African-inspired expressionism, symbolically representing human experience rather than adhering to a strictly sustained mimesis. His images exemplify his personal values, cultural heritage, and emotive experience, encapsulating personal anecdote, providing aesthetic stimulation, and generating topical commentaries that controvert old-world paradigms of order. His artworks are the means through which he is able to express a cumulative awareness of the universal human condition.

Dr. Courtney A. Howard is a science educator with a passion for teaching and learning. She has extensive experience teaching in formal classrooms and informal learning environments, such as afterschool programs. She has worked as a faculty member and administrator of educator preparation programs, and she has provided professional development to in-service teachers. Dr. Howard has served on the executive board of the South Carolina Association of Teacher Educators and Southeastern Association for Science Teacher Education. She has shared her expertise at national conferences of the American Educational Research Association, National Association for Research in Science Teaching, National Association of Professional Development Schools, and Foundations, Inc., as well as multiple local, state, and regional conferences. Dr. Howard has been invited to serve on education advisory boards, commissions, and task forces for a range of agencies, including the South Carolina Department of Education, Trident United Way, South Carolina Aquarium, Stevens Institute of Technology, and the Riley Institute at Furman University. Dr. Howard earned her undergraduate degree in biology from Florida A&M University. She later studied curriculum and instruction with a special emphasis on secondary science education at the University of Florida, where she earned her MEd and PhD. She is a member of the Honor Society of Phi Kappa Phi and Gates Millennium Scholars Alumni Association. Dr. Howard currently serves as the Director of the Center for Partnerships to Improve Education at the College of Charleston.

Dr. Jennifer Kohnke is an associate professor at Aurora University located in Chicago, Illinois. Dr. Kohnke specializes in social studies education with many years' teaching experiences in this area in terms of teaching and research. She teaches in both the undergraduate and graduate education programs. Her teaching and research interests are also focused on social justice and social studies education to educators of all levels. She also teaches reading methods for the primary grades and theories of learning for all students. In the graduate program she has taught almost every course in the ESL/Bilingual program and also designed and developed online versions of the courses. These courses allow teachers to obtain an ESL endorsement on their teaching license. She currently teaches Methods and Materials for Teaching English Language Learners each semester. In local school districts Dr. Kohnke has helped service English Language Learners by having her university students tutor primary grade ELLs in reading and writing. Dr. Kohnke has presented at a variety of international, national, and local conferences on research that focuses on social studies education, along with literacy instruction.

Mr. Frank C. Martin II is a graduate of Yale University and the City University of New York, Hunter College, with additional study in contemporary art and art theory at the Institute of Fine Arts of New York University. A former Curator and Director of the I. P. Stanback Museum, at South Carolina State University, Mr. Martin is a specialist in art theory and cultural interpretation, and has served as an academic advisor for the PBS documentary, *Shared History*, and as contributing critic in the fine arts for *The Charleston Post and Courier*, one of the South's oldest newspapers. A Carolina Diversity Professors Program Doctoral Scholar in the Department of Philosophy at the University of South Carolina, Martin's area of specialization is the study of Axiology concentrating in the field of Aesthetics. A faculty member in the discipline of art history at South Carolina State University, Mr. Martin also serves as an adjunct professor of art history at the Salkehatchie and Walterboro extensions of the University of South Carolina in Allendale, and has been a guest faculty member for special topics in the Department of Art History at The College of Charleston. Martin is a member of the International Association of Art Critics (*Association Internationale des Critiques d'Art—or AICA*) based in Paris. His recent projects include contributions to the encyclopedic *African American Biography* a publication and online project organized by Harvard University and the Oxford University Press, contributing research pertaining to American artists of the African diaspora. In 2014, Mr. Frank Martin was designated Professor of the Year, for the School of Education, Humanities, and Social Sciences at South Carolina State University.

Dr. Larisa A. Olesova is a professor at George Mason University in Fairfax, Virginia. Dr. Olesova received her PhD in Learning Design and Technology from Purdue University in 2011. She also has a doctorate in General Education and a masters in English Language and Literature from North-Eastern Federal University in Russia. Dr. Olesova is currently teaching as Instructional Designer in the Information Technology Services and Adjunct Faculty in the Instructional Design and Technology Program, Learning Technologies Division of the College of Education and Human Development at George Mason University. Prior to joining George Mason University, she also worked for 15 years as Associate Professor of English at North-Eastern Federal University in Russia. Her research focuses on distance education, specifically asynchronous online learning environments. Other areas of research and practice include aspects of online presence, the Community of Inquiry (CoI), instructional strategies and best practices in online teaching. Her works include the book *Feedback in Online Course for Non-Native English-Speaking Students* (Cambridge Scholars Publishing, 2013), articles in *Journal of Asynchronous Online Networks, Journal of Online Teaching and Learning,* and *Journal of Education,* and chapters in the books *Creating Teacher Immediacy in Online Learning Environments,* and *Assessment in Online and Blended Learning Environments.*

Dr. Luciana C. de Oliveira is Associate Professor at the University of Miami. She teaches courses related to ELLs in the Department of Teaching and Learning. Her research focuses on issues related to teaching English language learners (ELLs) at the K–12 level, including the role of language in learning the content areas, second language writing, and teacher preparation for ELLs. Her work has appeared in *Teachers College Record, Journal of Teacher Education, Journal of English for Specific Purposes, English Education, Multicultural Education, The History Teacher,* and other books and journals. She is the editor (with Tony Silva) of *L2 Writing in Secondary Classrooms:*

Academic Issues, Student Experiences, and Teacher Education (Routledge, 2013) and *Second Language Writing in Elementary Classrooms: Instructional Issues, Content-Area Writing and Teacher Education* (Palgrave MacMillan, 2016) and has several other authored, co-authored, edited, and co-edited books.

Dr. Aria Razfar earned his PhD from the University of California in 2003. Dr. Razfar is one of the leading scholars in the fields of applied linguistics and learning sciences. His research contributes to a growing body of work that merges sociocultural views of language and learning with critical perspectives for understanding the semiotic and learning processes of non-dominant communities. He has authored theoretically-driven empirical studies and conceptual pieces that draw on qualitative and quantitative methods, sociocultural theories of learning, and the application of language ideologies in urban schools. His publications have appeared in top-tier academic journals such as *Anthropology of Education Quarterly, Human Development, Linguistics and Education, Mind, Culture, and Activity,* and *TESOL Quarterly,* as well as in research handbooks, an edited volume (Bevin, Bell, Stephens, Razfar, 2013), and a book titled, *Applying Linguistics in the Classroom: A Sociocultural Perspective* (Routledge, 2014). The majority of his work is concerned with teacher development and teacher education of English learners across the life-span in urban communities (early literacy, K–12, Higher Education). His work has explicit and implicit implications for English learner policy, its impact on pedagogy and learning in the classroom, and national debates surrounding bilingualism and student achievement (especially Latinas/os and African American populations). He has written on the mathematics education of ELs in both school and non-school settings, especially focusing on the intersection of mathematics learning, language, and multilingual problem solving. He has secured major funding to conduct his research and training of teachers of English Learners (EL), with a focus on language learning, mathematics, and science from the U.S. Department of Education (Office of English Language Acquisition) and the National Science Foundation. In 2014, he was recognized for his scholarship by being named the University of Illinois at Chicago's Researcher of the Year for the Social Sciences.

Ms. Barbara Ragin is a first-grade teacher at Summerton Early Childhood Center in South Carolina. Ms. Ragin specializes in TESOL with extensive experiences working with K–12 teachers related to preparing and training the mainstream teachers through the ELL Center Project. Ms. Ragin is completing her Master's Degree at University of South Carolina with a concentration in TESOL. Ms. Ragin has also experience working on the program evaluation. She is a member of the TESOL International Association, Carolina TESOL Association, Phi Theta Kappa International Honor

Society, and a member of The National Society of Leadership and Success. She is also a member of the Daisy Pearson Chapter of the South Carolina Education Association and the Palmetto Teachers Association. Ms. Ragin received her Bachelor's degree in Early Childhood Education from Claflin University.

Dr. Lynn Atkinson Smolen is Professor Emerita of literacy and teaching English as a second language at The University of Akron. She co-directs Northeast Ohio ACHIEVE, a National Professional Development Grant funded by the U. S. Department of Education that provides professional development for teachers serving English learners in Northeast Ohio. Her academic credentials are in literacy and teaching English as a second language. She is the co-editor of *Multicultural Literature and Response* and has published numerous articles and book chapters on teaching culturally and linguistically diverse learners. Her areas of research are in literacy development of English learners, diversity issues, and multicultural literature.

Dr. Zayoni Torres earned her PhD in Curriculum and Instruction, with a concentration in Gender and Women's Studies, at the University of Illinois at Chicago (UIC). Dr. Torres was the project coordinator for the English Learning through Math, Science, and Action Research (ELMSA) program at UIC. She was a research fellow for the Center for the Mathematics Education of Latinos/as (CEMELA) funded by the National Science Foundation. Her research interests are grounded in sociocultural and feminists perspectives in exploring the teaching of mathematics and science literacy for English Learners (ELs). Her dissertation research focuses on (a) how teacher's construct language, gender, and race in relation to mathematics and science learning, and (b) how teachers' language, gender, and racial ideological stances mediate curriculum and instructional practices.

Dr. Wei Zhang holds a PhD and MEd degree and teaches undergraduate and graduate courses in linguistics, second language acquisition, and language teaching methodology at the University of Akron, Akron, Ohio. Dr. Zhang also co-directs a two-million dollar federal grant from the U.S. Department of Education to train in-service content teachers and special education teachers with a TESOL Endorsement. Her academic credentials are in linguistics and teaching English as a second language (TESOL). Her current research focuses on academic language development of English language learners, disciplinary literacy, TESOL program design, the acoustic-phonetic difference between native and non-native speech in English, Chinese phonology, and maintenance of Chinese as a heritage language.

Made in the USA
Columbia, SC
18 January 2021